THE POLITICS OF POWER

A CRITICAL INTRODUCTION TO AMERICAN GOVERNMENT

THIRD EDITION

THE
POLITICS
OF
POWER

A CRITICAL INTRODUCTION
TO AMERICAN GOVERNMENT

THIRD EDITION

Ira Katznelson
New School for Social Research

Mark Kesselman
Columbia University

Harcourt Brace Jovanovich, Publishers

San Diego   New York   Chicago   Austin   Washington, D.C.
London   Sydney   Tokyo   Toronto

To the memory of Paul Kesselman,
to Anne Kesselman
and to
Ephraim and Sylvia Katznelson

ISBN: 0-15-570735-3
Library of Congress Catalog Card Number: 86-81632
Printed in the United States of America

preface

Times change. Much has happened since the publication of the earlier editions of *The Politics of Power,* not least the presidency of Ronald Reagan which has reflected, and promoted, a major shift to the Right in political rhetoric, policy, and possibility.

Our aim in this book, however, remains the same: to introduce students to American government and to explore how the interplay of politics and power influence their lives. Though this edition has been recast and updated in numerous ways, it maintains a critical perspective. It is tempting to equate what exists with what is natural. Instead, we attempt in this book to explore the contours of America's political institutions and unequal social structure with an eye to raising questions not only about what exists but about what might be.

Although the aim of this book and most of its emphases have remained constant, this edition differs in several ways from its predecessors in organization and tone. After beginning with a discussion of democratic theory, the book essentially falls in three parts. First, we sketch the interconnections between the development of a distinctively American capitalism and politics. Second, we explore the key institutional features of the national state. With these tools, we turn, third, to an analysis of how the society (its class, gender, and race relations) and how domestic and foreign public policy have been shaped and limited by the state–business relationship and by the character of American political institutions. We conclude with a speculative assessment about the possibilities of change within these limits.

As the last chapter illustrates, this edition is also characterized by a change in tone of voice. The Reagan administration may not reflect a massive public shift to the Right, but it has managed to redefine in many ways what American politics are about and what choices we have. In that, Ronald Reagan has been the most successful president since Franklin Roosevelt. We attempt, in the conclusion, to suggest how the politics of power is still a politics of choice.

In our analysis, we underscore the mutually supportive, yet tense, relationship between American capitalism and political democracy. This is a complicated and multifaceted relationship. We put it at the center of our inquiries because the shifting boundaries between capitalism and democracy are fundamental to all else in our politics and society. Although we are certain our perspective on capitalism and democracy will not be shared by all, we do hope it will provoke thought and discussion, and, in so doing, help students develop their own approaches to American politics.

We continue to be assisted by numerous people. Amrita Basu's and Deborah Socolow Katznelson's thoughtful assistance, enthusiastic support for the book, and love stand out the most. In addition to the student and faculty friends and colleagues we thanked in the first two editions, we would like to express our gratitude to Gordon Adams, David Gold, Allen Kaufman, Margaret Levi, Helene Slessarev, and Philippa Strum.

For the third time we have benefited from the professionalism and dedication of the editorial and production staff at Harcourt Brace Jovanovich. In particular, we wish to thank Drake Bush, Robert Watrous, and Howard Owens.

Ira Katznelson

Mark Kesselman

contents

vii

THE
POLITICS
OF
POWER

A CRITICAL INTRODUCTION
TO AMERICAN GOVERNMENT

THIRD EDITION

the political economy of democratic capitalism

1

capitalism and democracy

Four of every ten Americans of voting age are not registered to vote. This degree of abstention from one of the key activities of democratic politics is unusual. In the other western countries that organize their politics by the competition of political parties, the vast majority of citizens vote. Many countries automatically register citizens when they reach the age of eighteen. Others conduct house to house surveys to find eligible voters.

In the United States, by contrast, it is not always simple to register to vote. In most states potential voters must travel significant distances to the offices of boards of elections to register in person. In 1977, President Jimmy Carter introduced a bill that would have allowed people to register on election day at the polls. He explained its overwhelming defeat by noting that most senior members of Congress prefer to keep the number of voters small because they fear the unpredictable outcome of elections with many new participants. "To have a 25 or 30 percent increase of unpredictable new voters is something they don't relish. I would suggest to you that this is the single most important obstacle to increasing participation on election day."[1]

In the spring of 1983, Richard Cloward, a professor of social work, Hulbert James, a longtime civil-rights activist, and Frances Fox Piven, a professor of political science, launched a new national organization that tried to promote voter registration at public and private social service agencies, such as hospitals, day care centers, welfare offices, and senior citizen centers. In this way, they sought to directly reach the part of the citizenry, principally poor or minority, that tends not to register or vote.

Their effort received much support from some unions, social service agencies, and a small number of important political figures, especially the governors of New York and Ohio. After a year and a half of effort, the campaign had added 275,000 people to the rolls of registered voters.

Still, according to Piven and Cloward, this result was a very limited one. Only 1 percent of the country's voluntary agencies were willing to participate. The main reason, they found, was fear of wealthy patrons and of politicians who managed grants to these agencies. Further, the federal government demanded the practice of using state government offices to register voters be stopped. Four of every ten Americans of voting age remain unregistered.

One in three adult Americans is functionally illiterate. Members of this group may read some, but they cannot read this book. Nor can they read the daily newspaper. Jonathan Kozol, a former schoolteacher, has recently written about these Americans. He observes that in terms of politics and democracy they live in a silent culture; they cannot participate in a minimally informed way in political discussion: "These people cannot read the blue-ribbon reports that document their plight. They cannot read the letters sent home with their children from the public schools to which they are entrusted, schools that threaten to turn out another and much larger generation of adult illiterates in the decade ahead. They cannot read instructions on a bottle of medication for their chil-

[1]Frances Fox Piven and Richard A. Cloward, "Prospects for Voter Registration Reform: A Report on the Experiences of the Human SERVE Campaign," *PS* XVIII (Summer 1985), p. 593.

dren. They cannot cast a vote based on informed and sensitive retrieval of the print-recorded past."[2]

The federal government spends less than $2.00 a year to teach each illiterate to read. President Reagan has sought to reduce this amount in every budget he has submitted to the Congress.

There are enormous disparities in the earnings and opportunities of hard-working Americans. President Reagan's Cabinet, reports *U.S. News and World Report,* contains a majority having assets of at least $1 million. Secretary of Labor William Brock has holdings worth over $3 million; Energy Secretary John Herrington, $2.3 million; and Defense Secretary Casper Weinberger, over 1.6 million dollars. Within the White House, Chief of Staff Donald Reagan possesses assets of at least the same amount.[3]

Ramona and Ruben Estrada, American citizens from South Texas, together with their seven children who range in age from 5 to 19, wake up each morning at 4 a.m. to begin an eight-hour day in the fields of the Yakima Valley in the state of Washington. They get paid 17 cents for each pound of asparagus they pick, which will be sold by their employer for 70 cents. Many of the farms they work have no toilets, and they must bring their own drinking water. The conditions of their work are not regulated by federal labor laws; and where they are protected by law, there is hardly any enforcement. They move all the time, first to pick asparagus, strawberries, and apples in Washington, then back to Texas for onions and cucumber, and then to Florida for oranges.

The Estradas are only one family of some 250,000 South Texan citizens of Mexican heritage who work as migrant workers. In their home counties, unemployment rates come close to 50 percent, water is sparse, education is often unavailable, and diseases common in the Third World—such as typhus, leprosy, and intestinal parasites from contaminated water—are rampant. As the *Wall Street Journal* observed in a report on these conditions, the migrant

<hr />

[2]Jonathan Kozol, "The Crippling Inheritance," *The New York Times Book Review,* Section 7 (March 3, 1985), p. 1.
[3]Michael Doan et al., "Measuring the Wealth of Reagan's Cabinet," *U.S. News and World Report* (June 17, 1985), p. 60.

workers pick to survive, fearful of losing even these jobs to other farmworkers.[4]

American politics is expensive to conduct. Much of the competition for public support takes place in the mass media. Advertising costs a great deal, and the candidate who spends the most usually wins. Elizabeth Drew's study of "Politics and Money" showed that in 1982 "the winners outspent the losers in twenty-seven of the thirty-three Senate races. In five of the six races where the margin of victory was four percent or less, the winners spent twice as much as the losers."[5]

The costs of elections thus tend to limit candidates to people who can fund campaigns out of their personal or family wealth, or to individuals who can attract large sums of money from powerful interest groups. In 1974, corporate America had established 89 political action committees (PACs) to fund campaigns; when Drew wrote her articles, there were 1,497. In addition, there were 613 PACs organized by such trade associations as the American Medical Association and the National Association of Realtors. Democratic Congressman David Obey of Wisconsin observed, "If you're on a committee with jurisdiction over big interests, you can be sure of raising a lot of money." Reporter Drew concluded, "The point is what *raising* money, not simply spending it, does to the political process. . . . It is not just that well-armed interests have a head start over the rest of the citizenry—or that often it is not even a contest. . . . What is relevant is what the whole thing is doing to the democratic process."[6]

The United States is the world's oldest political democracy. All adult American citizens today have the right to vote. The party system invites political participation, and parties compete actively to win the support of the electorate. Interest groups lobby to defend the interests of their members. Newspapers and television provide regular reports of government activities, debate the wisdom of government policies, and expose wrongdoing by high gov-

[4]Dianna Solis, "From Farm to Farm, Migrant Workers Struggle to Survive," *Wall Street Journal* (May 15, 1985), p. 1.
[5]Elizabeth Drew, "Politics and Money," *The New Yorker* (December 6, 1982), p. 68.
[6]*Ibid.*, p. 56.

ernment officials. In few countries is political debate as open, free, and extensive.

A democracy, like that of the United States, is composed of rules that tell who can govern and make laws and under what procedures they may do so. Compared to those in nondemocratic societies, public authorities are accessible and responsive. Rule is not arbitrary. Citizens are protected by rights and by laws, and they are invited into the political process as participants. Government is accountable to the people, who, in the last resort, are considered to be sovereign.

Is democracy to be judged only by formal procedures? What shall we make of uneven voting, the unequal distribution of reading skills, large divergences in the earnings and social class position of the population, and of the impact of monied interests on elections and the political process? More generally, to what extent is popular sovereignty possible in a society organized within a capitalist framework? In such societies, the divisions between those who privately own the means to produce goods and services have disproportionate power, not only because they have more money, but because governments must act in ways that promote the prosperity of private firms. In a capitalist society, the well-being of everyone for jobs and income depends on the investment decisions and the profits of private firms.

One consequence is that many political issues, including the very desirability of an economic system based on private property, are not debated in public. Further, many issues of manifestly public concern, such as where new automobile or computer plants will be built, are decided privately. The result is a contraction of public politics. The principle of majority rule, the very centerpiece of representative democracy, thus applies only to a limited sphere of questions and decisions. Just as it is frequently argued that the separation of economic from political power is beneficial for democracy, for it prevents the concentration of power in the hands of a single elite, so we may ask what the implications are for democratic citizenship when many key issues are not considered to be appropriate issues for public discussion and decision.

Further, the actions of business in pursuit of profit—indeed, the routine operation of a capitalist economic system—generate inequalities of wealth and income. In the United States, the pattern of income distribution has remained virtually unchanged in this century. In 1910, the top fifth of income earners received 46 percent of the national income; today, the richest fifth's share is still over 40 percent. The share of the bottom fifth, moreover, has actually declined from over 8 percent in 1910 to just over 5 percent today.

This pattern of inequality in income is tied directly to even greater disparities in the distribution of wealth—ownership of corporate stock, businesses, homes and property, cash reserves, government and corporate bonds, and retirement funds. Roughly 20 percent of personal wealth in the United States is owned by one-third of 1 percent of the population; the richest 1 percent own over 28 percent of the wealth; and the top 10 percent of Americans own over half (56 percent). The bottom 10 percent actually owe more than they own.

This basic structure underpins the complexity of everyday life in the United States. Although Americans have diverse ethnic and racial backgrounds, work in different kinds of jobs, live in different places, and hold widely different political opinions, all are part of the class structure and are affected by it. Capitalist production interpenetrates virtually every aspect of American society, including the place of racial minorities and women, the quality of city neighborhoods, and the political choices made by government officials and citizens.

The relationship of capitalism and political democracy poses very old questions. In the *Politics of Power,* we explore these issues by examining ties joining the democratic politics, governmental practices, and public policies of the United States; its capitalist economic and social system; and possibilities for fundamental change. Indeed, had the title, *Capitalism, Socialism and Democracy* not been used by Harvard economist Joseph Schumpeter in his classic treatment of these subjects in 1942, we would have selected it for this book.[7]

The connections between capitalism and democracy raise the most interesting and pressing questions about political life in all the advanced industrial societies of Western Europe and North America. Indeed, the central questions confronting modern social theory and political philosophy for the past century have been about the tensions inherent in societies that are simultaneously capitalist and democratic. The political content of debate in most of these coun-

---

[7]Joseph Schumpeter, *Capitalism, Socialism, and Democracy* (New York: 1942).

tries has been shaped principally by these questions. Even when these questions are not openly on the agenda, the relationship between capitalism—which routinely generates inequalities in life conditions—and democracy—which posits equal rights and responsibilities for all citizens—affects major features of political life. In the United States, it is impossible to understand the politics of power—and powerlessness—without attention to these concerns, because American society is both the most capitalist and one of the most procedurally democratic of all the countries of the West.

STANDARDS OF DEMOCRACY

In 1961, political scientist Robert Dahl published an influential study of politics in New Haven, Connecticut. By commonly accepted standards, he argued, the city was a democracy, since virtually all its adult citizens were legally entitled to vote, their votes were honestly counted, and "two political parties contest elections, offer rival slates of candidates, and thus present the voters with at least some outward show of choice." Although the city's residents were legally equal at the ballot box, they were substantively unequal. Economic inequality in New Haven contrasted sharply with its formal political equality. Fewer than one-sixteenth of the taxpayers owned one-third of the city's property. In the wealthiest ward, one family out of four had an income three times the city average; the majority of the families in the poorest ward earned under $2,000 per year. Only one out of thirty adults in the poorest ward had attended college, as contrasted to nearly half of those in the richest ward.[8]

Is the combination of legal equality and class inequality democratic? Dahl put the question this way, "In a system where nearly every adult may vote but where knowledge, wealth, social position, access to officials, and other resources are unequally distributed, who actually governs? . . . How does a 'democratic' system work

[8]Robert Dahl, *Who Governs? Democracy and Power in an American City* (New Haven, Conn., 1961), pp. 3–4.

amid inequality of resources?"[9] He placed quotation marks around the term *democratic* because its meaning in this situation is unclear. Should a democratic system be measured only by legal standards of equality, such as fair and open election procedures, or should it be measured by substantive standards, according to the control and distribution of resources? What, in short, is the relationship of capitalism and democracy?

PROCEDURAL DEMOCRACY: STRUCTURE IGNORED

In his study of New Haven, Dahl argued that, rather than one elite group making political decisions, different elite groups determined policy in different issue areas, such as urban renewal, public education, and the nomination of candidates for office. In each area, however, there was a wide disparity between the ability of politically and economically powerful people and average citizens to make decisions. As a result of such disparities, Dahl noted, New Haven was "a long way from achieving the goal of political equality advocated by the philosophers of democracy and incorporated into the creed of democracy and equality practically every American professes to uphold."[10]

Nevertheless, he concluded that "New Haven is an example of a democratic system, warts and all."[11] Dahl never resolved the problem of capitalist inequalities in a "democratic" system. Rather, he reached his conclusion by assessing democracy only according to the procedural test (Can citizens vote? Do they have a choice between candidates? Are elections honest and conducted freely?). The structure of society and class inequalities are ignored.

This approach has dominated much recent thinking about democracy. As mentioned at the start of this chapter, the most influential twentieth-century discussion of the relationship of capitalism and democracy is by Joseph Schumpeter in *Capitalism, Socialism, and Democracy.* Schumpeter defines democracy wholly in procedural terms. Even though we reject his proposed standard of democracy, it is important to review his arguments here because his work underpins the way that most American social scientists think

---

[9]*Ibid.,* pp. 1, 3.
[10]*Ibid.,* p. 86.
[11]*Ibid.,* p. 311.

about democracy and because the issues he raises are basic to the elaboration of the approach to democracy we propose in this chapter.

Schumpeter began his discussion by rejecting the "classical view of democracy," which held that democracy exists when the people decide issues in the interest of the common good of all. This view assumed that there exists a "common good"—that all the members of the political system share basic interests. Since all members of the polity share these interests, it is possible to talk of "the people" who actually make decisions—either directly by themselves or indirectly through representatives whose job it is to accurately reflect the "common good."

Schumpeter powerfully questioned the existence of these assumed entities in a capitalist society. He wrote, "There is . . . no such thing as a uniquely determined common good that all people could agree on or be made to agree on by the force of rational argument."[12] A "common good" does not exist in societies characterized by basic structural inequalities because of the absence of shared interests. So long as patterns of inequality persist, it is impossible to speak of a "common good," since the good of some depends on the subordination of others.

Hence it is also impossible to speak of "the people," for when members of a society have different interests, there is no single, natural direction their will can take. Rather, "the people" are divided into groups that reflect the unequal distribution of power. Schumpeter thus concluded that "both the pillars of the classical doctrine inevitably crumble into dust."

Because he found the classical approach to democracy out of touch with reality, Schumpeter proposed that we accept "another theory which is much truer to life and at the same time salvages much of what sponsors of the democratic method really mean by this term."

Whereas the classical doctrine saw democracy as a set of institutional arrangements for reaching decisions to realize the people's common good, Schumpeter viewed democracy as "that institutional arrangement for arriving at political decisions in which individuals acquire the power to decide by means of a competitive struggle for the people's vote." Democracy thus becomes a set of rules for choosing, by election, among competing political leaders;

---

[12]Schumpeter, p. 251.

the substance of what is decided by those selected is only secondary. Schumpeter's alternative to the classical doctrine of democracy is also rooted in a profound distrust of the governed. Indeed, for Schumpeter, it is best that political elites, not "the people," make decisions, because the people are incompetent:

> The typical citizen drops down to a lower level of mental performance as soon as he enters the political field. He argues and analyzes in a way which he would readily recognize as infantile within the sphere of his real interests. He becomes a primitive again.[13]

For Schumpeter, and for the vast majority of American social scientists who have accepted his approach, a political system is democratic when citizens are provided with an opportunity to vote either for the political leaders in office or for a set of competing leaders who wish to get into office. Democracy is seen as a method, a set of formal procedures by which citizens can select among a limited number of alternative sets of leaders.

The role of voters in this conception resembles the role of consumers in a market economy. Much as consumers choose among competing products packaged by business people, so voters choose among competing candidates packaged by political parties. "The psycho-technics of party management and party advertising," Schumpeter wrote, "slogans and marching tunes, are not accessories. They are of the essence of politics."[14] Since neither major party challenges the basic structure of capitalist inequality, the act of choice, a legal right, replaces the substance of choice at the heart of democratic theory.

This purely procedural definition of democracy has become an ideological tool of social control. Those who benefit most from the capitalist social structure may maintain, since citizens can choose their leaders, that they have little cause for grievance. The system, by definition, is open and democratic. Those with complaints can express them in the next election. In this way, the procedural approach to democracy requires and promotes a relatively passive citizenry.

"Democracy" emerges from Schumpeter's discussion without its cutting edge. The classical view of democracy, however flawed by its reliance on the concepts of "common good" and "the peo-

---

[13]*Ibid.*, p. 262.
[14]*Ibid.*, p. 283.

ple," was concerned fundamentally with the substance of political decision making and the rule of the many against the powerful few. For this reason, democracy commanded far from universal acceptance. The emasculation of the term by Schumpeter has made it far more acceptable to dominant interests. Democracy is not a standard against which existing practice can be measured critically but is rather an uncritical, incomplete description of present electoral arrangements. Not surprisingly, almost all those who define democracy in wholly procedural terms find that there is no clash between democracy and capitalist inequality.

In rejecting the classical definition of democracy, Schumpeter had three alternatives. The first was to abandon the term *democracy* altogether as hopelessly utopian. The second, which he opted for, was to retain the term but redefine it to conform to existing realities. The third alternative, which we support, was to maintain the term *democracy* as a yardstick against which to measure and test reality. Thus, in a preliminary way, we define *democracy* as *a situation in which all citizens have relatively equal chances to influence and control the making of decisions that affect them.*

This alternative recognizes that although formal democratic procedures are essential to democracy, they do not guarantee it. For democracy approached this way does not depend simply on a set of rules, important though rules may be, but on the nature of the social structure within which the rules of procedural democracy operate.

Broadly, we may distinguish three different, though related, approaches to our definition of democracy. The first stresses popular participation in decision making; the second, the representation of interests; and the third, the transformation of the social structure itself. Let us examine each of these approaches in turn.

THE IMPORTANCE AND LIMITS OF DIRECT PARTICIPATION

Citizen participation in decision making has traditionally been regarded as the centerpiece of democracy. Convincing arguments for a participatory form of democracy were put forward by Jean Jacques Rousseau, an eighteenth-century French philosopher. His influential political theory hinged on the *direct* experience of political participation. For Rousseau, participation has objective and subjective components. The objective component is that citizens exercise control by participating in decision making; the subjective component is that, because they feel they have been able to participate authentically in the making of decisions that affect them, citizens come to identify with the decisions taken and develop feelings of loyalty to the society. In addition, citizens learn to participate effectively. As social theorist Carole Pateman put it in her interpretation of Rousseau's *The Social Contract,* "the more the individual citizen participates, the better he is able to do so. . . . He learns to be a public as well as a private citizen."[15]

One of the by-products of authentic participation is that citizens learn to identify and interpret their own interests accurately and need not depend on the interpretations of others. Conversely, if participation is inauthentic, if individuals are given the feeling of participating in decision making but are not accorded the power to actually control the decision-making process, the inevitable short-term result is that they are prevented from arriving at an accurate perception of their interests. Though eighteenth-century New England town meetings were examples of direct democracy, many were dominated by a small elite who controlled the agenda and often successfully manipulated the group discussions. The key issue is thus not whether people participate in the political system but what the *terms* of their participation are.

In the past 20 years, many organizations—including communes, antiwar protest groups, and women's-rights groups—have been founded on classical, Rousseauian democratic principles. They reject the formal procedural approach to democracy and run themselves, instead, as participatory democracies. Their members have self-consciously sought to create open, democratic communities in which all members participate directly in decision making. For many political activists, this kind of direct democracy provides a model for how democracy should be practiced in American society as a whole.

The leap from the small group to the society, however, is impossible to make. The program of participatory groups, including

[15]Carole Pateman, *Participation and Democratic Theory* (Cambridge, Mass., 1970), p. 25.

face-to-face unanimous decision making and absolute equality of status and power, is actually based on principles of friendship. As political scientist Jane Mansbridge notes

> friendship is an equal relation, it does not grow or maintain itself well at a distance, and its expression is in unanimity. . . . As participatory democracies grow from groups of fairly close acquaintances to associations of strangers, friendship can no longer serve as the basis of organization. Distrust replaces trust, and the natural equality, directness, and unanimity of friendship are transformed into rigid rules whose major purpose becomes the prevention of coercion and the protection of the individual.[16]

In small groups where people know each other intimately and are present voluntarily, the principles of direct, unanimous democracy may work to produce a natural, organic consensus of the group's will. Beyond such small groups, however, consensus is likely to be the result of manipulation, since shared values and mutual respect can develop only in situations where group members share interests. Small groups may constitute a "people" with a "common good," but as Schumpeter demonstrated, these entities in a capitalist society are fictions on a larger scale.

If democracy is to be used as a yardstick to assess both what exists and what is possible, the direct-participation approach is ruled out, because society as a whole does not provide the "friendship" basis that direct democracy requires. Hence a second approach to our definition of democracy argues that the crucial issue is not whether people participate directly, but whether all groups of the capitalist social structure and their interests achieve political *representation*.

REPRESENTATIVE DEMOCRACY

There are four dimensions of representative democracy that provide us with an immediately useful yardstick against which to test present realities. The first is *procedures*. It is essential in a democracy that individuals and groups be able to make their views known

[16]Jane Mansbridge, "The Limits of Friendship," unpublished manuscript, pp. 1–2.

and fairly select their leaders and public officials. Hence, civil liberties are essential. Free speech, free assembly, and freedom of the press are basic aspects of procedural representation. When these procedural guarantees are suppressed, it is extraordinarily difficult for people to formulate and express their interests.

The electoral mechanisms available to citizens for selecting their representatives are also an important factor in procedural representation. How wide is the electorate? How is party competition organized? What, in short, are the rules of the electoral process? As we have seen, electoral choice is at the heart of the formal procedural standard of democracy developed by Schumpeter.

But, unlike those who advocate procedural democracy, we believe that it is a mistake to limit the discussion of procedures of representation to elections. Rather, we must consider the nature of all of the rules that determine whether an individual or group has access to the political system and whether that access is likely to have an effect on decision making. Thus the traditionally narrow focus of issues raised about the procedures of representation must be widened. Are workers permitted to join unions? How are congressional committee chairmen selected? How does an elected mayor exercise control over nonelected city bureaucrats? To whom and how is a school system's personnel formally accountable? How are key foreign-policy decision makers chosen? How, if at all, are they formally held accountable? What are the procedures for representation in areas such as the space program, where expertise is available only to a few? Who selects the experts and to whom are they accountable? What are the procedures of leadership selection in interest groups (unions, farmers' organizations, professional associations)?

The list could easily be extended. The procedural dimension of representative democracy depends not only on equitable electoral procedures but more broadly on the mechanisms of access, influence, and accountability in government and in organizations that claim to represent the interests of their constituents. It is essential that the "rules of the game" ensure that the line that divides representatives and represented not harden and that access to ruling positions be open to all and not limited by racial, class, sexual, or other forms of discrimination.

Let us briefly consider a historical example. In the early 1900s, the Democratic party Tammany Hall machine dominated politics in New York City. During this period, most of the city's population consisted of European immigrants and their children. Because the populations of ethnic neighborhoods were relatively homogeneous, the ethnic groups gained control over the Tammany political clubs in their area. Blacks, however, were excluded from these organizations. They participated in party affairs through a citywide organization called the United Colored Democracy, whose leaders were selected by the white leaders of Tammany Hall, not by other blacks. Not surprisingly, studies of political patronage in the period indicate that blacks did the least well of all the groups in the city in securing political jobs; and the jobs they did get were the least desirable.[17]

Thus both the blacks from the South and the white ethnics from Europe joined the Democratic party, but on very different procedural terms. Although both groups could vote, the differences blacks experienced in the rules of access to the Democratic party severely limited their chances of reaping the rewards of municipal patronage.

The second dimension of representation is *personnel.* Irrespective of the way in which representatives have been selected, those who govern may or may not accurately reflect the demographic characteristics of class, race, ethnicity, sex, and geography of those they formally represent. During the Cuban missile crisis of 1962, for example, which was resolved when the Soviet Union removed its offensive missiles from Cuba after an American blockade of the island had been imposed, fewer than twenty individuals made the decisions that, by their own account, might have resulted in 150,000,000 casualties. The executive committee of the National Security Council met regularly in the two-week period of crisis to recommend courses of action to President Kennedy. Almost all of the council's members were Protestant, all were white, male, and wealthy. They included an investment banker, four corporation lawyers, a former automobile company president, and a number of multimillionaires.

In this instance, a very small group of men, hardly representative of the population as a whole, had the power to make decisions of the highest consequences. Judged by the personnel dimension of representation, the absence of democracy in this case

---

[17]Ira Katznelson, *Black Men, White Cities* (New York, 1973), chapter 5.

is beyond doubt. The demographic representativeness of those who make political decisions is not important just in order to fulfill abstract numerical quotas of representation. Rather, the personnel dimension of representation is important because the more demographically representative a political system is, the more likely it is that the interests of the basic groups of the social structure will be adequately and substantively represented. It is highly unlikely, for example, that a group of business leaders will accurately represent the interests of workers or that the interests of blacks will be best represented by whites. This might occasionally be the case, but group members are much more likely to represent their own interests than those of their structural antagonists. It is not surprising, therefore, that workers in unions earn better wages than those whose wage levels are entrusted to the discretion of their employers; nor is it surprising that Southern blacks have been treated more equitably by police since the passage of the Voting Rights Act of 1965 than they had been when they had to depend on the goodwill of the white community.

To represent group interests adequately, representatives must also fulfill the dimensions of *consciousness*—they must be aware of and responsive to their constituents' concerns. In this respect, subordinates often find it much more difficult than the privileged to achieve representation of their interests, since those with more resources tend to perceive their interests more accurately than subordinates. The privileged are also in a better position to put pressure on their representatives than those who are politically powerless. Thus representation concerns not only *who* rules but also the *uses* to which power is put by those who rule. The first two dimensions of representation—procedures and personnel—refer to the first of these two issues. But the dimension of consciousness asks how representatives see the interests of their constituents and how they act on behalf of these interests. To satisfy the requirements of representative democracy, those who formally represent the population must use the power conferred by their positions to promote the interests of the represented.

But even where the first three dimensions of representation are satisfied, political democracy cannot be said to exist. The last dimension that must be realized is *effectiveness*—the ability of representatives to produce the results they desire. A system cannot be democratically representative if effectiveness is distributed very unequally among representatives. For example, given the fact that most congressional legislation is decided by the various committees, it would be difficult to argue that Polish working-class citizens who select a Polish working-class representative will be democratically represented if the representative is placed on committees irrelevant to their concerns.

Thus representative democracy is achieved only when all four dimensions are satisfied: when leaders are selected by regular procedures that are open to all people and all groups have relatively equal access to the political system; when representatives reflect the demographic composition of the population as a whole; when they are conscious of and responsive to their constituents' interests; and when they can effectively act on behalf of those interests.

SUBSTANTIVE DEMOCRACY:
STRUCTURE TRANSFORMED

Unlike the purely procedural approach to democracy, the standard of representative democracy does not simply endorse present practices as democratic. Rather, it allows us to measure the degree of representative democracy that exists and, conversely, shows us how much needs to be done to achieve a fully representative democracy. As such, this standard is the best available to test the democratic content of existing political institutions and processes.

Nevertheless, it is limited. It leaves us with the basic dilemma posed earlier in the chapter: in Dahl's words, "How does a 'democratic' system work amid inequality of resources?" What is the relationship between a political system based on equality of representation and an economic system based on the inequality of capital and labor?

The answer to this question is that the two systems may coexist, as they have in much of the West for more than a century, but the routine operation of a capitalist economy prevents the full achievement of representative democracy: a situation in which all citizens have relatively equal chances to influence and control the making of decisions that affect them. This demanding, critical standard of democracy—a standard of substantive democracy—is based not only on the dimensions of representation but on the criterion of structural change. The basic contradictions between capitalism and democracy can be finally resolved only by the transformation of the social structure.

PARADOXES OF CAPITALIST DEMOCRACY

Of course, basic change in American capitalism represents just one, and at present hardly the most likely, outcome in the forseeable future. From the vantage point of the relationship of capitalism to democracy, this situation presents us with a puzzle. It is in the interest of members of the capitalist class to use their resources to maintain existing arrangements, and thereby freeze inequalities. At the same time, logically, it should be in the interest of noncapitalist groups and classes to seek fundamental change.

If this logic were to play itself out in American democracy, widespread challenges against the basic social structure would dominate American politics. Yet, obviously, these challenges only rarely occur. Much of everyday political life—speechmaking, elections, congressional debates—do not appear to reflect fundamental antagonisms of interest. We are thus confronted with our first paradox of American politics and society: political stability despite structural class inequality.

This paradox is expressed clearly in taxation policy. The most progressive tax is the income tax. The more income individuals or families earn, the higher percentage they pay in taxes. Yet even before the tax cuts successfully introduced by the first Reagan administration in 1981 (and implemented in the subsequent three years) that disproportionately aided the wealthy and the upper middle class, the income tax had virtually no effect on the country's overall distribution of income. A study conducted by the Congressional Joint Committee on Taxation during the administration of President Carter found that the richest fourth of households in America took home 55.5 percent of the income in the country in 1977 and yet still had 53.2 percent after paying income taxes. And even this minor amount of redistribution was offset by the regressive nature of sales and excise taxes (which tax by a flat percentage regardless of ability to pay) and of social security taxes (which only tax just under the first $40,000 of income, leaving higher earners untaxed over that amount).[18]

Nevertheless, there is a lack of enthusiasm among most Americans for a more equitable tax system. As the 1986 changes in the tax code have shown, tax reform has become a synonym for lower tax rates, irrespective of the consequences for the distribution of income and wealth. Although Americans are often cynical about the ways tax dollars are spent and think taxes are too high, "when redistributive issues are clearly raised, . . . it appears that most Americans do not want steeply progressive taxation." In responding to survey questions, Americans say they favor tax breaks that disproportionately aid the wealthy and prefer sales to income taxes.[19] These findings strongly indicate that political and social stability in the United States, fashioned in the face of a high degree of inequality (higher than anywhere else in the West)[20], is based principally not on a high degree of repression, though such coercion exists, but on a high degree of consent.

Democratic institutions and political freedom in the United States make America's strong political stability particularly noteworthy. No other nation, among the nearly two hundred existing today, has been governed by the same Constitution since the eighteenth century. Although there have been opposition movements calling for fundamental change in the United States, they have been relatively rare. In light of the freedom to organize, the weakness of opposition political movements suggests that there is substantial popular support for existing arrangements. In a public opinion poll of citizens in England, Italy, Germany, Mexico, and the United States, Americans expressed most pride in their political institutions.[21]

But popular support for American political institutions provides a clue to the persistence of inequality. In contrast to the United States, in every European country workers and the poor

---

[18]Art Pine, "Income Tax Doesn't Redistribute U.S. Wealth," *The Washington Post* (March 27, 1978); U.S. Department of the Treasury, Internal Revenue Service, *Individual Income Tax Returns, Preliminary Statistics of Income, 1976* (Washington, D.C., 1978); Harvey Galper, "Tax Policy," in Joseph Pechman, ed., *Setting National Priorities: The 1984 Budget* (Washington, D.C., 1983).

[19]Benjamin I. Page, "Taxes and Inequality: Do the Voters Get What They Want?" unpublished manuscript.

[20]For a discussion, see Ira Katznelson, "Considerations on Social Democracy in the United States," *Comparative Politics* II (October 1978): 77–99.

[21]Gabriel Almond and Sidney Verba, *The Civic Culture* (Princeton, N.J., 1963).

have organized political parties and long-term social movements to pressure government to respond to their needs. Large worker-based political parties in these countries have been responsible for obtaining benefits from governments for the working class. The absence of a strong working-class political movement in the United States means that workers and the poor have no regular organized way to press political demands. Government policies are bound to be less responsive to the working class if it fails to organize and use its political resources effectively. But what explains the relative political quiescence of the American working class? Why have those groups suffering systematic unequal treatment not used their right to vote and other political resources to press not only for modest but for substantial social change as well?

A second paradox is that of want and insecurity amidst plenty. Although, as we shall see, the kind of market capitalism that many economists assume to exist does not, in fact, operate in the United States, there are far fewer government constraints on the operation of the private economy than elsewhere in the capitalist world. No industries have been nationalized. No mechanisms of national economic planning exist. The American welfare state is fairly small.

This relatively unbridled capitalism produces goods and services in abundance. One hundred years ago, most of the technological innovations that now make for material ease did not exist. Automobiles, airplanes, computers, plastics, modern medicine, synthetic fabrics, indoor plumbing, cheap printing, television, washing machines, and telephones were all invented in the twentieth century—most of them in the United States. This country pioneered the mass-production techniques that make it possible to produce goods cheaply so that the fruits of modern science and industry can be distributed widely.

But far from equally. Although American industry churns out a vast quantity of products—$4 trillion ($4,000,000,000,000) yearly—millions of citizens lack adequate health care, housing, safe working conditions, even the chance to get a job. In the last several years, in some sections of the economy, there has been a shortage of workers, while overall there are nine million or more unemployed workers, and others so discouraged from looking that they are not even included in the official counts of the unemployed. One in ten families, and one in four individuals not living in families, earn incomes below the level of poverty as defined by the federal government; for blacks, the relevant figures are one in four, and two in five, respectively. The routine operation of American capitalism also produces regional disparities. While large cities in the Northeast and Midwest are decaying, suffering fiscal crises, and have many poor and unemployed workers, industries are spending heavily in other regions of the country. One may reasonably ask, why, in the most affluent nation in world history, is there so inadequate a provision of employment and public services, and so skewed a distribution of opportunities?

Our third paradox concerns the activities of government. It has rightly become a commonplace to comment on the spectacular growth of government in this century. For every $10 of the country's Gross National Product in 1900 less than $1 was spent by government. Today, that figure has increased to $4 in $10. Of course, much of that dramatic rise is accounted for by spending on military affairs, but a great deal of governmental activity is directed at alleviating hardship and inequalities. Such spending is more than sixty times greater than at the turn of the century, and at least six times what it was during the height of the New Deal of President Franklin Roosevelt in the 1930s. Why has such massive government intervention failed to reverse inequalities of wealth, income, and power, or assure that minimum social needs are met?

2

capitalism as private government

On September 19, 1977, disaster struck at Youngstown, Ohio, with effects as devastating as an earthquake, flood, or hurricane. Yet this was not a natural disaster. It was the announcement by the management of the Lykes Corporation, which owned the Youngstown Sheet and Tube steel company, that it had decided to close the local steel mill.

At one stroke, 4,000 steelworkers in the area lost their jobs. One commented, "We'll just about lose it all," referring to the life his family had built during the eight years he had worked for Youngstown Sheet and Tube.[1] The effects of the closing reverberated throughout the Mahoning Valley, harming thousands of other area residents. Food, clothing, furniture, and other retail stores whose business depended on steelworkers experienced a drop in sales, which resulted in further layoffs. Schools and other public services were cut back as a result of the decline in tax revenues

[1] *New York Times*, September 21, 1977.

from the company and its employees. The blow that was dealt to the area will last for years to come.

It is rare that the social effects of management decisions can be pinpointed so precisely. Yet the case of Youngstown is far from unique. In the steel industry alone, Bethlehem, Johnstown, and Conshohocken in Pennsylvania, as well as cities in New York and Ohio, have been crippled by layoffs of thousands of steelworkers. The cutback in steel production is part of larger changes going on worldwide. The abrupt slowdown of the American and other capitalist economies has reduced the demand for steel. Further, American steel plants are at a particular disadvantage: they are technologically backward, since American steel executives have been slow to introduce the latest steelmaking techniques. As a result, American steel companies are being squeezed by foreign competition, especially Japanese firms using modern methods. American steelworkers are bearing the burden of management misjudgment.

The preceding paragraphs, written for an earlier edition of this book, remain relevant. Since then, in fact, the tempo of disinvestment and layoffs in steel has accelerated. Between 1979 and 1980, U.S. Steel, the nation's largest steel company, cut steel production from 30 to 23 million tons, shut down 19 of its 46 blast furnaces, and laid off 15,000 of its 170,000 employees.[2] But cutbacks in steel had not ended. In December 1982, Bethlehem Steel Corporation laid off 10,000 steelworkers and one year later U.S. Steel (now known as USX) laid off an additional 15,000 workers and closed all or part of 29 mills, the largest shutdown in the history of the American steel industry. In all, 130,000 American steelworkers have lost their jobs since 1977.[3]

Analyzing the way that the crisis hit Youngstown can illuminate basic features of capitalist democracy in the United States. Since the Lykes management had virtually complete freedom to decide the fate of workers at the plant, as well as that of other area residents, we suggest that capitalism can be considered a

[2]Seymour Melman, *Profits Without Production* (New York, 1983), p. 198.
[3]Bruce Schmiechen, Lawrence Daressa, and Larry Adelman, "Waking from the American Dream," *The Nation*, March 3, 1984, p. 241; and Diane Feeley, "Unemployment Grows, A New Movement Stirs," *Monthly Review* 35 (December 1983): 18.

system of private government. This chapter describes its overall characteristics.

What was the basis on which management reached the decision to close the Youngstown steel mill? How much say did workers, other area residents, or the Youngstown city government have in the decision? The answer is that the management of Lykes decided alone, without consulting its workers or the community. The fact that workers were dependent for their livelihood on their jobs at the plant (some had worked there all their lives) did not give them the slightest right to participate in the decision. The fact that the Youngstown community was dependent on the plant for tax revenues—and that local taxes had provided services for the plant—did not give the city government the slightest right to participate in the decision.

It is a safe guess that the Lykes management decided to close the plant on the basis of what would be best for Lykes stockholders and executives, not Lykes workers or Youngstown. But it was less the personal intentions of management than the imperatives of profit-seeking in a capitalist system, as it has developed in the American setting, that dictated the decision. Following the logic of capitalism, and not constrained by the kind of government regulation of plant closings that exists in West European capitalist democracies, steel company executives were able to ignore the costs to workers, their families, and the community of closing down the plant. However great these costs to others, they were invisible from the perspective of Lykes' balance sheet. The costs were an unintended by-product of management's attempt to secure maximum profits. In the same way, the large proportion of American coalminers afflicted by black lung disease, as well as the polluted air, water, and soil of America's natural environment, and scores of devastated American cities are by-products of the day-to-day functioning of American corporate capitalism.

The Youngstown case illustrates the enormous power wielded by private management in a capitalist society and how that power is used to benefit companies, not communities. A *New York Times* reporter observed that executives of the Lykes Corporation

> made the decision in private the day before [it was announced]. They were under no obligation to give any notice or to assume any responsibility for the consequences in the areas from which they were drawing labor and resources. . . . Lykes was exercising a traditional and

jealously guarded right of the management of American business: to be the sole determiners of when a plant should be built, expanded or closed.[4]

What was government's role in the decision? In a democracy, do not the people or their elected representatives make the important decisions that affect the whole community? The answer is: not in the United States. Although the decision vitally affected the citizens of Youngstown, they had no say in the matter, nor did their local government, their congressional representatives, the Ohio state government, or federal officials. By contrast, plant closings in other capitalist democracies require advance notice and government approval.

The crisis of the American steel industry did elicit government action. But, as described by economists Gar Alperovits and Jeff Faux, "The political response to the Youngstown layoffs has not centered on saving the town, but on saving the *steel industry.*"[5] The federal government has provided steel companies with tax credits and other incentives to modernize their equipment. Much of the new investment will go into "labor-saving" technology, which is another way of saying that it will displace workers. Steel companies have used new funds, obtained with federal tax and other assistance, to diversify out of steel. Between 1977 and 1980, U.S. Steel increased its nonsteel assets by 80 percent and its steel assets by 13 percent. In 1982, it purchased Marathon Oil Company for $6 billion.

How can one make sense of these illogical actions? The answer is that they are not illogical from the standpoint of capitalist profit-seeking.

CAPITALISM AS A SYSTEM
OF PRIVATE GOVERNMENT

Capitalism may be defined as a system in which production is privately controlled and carried on for sale and profit rather than for consumption (use). Those who own and control the means of pro-

---

[4]*New York Times,* December 26, 1977.
[5]*New York Times,* November 3, 1977. Italics in original.

duction—the factories, machines, and raw materials used to produce commodities for sale—set the process in motion by hiring
workers to carry on the actual work of production. The aim of the
capitalist in doing so is to make a profit, which can then be used for
further investment and the accumulation of additional profits.
Economist Paul Sweezy, following Marx, suggests that capital can
be defined as self-expanding value: "Capitalism therefore can exist
only if there is some way that capitalists can regularly sell their
products for more money than they had to lay out to produce
them."[6]

This difference between a commodity's cost of production and
its sale price is profit, or surplus value. Profit derives from the fact
that workers produce more value than the wages they receive for
their labor (after other costs of production are subtracted). The
capitalist (either an individual employer or a corporation) appro-
priates this surplus value produced by workers.

The second phase of the process is the realization of profit
through the sale of the commodities that workers produce. Unless
goods are sold, profits cannot be realized. Thus, the capitalist attempts to maximize profits by organizing production at the lowest
possible cost (for example, by squeezing workers to work hard) and
selling the commodities that are produced at the highest possible
price.

The third phase of the capitalist production process is investment in new means of production. Expanding production—capital
accumulation and new investment—is a necessity if capitalist production is to continue.

This highly simplified model of the capitalist system raises
many questions. Why do capitalists have the legal right and the
material resources to hire others to work at their direction? Why
are they entitled to take the surplus created by workers? Why are
most members of the society forced to work for a wage or salary
and follow the dictates of capitalist management?

A crucial feature of capitalist production is that most people
do not control the means of production and must therefore work
for those who do in order to earn the necessities of life. Further,
capitalism requires a political framework that protects the right of

---

[6]Paul Sweezy, "The Present Stage of the Global Crisis of Capitalism," *Monthly
Review* 29 (April 1978): 9.

capital both to hire workers and appropriate the surplus value workers create. These characteristics have pervasive political consequences.

No matter how democratic formal political institutions are, the exploitation of workers is inherent in a capitalist society. Exploitation occurs through the process by which workers are compelled to work at capitalists' direction in order to produce surplus value that is appropriated by capital. This process—what is often described as the functioning of a healthy economy—reproduces a society in which the means of production are privately owned and controlled and in which workers are forced to enrich capital in order to survive. Although these harsh facts are rarely noted, they are the daily reality of capitalist society. It is only at unusual moments, like at Youngstown, that the reality of capitalism becomes painfully apparent. In most cases, it is obscured by the illusion (and, to some extent, the reality) of free choice and democratic government.

Yet capitalist domination is never free from challenge. Three kinds of conflicts warrant special mention. First, capitalists are continually struggling with each other. Because they are divided by economic competition (despite attempts described in this and the following chapter to limit competition), capitalists find it harder to unite for common action. Second, workers struggle with their employers to obtain higher wages, safer working conditions, and more autonomy on the job. Although these conflicts have rarely posed a threat to overall capitalist control in the United States, militant strikes or even workers' day-to-day resistance in the office or on the shop floor poses a challenge to management.

Third, in a capitalist democracy like the United States, citizens often seek to use government to make capitalist firms serve their interests. For example, as was mentioned previously, in most capitalist democracies governments have passed laws limiting management's right to close a plant and requiring management to provide for workers' retraining and relocation. Given the relative weakness of the American labor movement and the federal political structure that fragments power, this has not occurred in the United States. But labor unions and citizens' groups in Massachusetts, Connecticut, Maine, and Wisconsin have passed laws regulating plant closings, and many other states are considering similar laws. Yet, so long as a capitalist system of production remains in place, capitalists will possess extraordinary influence over the entire political economy. The major reason is that, by their day-to-day investment decisions, capitalists affect the fate of local communities, regions, and the entire nation. A fuller picture of capitalism as a system of private government can be gained by reviewing the rights conferred by control of capital.

What to produce

Investment decisions, especially major ones, made by giant corporations, determine the kinds of goods available in the society. As at Youngstown, the decision to invest or disinvest (that is, reduce or close down production) is made on the basis of what promises to fetch the highest profit. The whole community is affected by capitalist investment decisions. When investment lags, then production lags, wages stagnate, and many workers are unable to find jobs. When investment booms, then production booms, jobs are more plentiful, and wages rise as employers compete for workers.

A profoundly important consequence of this process is that citizens tend to identify their individual welfare with the welfare of capitalism. This helps explain the widespread support for capitalism in the United States. In addition to the intensive propaganda on behalf of capitalism by schools, business, political parties, and other institutions, there is a rational basis for pro-capitalist beliefs. Citizens engage in a kind of cost-benefit analysis—rational within the confines of capitalist democracy—that their interests are served by helping capitalism flourish. This does not mean that citizens do not perceive conflicts between their interests and capitalist interests. (Workers at Youngstown hardly needed to be reminded of this fact.) Nor does widespread support for capitalism mean that workers and other citizens do not struggle against specific features of capitalist domination. But what has been missing in the United States during much of its history is a *generalized* struggle against the entire system of capitalist production.

Capitalism is often described as a system of consumer sovereignty, in which the market accurately reflects individual consumer preferences. Thus, it is argued, a system of free enterprise rather than government control maximizes individual freedom, equality, and choice. However, three factors prevent the free expression of consumer choice. First, given the highly unequal distribution of income in the United States (described elsewhere in this book), what is rational from the standpoint of profitable investments is irrational for many citizens. Thus, many citizens do not have the economic resources to be "free." For example, large numbers of Americans cannot afford to pay for adequate housing. Consequently, the fact that there is a pressing need for decent housing does not mean that it is profitable to provide it.

Second, giant corporations and capitalism as a productive system shape as much as they reflect people's needs and preferences. The situation is often described as a choice between individual decision making (capitalism) and government control. For example, according to President Reagan in his 1985 State of the Union address, "Every decision government doesn't make, makes us freer." But this neglects the enormous power exercised by another set of participants: individual capitalist firms and the even greater power of corporate capitalism as a whole. We are all to a considerable extent captive of corporate marketing and advertising strategies. Far more important than fostering reliance on specific products is that capitalism encourages the development of individualistic, acquisitive desires (precisely those that can be satisfied by purchases in the market) as opposed to cooperative, communitarian desires.

Third, the market is designed to satisfy individual, not social preferences. Economist Frank Ackerman points out, "There is no way for a single individual to freely choose mass transit, pollution control, a ban on nuclear power, clean streets, fire protection, [and] guaranteed incomes for senior citizens. . . . Collective choice and government are required. . . ."[7] By choosing a capitalist system, Americans delegate to capitalists much of the power to decide what to produce. Although seldom recognized as a political choice, it is one of the most fateful political decisions made in the United States.

Where to produce

In a capitalist system, those who own and control the means of production are free to decide the geographic location where production will be carried on. This decision is made strictly on the basis

---

[7]Frank Ackerman, *Hazardous to Our Wealth: Economic Policies in the 1980s* (Boston, 1984), pp. 87–88.

of which location will reap the greatest profits or (another way of describing the same thing) which location will minimize the costs of production and maximize sales. Among the different factors taken into account are proximity to suppliers, raw materials, and markets, as well as adequate transportation facilities.

Two factors that affect the attractiveness of new plant sites are especially relevant for political analysis. One is the tax advantages and other benefits promised a company by state and local governments. Governments bid against each other in an attempt to attract private industry, offering companies low taxes, custom-built factories, roads, and waste treatment facilities. Who pays for these inducements? The answer is local residents, often workers.

The second, and more important, factor in determining a company's choice of plant location is the characteristics of workers. Companies search for areas where workers are willing to accept low wages. Wage rates and the militance of workers (for example, their readiness to strike) vary in different sections of the country. Where workers are unionized, wages are higher. A company may prefer to hire nonunion labor to keep wages low and workers divided. By paying low wages, capital extracts an additional bonus from working people.

The Youngstown case illustrates what can happen when management is entrusted to decide where to invest or disinvest. A pattern of decisions made by many corporations has nationwide consequences. Scores of companies have moved from the Northeast and Midwest (the "Frostbelt" or "Rustbowl") to the South and West (the "Sunbelt"), leaving behind a trail of blight.

Many corporations have found that the wage bill is lower yet if they invest in manufacturing facilities outside the United States. (The process of multinational expansion abroad will be examined in Chapter 10.) Not only are corporations not required to pay for the damage they cause when they leave an area; the federal government provides tax breaks for new investments, thereby subsidizing the costs of corporate flight.

How production is carried on

In a capitalist society, the workplace is not organized democratically. Private managers—not workers, consumers, or government—decide the key questions about production, including what will be produced; who will be hired, promoted, and fired; the level of wages that will be offered; the length of the working day; the kind of technology used; and how to dispose of toxic wastes resulting from production. Workers are paid to take orders, not exercise initiative. In a capitalist democracy, many citizens' rights end at the factory gate or office door.

However, there is a continual possibility of government intervention to limit capitalists' freedom to decide these questions. The sphere of capitalist decision making may be restricted as a result of popular pressure and government action. If not for such pressure, culminating in government regulation, the working day would continue to be over 14 hours long, as it was for the average steelworker until the First World War.

The price of commodities

In a capitalist system, people acquire most goods and services by purchasing them in the market. Those owning and controlling capital are free to set the level of prices they charge, although competition from U.S. and foreign capitalist producers sets limits on the prices that can be charged. (For years, American producers have been losing ground in domestic and foreign markets because they charge high prices for low quality goods.) Of course, consumers are free to refuse to purchase. But this becomes a hollow right when people are dependent on capitalist production for food, energy, clothing, shelter, and other necessities.

What is the significance of this picture of capitalist production? From the standpoint of capitalists, it means business as usual, the normal calculations of profit and loss that guide capitalist investment, production, and sales. Yet from a wider viewpoint, it is a system of private business firms pursuing their self-interest. As political economist Charles Lindblom points out, "Because public functions in the market [capitalist] system rest in the hands of businessmen, it follows that jobs, prices, production, growth, the standard of living, and the economic security of everyone all rest in their hands."[8]

This book attempts to study the conflict between the needs of capitalist production and the needs of the whole society, as well as the tension between the undemocratic organization of the economy

---

[8]Charles E. Lindblom, *Politics and Markets: The World's Political-Economic Systems* (New York, 1977), p. 172.

and the formally democratic character of the political system. The scope of democratic politics is severely limited by the capitalist organization of the economy. In the next section, we will review the overall characteristics of the private government exercised by corporate capitalism in the United States.

CORPORATE CAPITALISM

Suppose it was learned that a small group had obtained critical power in the United States. Imagine that, in a country with a population of 236 million people, several thousand Americans—unrepresentative, not democratically chosen nor even known to most people—controlled many of the key aspects of American life. This small group decided what kinds of products Americans would manufacture. It owned and controlled the factories in which production occurred. It not only employed but could also promote or fire a large proportion of Americans. This group produced dangerous and expensive weapons for the military. It directed radio and television networks and deeply influenced Americans' values and attitudes. It dominated the companies that produce the automobiles, televison sets, and electric appliances found in most American homes.

Because members of this group controlled much of the country's productive capacity, their decisions affected every American. Yet they based their decisions not on what the country needed but on what would be profitable for them. As a result, some Americans were saturated with a profusion of possessions, while many others could barely obtain basic necessities, such as food, housing, and medical care.

Further, this group had enormous political influence. Its contributions to political parties were vital for candidates to be nominated and elected to office. It developed close ties to Congress, the president, and government agencies, which helped it to receive preferential treatment.

One can imagine the outcry that would greet the announcement that such a group existed. After all, its existence would make democratic government an illusion.

And yet, such a group does exist. All that has been described is fact, not fiction. A convenient shorthand label for the process of production, distribution, and consumption, over which this group exerts control, is corporate capitalism. What makes it such a powerful force in America?

There are approximately twelve million economic enterprises in the United States, from small family farms and shoe repair shops to U.S. Steel Corporation and Gulf Oil Corporation. In terms of value, their individual net worth ranges from several hundred dollars to the $69 billion in assets controlled by Exxon.

We can distinguish between two sectors of private production: corporate capital, which includes the largest mining and manufacturing corporations, banks, large commercial and investment retail chain stores, insurance companies, utilities, television networks, and corporate law firms; and small-scale capital, which include restaurants, small-town newspapers and banks, clothing stores, small construction companies, and small manufacturers (such as garment factories). In terms of the number of workers employed, the two sectors are nearly equal. However, that is about all they have in common. Productive resources are owned, organized, and managed very differently in the two sectors: the sphere of corporate capital is far more productive, centralized, and powerful than the sphere of small-scale capital. Measured by the ability to shape the major decisions regarding their organization of society and the distribution of benefits, corporate capital far outdistances small-scale capital.

Some idea of the raw power concentrated within the corporate sector can be conveyed by the following figures. Among the over 400,000 manufacturing concerns in the United States, a fortunate few—about 260—have assets worth over $1 billion. They are the industrial giants of America, whose names are household words: Ford, General Electric (GE), Exxon, International Business Machines (IBM), Chrysler. These corporations are immense individually; their combined worth and power are staggering. The top 500 corporations control three-quarters of all industrial assets in the United States—leaving the remaining one-quarter to the other 400,000 firms. The same 500 corporations had $1.8 trillion in sales in 1985—nearly half the total sales of the entire American economy.

Yet, there are further inequalities between the biggest and smallest corporations in the top 500: the largest (General Motors) had sales in 1985 that were 227 times greater than the smallest corporation (Winnebago Industries). The 200 largest corporations

Table 2-1
The 20 largest industrial corporations, 1986 (ranked by sales)

RANK '85	'84	COMPANY (Headquarters)	SALES ($000)	ASSETS ($000)	NET INCOME ($000)	EMPLOYEES
1	2	General Motors (Detroit)	96,371,700	63,832,800	3,999,000	811,000
2	1	Exxon (New York)	86,673,000	69,160,000	4,870,000	146,000
3	3	Mobil (New York)	55,960,000	41,752,000	1,040,000	163,600
4	4	Ford Motor (Dearborn, Mich.)	52,774,400	31,603,600	2,515,400	369,300
5	6	International Business Machines (Armonk, N.Y.)	50,056,000	52,634,000	6,555,000	405,535
6	5	Texaco (White Plains, N.Y.)	46,297,000	37,703,000	1,233,000	54,481
7	11	Chevron (San Francisco)	41,741,905	38,899,492	1,547,360	60,845
8	8	American Tel. & Tel. (New York)	34,909,500	40,462,500	1,556,800	337,600
9	7	E.I. du Pont de Nemours (Wilmington, Del.)	29,483,000	25,140,000	1,118,000	146,017
10	9	General Electric (Fairfield, Conn.)	28,285,000	26,432,000	2,336,000	304,000
11	10	Amoco (Chicago)	27,215,000	25,198,000	1,953,000	49,545
12	12	Atlantic Richfield (Los Angeles)	22,357,000	20,279,000	(202,000)	31,300
13	14	Chrysler (Highland Park, Mich.)	21,255,500	12,605,300	1,635,200	107,850
14	13	Shell Oil (Houston)	20,309,000	26,528,000	1,650,000	35,167
15	15	U.S. Steel (Pittsburgh)	18,429,000	18,446,000	409,000	79,649
16	16	United Technologies (Hartford)	15,748,674	10,528,105	312,724	184,800
17	17	Phillips Petroleum (Bartlesville, Okla.)	15,676,000	14,045,000	418,000	25,300
18	19	Tenneco (Houston)	15,400,000	20,437,000	172,000	111,000
19	18	Occidental Petroleum (Los Angeles)	14,534,400	11,585,900	696,000	42,353
20	20	Sun (Radnor, Pa.)	13,769,000	12,923,000	527,000	37,818

Source: *Fortune*, April 28, 1986. The Fortune 500 © 1986 Time Inc. All rights reserved.

control nearly two-thirds of all manufacturing assets in the United States, and the top ten alone account for about one-seventh of America's total annual gross national product (GNP).

These statistics indicate the overall dimensions of corporate capitalism. Some additional important features of corporate capitalism include:

Size   The largest corporations, which dominate production in the United States, are immense. For example, General Motors (GM) employs 811,000 people, has assets of $63 billion, annual sales of $96 billion, and profits of about $4 billion. General Electric employs workers in 240 factories in over 20 countries. GE produces 230,000 different products. The output of GE, GM, or Exxon exceeds the total gross national products of hefty countries like Austria, Denmark, or Yugoslavia.

Most of the products Americans buy, from toothpaste to automobiles, are produced by corporate capitalism. The top 500 corporations employ 14 million workers—half of the industrial workers and one-third of all workers in the United States. Many Americans who are not directly dependent on giant corporations for their livelihood are indirectly dependent. Small manufacturers produce parts and other supplies that they sell to these corporations. Retail dealers sell and repair workers service what corporate capitalism produces. Many local retail stores, gasoline stations, bus companies, and banks would not exist were it not for the economic activity of the corporate giants. Newspapers and television stations also would not survive without the advertising revenue they receive from corporate capitalism.

A typical mammoth corporation constitutes a powerful force in American politics. Together, the few hundred largest corporations control most of the country's productive resources. The requirements of corporate capitalism are a first priority on the American political agenda.

Concentration   Economists call an industry *concentrated* if a few large firms dominate production and sales. Automobile production is one such industry. Four companies—GM, Ford, Chrysler, and American Motors—produce 95 percent of the nine million automobiles made in the United States each year. (More than half of these—about five million—are produced by GM alone.)

Firms in a concentrated industry behave differently than firms in a competitive industry. The critical difference is the extent of

their power. In a competitive industry, many small companies compete with each other and none get a large share of the market. In a
concentrated industry, firms enter into long-term arrangements
with other firms to stabilize their supplies and sales. Through a
process known as administered prices, they informally cooperate
to set prices high enough to assure profits even when demand for
their products may lag. (One study found that the average rate of
profit before taxes was 20 percent in concentrated industries, but
only 13 percent in nonconcentrated industries.[9])

When production becomes concentrated, in brief, control over
the society's productive resources becomes centralized. Giant corporations are powerful, stable institutions, able to exercise considerable control over their environment—including consumers,
workers, and (as we shall see in the next chapter) government. The
trend toward concentration in the American economy has been
rapid. In the period from 1948 to 1968, the 200 largest corporations
increased their share of total manufacturing assets in the United
States from 46 to 60 percent. The same proportion of sales that the
top 200 firms controlled in 1950 was controlled by only half as many
firms 20 years later. (As can be seen in Figure 2-1, the trend slowed
during the 1970s and picked up at the end of the decade.)

Concentration thus occurs not only within given industries but
in the economy as a whole. The American economy has become
nationalized, integrated, concentrated, and centralized around a
cluster of privately owned industries and firms. In describing the
contours of concentrated industries, we are also describing the results of private decisions about the allocation of resources in the
United States.

Expansion and contraction   Economist Douglas Dowd has
pointed out, "Expansion may be seen as the essence of the capitalist *process,* as the heartbeat of capitalism."[10] One aspect of this
expansion is that corporate capital has extended its control beyond
the traditional spheres of industrial and mining activity. Corporations have moved into the entertainment and leisure fields, including motion picture companies, hotels, travel and tour companies,
and restaurants (Howard Johnson's and McDonald's, rather than
the corner drugstore, now supply Americans with hamburgers). In

[9]Howard Sherman, *Radical Political Economy: Capitalism from a Marxist Humanist
Perspective* (New York, 1972), p. 108.
[10]Douglas F. Dowd, *The Twisted Dream: Capitalist Development in the United States
Since 1776,* 2nd ed. (Cambridge, Mass., 1977), p. 36.

Figure 2-1
Real assets of all large manufacturing and mining companies acquired:
1948–79 (1967 = 100)

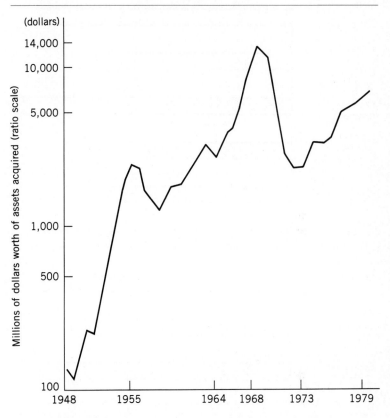

Source: Barry Bluestone and Bennett Harrison, *The Deindustrialization of America: Plant Closings, Community Abandonment, and the Dismantling of Basic Industry* (New York: Basic Books, 1982), p. 125. Reprinted by permission. Sources listed in original.

the field of agriculture, "agricorporations" are fast replacing the family farm, centralizing the production, processing, and distribution of food. (By 1966, the 100 largest food manufacturers accounted for nearly half of all food commercially marketed.)[11]

[11]James Hightower, "The Case for the Family Farmer," *Washington Monthly* (September 1973), p. 28.

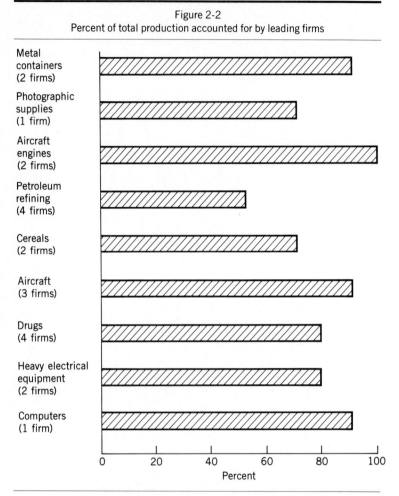

Figure 2-2
Percent of total production accounted for by leading firms

Source: William G. Shepherd, *Market Power and Economic Welfare: An Introduction* (New York: Random House, 1970), pp. 152–54. Reprinted by permission.

Hospital care is a relatively recent profit-making "industry." Among the winners in this lucrative field are Hospital Corporation of America (over $4 billion in annual revenues) and Humana, a rapidly growing new entrant that sponsored the world's second artificial heart transplant at its Louisville hospital. Given their profit-making goal, such hospitals reserve their facilities for

Figure 2-3
The 500 largest corporations:
changes in sales, income, and employees, 1954–1983

Source: *Fortune,* April 30, 1984, p. 275.

wealthy patients, directing the poor to nonprofit and public hospitals. (The result is to overstrain and discredit public-sector services.)

The expansion of corporate capital often means the contraction of jobs, as workers are replaced by machines. In 1983, a boom period, the top 500 corporations employed 300,000 fewer workers than the previous year. *Fortune* magazine, a business publication, found that, since 1954, the top 500 corporations have increased sales twelve times and net income eight times, yet have only doubled their work force.[12]

[12] *Fortune,* April 30, 1984.

The process is illustrated by the corporate takeover of agriculture. Since 1940, as agriculture has become penetrated by corporate capital and transformed into agribusiness, the resulting mechanization has forced 20 million people off the land. Since 1950, mechanical harvesters have eliminated jobs for 2 million of the 4.3 million farm workers.[13] The remaining farmers are becoming hired hands for large agricorporations that produce farm machinery, pesticides, and fertilizers and then process the food, which is grown to their specifications. Corporations have also been moving onto the land directly. Among the nation's largest "farmers" are Boeing, Dow Chemical, and Tenneco.

A massive restructuring of the U.S. economy has been occurring in recent years, producing dislocations for millions of workers. In a thorough study of the process, what they term deindustrialization, economists Barry Bluestone and Bennett Harrison find that 39 million jobs were eliminated by plant cutbacks and closings between 1969 and 1976 alone. This far outweighed the 25 million new jobs created by private industry during the same period.[14]

Contrary to those who argue that this is a healthy process of economic renewal that benefits everyone, Bluestone and Harrison find that many closings are motivated by the search to obtain greater advantages by weakening workers' power. This also helps explain why there were many more new jobs created in the Sunbelt than in the Frostbelt. Why? One indication is provided by the Conference of State Manufacturers' Association, a business organization that developed an index rating each state's "business climate." The ingredients were "low taxes, low union membership, low workers' compensation insurance rates, low unemployment benefits per worker . . . in that order."[15] Business moves are profitable because laid-off workers, the community, and government bear the costs.

In the process of economic restructuring, as carried out under capitalist auspices, displaced workers rarely land comparably well-paying and skilled high-tech jobs. "For example, automobile work-

---

[13]Douglas Zoloth Foster, "Weeding Workers: How the University of California is Underwriting the Loss of 170,000 Jobs," *In These Times*, May 10–16, 1978, pp. 12–13.

[14]Barry Bluestone and Bennett Harrison, *The Deindustrialization of America: Plant Closings, Community Abandonment, and the Dismantling of Basic Industry* (New York, 1982), p. 30.

[15]*Ibid.*, p. 182.

ers who lose their jobs in this high productivity industry are found two years later to be in jobs that pay on the average 43 percent less."[16] Most new jobs are created by small firms, where unions are less likely to be organized and pay is low. For example, in the 1970s, the *increase* in employment in the "food and drink" industry was larger than the *total* employment in the automobile and steel industries combined.[17] Bluestone and Harrison observe, "A family is required to take two full-time jobs at a McDonald's fast food outlet or in a discount department store to make up for the loss of one job in a unionized woolen mill."[18]

There are substantial disparities in wages between the declining and growing industries. The motor vehicles, blast furnaces, and farm machinery industries are all expected to grow at less than 2 percent annually into the 1990s. The fast growth industries—electronic components, computer office equipment, and medical instruments and supplies—are expected to grow several times as fast. (In any case, since these are relatively small industries, they will not create sufficient new jobs to offset the job losses in basic industries.) In 1982, whereas wages in the slow growth sector exceeded $10.00 an hour, wages in the fast growth sector were in the $7.00 to 8.50 range.[19]

But the worst—or the best—news regarding economic restructuring is yet to come. (Which of the two it will be hinges on the outcome of political struggles and decisions.) Sociologist Fred Block emphasizes the importance of a little-noticed feature of the micro-electronic revolution presently occurring, which involves the miniaturization of computer circuitry, fibreoptics, and the linking of rapid means of communication and data processing, including satellite transmission, telephone, and cable TV: "Many of the new technologies based on microelectronics are capital-saving as well as labor-saving."[20] Not only do the new technologies displace workers in the industries where they are introduced (robots replacing workers in the automobile industry), but the industries producing the new technologies themselves incorporate these technologies in the

[16]*Ibid.,* p. 10.
[17]*New York Times,* May 31, 1984.
[18]Bluestone and Harrison, p. 95.
[19]Richard Corrigan and Rochelle L. Stanfield, "Casualties of Changes," *National Journal,* February 11, 1984.
[20]Fred Block, "The Myth of Reindustrialization," *Socialist Review,* no. 73 (Jan.–Feb. 1984), p. 70.

production process and produce more with fewer workers. For example, in the robotics industry, robots produce robots. The outlook is thus for increasing structural unemployment as the fast-growth industries produce more output with fewer workers, and traditional heavy industries continue to lay off workers. Nobel prize-winning economist Wassily Leontief estimates that in 1990 11 million fewer workers will be needed to produce the same amount of goods and services as in 1983, while by the year 2000 20 million fewer workers will be needed to produce the 1983 output.[21]

The process of producing more output with fewer workers is presently a curse because it signifies a dwindling number of jobs in the future and therefore the prospect of unemployment or under-employment for millions of Americans. In a rationally organized society, automation would prove a blessing, permitting a substantial reduction in the length of the work week, more flexible scheduling of work, and the like. Under capitalist domination of the workplace, however, the benefits of the new developments accrue to capital, in the form of lower wages, a smaller work force, and greater managerial control over work and workers.

Who are the people behind the impersonal mask of "capital"? Although corporate capitalism is a *system,* it is also flesh and blood human beings.

WHO OWNS AMERICA'S PRIVATE GOVERNMENT?

The answer to this question begins with tracing the ownership of stock in giant corporations. In the corporate form, people who invest money receive shares in the assets or stock of the corporation. They share in the corporation's profits in proportion to the amount of stock they own. Stockholders are entitled to vote for the board of directors of the corporation. They have a number of votes proportional to the amount of stock they own. The board of directors chooses the corporation's top management and reviews management decisions. Since corporations control most of America's productive assets (means of production), those who control corpo-

---

[21]Corrigan and Stanfield, op. cit.

rations are influential in deciding what America will produce and consume.

If corporate stock ownership were widely and equally distributed, then the following frequently heard claim would be valid: "In our system of free enterprise, the capitalist system, industry is owned by the American public."[22] However, such cheery pronouncements are belied by the fact that less than one family in six owns stock. Most Americans are forced to devote their income to purchasing necessities. Over half of all savings in the United States is supplied by the richest 5 percent of the society.

Even among the small stock-owning group, the distribution of stock is highly unequal. Two-thirds of all stockholders own less than $10,000 in stock, a negligible investment. For gaining influence in the corporation depends not only on owning stock in the corporation but on how *much* one owns: a person owning 1 share has 1 vote at the annual stockholders' meeting, while a person with 100 shares has 100 votes, and a person with 10,000 shares has 10,000 votes. Small stockholders are lavishly praised at the annual meeting, but they are "owners" of a corporation only in legal appearance for, in reality, it requires a large bloc of stock in a corporation to have an *effective* voice.

Most stock is held by a tiny proportion of Americans. An examination of the upper range of the stock-owning pyramid indicates that less than one-tenth of all stockholders own 80 percent of all stock. In its 1982 Annual Report, the Joint Economic Committee of Congress pointed out that 1.2 percent of all stockholders (about .2 percent of all Americans) receives over 40 percent of all stock dividends. In a nation of 236 million people, the means of production are owned by a group no larger than the population of Denver, Colorado.

The professionalization of capital

Despite their strategic position, the fabulously wealthy upper class does not rule corporate capitalism by itself. In recent decades, there has been a trend toward professionalizing the management

---

[22]William Lynch, an executive of the stockbroker firm Dean Witter Reynolds, interviewed by the Voice of America, February 3, 1985. Note that this statement was broadcast around the world as a description of the American system.

of capital. The new breed of corporate managers are usually engineering or business school graduates trained to apply modern methods to furthering the search for corporate profits. Relatively anonymous bureaucrats, the new managers are quite different from the colorful magnates of an earlier era. And because they are out of the public eye, they are less likely than old-time tycoons like J. P. Morgan or John D. Rockefeller to provide a target for popular discontent. (Has anybody heard of Roger Smith? He is chairman of GM.)

Most corporate executives, even those not in the ranks of the superwealthy, own large blocks of shares in the corporations they manage. About one-half of an executive's pay is in the form of stock bonuses and options, deferred compensation, and profit sharing rather than straight salary. (This does not mean that corporate executives do not receive handsome salaries: the country's highest-paid corporate executives have an annual salary exceeding $1 million.) Economist Edward Herman found that, in four-fifths of the 100 largest corporations, the chief executive owned at least $1 million in stock in the corporation.[23] Although this is a paltry sum, measured by the total stock outstanding, it does mean that top managers have similar interests to the corporation's other large stockholders. Moreover, the alliance of management and large stockholders is sealed by the fact that many top corporate executives sit on the firm's board of directors. (About one-third of the average corporate board is composed of these so-called "inside" directors.)

It apparently makes little difference for corporate performance whether a corporation is controlled by large stockholders, as was typical for corporations in the past, or whether, as is becoming more common, professional managers play a dominant role. Contrary to those who assert that manager-controlled corporations in the modern era are more "mature," less aggressive, less interested in profits, and more interested in stability than were owner-controlled corporations in the past, both types of corporations act about the same.

In the present period, capital is organized in collective units rather than by individual capitalists. Economists Paul Baran and

---

[23]Edward S. Herman, *Corporate Power, Corporate Control* (Cambridge, England, 1981), p. 93.

Paul Sweezy suggest that "the real capitalist today is not the individual businessman but the corporation."[24] That corporations have become increasingly large and complex, drawing on the skills of diverse technical specialists, and run by professional managers, means that they are more effective in pursuing the quest to cut costs and increase profits.

Competition and coordination

Although a corporation can be considered a single unit of capital, competing with other units of capital (rival corporations), the relationship among corporations is characterized by cooperation and coordination as well as competition. A number of informal mechanisms serve to reduce competition among corporations and develop a common point of view for capital as a whole. First, corporations in a given industry share an interest in reducing competition, or at least limiting its scope. The most common result is a pattern known as "administered prices," in which corporate rivals tacitly agree to maintain prices at levels sufficiently high to permit a target rate of return (profit). Trade associations within given industries also seek to coordinate and harmonize the interests of rival firms.

Banks, especially the largest New York commercial and investment banks, achieve direct integration through purchase of stock in corporations, usually using investment and union pension funds they manage. For example, the Morgan Guaranty Trust (a leading investment bank) controls more than 7 percent of the stock in American Airlines, United Airlines, and TWA, the three largest domestic airlines. Chase Manhattan Bank holds over 5 percent of all stock in four competing airlines, six railroads, and seventeen industrial companies.[25] One study finds that these two giant banks alone exercise substantial control over 36 of the 200 largest industrial corporations.[26]

---

[24]Paul Baran and Paul Sweezy, *Monopoly Capital* (New York, 1966), p. 4
[25]U.S., Congress, Senate, Committee on Government Operations, *Disclosure of Corporate Ownership,* 93rd Cong., 1st sess., December 27, 1973, p. 22.
[26]David M. Kotz, "Finance Capital and Corporate Control," in Richard C. Edwards, Michael Reich, and Thomas E. Weisskopf, eds., *The Capitalist System: A Radical Analysis of American Society,* 2nd ed. (Englewood Cliffs, N.J., 1978), p. 153.

Another method of integrating corporate competitors is the device known as the interlocking directorate, in which corporation A appoints the president or chairman of corporation B to its board of directors. (Two corporations may be indirectly interlocked when their executives share common membership on the board of a third corporation.) Large corporations, commercial and investment banks, Wall Street law firms, and giant insurance companies are interlocked in a dense network. Once again, a few New York banks play a central role in the process.[27] It is common for corporations to have interlocking directorates with large suppliers of parts and raw materials, with favored customers, and even (although this is illegal) with competitors. Interlocking directorates create a tight network reaching throughout corporate capitalism. One study notes, "Less than 4,000 managers of large corporations hold the directorships that interconnect the elite classes of officers and managers of the major corporations that employ most of the workers and do most of the business in American life."[28] Economist Peter Dooley found that by 1965 all but 17 of the 250 largest corporations had interlocks with each other.[29] A study prepared for a Senate subcommittee in 1978 found that interlocks are especially high among the very largest corporations. Each large corporation is directly or indirectly interlocked with nearly every other giant corporation.[30]

Additional informal coordination among corporations occurs through trade association "umbrella" organizations like the National Association of Manufacturers, the National Industrial Conference Board, the United States Chamber of Commerce, and the Committee for Economic Development. All of these prestigious organizations conduct pro-business research, develop policy positions, command the attention of political officials and the media when they propagandize on behalf of business, and seek to harmonize the conflicting interests of their corporate members. Particular mention should be made of the Business Roundtable, composed of the chief executives of the nation's 200 largest corporations. Given

[27]Beth Mintz and Michael Schwartz, "Interlocking Directorates and Interest Group Formation," *American Sociological Review* 46 (December 1981): 851–69.
[28]L. Lloyd Warner, *The Emergent American Society* (New Haven, 1967), p. 157.
[29]Peter C. Dooley, "The Interlocking Directorate," *American Economic Review* 59 (June 1969): 315.
[30]*New York Times,* April 23, 1978.

its prominent and powerful membership, the Business Roundtable acts informally as a peak representative of American corporate capital; its members personally transmit the organization's positions to the president, cabinet officers, and members of Congress.

While particular corporations and entire industries are in ceaseless competition, they all share a fundamental interest, which David Rockefeller, former chairman of Chase Manhattan Bank, has defined as "a community of interests and search for stability in which business can thrive and capital be protected."[31] However bitter their differences, corporations are unanimous in seeking to preserve a capitalist economy based on private ownership of the means of production, with a minimum of government interference in corporate decision making.

Professor Michael Useem has argued that the growth of coordinating mechanisms signifies a new era for capitalism, in which managerial capitalism is replaced by what he terms institutional capitalism. The new situation is characterized by "classwide organization, the creation of transcorporate networks of ownership and directorships as extensions of individual corporate strategies. . . ."[32]

This claim is partially valid but probably exaggerated. Even in past decades, when business mobilized to seek tax concessions and roll back environmental regulation, divisions remained on a host of other issues, including the wisdom of subsidies to particular industries (depending on whether they were among the beneficiaries), import quotas and tariff barriers (again depending on their own self-interest), and on and on.

Given severe conflicts among segments of capital, as well as between capital and workers, citizens, and groups abroad, the relationship between capital and government becomes especially important. Although capital has vast resources and a key structural position that provide it with favorable political treatment, it cannot simply bend government to its bidding. Moreover, the relationship between government and capital is not fixed once and for all but varies with the historical period and the outcome of political strug-

[31] *New York Times,* November 7, 1973.
[32] Michael Useem, "Business and Politics in the United States and United Kingdom: The Origins of Heightened Political Activity of Large Corporations During the 1970s and Early 1980s," *Theory & Society* 12 (May 1983), p. 303. Also see Useem, *The Inner Circle: Large Corporations and the Rise of Business Political Activity in the U.S. and U.K.* (New York, 1983).

gles. We begin studying the relationship between capitalism and government by analyzing the unstable evolution of capitalism and the necessity for government assistance to protect "free markets" and "free enterprise."

THE UNSTABLE CHARACTER OF CAPITALISM

As we just saw, in a capitalist society those controlling portions of capital compete with each other to secure maximum profits. It follows, then, that maximum profits require continued economic growth. Yet capitalism seems incapable of sustaining growth. In order for capitalist production to flourish, periods of contraction must alternate with periods of growth. There are three reasons why this is so. All stem from the fact that the competition inherent in a capitalist system means that there is no way to assure economic stability. The economy is thus constantly oscillating from one crisis to the next. In particular, periods of economic expansion are eventually followed by periods of economic contraction and recession. One reason is that there is a constant tendency for productive capacity to outstrip demand. During periods of economic growth, capitalists estimate that the chances of making a profit are high and they invest in new equipment to expand output. But this eventually leads to overproduction because workers (who, along with their families, form a majority of the society) are paid such low wages that they cannot afford to purchase the commodities that the system is capable of producing. As economist Roger Alcaly points out, "The small incomes of the majority of the population limits their ability to consume the output that the economy is increasingly capable of producing."[33] When production exceeds demand, factories begin to run at partial capacity and workers are laid off, thus further reducing the demand for goods, and a downward spiral toward recession begins.

A second way in which an economic boom turns to a recession is through the workers' demand for higher wages. When the econ-

---

[33]Roger E. Alcaly, "An Introduction to Marxian Crisis Theory," in Union for Radical Political Economics, *U.S. Capitalism in Crisis* (New York, 1978), p. 18. This section draws heavily on Alcaly.

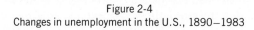

Figure 2-4
Changes in unemployment in the U.S., 1890–1983

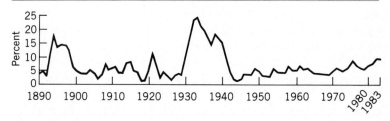

Source: 1890–1975: Thomas E. Weisskopf, "Sources of Cyclical Downturns and Inflation," in Richard C. Edwards, Michael Reich, and Thomas E. Weisskopf, eds., *The Capitalist System: A Radical Analysis of American Society,* 2nd ed., (Englewood Cliffs, N. J., 1978), p. 444. 1975–83: *Statistical Abstract of the United States* (Washington, D.C., 1985), p. 406.

omy is expanding, more workers are hired in order to produce more goods. As the number of people looking for work goes down, employers are forced to raise wages to attract new workers. The result is to increase the cost of producing commodities. After profits are squeezed beyond a certain point, workers begin to be laid off, contributing to the downward spiral.

A third way prosperity generates recession under capitalism is that machines are used to replace workers: technological innovation and mechanized production are central to capitalism. In a society where all shared in the gains from technological innovation, it could be socially beneficial. However, in a capitalist society technological innovation often spells unemployment; workers displaced by mechanization are forced to absorb the costs of the change.

Although the driving force of capitalism is the search for profitable investments and, hence, expansion, we have seen how inner tendencies of capitalism periodically produce stagnation. The alternation of boom and bust, what is referred to as the business cycle, is a universal characteristic of capitalism. The tendency to contract is as central to a capitalist economy as the tendency to expand.

Thus, a recession is both a logical outcome of capitalist production and, within limits, even beneficial for capitalism. A recession sets the stage for a new period of profitable investment and economic growth. First, it weeds out inefficient producers; firms that cannot turn a profit during the harsh conditions of a recession are forced out of business. Second, a recession weakens the working class and thereby strengthens the dominance of capital. During a recession, the working class is divided, more ready to accept low wages, and compliant. As some workers lose their jobs, all workers begin to fear the coming of hard times, to appreciate what they have gained, and to demand less of their employers.

However, when the economy slides from a mild recession to a deeper and more durable depression, the costs to capital begin to outweight the benefits. All capitalist firms, not only the least efficient, are damaged by the economic collapse. Further, the working class actively resists the sacrifices that it is called upon to make. In a mild recession, the relatively few workers who are laid off act as a warning to employed workers to moderate their wage and other demands. In a depression, the vast number of unemployed workers and the bleak prospects for those still employed serve to unite the working class to challenge the irrationality of a capitalist system. Periods of depression in the United States (most recently, the 1930s) are periods of widespread worker protest.

Depressions are thus periods of capitalist crisis and upheaval. Yet, just as there are built-in tendencies toward at least mild recession every several years, so there have historically been fundamental tendencies in capitalist economies, including the United States, to experience depressions at longer intervals.

N. D. Kondratieff, a Soviet economist in the 1920s, was the first to detect long waves of growth and stagnation within capitalist economies, moving in approximately fifty-year cycles from the early nineteenth century. During the first half of such a cycle, there is a steady, often vigorous, economic expansion; during the second half, there is the onset of stagnation, deepening into depression and crisis toward the end of the cycle. The movement of long historical waves is associated with fundamental changes in the economic, social, and political spheres.

Scientific and technological breakthroughs that make possible major shifts in a society's patterns of production and consumption set the stage for long waves. During the expansionary phase, major new technological discoveries and investments shape the society's future development. The boom is set off by the development of new sources of energy and locomotion, cheap sources of labor and raw materials, and advances in transportation, communication, and production. These innovations involve the whole society, creating a demand for the new products made possible by the break-through and increasing employment. The period of expansion produces a spirit of optimism, vitality, and commitment. For several decades, the society experiences prosperity and purpose.

The beginning of a new era is associated with the development of quite harmonious class relations and political arrangements. Class struggles temporarily take a back seat to the pursuit of happiness. The society works hard and lives well.[34]

New governmental policies and programs provide a framework for political stability by satisfying the demands of many powerful social groups and classes. Stability is enhanced by the emergence of a new majority political coalition, grouping major social forces within one of the two political parties. The majority party provides leadership by sponsoring innovative programs that provide benefits and, in turn, strengthen the party's appeal. Unable to find an effective alternative program, the minority party often weakly echoes the majority party's approach. Thus, there is a convergence of technological innovation, economic expansion, stable party leadership, and political stability.

However, like the self-limiting tendencies of the short-term business cycle, there are limits to long periods of expansion. Both economic expansion and political stability eventually begin to falter. Fewer new outlets for profitable investments are evident as the new infrastructure is completed. Economist David Gordon suggests that the "size and inflexibility [of infrastructural booms] channel economic growth along increasingly unprofitable paths."[35] In a long wave, the tendency toward stagnation occurs slowly and is overlaid by the short-term swings of the business cycle, where periods of upswing continue to occur, though with less frequency than declines. (By contrast, during the expansionary phase of a long wave, the upturns of the business cycle are more durable than downturns.) The downward slide does not occur all at once, although the arrival of crisis may be heralded by a dramatic event, such as "Black Friday," the outbreak of the financial panic in October 1929 that devastated the New York Stock Exchange, or the tripling of petroleum prices imposed by the Organization of Petro-

---

[34]This is not to imply that conflicts and repression are not present; but they are less severe.

[35]David M. Gordon, "Up and Down the Long Roller Coaster," in *U.S. Capitalism in Crisis*, p. 31.

leum Exporting Countries (OPEC) in 1973. Although economic stagnation may be obscured by short-term prosperity, government measures, and popular misconceptions, eventually there is no mistaking the fact that economic growth has given way to stagnation and rising unemployment.

During periods of deepening economic crisis, political stability is undermined. The majority coalition becomes divided as the dominant party is less able to harmonize the interests of its diverse supporters. Groups that were satisfied in the past voice grievances and new groups with new demands arise, partly a result of economic expansion in the preceding period. Groups in conflict cannot be reconciled within the existing framework and the majority party is ill-equipped to devise new solutions. It therefore suffers a decline in support. Government appears ineffective and political harmony is replaced by strife.

In the past, such crises have been resolved by major changes in economic and political institutions. After each crisis, there has been increased centralization and interpenetration of government and the economy. New technological innovations and new mechanisms of government intervention have helped to resolve the crisis and have facilitated a new period of economic growth and political stability. The middle 1980s may have marked the beginning of a new expansionary phase. More likely, however, is that the period represented a temporary respite in a deepening economic and political crisis.

3

government and corporate capitalism

LONG WAVES IN AMERICAN HISTORY

There have been three long waves of expansion and stagnation in American history since the early nineteenth century. In the present era, a new wave of expansion began around the time of the Second World War, peaked in the 1960s, and was replaced by a combination of stagnation and inflation through the early 1980s. After the most severe recession since the 1930s in 1981–82, an upturn occurred in 1983–84. While the outcome of the present period is unclear, the future will probably exhibit further instability and deepening crisis. In the account that follows, we will focus on the changing role of government in seeking to facilitate economic expansion, while analyzing government's inability to overcome the fundamental tendency toward instability within capitalism.

The expansionary phase of the first long wave in American history, starting in the 1840s, was based on a shift in power sources from water-driven devices to the steam engine. New transportation facilities—canals, roadways, and especially railroads—made it economically feasible to produce for regional and even national markets.

According to historian Morton Keller, "The postwar economic boom [following the Civil War] was sparked by government-supported railroad construction."[1] The federal government contributed 100 million acres of land and $100 million to subsidize the building of railroads. In ten years, trackage doubled to 74,000 miles, making possible the vast westward expansion.

Economist Douglas Dowd sums up the new developments:

> The transportation network . . . constituted an enormous demand for a whole range of products—most importantly, metals and machinery and coal, the heart of nineteenth-century industrial development. A new technology was required to dig canals, to tame the plains and mountains with rail and powerful locomotives, and to exploit the surface and subsurface resources of America's varied lands. All this, taken together with a persisting labor shortage, meant that the United States became the first of all industrial nations to develop a comprehensive machine technology for all aspects of production—agriculture, mineral, manufacturing, and transportation.[2]

This was the classic era of competitive capitalism and decentralized government. The federal government's role was quite limited: "The national government throughout the nineteenth century routinely provided promotional and support services for the state governments and left the substantive tasks of governing to these regional units."[3] Governments acted vigorously to suppress working-class strikes and challenges, and provided business with extensive subsidies. But government's major function was to provide law and order within a capitalist setting, which included guaranteeing the sanctity of contracts and protecting private property.

It was the competitive nature of early capitalism that led to the downturn of the late nineteenth century and, eventually, a new

[1]Morton Keller, *Affairs of State: Public Life in Late Nineteenth Century America* (Cambridge, Mass., 1977), p. 165.
[2]Douglas F. Dowd, *The Twisted Dream: Capitalist Development in the United States since 1776*, 2nd ed. (Cambridge, Mass., 1977), pp. 63–64.
[3]Stephen Skowronek, *Building a New American State: The Expansion of National Administrative Capacities, 1877–1920* (Cambridge, England, 1982), p. 23.

configuration of economic and political institutions. Fierce competition meant that new efficient production methods were quickly
translated into falling prices. Beginning in 1873 and lasting until the
end of the nineteenth century, there was an era of sagging employment, prices, profits, and production. The railroads, once hailed as
an engine of progress, were a major target of popular wrath. The
late nineteenth century became the first major crisis of American
capitalism. The Granger, Populist, Free Silver, and other popular
movements called not only for extensive reforms but also challenged the manner in which industrialization was carried out under
the control of private business, with government a cooperative
junior partner.

The crisis was resolved in a way that permitted a surge of
growth under capitalist auspices. The second long wave, which
began in the late nineteenth century, was sparked by technological
developments based on new power sources—notably the electric
motor and internal combustion engine—and their application to
transportation and manufacturing.

Intertwined with the new technological developments was a
centralization of production in the corporation. Corporate concentration made possible the limiting of competition, the control of
prices, and greater stability of profits. Historian David Noble
points out that in such varied industries as petroleum, steel, rubber,
and transportation, "the systematic introduction of science as a
means of production presupposed, and in turn reinforced, industrial monopoly."[4] The movement toward mergers and industrial
concentration represented a social and organizational transformation as significant as the shift in technology.

The federal government, under the leadership of the revitalized Republican party, also played a critical role in the change,
helping to protect and stabilize corporate concentration under the
guise of limiting and regulating corporations.

Government regulation and corporate production

As long as there were many manufacturers in a given industry, they
had no choice but to compete. But the corporate form offered a

---

[4]David F. Noble, *America by Design: Science, Technology, and the Rise of Corporate Capitalism* (New York, 1977), p. 6.

means of thwarting the free market. A large company could profit from its power over the market to undercut its competitors, monopolize sources of supply, and coerce or buy out smaller competitors. A further extension of the trend was the creation of trusts, in which many producers within an industry were merged into a single large firm. The result was a monopoly in which, unrestrained by competition, the trust could raise prices and achieve huge financial gains. (A modified form was oligopoly, where a few giant corporations dominated an industry and reached an informal agreement to set prices high enough to secure generous profits.)

Small business and farmers tried to unite in the face of the corporate threat to their survival. The Greenback, Granger, and Populist parties were moderately successful. Many state governments passed laws that regulated the new monopolies. For example, Wisconsin, New York, and other states prohibited railroad freight carriers from giving rebates (lower rates) to large shippers. Nationally, the Sherman Antitrust Act of 1887 prohibited "combinations in restraint of trade." The law empowered the federal government to break up conspiracies among competitors. Yet a pattern originated with the Sherman Act that was repeated often in the future. When public opposition was strong, the government stepped in to curb the worst excesses of business and to provide the appearance of regulation—without mortal damage to business interests. As described by historian Richard Hofstadter, the Sherman Act was "recognized by most of the astute politicians of that hour as a gesture, a ceremonial concession to an overwhelming public demand for some kind of reassuring action against the trusts."[5]

The critical period: 1897–1912

That the Sherman Act failed to prevent combinations in restraint of trade can be seen from the fact that the largest merger movement in American history (to that time) began in 1897, ten years *after* its passage.

By 1900, however, the merger movement began to slow. Moreover, the giant corporations that developed from the merger movement do not appear to have outperformed their smaller rivals. The point of diminishing returns in achieving efficiency through large

---

[5]Richard Hofstadter, *The Age of Reform* (New York, 1960), p. 245.

size seems to have been reached in the early 1900s. The best example was the United States Steel Corporation, organized in 1901 under the leadership of J. P. Morgan, leading financier of the period. It was the largest industrial corporation formed until then. Its assets of over $1 billion made it bigger than other leviathans organized during this period, such as Standard Oil of New Jersey, American Smelting and Refining Company, and Consolidated Tobacco Company. J. P. Morgan created U.S. Steel not to achieve greater efficiency but to eliminate competition. There were already a number of large, efficient steel companies. The most notable of these was Andrew Carnegie's, which Morgan was able to buy out and merge with the other companies he had captured to form the new industrial monolith. When it was formed, U.S. Steel had 800 plants and controlled 60 percent of American steel production. It was a gigantic test of whether bigness and near-monopoly conditions could prevent competition.

In fact, however, U.S. Steel was neither more efficient nor more profitable than its remaining competitors, nor could it prevent new competition from arising in the steel industry. In the years following its creation, the price of U.S. Steel's stock declined, and its share of total steel output fell from over 60 percent to 40 percent. Its failure was due mainly to its large size, which made it inflexible and slow to innovate, compared to its smaller competitors. Moreover, U.S. Steel was unable to persuade other steel companies to abide by price-fixing agreements.

What happened in the steel industry occurred in other industries in which there were huge new trusts. After its creation, Standard Oil failed to increase its control over the petroleum industry. In the automobile, copper, telephone, and meat industries, trusts were unable to outperform their competitors or dominate the industry. They, too, were unable to prevent new firms from entering the industry and to enforce price-fixing agreements among competitors. If it had not been for government intervention, the breed of industrial giant might have continued to decline. Thus, technological innovations and government-regulated protection for the emergent corporate giants helped make possible renewed economic expansion in the early years of the twentieth century. The irony is that government has often been perceived as being directed against big business when in fact government contributed to its survival.

Gabriel Kolko, the first historian to analyze this crucial transition in American history, notes: "The dominant fact of American politics at the beginning of this century was that big business led the struggle for the federal regulation of the economy. . . . Federal economic regulation was generally designed by the regulated industry to meet its own ends, and not those of the public." Kolko adds that the method used by big business to secure dominance over small business, agrarian interests, and labor was "the utilization of political outlets to attain conditions of stability, predictability, and security."[6] To cite one example, the Interstate Commerce Commission, created in 1887, has often been perceived as a move to curb and regulate the railroads. Yet "the intervention of the federal government not only failed to damage the interests of the railroads but was positively welcomed by them."[7] As in other comparable cases of government "regulation" of industry, the railroads used the government to control competition, calm an outraged public, and limit competition—ends that they could not achieve by themselves. The assurance given by Attorney General Richard Olney (himself a former railroad company executive) in a letter in 1892 to a disturbed railroad president suggests the value of regulation to railroad interests:

> The [Interstate Commerce] Commission, as its functions have now been limited by the courts, is, or can be made, of great use to the railroads. It satisfies the popular clamor for a government supervision of railroads, at the same time that the supervision is almost entirely nominal. Further, the older such a Commission gets to be, the more inclined it will be found to take the business and railroad view of things. It thus becomes a sort of barrier between the railroad corporations and the people and a sort of protection against hasty and crude legislation hostile to railroad interests.[8]

Thus, the turmoil of the late nineteenth century ended in the triumph of big business and conservatism—under the guise of reform: "By 1918 the leaders of the large corporations and banks emerged secure in their loose hegemony over the political struc-

[6]Gabriel Kolko, *The Triumph of Conservatism: A Reinterpretation of American History, 1900–1916* (New York, 1963). This account relies heavily on Kolko.
[7]Gabriel Kolko, *Railroads and Regulation, 1877–1916* (Princeton, 1965), p. 3.
[8]Quoted in Marver H. Bernstein, *Regulating Business by Independent Commission* (Princeton, 1955), p. 265.

ture."[9] The contrast with the earlier period could not have been greater. Manufacturers had never constituted a cohesive group in America; instead, they had consisted of many competing small producers, split by regional and economic rivalry. Moreover, business had been only one economic interest in the United States, no more powerful—probably less powerful—than farmers and merchants. The shift to corporate capitalism signified a fundamental transformation of the political and economic structure. A centralized economy (particularly following the New Deal in the 1930s), controlled by large corporate producers with the help of big government, replaced an economy divided by conflicting interests and controlled by none. This new alliance of giant corporate producers and an interventionist government can be called the corporate complex.

The combination of new technology, corporate concentration along with government regulation and a sharp increase in demand, led to sustained economic growth during the period of the First World War. The expansion transformed American society. The mass-produced automobile gave rise to related industries, including glass, rubber, and paint. Along with the radio and telephone, the automobile changed consumer patterns and, thanks to the birth of the advertising industry, helped produce the first consumer society. During the period following the First World War, the United States became the world's leading power, accounting for about half the world's total production.

Yet toward the end of the 1920s there were already signs of an approaching economic collapse. The downturn was obscured by financial trickery and frantic speculation. But, beginning with the collapse of the stock market in 1929, there erupted the worst depression ever for American capitalism. At the height of the Great Depression in 1933, production plunged to half its former level and unemployment soared to 25 percent. For ten years, under presidents of both parties, the government sought a way out; but all approaches failed. Republican president Herbert Hoover followed the traditional course of limiting government expenditures, balancing the federal budget, and hoping that the downturn would eventually reverse itself. Instead, the crisis deepened, and he was

[9]James Weinstein, *The Corporate Ideal in the Liberal State, 1900–1918* (Boston, 1968), p. 3.

swept from the presidency in the 1932 elections, thus ending more than one-half century of Republican dominance.

Democrat Franklin Roosevelt promised a New Deal and bravely proclaimed in his inaugural address, "the only thing we have to fear is fear itself." Although his attempts to use government power to check the depression failed in the short run, Roosevelt created the framework for a new wave of economic expansion, government–corporate cooperation, and Democratic party dominance. Roosevelt first worked directly with business in an attempt to coax a revival. The National Recovery Administration (NRA), launched in 1933, developed codes of business conduct designed to reduce competition and keep prices high enough to assure profits. The NRA was declared unconstitutional by the Supreme Court, dominated by justices who harked back to the days of small business and competition. Roosevelt's next approach, informally known as the second New Deal, was to grant relief directly to the poor and unemployed. The measures Roosevelt sponsored looked like a direct attack on business and the individualist values of capitalism. However, although Roosevelt's program of government assistance to retired workers, the poor, and the unemployed was partly a response to the militant protest developing in the 1930s, the New Deal was far from constituting a fundamental attack on corporate capitalism.

The New Deal accepted the basic legitimacy of corporate dominance. Aside from the government's one notable attempt to organize production directly (the Tennessee Valley Authority, which developed a system of flood control, and electric power and fertilizer production), the New Deal did not challenge corporate production. The top 100 corporations increased their control of all corporate assets during the New Deal, and the highest income group increased its share of the country's personal wealth.[10] The New Deal was an innovative attempt to save corporate capitalism from the crisis of its own making. As political scientist David Greenstone observes, "In general, the New Deal may have functioned to forestall radical change by eliminating the most unpopular features of American capitalism."[11]

---

[10] Kenneth Prewitt and Alan Stone, *The Ruling Elites: Elite Theory, Power, and American Democracy* (New York, 1973), p. 45.
[11] J. David Greenstone, *Labor in American Politics* (New York, 1969), p. 46.

Nonetheless, peacetime government expenditures failed to end the depression. "The Great Depression of the thirties never came to an end," economist John Galbraith has pointed out. "It merely disappeared in the great mobilization of the forties."[12] Only in 1940 did per capita income climb back to the peak reached in 1929.

The New Deal, as well as the requirements of production for total war, led to government assuming responsibility for regulating overall demand in the economy, with the goal of preventing economic crisis. As a result of the tremendous expansion of the federal government, its taxing and spending pattern (fiscal policy) began to have a significant impact on the entire economy. And, thanks to the technological developments and investment possibilities made possible by the Second World War, the United States entered the third long wave of economic growth.

The postwar capital-labor government accord

Following the Second World War, the United States experienced the greatest period of growth that the world has ever seen. The massive war effort stimulated innovations in electronics, telecommunications, radar, data processing, aircraft, and nuclear power. These developments, along with a backlog of consumer demand from the war, triggered a postwar surge in civilian production. Another factor in the long wave of growth was the privileged position of the United States, described in chapter 10, which enabled the United States to gain access to foreign markets for American goods and to obtain raw materials abroad at cheap prices. Of prime importance was that the New Deal and wartime conditions helped forge a new political framework that facilitated economic growth. The National Labor Relations Act (1935) accorded government recognition to labor unions, during a period of militant working-class challenge. In return for government protection, however, labor unions were legally obliged to confine demands to the narrow sphere of wages, hours, and working conditions while accepting overall capitalist domination of the workplace. Working-class sup-

---

[12]John Kenneth Galbraith, *American Capitalism: The Concept of Countervailing Power* (Boston, 1952), p. 69.

port for the New Deal coalition was bolstered by the Social Security Act, providing old-age pensions for stably employed workers.

Although corporate capital remained generally hostile to labor unions, its opposition softened as the benefits of unions to management became clear. This proved to be an instance of enlightened self-interest as a business school textbook makes clear: "Unionization may be credited, in part, with fostering sufficient integration of labor and management interests to protect the private enterprise system from the threat of radical political movements."[13]

An important feature of the new arrangements was that the federal government developed a capacity to counter tendencies toward economic instability. The Democratic party organized a political coalition uniting organized labor, Catholic immigrants from Southern and Eastern Europe, Jews, blacks, and the South. Although most corporate executives personally detested the Democratic party, the new political framework organized by the Democrats offered them handsome benefits and a tacit accord developed linking organized labor, corporate capital, and the federal government.

In the approach forged in the New Deal, government assumed overall responsibility for counteracting unstable tendencies and steering the economy toward steady expansion. The theoretical inspiration derived from British economist John Maynard Keynes, who in the early 1930s analyzed why, left to the unregulated free market, capitalism could slide into long periods of economic stagnation. However, Keynes asserted, economic instability could be avoided if government would actively intervene to maintain adequate demand and counter the boom and bust tendencies within capitalism.

Government could perform this role through the adroit use of central planning, and monetary and fiscal policy. By vigorous government intervention when the economy was stagnating, through deficit spending for welfare programs ("pump priming"), government could increase total—aggregate—demand and thereby stimulate economic growth. Conversely, government could counteract inflationary tendencies by running a budgetary surplus to reduce aggregate demand.

[13]John D. Aram, *Managing Business and Public Policy: Concepts, Issues and Cases* (Boston, 1983), p. 169.

Keynes saw his prescription producing economic growth through government planning and redistribution to the working class. However, the United States adopted a conservative form of Keynesianism: government was entrusted with minimum discretionary power and automatic stabilizing measures were substituted for central planning. Further, Keynesianism in the United States sought growth not in *conjunction* with redistribution toward the working class and poor but as a *substitute* for redistribution.[14] According to historian Robert Collins, this conservative approach "opted for an active monetary policy and a passive fiscal policy, for automatic stabilizers over discretionary management, for reductions in taxation and increases in private spending over increases in public spending, for a modicum of unemployment over a modicum of inflation, and for economic stability over the redistribution of income. . . ."[15]

One means that government used to avoid the redistributive features of Keynesianism was to channel expenditures through military purchases rather than welfare programs. (The United States spends more on the military and less on welfare than any other capitalist democracy.) As *Business Week,* a management publication, pointed out when the new approach was being developed, "There's a tremendous social and economic difference between welfare pump priming and military pump priming. . . . Military spending doesn't really alter the structure of the economy. It goes through regular channels. As far as a business man is concerned, a munitions order from the government is much like an order from a private customer." By contrast, social spending "redistributes income."[16]

The Keynesian approach was bitterly opposed by conservatives on the grounds that it gave too much power to government and interfered with the free market. But, as business succeeded in shaping Keynesianism in a pro-business manner, bringing economic growth and relative social peace, Keynesianism attracted near-universal support. By the 1970s, Republican President Richard Nixon could declare, "We are all Keynesians now."

---

[14]Alan Wolfe, *America's Impasse* (New York, 1981).
[15]Robert M. Collins, *The Business Response to Keynes, 1929–1964* (New York, 1981), p. 17.
[16]*Business Week,* February 12, 1949, quoted in Collins, p. 199.

As described in Chapter 9, the urban-based black revolt of the 1960s, as well as the environment movement described in this chapter, shifted the welfare state in a more progressive direction. These developments were an important reason why capital began to oppose "big" government in the 1970s, after being quite satisfied with it in the 1950s and 1960s. Capital's opposition was manifested in a refusal to invest during the 1970s, which helped to intensify the economic crisis. By the late 1970s, Keynesianism became a favorite target of conservatives. It was rejected by the Republican party in favor of approaches that give capital greater control and government a smaller role in economic management. Yet even opponents of Keynesianism rely (however unwillingly) on certain of its elements. For example, deficit spending for military purposes played an important role in the Republican-sponsored economic revival of 1983–84. And it will never again be possible for the federal government wholly to escape responsibility for the performance of the economy.

GOVERNMENT AND THE ECONOMY

Although the "private government" that owns and controls capital has enormous power, since the Keynesian "revolution" government has gained a key economic role as well. Big government developed after the growth of big capital in the United States, and in part as a response to it. But big government is now a central feature of American economic life. There is one federal official for every 60 citizens. Few areas of human activity escape government involvement. To some extent, the balance of power between government and business has drifted toward government, as tax revenues and government expenditures have grown and business has become more dependent on government assistance.

However, the growth in government power had not been at the expense of business since, we have seen, there was a massive expansion and centralization of corporate power in the twentieth century. Given the fact that government does not directly control production, it is forced to rely on corporate capital to perform the functions essential for the survival and prosperity of the society.

So long as production remains privately controlled by corporate producers, government is compelled to put the needs of corporate capitalism high on the political agenda. "Not many Government officials are so witless as to overlook their own dependence on business," observes economist Charles Lindblom. "If business is not induced to perform, the result is economic distress. When the economy fails, the Government falls. . . . Hence, no category of persons is more attentive to the needs of business than the Government official."[17]

One might add that when the economy is expanding, employment is high, and living standards are rising, the incumbent government benefits. In 1980, Ronald Reagan may have won the presidential election against incumbent Jimmy Carter because Reagan dramatically asked the American people to decide "Are you better off today than four years ago?" (when Carter was first elected). If the 1984 presidential election had been held two years earlier, during the severe recession in 1982, President Reagan would doubtless have been defeated for reelection. Thus, government's fortunes are closely intertwined with the fortunes of capitalism. Yet this does not mean that the process by which business gains and retains its privileged position is easy, automatic, or assured. There are continuous struggles around the question. For example, in the 1970s, as we describe later in the chapter, the environmental movement was quite successful in limiting corporate freedom in an important (if limited) domain.

Furthermore, government is not a passive participant in struggles involving business interests nor is it a blind captive of business. Given sufficient pressure from citizens' groups, government may be forced to oppose business, as it did on environmental issues. Moreover, government has separate interests of its own. For example, beyond corporate interests abroad, it seeks to preserve U.S. power in the international arena.

Yet, short of massive pressure from social movements opposed to capitalism (which is not the case in the United States), government will doubtless seek to favor capitalist interests. However, even in this regard, if government were simply a prisoner of business capitalism would have long since disappeared. Government

---

[17]Charles E. Lindblom, "The Business of America Is Still Business," *New York Times*, January 4, 1978.

Figure 3-1
The unemployment rate and Reagan's popularity

¹Not including military

Source: *New York Times*, October 26, 1984.

must be free to oppose individual corporations or even, on rare occasions, the whole business community if it is to preserve the larger framework within which profitable corporate production (what is also called capital accumulation) can occur. No single corporation or business organization possesses government's central vantage point to judge what is needed for the whole capitalist system. For example, automobile producers bitterly opposed federally imposed gasoline efficiency requirements in the 1970s on the grounds that they would cut into auto sales. Yet these requirements, aimed at achieving reduced energy consumption, were in the long-term interests of American capitalism and of the automakers themselves.

Economist James O'Connor has distinguished two broad functions of a capitalist government: assisting capital accumulation (which will be studied in the remainder of this chapter) and maintaining a framework of social control so that capital accumulation can occur.[18] Social control (which O'Connor calls legitimization) consists of obtaining popular assent within the United States for the capitalist system—for example, through mobilizing electoral majorities, providing government welfare payments, and using force (as a last resort if peaceful means fail). Social control abroad (which will be discussed in Chapter 10) is also necessary if American capitalism is to flourish.

Regulating demand

Government uses an arsenal of techniques in attempting to counteract the cyclical tendencies within capitalism. In the period following the Second World War, the government's major aim has been to maintain a rising level of total (aggregate) demand that was in rough balance with rising productive capacity. It did so through monetary and fiscal policy.

Monetary policy   The Federal Reserve Board regulates the amount of money in circulation by varying the interest rates it charges to private banks within the Federal Reserve system. Although the Federal Reserve Board is a government agency, private banks choose most of the members of the regional Federal Reserve Bank boards. The Federal Reserve Board is closely allied with the banking industry and its monetary policies often have the effect of restricting economic growth and raising unemployment.

Fiscal policy   Fiscal policy refers to the taxing and spending activities of the government. Government expenditures increase the demand for privately produced goods and services when government spends more than it receives in tax revenues, a process

---

[18]James O'Connor, *The Fiscal Crisis of the State* (New York, 1973).

that is called deficit spending or (more informally) pump priming. When government collects more in tax revenues than it spends, the result is a budget surplus. This reduces purchasing power (demand) and thus slows up economic activity. Since the Second World War, federal spending has been at a high level and government-created demand was a major source of the long expansionary wave in the postwar years.

The collection of taxes is another element in fiscal policy. The importance of government can be appreciated from the fact that over one-third of the entire gross national product (GNP—the entire national output) is collected by federal, state, and local governments in tax revenues and then redistributed through government expenditures.

As with its other activities, government tax policies serve the dual (and conflicting) purpose of assisting business and building popular support for the economic and political system. On the one hand, the tax system is designed to assist capital accumulation. On the other hand, the tax system is often said to help redistribute income from the wealthy to the poor, justified on the grounds of social solidarity and equity. The principle is given expression in the graduated federal income tax, in which the proportion of the tax levy (marginal tax rate) increases for higher income brackets. Prominent display is given each year to the federal income-tax rates on the tax forms sent to millions of families. A simple way to measure how well the personal income tax redistributes income is to compare the distribution of income among different income groups before and after they pay taxes.

The surprising result is that, according to the tax system in use until 1986, (and the present system is little different in this respect) tax laws had little effect on the relative distribution of income among most income groups. Most Americans—those earning between $2,000 and $30,000 annually—pay about the same proportion of their income in taxes (about one-quarter). Those earning more than $30,000 pay a slightly higher tax—but nowhere near the rate given in the tax table. The cruelest irony is that the lowest income group also pays a higher proportion of taxes than many Americans.

What accounts for the discrepancy? First there a bewildering variety of other taxes beside the federal income tax. Most are regressive: instead of levying a higher rate on the wealthy, they levy a lower rate. One important example is payroll (social security)

Table 3-1
Distribution of Tax Revenues

Period	Corporate Tax	Personal Income Tax	Social Security	Sales Tax
1959	17%	33.6%	12.9%	8%
1981	7.9%	37.2%	22.5%	10%

Source: Martin Carnoy, Derek Shearer, and Russel Rumberger, *A New Social Contract: The Economy and Government After Reagan* (New York, 1983), p. 10.

taxes, which are deducted directly from an employee's salary by his or her employer. Since social-security taxes are collected only on the first $46,000 of one's income, those earning above this amount pay proportionately less tax. (Nor is this a minor example: nearly one-fourth of all federal tax revenue is now raised through payroll taxes.) Local sales taxes, levied on clothing and other necessities, also fall more heavily on the poor.

Special features of the tax laws further permit the wealthy to shelter earnings from the progressive income tax. Such provisions, which result in a lower tax bill, are equivalent to granting a subsidy to affluent taxpayers. For example dividends from state and municipal bonds—two-thirds of which are owned by .1 percent of the population—are not taxed at all.[19] Through such devices, the wealthy exempt much of their income from high tax rates. Rather than redistributing income to the poor, two economists conclude that tax laws "provide a vehicle of redistribution to the wealthy."[20]

In 1986, Congress passed a fundamental overhaul of the federal income tax system. The reform was defended on the grounds of achieving greater fairness and simplicity—but the latter was especially influential. The 1986 changes, along with tax reforms passed in the first years of the Reagan administration, reversed the pattern of previous tax reforms, which sought increased progressivity in the tax system. The 1986 plan tried to bring *effective* tax rates (what is actually paid in taxes) closer to *statutory* rates (those officially enshrined in the tax code). It coupled a drastic reduction in the number of personal income tax brackets (from fourteen to

[19]Philip M. Stern, *The Rape of the Taxpayer* (New York, 1973), p. 62.
[20]Martin Pfaff and Anita Pfaff, "How Equitable are Implicit Public Grants? The Case of the Individual Income Tax," in Kenneth E. Boulding and Martin Pfaff, eds., *Redistribution to the Rich and the Poor* (Belmont, California, 1972), p. 191.

two), a drop in the highest marginal tax rate (from 50 to 28 percent), and the elimination of many tax loopholes with an increase
in the volume of taxes collected from corporations through reducing corporate tax loopholes. However, it made little attempt to
achieve greater fairness. Although it removed six million low-
income families from the tax rolls, wealthy taxpayers (those with
incomes over $200,000 annually) obtained several thousand dollars
a year in tax savings.[21]

Government expenditures   Government spending has been
climbing steadily throughout the twentieth century: from less than
one-tenth of GNP at the turn of the century, it now constitutes
about one-third of GNP. (As the late Senator Everett Dirksen once
said, "A billion here and a billion there and pretty soon it adds up
to real money.") In recent years, however, annual increases in federal government spending have not exceeded the rise in GNP. (Federal government expenditures now constitute about one-fifth of
GNP.) The major reason that total government spending absorbed
a rising share of national output in the 1970s was a sharp increase
in state and local government expenditures. In 1957, state and local
governments collected one-fourth as much in tax revenues as the
federal government; by 1977, the proportion of the revenues collected by state and local governments increased to more than one-
third of federal tax revenues.[22] This helps account for the "tax
revolt" occurring in many states and communities which helped
elect Ronald Reagan in 1980 on a platform of lower taxes and
reduced government spending.

Total federal expenditures since the Second World War have
run into many trillion dollars. What was obtained for these colossal
sums?[23] Three major categories of federal expenditures can be
identified. By far the largest amount—over three-quarters of the
total—has gone for military purposes. The second largest category
has been welfare-state payments. Both of these can be considered
expenses to obtain social control—the first, abroad; the second,
within the United States. They are analyzed in later chapters.

[21]This analysis relies heavily on "Tax Reform Hoopla," *Dollars & Sense*, no. 121
(November 1986): 6–8.
[22]*Dollars & Sense*, no. 40, October 1978, p. 4.
[23]One result that was *not* obtained was income redistribution. Political scientist
Benjamin Page notes, in a thorough study of government fiscal policy, "Over time,
greatly increased government activity has not led to more income equality." Benjamin I. Page, *Who Gets What from Government?* (Berkeley, 1983), p. 144.

Socializing the costs of production

Most remaining federal government expenditures go for physical facilities and services that can be considered a direct or indirect subsidy to affluent citizens and business. Business is the largest beneficiary of most government-provided services and facilities, including government statistical services, transportation facilities, and subsidies for R&D. However, these government outlays are financed by all taxpayers. Were it not for public largesse, private business would have to pay for many of these services directly. The costs of production are thus paid for by the whole society, but the major benefits go to private producers. Government-provided benefits can consist of a direct subsidy to private producers—a subsidy to develop new products that can be patented and sold by a private firm, for example, or facilities available to all but which benefit business disproportionately. For example, the interstate highway system was built at a cost to taxpayers of $80 billion (the largest public works project in history), it represents an indirect subsidy to corporate producers—the major users—for it enables them to ship their products quickly and cheaply throughout the country.

A distinguishing feature of U.S. capitalism, which underlines its especially conservative character in comparison with other capitalist democracies, is the extent to which American government avoids organizing production directly. Although it is often argued that private ownership minimizes bureaucracy and maximizes individual freedom and efficiency, these virtues are hardly evident from a comparison of privately owned (although heavily subsidized) American railroads with the public rail systems of West Europe.

Government's economic activities have an immense impact on the economy and affect individual workers and their families, business firms and industries, and entire regions. For example, federal fiscal policy has been an important factor in the decline of the Frostbelt and rise of the Sunbelt in recent years. Between 1975 and 1979 alone, the 18 states of the Northeast and Midwest (the Frostbelt) spent $165 billion more federal taxes than they received back in federal spending; the 32 states of the South and West (Sunbelt) got back $112 billion more than they spent.[24] These large sums help explain the opposite fortunes of these two sections of the country.

[24]Seymour Melman, *Profits Without Production* (New York, 1983), p. 94.

Figure 3-2
Extent of state ownership

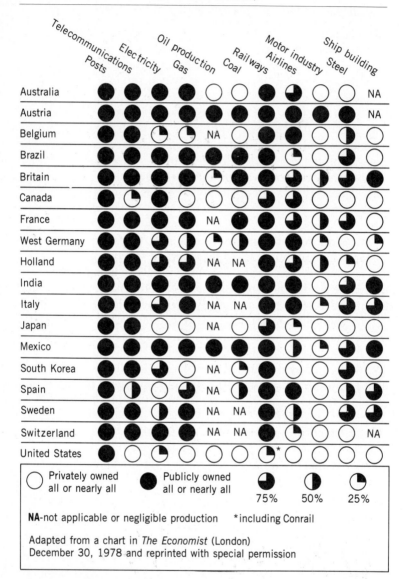

Privately owned all or nearly all — Publicly owned all or nearly all — 75% — 50% — 25%

NA-not applicable or negligible production   *including Conrail

Adapted from a chart in *The Economist* (London)
December 30, 1978 and reprinted with special permission

Despite extensive government intervention since the Second World War, the expansionary phase of the third long wave lasted no longer than the two previous long periods of growth of American capitalism in the nineteenth and early twentieth centuries. Indeed, whereas in the 1960s government spending was praised as helping to prevent economic crisis, in the 1970s and 1980s government spending has been singled out as one of its major causes.

During the long expansion beginning in the 1940s, severe economic crisis seemed a thing of the past, although there continued to be periodic ups and downs of the business cycle. Then, beginning in the middle 1960s, ominous warning signs began to appear on the horizon: an international trade deficit (signifying that other nations were producing more efficiently than the United States), inflation, and a slowdown in productivity gains (output per worker).

The full extent of the crisis was obscured for several years. The Vietnam war kept the economy booming when it would have otherwise turned slack. Moreover, the financial costs of the war were concealed by President Lyndon Johnson, who decided not to raise taxes for fear of further provoking public opposition to the war. The result was to fuel inflationary pressures as government competed with business and consumers for scarce resources. A tripling of petroleum prices by the Organization of Petroleum Exporting Countries (OPEC) in 1973 along with soaring food prices made the dimensions of the crisis dramatically clear.

Stagflation   Since then, unemployment has been higher than at any time since the 1930s, while prices rose faster than at any period in American history. A new term—*stagflation*—had to be coined to describe the unprecedented coexistence of *stagnation* and *inflation*.

An indication of the crisis is that there were three recessions in the 1970s compared to one in the 1960s, and the most severe recession since the Great Depression occurred in the 1980s. Whereas in the 1950s and 1960s, wages rose continually, wages were lower at the end of the 1970s than at the beginning of the decade. A price rise of 3 percent annually was considered high prior to the 1970s. In the 1970s, the *lowest* yearly price rise was 6 percent, and double-digit inflation (over 10 percent) became typical. Highly restrictive monetary policy brought down inflation in the early 1980s—while pushing unemployment to a postwar record high.

FROM ACCORD TO DISCORD

What can explain the economic crisis that began in the late 1960s? What are the prospects for a fourth long wave of economic expansion, lasting through the rest of the century, that will spell an end to economic crisis? Some of the same ingredients of the postwar capital–labor–government accord that initially produced economic growth and political stability later produced stagflation and political instability. First, organized labor was quite successful in using the accord to achieve yearly wage increases, a principal reason for the labor peace that prevailed until the early 1960s. Until that point, steady productivity gains and economic growth produced a surplus to finance wage gains. When productivity failed to maintain its upward course from the mid-1960s, this both made it harder to finance wage hikes and meant that they would prove inflationary as well as cut into profits. Between the mid-1960s and early 1970s, wages as a share of Gross National Product (GNP) increased from 52.5 percent to 55.3 percent, while before-tax profits fell from 15.6 percent of GNP to less than 11 percent.[25] Capitalists reacted to this profit squeeze by (1) raising prices to protect profit margins (which fueled inflation and made U.S. products less competetive against foreign imports), (2) refusing to invest (increasing unemployment), and (3) trying to coerce workers into producing more. (Later in the 1970s, this took the form of an all-out assault on labor unions.)

The top-heavy character of work-place organization deserves special emphasis in understanding America's declining productivity, for an increasing proportion of resources were poured into unproductive supervisory positions. For example, at Toyota, there are seven layers of management between the company chairman and the shop-floor production worker; at Ford, there are twelve.[26] Between 1948 and 1966, the ratio of supervisory to nonsupervisory employees in U.S. industry increased from 13 per hundred to 22 per hundred.[27]

[25]This is analyzed well in Martin Carnoy, Derek Shearer, and Russell Rumberger, *A New Social Contract: The Economy and Government After Reagan* (New York, 1983).

[26]Melman, p. 80.

[27]Samuel Bowles, David M. Gordon, and Thomas E. Weisskopf, *Beyond the Wasteland: A Democratic Alternative to Economic Decline* (Garden City, N.Y., 1982), p. 74.

Yet, predictably, the attempt to coerce workers met with increased resistance, and so the vicious circle continued. As productivity fell further, American industry was unable to compete with foreign competitors in supplying U.S. markets: the share of imports increased from 5 percent of GNP in 1965 to 12 percent in 1981 and provoked a soaring international trade deficit.[28]

These shifts signify a bedrock change in the position of U.S. capitalism with respect to the international capitalist system. For decades after the Second World War, the United States enjoyed international economic dominance as a result of the devastation caused by war to its economic rivals. However, in such key industries as steel, automobiles, and electronics, American managers were slow to innovate and respond to increasingly effective foreign competition.

When jolted into action, their response was not long-term economic renovation but short-term financial manipulation. Robert Reich, professor of business and public policy, points out, "Instead of generating new wealth, corporations are playing a giant game of asset rearrangement that is largely unproductive."[29] Economist Seymour Melman describes the process as "profits without production." It involves complex corporate mergers, which bring lucrative fees to lawyers, financial consultants, and investment bankers while adding nothing to productive capacity. To provide some idea of the immense waste involved, for every 10,000 citizens, there are twenty lawyers in the United States compared to one lawyer in Japan.[30] One careful estimate is that one-half of the entire U.S. GNP is devoted to wasteful, unproductive, and unnecessary purposes.[31] Further, the major source of this waste is not "welfare chisellers" or workers receiving high wages. For example, although American autoworkers earn moderately higher wages than Japanese autoworkers, American automobile executives receive five times higher salaries than their Japanese counterparts.[32] In 1984, after U.S. autoworkers had provided wage concessions and negotiated a modest pay raise for future years, automobile executives

---

[28]*Ibid.*, p. 80.
[29]*New York Times,* July 3, 1984.
[30]Ira C. Magaziner and Robert B. Reich, *Minding America's Business: The Decline and Rise of the American Economy* (New York, 1982), p. 117.
[31]Bowles, Gordon, and Weisskopf, *passim.*
[32]Melman, p. 187.

awarded themselves bonuses of up to $900,000 each in addition to their million-dollar annual salaries.

Another important source of waste in the U.S. economy, which reduces American civilian productivity and international competitivity, is the fabulous sums devoted to military purposes. The arms budget now absorbs over $300 billion annually and more than two-thirds of federal funds for research and development (R and D). In addition to the dangers these expenditures pose to national security, the result is to deprive civilian production of resources and talent.

The irony is that the very attempts by capitalist producers and the U.S. government to deal with the growing crisis in their relations with workers, disgruntled citizens, and groups abroad intensified crisis tendencies.[33] In later chapters, we will examine U.S. capital's inability to manage relations with labor and international forces. In the section that follows, we describe the growing militance of citizens' groups in face of corporate abuses within the United States.

CHALLENGE TO CORPORATE DOMINANCE: THE ENVIRONMENT MOVEMENT

In the late 1960s and 1970s, a wide range of social movements—including organized labor, the women's rights, civil rights and black groups, and environmental protection organizations—came together to challenge the right of corporate capitalism to produce what it wished, as it wished, and without regard to damage caused to workers, consumers, the physical environment, and the democratic political process. The loose coalition of grass-roots activists was not centrally directed, tightly coordinated, nor highly cohesive. Nor did it have a single programmatic focus or common ideology. What linked these diverse groups was the attempt to substitute democratic procedures for corporate decision making. No single term can encompass the various causes that these organizations

---

[33]Bowles, Gordon, and Weisskopf analyze the crisis in these terms.

Table 3-2
Changes in productivity and wages, 1948–1981

Period	Productivity Increases	Wage Increases*
1948–66	3.2%	2.9%
1966–73	2.3%	2.0%
1973–79	.8%	.6%
1979–81	.4%	.3%

*Rise in hourly income

Source: Samuel Bowles, David M. Gordon, and Thomas E. Weisskopf, *Beyond the Wasteland: A Democratic Alternative to Economic Decline* (Garden City, N.Y., 1982), pp. 29–30.

advocated. We will adopt here the most commonly used designation, the environment movement. However, "environment" should be understood in a broad sense to include the social, work, and natural environments.

Among the examples of abuses that provoked the environment movement is the fact that 100,000 workers die annually from occupational hazards and accidents, and 400,000 are disabled from exposure to toxic substances. (Thus, each year, twice the number of Americans are killed than died in Vietnam throughout the decade of American troop involvement there.) Countless disasters have occurred from hazardous industrial production and reckless waste disposal, including injuries and deaths at Love Canal, near Buffalo, New York; Times Beach, Missouri; and Three Mile Island, Pennsylvania. But even more deadly than the isolated disaster that periodically dominates TV news and newspaper headlines is the routine and largely unregulated industrial production by corporate capital of plastics, pesticides, and thousands of products that pose dangers to workers, consumers, and the environment.

In recent decades, there has been vastly expanded production of synthetic organic chemicals because corporate producers found the switch to synthetics profitable. As with the decision to close factories (described in the last chapter), little consideration was given to the risks and costs involved to others. Moreover, corporations strenuously resisted restraints on their activities. Until pressured by the environment movement, government took industry's side.

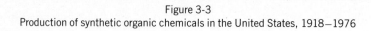

Figure 3-3
Production of synthetic organic chemicals in the United States, 1918–1976

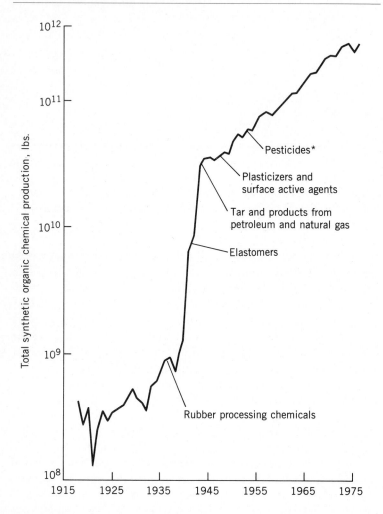

*Labels indicate year when usage became sufficiently "significant" to be included as specific categories in Commission reports.

Source: Samuel S. Epstein, *The Politics of Cancer* (Garden City, N.Y., 1979), p. 31.

Take the case of asbestos, used in manufacturing insulation and fibreboard.[34] As far back as the First World War, the federal government and asbestos companies knew that asbestos caused severe respiratory illness and cancer. (Insurance companies stopped selling life insurance policies to asbestos workers in 1918). Approximately 10,000 Americans will die annually as the result of cancer caused by past exposure to asbestos. Yet asbestos manufacturers bitterly opposed efforts by asbestos workers, unions, and health activists to limit worker exposure to asbestos and to curtail asbestos manufacture.

The industry's criminal negligence came to light when product liability suits by cancer-stricken asbestos workers in the 1970s produced company documents dating back to 1933. They demonstrated that asbestos manufacturers engaged in extensive propaganda efforts to mislead and suppress evidence of the murderous effects of asbestos. When the medical director of Johns Manville, the largest asbestos maker, was asked at a congressional hearing why the company did not comply with legislation passed in the 1970s requiring warning labels to be placed on dangerous products, he replied

> The reasons why the caution labels were not implemented immediately, it was a business decision as far as I could understand. Here was a recommendation, the corporation is in business to make, to provide jobs for people and make money for stockholders and they had to take into consideration the effects of everything they did, and if the application of a caution label identifying a product as hazardous would cut out sales, there would be serious financial implications.[35]

The environment movement proved highly successful in pinpointing a range of specific corporate abuses and pressuring Congress and the president to sponsor remedial legislation. New

---

[34]This account relies on Samuel S. Epstein, *The Politics of Cancer* (Garden City, N.Y., 1979). A similar story could be told of the tobacco, automobile, coalmining, and scores of other industries. Note that, as a result of struggles against asbestos manufacture, production has mostly ended, and damage claims are pending against asbestos manufacturers. Johns Manville, the largest asbestos producer, filed for bankruptcy on the grounds that it could not afford to compensate stricken workers.

[35]*Ibid.*, p. 94.

regulatory machinery was created to limit corporate political contributions in the United States and abroad, after disclosures that
corporations had channelled corporate funds into payments to
American and foreign politicians. (As described in Chapter 8, corporations soon circumvented restrictions on political contributions
within the United States.) The environment movement achieved
its most noteworthy gains with the creation of government agencies
to administer new legislation in the fields of employment opportunity for women, blacks, and other minorities (the Equal Employment Opportunity Commission—EEOC), occupational safety and
health (Occupational Safety and Health Administration—OSHA),
product safety (Product Safety Commission), and environmental
protection (Environmental Protection Administration—EPA).
The Federal Trade Commission (FTC) was also revamped and
strengthened.

The new "social regulation" resulting from the environment
movement's struggles was an unprecedented and quite effective
attempt to limit corporate freedom. Unlike earlier regulatory
movements in the Progressive period and New Deal years, which
dealt with specific industries like railroads or broadcasting, the new
wave of social regulation in the 1970s applied to all industries
(which explains why business later proved able to unite so successfully in opposition to this regulation). Social regulation also differed from earlier governmental activity in that it was explicitly
anticorporate; in contrast, as we have seen, in the past business
actively sought governmental regulation.

Moreover, the sheer scope and volume of social regulation in
the 1970s went considerably beyond earlier regulatory efforts. In
the area of consumer health and safety, five laws were enacted by
the federal government during the Progressive period, eleven during the New Deal years, and 62 between 1964 and 1979. Regarding
occupational health and safety, five laws were passed in both the
Progressive and New Deal years; 21 were voted between 1960 and
1978. In the fields of energy and the environment, two laws were
passed during the Progressive period, five in the New Deal years,
and 32 in the recent period.[36] Political scientist David Vogel argues

---

[36]David Vogel, "The 'New' Social Regulation in Historical and Comparative Perspective," in Thomas K. McCraw, ed., *Regulation in Perspective: Historical Essays*
(Boston, 1981), p. 162.

that the conflicts over social regulation raised basic issues regarding the place of corporate producers in the United States: "In essence, during the seventies, the controversy over the social regulation of business became the focus of class conflict: it pitted the interests of business as a whole against the public interest movement as well as much of organized labor."[37]

Where the new laws had teeth, were administered by agencies committed to their enforcement, and supported by mobilized grass-roots activists, regulation worked. For example, mine accidents fell by three-fourths, accidental work-place deaths were cut in half, automobile emissions were reduced by one-third, and particle emissions in the air were halved.[38] But corporate capital retained considerable freedom to conduct operations as it saw fit. The new regulatory agencies had neither the resources, legal mandate, nor political support to go beyond addressing a few of the most glaring problems. Take synthetic chemicals, one of countless examples. In 1977, the Chemical Abstracts Service registry listed over 4 million chemical compounds, and the list grows by 6,000 a week. Although over 33,000 chemicals are used in industry, only a fraction have been thoroughly checked for safety.[39]

The confrontation over social regulation illustrates the conflict between the logic of capitalism and the logic of democracy. Here was a case where, by peaceful, legal means, citizens' groups elected representatives to address crying public needs for limiting corporate abuses. (One shudders to think how many Three Mile Islands, where a near-meltdown occurred at a nuclear power plant, would have occurred were it not for the antinuclear movement.) While the environment movement was highly successful, it never threatened capital's core privileges, even during the brief period in 1977–78 when its influence was greatest. Given the immense disparity of resources, the deck remained stacked in favor of corporate capital. Specific corporate misdeeds were addressed, but the power, privilege, and legitimacy or corporate capital were barely affected. Nor were the new regulatory agencies especially oppressive. Commenting on the activities of OSHA, *Business Week* observed, "The typ-

[37]*Ibid.*, p. 165.
[38]Barry Bluestone and Bennett Harrison, *The Deindustrialization of America: Plant Closings, Community Abandonment, and the Dismantling of Basic Industry* (New York, 1982), p. 207.
[39]Epstein, p. 30.

ical business establishment will see an OSHA inspector every 76 years, about as often as we see Halley's Comet."[40]

Vulnerable to attack, given public indignation at corporate abuses and the militance of the environment movement, business first reacted cautiously. A policy statement on "Social Responsibilities of Business Corporations," issued by the respected business organization, the Committee on Economic Development, warned that "indiscriminate opposition to social change not only jeopardizes the interest of a single corporation, but also affects adversely the interests all corporations have in maintaining a climate conducive to the effective functioning of the entire business system."[41]

Soon, however, business began to counterattack. It responded on two fronts, economic and political. In the economic sphere, business argued that social regulation substantially increased production costs and hence prices to consumers. This claim was misleading, since the costs of social regulation adds less than 1 percent annually to consumer prices.[42] But, in a period of high inflation, the message, however exaggerated, was quite effective.

But what capital most feared was not the additional expense of producing in a safe manner. The real danger was the precedent set by citizens' groups effectively exercising their democratic rights in order to limit corporate freedom. Faced with this threat, capital struck back with its most formidable economic weapon: an investment strike. Since its control was becoming less secure, business retaliated by refusing to invest new capital to create productive capacity and jobs. It worked: in the 1970s, private investment stagnated and unemployment soared.

In the political sphere, business mounted a sharp counteroffensive in the late 1970s. As described in Chapter 8, business executives, corporations, and trade associations poured vast sums into the effort to reverse the political tide. One observer suggests, "Corporate money has now become a fundamental force in American politics."[43] Corporations stepped up funding for conservative

[40]*Business Week,* June 14, 1976, p. 65.
[41]Committee on Economic Development, *Social Responsibilities of Business Corporations* (New York, 1971), p. 29.
[42]Bowles, Gordon, and Weisskopf, p. 45.
[43]Michael Useem, "Business and Politics in the United States and United Kingdom: The Origins of Heightened Political Activity of Large Corporations during the 1970s and Early 1980s," *Theory & Society* 12 (May 1983), p. 296.

"think tanks," which churned out reports warning of the high costs of regulations and neglecting the enormous benefits (not always calculable in dollar terms) of reduced accidents, improved health, and a cleaner, more attractive environment. Corporations organized grass-roots lobbying campaigns, in which stockholders, employees, and executives were mobilized to pressure politicians.

Business funded chairs of free enterprise at universities and colleges to increase the number of professors preaching the value of free enterprise and denouncing government regulation. Business schools added courses on business and public policy. A textbook designed for such a course states that managers must learn how "to articulate a business position on complex public issues and persuade people not under the manager's control that the position is in their best interests and the interests of society as a whole."[44] In the 1970s, business increasingly turned to advocacy advertising, which emphasized the value of free enterprise and the dangers of regulation. (Business now spends $2 billion annually on advocacy advertising and grassroots lobbying, compared to under $10 million spent by consumer and environmental groups to present the other side.) Business also directed its fire at Washington. By the middle 1980s, over 500 corporations had established Washington offices, a fivefold increase from a decade before.[45]

Perhaps the most effective political response by business was to lavish handsome sums on conservative political candidates, usually Republicans, as well as on the Republican party. Its most profitable political "investment" was Ronald Reagan, who pledged to "get government off the people's backs," by which he meant off business' back. As will be described next, deregulation was a key element in Reagan's program for dealing with the economic crisis.

THE REAGAN COUNTERREVOLUTION

In the late 1970s and early 1980s, the only major alternative proposed to the Republican program has been a continuation of Keynesianism, linked to a more interventionist economic role for

[44]Rogene A. Buchholz, *Business Environment and Public Policy: Implications for Management* (Englewood Cliffs, N.J., 1982), p. 11.
[45]Gordon Adams, *The Iron Triangle: The Politics of Defense Contracting* (New York, 1981), p. 129.

government known as industrial policy. As *Business Week* noted in a cover story on the question:

> Thus, the U.S. is searching frantically for ways to revive its economic vitality. And that search increasingly is zeroing in on industrial policy, or IP as economists call it. In broad terms, an IP can be anything from a plan to aid semiconductors, for example, with subsidies, tariffs, or tax breaks to a centralized planning approach that attempts to choose future growth areas—the so-called sunrise industries—as part of an overall economic growth strategy.[46]

Defenders of industrial policy argue that, since there is no way to avoid having one, in the sense that government actions have important economic consequences, it is preferable to have a consciously planned policy. Presently, however, industrial policy is a patchwork: the Pentagon is the world's largest "consumer," "voluntary" quotas are imposed on foreign steel, automobile, and other imports, and the federal government provides a host of subsidies to industry and agriculture. Advocates of industrial policy argue that consciously targeting government assistance to corporate producers will prove more effective than the present haphazard methods. These proponents of industrial policy are as eager as the critics to help capitalism flourish: their goal is to improve capitalist efficiency through selective government intervention. A minority of those advocating industrial policy, whose works are cited in these pages, seek to use industrial policy, along with other modes of public intervention, to democratize production. Conservative opponents of industrial policy fear precisely this. They argue that industrial policy would require larger government and increased central planning capacity. This would distort the operation of free markets and create a dangerous precedent to use government to democratize production.

The Republican victories of 1980 and 1984, on a platform radically opposed to industrial policy, at least temporarily eclipsed the debate, although it will doubtless reemerge when economic instability returns. However, in the 1980s, the government's relationship to corporate capital has moved in a very different direction.

---

[46]*Business Week,* July 4, 1983, p. 54.

The Reagan years: A fourth long wave or deepening crisis?

In the late 1970s, under Democrat Jimmy Carter, the business counterattack began to bear fruit. Carter ordered that cost-benefit analysis be used to evaluate new environment regulations issued by administrative agencies (which ignores nonmonetary benefits). He sponsored partial deregulation of the airlines, trucking, banking, and energy industries (a process distinct from the rolling back of social regulation). He proposed cuts in welfare programs and a buildup in military spending. Thus, a decidedly conservative shift was already under way before the 1980 election. But Ronald Reagan and the Republican party made a virtue of what Carter and the Democrats proclaimed to be a necessity. The Republicans accelerated the conservative thrust, and, by adding a highly biased tax cut, produced the most reactionary program sponsored by a major party in over half a century. To top it off, "the new class war," as social analysts Frances Piven and Richard Cloward describe it, was skillfully sugar-coated as the American dream.[47]

The Republican political formula of the 1980s has two aspects: a generous, optimistic public face and a harsh, vindictive private face. On the other hand, the program has been presented as a progressive recipe to increase material abundance, individual initiative, and political freedom for all. Rather than imposing a heavy tax burden on citizens to nourish an already bloated oppressive government, which reduces the resources that citizens have available for personal consumption, saving, and investment, the formula claims to lower taxes. Moreover, "getting government off people's back" by reducing environmental regulation and welfare assistance is said to increase personal freedom and self-reliance.

Although not publicly discussed by its Republican sponsors, the harsh features of the program reveal its true significance. An

---

[47]Frances Piven and Richard Cloward, *The New Class War: Reagan's War Against the Poor* (New York, 1982). The major elements of the Republican economic program were partially contradictory, as its own defenders admitted. For two analyses by Republican economists, see Paul Craig Roberts (who was assistant secretary of the treasury for economic policy in 1981–82), *The Supply-Side Revolution: An Insider's Account of Policymaking in Washington* (Cambridge, Mass., 1984), and Herbert Stein (who chaired the council of economic advisers under President Ford), *Presidential Economics: The Making of Economic Policy from Roosevelt to Reagan and Beyond* (New York, 1984).

enormous military buildup has consumed any savings from domestic spending cuts and, more disturbing, has purchased greater insecurity and the risks of war (see Chapter 10). Rather than a redistribution of power and resources from government to "the people," the program has redistributed power and resources from the poor to the rich, as well as from democratically elected government to private capital. Rather than increasing personal freedom, the shift increases business freedom, and other changes (discussed in Chapter 6) sharply expand government intrusion into people's personal lives, including reproductive rights. The Republican program represents an attempt to reverse decades of struggles to increase democratic control of the capitalist economy. Rather than uniting Americans and increasing social solidarity (presumably intended by the martial, patriotic rhetoric used to describe the approach), the formula polarizes Americans and increases class, racial, and gender inequalities. It uses the lash of economic hardship and fear to "motivate" workers, by weakening labor unions, reducing welfare assistance, and holding out the threat of unemployment to increase workers' dependence on management.

The unavowed goal of the Republican program is to reverse the redistribution of power from capital to citizens that had occurred in the 1970s. The Republican program is designed to restore capital's dominance in its relations with organized labor, citizens groups, and forces outside the United States.

Five major elements in the Republican program will be described, following which their impact will be assessed, as well as the possibility that the program will succeed in stimulating a fourth long wave of economic growth and political stability.

Reduced government domestic spending, especially welfare spending   The Republicans argued that government had grown large, oppressive, and inefficient. By eliminating "unnecessary fat," government could be restored to its proper and limited role. However, despite the huge size of the American military budget, government spending as a proportion of GNP is lower in the United States than in nearly every other capitalist democracy. The reason is that spending for social programs is meager in the United States—and this was true *before* the Republicans slashed a host of welfare programs.

A related aspect of the proposal to roll back federal spending and the federal government's role was to return power to state governments. The "new federalism" was to transfer responsibility for many welfare programs to the states, with federal subsidies promised for a limited period to help state governments finance their new responsibilities. Since the state governments would be free to reduce benefits or eliminate programs altogether, the "new federalism" represented a veiled attempt to reduce further the scope of the welfare state.

Supply-side reform   According to supply-side theory, Keynesianism was concerned only with demand, whereas the real problem with the economy was inadequate private savings and investment. Tax cuts would provide the funds and incentives to stimulate fresh investment. The principal measure proposed was a sharp income tax cut, aiming to provide new incentives for people to work, save, and invest.

The more optimistic supply siders argued that a tax cut would have such a powerful expansionary impact that it would pay for itself, since the economic pie would grow sufficiently fast to produce higher tax revenue despite the cut in marginal tax rates. (The untested theoretical basis for this optimistic view was supplied by economist Arthur Laffer; the Laffer curve described how dropping taxes would boost output.) The supply-side tax cut was the boldest and most unorthodox feature of the Republicans' approach.

First proposed by Congressman Jack Kemp, the supply-side tax cut was the culmination of a conservative populist "tax revolt" that began in the 1970s. (The most notable example was California's Proposition 13, in which citizens voted by referendum to slash property taxes and state government services.) According to Kemp and others, the low rate of private investment in the 1970s resulted from ever-higher personal income taxes, which consumed an increasing share of hard-working Americans' income, reduced incentives to work and save, and thereby starved business of needed investment capital. Cutting personal income taxes was also justified as providing relief to working-class and middle-income Americans. In fact, however, only the affluent have sufficient savings for investment. The tax cut was brilliantly designed to build an alliance between the working class and the affluent on a program of conservative economic revitalization. The real beneficiaries of the tax cut were not workers, who, as we shall see, received a small proportion of the personal tax reduction (and paid higher taxes overall), but wealthy citizens. In supply side theory, however, as a result of the personal income tax cut, as well as reductions in other taxes for business and individuals, business would gain access to new capital and would have the incentive to find profitable investments for it.

Monetarist orthodoxy   Coexisting in a somewhat contradictory fashion with the supply-side approach, another element in the Republican program aimed to break inflationary expectations through the use of Federal Reserve Board policies of monetary control. The monetarists argue that the Fed should follow an inflexible policy of slow monetary growth, regardless of economic conditions. By breaking inflationary expectations, half the battle against inflation would be won.

Deregulation   Government intervention had far exceeded what was needed and constituted an expensive and meddlesome intrusion. Deregulation promised to roll back unnecessary and undesirable government intervention.

The militarized economy   One area was not only spared the budget-cutting axe but given a lavish boost. President Reagan argued that a dangerous military imbalance had developed in the 1970s and a crash program of rearmament was necessary to achieve American superiority. (We will analyze this issue in Chapter 10.)

Especially in its reliance on the supply-side tax cut, President Reagan's program promised a painless way to restore economic growth. It was thereby in marked contrast to the traditional conservative argument that the road to fiscal soundness lay through raising taxes. Further, by his attack on the so-called excesses of the welfare state, Reagan skillfully divided former allies in the Democratic party coalition: stably employed workers, who resented rising taxes, as opposed to welfare recipients (who were members of the working poor, underemployed, unemployed, and/or single parents with young children to support). The Republican program also sought to reverse the trend since the New Deal toward government's assumption of responsibility for achieving economic growth and social solidarity. The new approach equated the freedom of individual citizens with the freedom of business from government "interference." *Business Week* described it best: "Politically, the Reagan administration's program represents an agenda for the revival of American capitalism."[48] In order to assess the success of the attempt, we will review how Reagan's proposals fared.

[48]*Business Week,* December 28, 1981, p. 76.

Spending cuts In his first year in office, President Reagan succeeded in cutting domestic spending by more than $40 billion. Additional cuts were made in succeeding years, although grass-roots pressure forced Congress to resist Reagan's proposals for major new cuts. Welfare programs for the poorest income groups were the major target of cuts; programs like Social Security and Medicare, for middle- and upper-income groups, were less affected. The Congressional Budget Office estimated that the poorest one-fourth of all families absorbed 40 percent of spending cuts.[49] This "war against the poor," as Piven and Cloward describe it, will be analyzed in Chapter 9.[50]

Another aspect of the Republican program to cut spending and reduce the role of the federal government was dubbed the "new federalism." Thanks to skillful legislative tactics in 1981, the administration persuaded Congress to consolidate 77 federal categorical grants to the states for health, education, social services, and community development into 10 broad block grants; 62 other categorical grants were eliminated. Overall, the total number of federal programs were cut by one-quarter.

Consolidating categorical grants into block grants enabled states to shift funds from programs providing benefits for lower income groups. For example, educational funds could be redirected from inner schools to buying computers for wealthy suburban school districts.[51]

The spending cuts were large in themselves and caused suffering for millions of people. But the effects of the cuts go beyond the specific programs reduced or eliminated. First, some of the cuts, while relatively small in financial terms, have great political importance, for example, slashes in the Legal Services Corporation, a government program of legal advocacy for the poor. Second, once a given cut is made, spending remains at the lower level unless there is sufficient pressure to reverse the trend. Third, the total size of the federal budget was *not* reduced: priorities were shifted from social to military spending. Whereas domestic spending was cut,

---

[49] *New York Times,* August 26, 1983.
[50] Piven and Cloward.
[51] Art Levene, "Easing of State-Local Regulatory Burden Leaves Some Pleased, Others Grumbling," *National Journal,* April 8, 1984; and Timothy J. Conlan, "The Politics of Federal Block Grants: From Nixon to Reagan," *Political Science Quarterly* 99 (Summer 1984): 249–70.

military spending was sharply increased. Thus, the net effect of the changes—both domestic cuts, military increases, and other changes reviewed here—signifies a fundamental reorientation of the federal government's priorities: a wholesale reversal of the trend toward an expanded welfare state that began in the 1960s.

Spending cuts and the new federalism were justified on the grounds that they reduced the role of government. But in fact the federal government's power increased substantially under the Republican administration as a result of increased military spending. Moreover, by proposing to outlaw abortion, President Reagan sought to restrict personal freedom and promote a massive new intrusion of government into people's (especially women's) lives. Further, the new federalism, which supposedly was to reduce federal supervision of state governments and increase their freedom, was contradicted by President Reagan's proposal that the federal government compel state governments to limit their own regulatory activity.

Supply-side tax cuts   In 1981, the Republican administration sponsored the largest tax cut in American history, an across-the-board 23 percent reduction in personal income taxes. While appearing to be income neutral, by applying equally to all taxpayers, the same percentage reduction was worth far more to the wealthy, both in terms of dollars and as a proportion of income, since it substantially reduced progressive features of the tax laws. Moreover, the wealthiest group received an even larger bonus when, as part of the same "reform," the highest marginal tax rate was dropped from 70 to 50 percent. President Reagan's director of the budget privately termed other features of the tax plan a "Trojan horse" to disguise this reduction in the top tax bracket.

The combined effects of cuts in the personal income tax affected various income groups very differently: for the vast majority of the population earning under $50,000, the tax cut made little difference; for those earning over $50,000 it provided substantial benefits, and for the $100,000 plus group (fewer than 1 percent of the population), it was a real bonanza. Overall, the wealthiest 6 percent received 40 percent of the total tax savings.

But this is not the end of our survey of tax reform under the Reagan administration. First, the wealthy received a number of other important breaks, including a drop in the capital gains tax from 28 to 20 percent. (This is what even the government terms "unearned income"—it derives from gains in the value of capital and does not include interest and dividends.) Inheritance taxes for all but the wealthiest citizens (1 percent of the population) were completely eliminated. Second, alongside tax cuts for the wealthy was a tax increase for lower income groups, notably a substantial rise in Social Security taxes, which falls most heavily on workers.

Various calculations of the combined effects of the tax changes suggest how class biased the tax plan was. Whereas in 1980, families earning less than $10,000 paid 9.9 percent annually of their income in taxes, in 1984 they paid 12.2 percent of their income in taxes. At the top of the income pyramid, families receiving over $250,000 in income paid 50.8 percent in taxes in 1980 and 40.9 percent in 1984.[52] The Congressional Budget Office calculated that, in 1983, a family receiving over $80,000 gained $7,100 from the tax changes, a family earning between $10,000 and $20,000 gained $130, and a family earning less than $10,000 paid $160 in additional taxes.[53]

A final measure of the impact of the Reagan economic program on different classes of Americans derives from combining the effects of spending cuts and tax changes. The cumulative impact is even more generous to the wealthy and damaging to the poor. According to the Congressional Budget Office, between 1983 and 1985, the one-fifth of all families with income under $10,000 lost $23 billion while the 1 percent of all families with income over $80,000 gained $35 billion.[54]

This was redistribution with a vengeance. As a result of fiscal changes and the 1981–82 recession, also partially provoked by government policies, the number of Americans officially classified as living below the poverty line increased for the first time in over a decade. Between 1980 and 1984, 6 million more Americans were added to the ranks of the official poor, bringing the total to 35.3 million. (The actual total is far larger, as explained in Chapter 9.)

The enormous redistribution of economic resources and political power up the class ladder was not an unintended consequence. The Reagan approach sought, quite successfully, to turn back the

[52]Frank Ackerman, *Hazardous to our Wealth: Economic Policies in the 1980s* (Boston, 1984), p. 36.

[53]*New York Times,* May 15, 1984.

[54]*In These Times,* May 2, 1984. Also see, for similar figures, Carnoy, Shearer, and Rumberger, p. 23; and Joel Haveman, "Sharing the Wealth: The Gap Between Rich and Poor Grows Wider," *National Journal,* October 23, 1982, p. 1795.

clock before the expansion of the welfare state in the 1960s and 1970s and, to an extent, before the New Deal made government responsible for overall economic management.

Did the fiscal changes achieve the stated goals of reducing inflation, stimulating economic growth, and reducing the federal deficit? Government policies did bring inflation down—although not through supply-side methods but by the time-honored method of the Federal Reserve Board's restricting monetary growth. The Fed's policy of high interest rates, begun under Jimmy Carter and inflexibly maintained despite ample indication of what lay ahead, plunged the United States into its worst recession since the 1930s. Economists Bowles, Gordon, and Weisskopf point out, "The Reagan administration has simply purchased lower inflation with high unemployment."[55]

But recession was not unintended by government policy makers although its severity and duration exceeded their expectations. The recession was meant to deliver a political message to workers and other citizens by stressing the need to sacrifice on behalf of capitalist growth. The recession was a resounding success in moderating wage demands and weakening organized labor. (See Chapter 7.)

And yet the recession failed to produce durable recovery. After reaching a low point in 1982, the economy began to revive. For two years, GNP increased at an annual rate of over 7 percent, higher than in other expansionary periods, and unemployment fell from its recession high of over 11 percent. However, this did not signify the promised era of stable expansion. Considering that GNP had stagnated during the recession, its upward course was less remarkable. And from late 1984 through 1986 growth slowed significantly. The decline in unemployment must also be placed in perspective. During the peak of the 1983–84 recovery, unemployment fell to 7.4 percent, the precise level as when President Reagan was elected in 1980—during what was then considered a period of economic slow down.

Economic growth was highly uneven and increased regional inequalities. According to a staff report by the Congressional Joint Economic Committee in 1986, while income in coastal states grew by 4 percent annually between 1981 and 1985, income rose only 1.4

[55]Sam Bowles, David M. Gordon, and Thomas E. Weisskopf, "Perspectives," *In These Times,* May 30, 1984, p. 17.

percent annually in the rest of the country. The 16 coastal states, with 42 percent of the nation's population, accounted for 70 percent of income growth during this period. Moreover, economic growth was distributed highly unevenly among social categories. While many affluent citizens experienced a sharp rise in income, unemployment rates remained at high levels among low-income groups.

Moreover, third, the stagnation of productivity, an important feature of the crisis, persisted. Productivity advanced less during this recovery than in other postwar recoveries. Bowles, Gordon, and Weisskopf observe, "We were promised a more than usually vibrant recovery of the economy's efficiency, for all our troubles, and we got the worst on record since World War II."[56]

Thus, rather than a new era of stable growth, the 1983–84 recovery resembled the stop-go boom and bust pattern typical of the capitalist business cycle. Moreover, whether the recovery should be interpreted as a victory for supply-side theory is open to doubt. *Business Week* commented, "In the short run at least, the combination of budget deficits and tax cuts has produced a recovery that looks less like a supply-side miracle than an old-fashioned super-Keynesian expansion."[57]

A dramatic indication of supply-side failure was the federal deficit, which soared to unprecedented heights. The 1983 deficit was not $23 billion, as the administration had officially forecast in 1981, but $195 billion; rather than a balanced budget in 1984, as forecast, the deficit hovered around $200 billion. The interest payments on the post-1981 deficits exceed the amount of welfare cuts, with the difference that they are paid to affluent holders of treasury notes. Whereas in 1975 interest charges represented 6.6 percent of federal spending, in 1984 the figure was 12.4 percent; in 1989, it is predicted to reach 16 percent.

Monetarism As noted above, with President Reagan's support, the Federal Reserve Board's restrictive monetary policy helped provoke the severe recession of 1981–82. Only when the Fed relaxed rates, contrary to monetarist orthodoxy, did economist expansion begin.

High interest rates help account for the fragile state of American banks. Over 70 failed during the presumably prosperous year 1984 (compared to 48 in 1983 and 10 in 1981). Continental Illinois

[56] *Ibid.*
[57] *Business Week,* September 3, 1984.

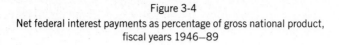

Figure 3-4
Net federal interest payments as percentage of gross national product,
fiscal years 1946–89

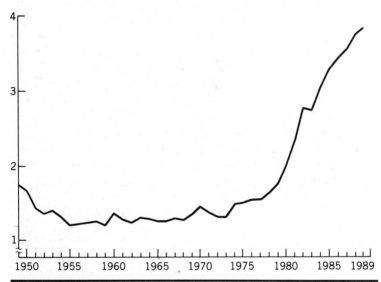

Source: Adapted from Paul E. Peterson, "The New Politics of Deficits" in John E. Chubb and Paul E. Peterson, eds., *The New Direction in American Politics* (Washington, D.C.: The Brookings Institution, 1985), p. 370. Data for 1985–89 are projected.

of Chicago, the nation's sixth largest bank, was narrowly saved from bankruptcy by a Federal Reserve bailout in 1984.

In 1985, during the first year of his second term, President Reagan sought to repeat the pattern of fiscal changes that he achieved in his first term. Using as a pretext the gigantic federal deficits, as well as his pledge not to raise taxes, he proposed a further $30 billion of domestic spending cuts in his $950 billion 1986 budget. As with the earlier changes, the brunt of cuts fell on the poor; the affluent continued to receive the lavish benefits from the first tax cut. Total federal spending continued to rise because of military spending increases. In a final irony, the president who produced the largest budget deficits in history ($220 billion in 1985 and $150 billion in 1987) proposed a constitutional amendment requiring a balanced budget. There has not been a balanced budget in decades and the requirement to balance the budget every year would be economically disastrous and socially reactionary (since spending cuts would doubtless affect welfare programs most heavily). The proposal was designed to appeal to conservative populist groups for whom a balanced budget is an article of faith.

By passing the Gramm-Rudman-Hollings deficit reduction plan in 1985, Congress accorded highest political priority to budget-cutting. The reform mandated large spending cuts to achieve a balanced budget by 1991. Although a key feature of the plan was declared unconstitutional by the Supreme Court because it violated the separation of powers, the law provided for across-the-board spending cuts in most federal programs. This produced further cutbacks in programs already reduced by previous decisions. Gramm-Rudman bill suggests the extent to which the structural deficits generated by the Reagan tax cuts have helped reshape the American political agenda.

Deregulation   President Reagan amply fulfilled his pledge to deregulate; he achieved a sweeping reduction in social regulation by administrative fiat, underfunding regulatory agencies, and appointing administrators hostile to the purposes of the agencies they directed. The impact was immediate. For example, during the first two years of the Republican administration, OSHA halved its work-place inspections and the number of penalties imposed by OSHA inspectors declined by three-fourths. In 1981, the EPA referred one-quarter as many business violations to the Justice Department for prosecution as in 1980. The EPA was soon crippled by collusion between Reagan appointees and corporate polluters. The entire top tier of administrators was forced to resign and criminal charges were brought against several EPA executives. The number of mining deaths increased by one-sixth in 1981, and the number of mine disasters increased for the first time in a decade.[58]

Reagan's appointees to head regulatory agencies were good friends of industry. His choice to head OSHA was a 35-year-old businessman whose family construction firm had been cited 48 times for OSHA violations. The person appointed to head EPA's program for cleaning up the most toxic waste sites (the "Superfund") was formerly public relations director for Aerojet-General,

[58]Susan J. Tolchin and Martin Tolchin, *Dismantling America: The Rush to Deregulate* (Boston, 1983), p. 94.

one of California's worst polluters. (She was later convicted of perjury as a result of her activity while at EPA.) One study of the deregulation process under Reagan suggests:

> Environmental regulation became a thing of the past as the EPA studiously ignored the laws and regulations dealing with clean air and water, as well as hazardous waste. . . . No area of social protection was left untouched by White House efforts. . . . What had taken years to build was dismantled in the first twelve months of the Reagan administration.[59]

An indication of the need for more, not less, regulation was the disaster that struck Bhopal, India, in 1984, when American-owned Union Carbide's pesticide manufacture plant leaked highly toxic chemicals that killed more than 2,500 people and injured over 100,000 because of inadequate fail-safe procedures. When the environment movement produced new evidence of environmental dangers, such as acid rain produced by disposal of acid wastes by manufacturing plants in the Midwest, the administration evaded action. By abdicating responsibility for safeguarding the environment from corporate capitalism, the government created a time bomb for future generations.

Remilitarization   The Reagan administration accomplished the largest peacetime military buildup in history. In four years from 1980, the military budget doubled; it was scheduled to triple by 1988, according to administration projections. This shift transformed the composition of the federal budget, with military spending rising from one-quarter to one-third of all federal spending, and it further militarized the entire U.S. economy. Even President Reagan's Republican supporters in Congress balked at approving further military increases of $40 billion in 1985. (Chapter 10 will analyze the effect on American security of these colossal sums.)

Conclusion

The revival of the economy in 1983–84 and President Reagan's resounding reelection in 1984 testified to at least the short-term success of the new approach. Further, as was emphasized previ-

[59] *Ibid.*, pp. 21–22.

ously, the class biased features of the program, involving a vast redistribution from poor to rich, are also evidence of the Republicans' success in reallocating benefits from their political opponents to their supporters.

Yet it is doubtful whether the Republican achievements will prove durable. As their costs mount, they may well provoke a strong reaction. Reasons include:

1. The economic recovery of 1982–84 was a product of wage cuts (made possible by the previous recession) and cuts in government social expenditures, both of which weakened the working class and reestablished capitalist dominance. In addition, government stimulated the economy through the "pump priming" of military spending increases and huge budget deficits. This pattern will not be able to be repeated to counter the next recession. For one thing, social cuts have already been severe. For another, the fact that deficits increased to record levels even during the 1983–84 recovery meant that deficit reduction assumed high priority, ruling out deficit spending in the future. The editors of *Monthly Review* observe, "Deficit finance considered as part of the government's stockpile of anti-cyclical ammunition has been used up. In this respect, at least for the foreseeable future, a significant chapter in the twentieth-century history of U.S. capitalism must now be considered closed."[60]

2. The new approach constitutes a direct assault on a host of groups—blacks, the poor, women, and organized labor, thus sowing the seeds of future conflict.

3. The approach fails to cope with increasing structural unemployment, caused by the microelectronic revolution, decline of basic industries, and increased international economic competition. Instead, it shifts the costs of economic adjustment to displaced workers—the same groups enumerated previously.

4. Deregulation is producing incalculable social and environmental damage that will haunt Americans in the future.

5. Remilitarizing the economy has harmful economic effects and potentially devastating consequences for national security.

---

[60]Editors of *Monthly Review,* "Four More Years—Of What?" *Monthly Review* 36 (January 1985): 10.

Thus, despite the short-term political and economic success of the Republican approach, it appears to be creating the basis for fresh conflicts in the future. Yet, the Republican approach provides opportunities as well as costs. It has graphically demonstrated the possibilities of movement along the capitalist–democratic axis, in a pro-capitalist direction. The failure of the Republican approach, both to restore growth and to mobilize electoral majorities on behalf of capitalist domination, would create space for movement in a democratic direction.

Institutional Patterns

4

the president as manager of corporate america

When delegates to the Constitutional Convention were meeting in Philadelphia in 1787 to consider ways to revise the Articles of Confederation, Alexander Hamilton, a thirty-year-old delegate from New York, shocked the gathering by praising the British monarchy—against whom the colonies had revolted a mere decade before—as "the best in the world." Recognizing that hereditary monarchy would never be accepted in America, Hamilton suggested that the new federal government should be directed by an elected monarch, holding office for life. Hamilton later returned to this idea in *The Federalist* No. 70, one of a series of papers written by Hamilton, James Madison, and John Jay to persuade voters to ratify the proposed Constitution.

Hamilton's proposal was ignored by the Convention and it occupies barely a footnote in histories of the founding period. Instead, the Constitutional Convention proposed a government of separated institutions, embodying the delegates' belief in the necessity for a system of checks and balances to prevent any one branch from overpowering the others and gaining the chance to exercise tyranny.

Yet, taking account of the fact that the president is elected every four years, rather than holding office for life as Hamilton favored, the term *elected monarch* is as accurate as any to describe the contemporary presidency. Former senator Jacob Javits has observed that the United States had lodged "more power in a single individual than any other system of government that functions today," a strange irony in a country that once prided itself on limited government and that regarded "the accumulation of all powers, legislative, executive, and judiciary in the same hands," according to James Madison's formulation in *The Federalist* No. 47, as "the very definition of tyranny." Contrary to the intention of the framers—who attempted to distribute the legislative (policy making), executive, and judicial functions of government among separate branches of government, with the three responsive to different constituencies but sharing the functions of government—the contemporary presidency has substantially absorbed many of the powers of government.

The modern presidency (which, as we will describe, extends far beyond the president) is at the center of the executive branch of government, the sprawling bureaucracy that numbers two million federal civil servants. The president commands the most powerful military establishment in the world. The presidency has taken over much of the function of policy initiation, although Congress, "think tanks," social movements, and other forces make policy proposals as well. The courts curb presidential power only in extreme instances, such as Watergate. In recent years, Congress has assumed substantial new powers, as detailed in the next chapter. But the president continues largely to determine the legislative agenda. In brief, there is no political office anywhere, whether it be in capitalist democracies, authoritarian regimes, or soviet systems, that represents a comparable concentration of power to the American presidency.

During the 1970s, however, it was common to characterize the presidency as a weak and ineffective institution. An indication was that, for more than one quarter of a century—since Dwight D. Eisenhower in the 1950s—no president served two full terms, and every single president was forced from office. John F. Kennedy was assassinated in 1963 before completing his first term, Lyndon B. Johnson chose not to seek reelection in 1968 because of deep divisions provoked by his conduct of the Vietnam War, Richard M. Nixon was forced to resign from office in 1973 to avoid impeachment in the Watergate scandal, and incumbent presidents Gerald Ford and Jimmy Carter were defeated at the polls. Ronald Reagan's reelection in 1984 marked a sharp contrast with recent decades.

A factor that helps to explain what one analyst calls the "no win president" was a shift in public attitudes toward the president and the entire political system as a result of Johnson's Vietnam War policies, Nixon's duplicity about Watergate, and widespread criticism of corporate and political abuses.[1] Whereas until the 1960s, most citizens assumed that the government acted in the public interest, few displayed such trust by the 1970s. Part and parcel of this trend was that public opinion, the mass media, and Congress showed more readiness to resist presidential leadership.

A second factor explaining the decline of the presidency, and partially linked to the first, was the growing economic crisis. Since at least the New Deal, the president's fortunes have been closely tied to the fate of the economy. The power and prestige of the president (as well as of the entire government) have prospered when corporate capitalism has prospered; and when the economy stagnates, the president's popular and professional standing falls. Beginning in the middle 1960s, just when presidents were falling from popular favor, the American economy was beginning to show signs of the economic crisis that is still not resolved.

A third cause of presidential weakness was the growing fragmentation of the federal executive, the government, and the entire American society. One observer points to the breakdown of stable political support for the president. In its place, he suggests there has developed the "single issue presidency," in which presidents and their advisers are forced to assemble an ad hoc coalition of interests within Congress and the society for each policy proposal.[2]

---

[1] Paul Charles Light, *The President's Agenda: Domestic Policy Choice from Kennedy to Carter (with Notes on Ronald Reagan)* (Baltimore, 1981).
[2] Joseph A. Pika, "Interest Groups and the Executive: Presidential Intervention," in Allan J. Cigler and Burdett A. Loomis, eds., *Interest Group Politics* (Washington, D.C., 1983), p. 320.

Moreover, as the scope of government increased and issues became more complex, it became more difficult to develop broad policy syntheses. Each proposal required endless scrutiny by policy experts and interested groups, with increased likelihood of delays and stalemate.

Other observers describe the increasing fragmentation and conflict within American society, identified as a process of "Balkanization" or "atomization." The result has further hindered the exercise of presidential leadership.[3]

Yet another argument has stressed the importance of increased grass-roots participation and conflict that overburdened political institutions and created a veritable "crisis of democracy."[4] The root problem was that the president could no longer expect to be supported when repression was used to control dissent.

Whether these views were a fully accurate description of American politics in the 1970s can be questioned, given the continued preeminence of the president and the basic stability of political institutions. For example, during the entire period, no major movement or political party challenged in a sustained way the basic legitimacy of American economic and political arrangements. Furthermore although social movements like the women's movement, black militants, and environmental activists achieved significant changes, American corporate capitalism remained intact.

In any event, since Ronald Reagan's election in 1980, there is little question of the president's ability to command government and the nation in pursuit of broad, coherent, and activist policies. As described in Chapter 3, the Reagan administration has sponsored a sharp reduction in environmental regulation of corporate activity, a vast redistribution of economic and political power from the working class to business and the affluent, and the largest peacetime military buildup in history. So much for political paralysis!

However, this fundamental reorientation of federal policies, as well as of the entire political economy, raises anew the question with which the framers grappled concerning the dangers inherent

[3]Kevin P. Phillips, *Post-Conservative America: People, Politics and Ideology in a Time of Crisis* (New York, 1982), chapter 6; Anthony King, ed., *The New American Political System* (Washington, D.C., 1978).
[4]Michel Crozier *et al., The Crisis of Democracy: Report on the Governability of Democracies to the Trilateral Commission* (New York, 1975).

in concentrating vast powers in a single institution. How did the presidency become so powerful?

The presidency did not assume its present character overnight nor was the development inevitable. In constitutional doctrine and in political practice through much of American history, the presidency was at most first among equals—and not always that. Prior to the twentieth century, most presidents exercised relatively few powers, and the entire national government had limited influence. Bold innovators like Andrew Jackson, Abraham Lincoln, Theodore Roosevelt, and Woodrow Wilson were isolated exceptions, not the rule.

As late as the end of the nineteenth century, the presidency was viewed by many scholars as a weak branch of government. In 1885, a young Princeton professor published an influential study of American politics, entitled *Congressional Government,* in which he asserted that Congress was the foremost policy-making institution of American government. Indeed, the president was powerful only to the extent that he participated, by his limited veto power over bills passed by Congress, in the legislative domain. Twenty-three years later, the author changed his view and, in *Constitutional Government in the United States,* developed a far more expansive theory of the presidency. Soon after, by his actions as president, Woodrow Wilson, the former Princeton professor, contributed even more directly to the creation of a powerful presidency.

Through much of the nineteenth and early twentieth century, there were swings between strong and weak presidents, between presidential and congressional supremacy, and between an interventionist and a restrained federal government. Underlying the particular changes, however, was the slow but steady growth in size and power of the federal government. A decisive shift occurred in the early twentieth century. The development of the modern presidency has accompanied the growth of big government, which, as described in the previous chapter, was a product of the rise of corporate capitalism within the United States and its penetration abroad. Particularly since Franklin D. Roosevelt, the balance of power among the three branches of government has tilted toward the president.

The rapid growth in size and power of the presidency can be illustrated by one statistic. When Herbert Hoover served as president from 1928 to 1932, he was aided by a personal secretary and two assistants. The Executive Office of the President (EOP) presently exceeds 5,000 staff members, including 600 members of the White House staff.[5]

Every president for half a century has probably been more powerful than even the most powerful presidents of the nineteenth century. The bold innovations of one president have come to be accepted as a normal feature of presidential rule by the next. "In instance after instance," Richard Neustadt, a student of the presidency, has observed, "the exceptional behavior of our earlier 'strong' Presidents has now been set by statute as a regular requirement."[6] As political scientist Robert Gilmour describes it, "At least in part, routinization of the presidency represents a formalization of presidential actions that were once thought to be extraordinary."[7] Gilmour cites both Grover Cleveland's and Theodore Roosevelt's interventions to end strikes—actions that became institutionalized in later congressional legislation empowering the president to submit strikes to arbitration or to prohibit them.

Until the Watergate scandal, it was fashionable for presidents unabashedly to proclaim the need for wide-ranging power. The president, stated John F. Kennedy during the 1960 presidential campaign

> must be prepared to exercise the fullest powers of his office—all that are specified and some that are not. . . . For only the president represents the national interest. And upon him alone converge all the needs and aspirations of all parts of the country, all departments of the government, all nations of the world.[8]

During a television interview in 1964, Lyndon Johnson asserted:

> The office of the Presidency is the only office in this land of all the people. . . . At no time and in no way and for no reason can a President allow the integrity or the responsibility or the freedom of

[5]Arthur M. Schlesinger, Jr., *The Imperial Presidency* (Boston, 1973), p. 221.
[6]Richard E. Neustadt, *Presidential Power: The Politics of Leadership* (New York, 1963), p. 5.
[7]Robert S. Gilmour, "The Institutionalized Presidency: A Conceptual Clarification," in Norman C. Thomas, ed., *The Presidency in Contemporary Context* (New York, 1975), p. 155.
[8]Campaign speech by John Kennedy, quoted in Robert S. Hirschfield, ed., *The Power of the Presidency: Concepts and Controversy*, 2nd ed. (Chicago, 1973), pp. 130, 133.

the office ever to be compromised or diluted or destroyed, because when you destroy it, you destroy yourselves.[9]

In a 1968 election campaign address, Richard Nixon stated:

The days of a passive Presidency belong to a simpler past. Let me be very clear about this. The next President must take an activist view of his office. He must articulate the nation's values, define its goals and marshal its will. Under a Nixon Administration, the Presidency will be deeply involved in the entire sweep of American public opinion.[10]

On another occasion, Nixon suggested, "Only the President can hold out a vision of the future and rally the people behind it."[11]

However, it was partly Richard Nixon's excesses and the resulting public disgust surrounding his resignation following the Watergate affair that led Presidents Ford and Carter to display a more modest approach to presidential activism. Perhaps even more important to this trend was that when the political and economic crisis emerged in the 1970s, presidents sought to lower population expectations, not raise them—until Ronald Reagan. Reagan's alchemy was to pooh-pooh those who sought to lower expectations, like his 1984 Democratic opponent Walter Mondale, but to ground his appeal for boundless expectations in a rhetoric of agrarian self-reliance and individualism that ignored class divisions and the immense concentration of corporate power in the late twentieth century.

All modern presidents aim to be remembered as innovators. The precedent was set by Theodore Roosevelt's Square Deal, followed by Woodrow Wilson's New Freedom, Franklin Roosevelt's New Deal, John F. Kennedy's New Frontier, and Lyndon Johnson's Great Society. Richard Nixon continued this tradition when he proclaimed, "This will be known as an Administration which advocated . . . more significant reforms than any Administration since Franklin Roosevelt in 1932."[12] Presidents Ford and Carter had more modest ambitions, a function of their particular personalities, the economic crisis, and the turmoil of the times. President Reagan returned to the tradition of policy innovation—but with a

---

[9]*Ibid.*, p. 150.
[10]*New York Times*, March 4, 1973.
[11]Hirschfield, p. 165.
[12]*New York Times,* November 10, 1972.

twist. He sought to use government's power in a highly activist manner—with the goal not of expanding but reducing government's role in social welfare and economic management. Yet this hardly signified a return to limited government. At home, it meant an intense burst of government activity to alter popular expectations and government programs. Moreover, alongside domestic retrenchment was a substantial military buildup and stepped-up American intervention abroad.

A good way to understand the political significance of the presidency is to study the various areas in which the president exercises power. Different scholars have suggested alternative classifications. Clinton Rossiter, a student of the presidency, identifies various "hats" or roles of the president, including (following Rossiter's terminology) chief of state, chief executive, commander in chief of the armed forces, chief diplomat, chief legislator, chief of party, voice of the people, protector of the peace, manager of prosperity, and world leader.[13] Political scientist Thomas Cronin describes four spheres, or subpresidencies: foreign policy, aggregate economic functions, domestic-policy functions, and symbolic and moral leadership.[14] Aaron Wildavsky, a specialist in public policy, has pointed to two presidencies, one for foreign and the other for domestic affairs.[15]

Adapting these classifications, we suggest three broad purposes on behalf of which contemporary presidents exercise power: to foster economic growth and assist corporate production at home, defend corporate capitalism and American power abroad, and maintain social control. The three represent major founts of modern presidential power, resulting from the growth of corporate production, corporate and government expansion abroad, and the nationalization of American political and cultural life through the mass media. Each sphere can be identified with particular constitutional grants of authority and particular agencies within the Executive Office of the President.

Before examining each of these areas, however, a warning is in order. Richard Neustadt has questioned the validity of dividing the presidency into separate roles. In his view, the various presiden-

[13]Clinton Rossiter, *The American Presidency*, revised ed. (New York, 1960), chapter 1.
[14]Thomas E. Cronin, "Presidents as Chief Executives," in Rexford G. Tugwell and Thomas E. Cronin, eds., *The Presidency Reappraised* (New York, 1974), p. 235.
[15]Aaron Wildavsky, "The Two Presidencies," *Trans-action* (December 1966): 7–14.

tial functions are woven together into an indistinguishable whole. Their common ingredient is the exercise of presidential power. Presidential activity can be understood as the attempt to exert influence rather than the mechanical performance of separate roles.[16]

In our view, Neustadt is correct in stressing the need to understand the overall coherence of presidential activity. Yet he does not specify the ends served by the exercise of presidential power. Our interpretation is that presidential power can best be understood as an attempt to reconcile the conflict between the need to aid corporate capital at home and overseas (the goal of fostering capital accumulation) and the need to gain the assent of the broad majority (the goal of maintaining social control). The two goals would dictate very different policies: one serving the corporate sector, the other serving the broad majority. Presidents generally try to obscure the conflict between the two under the cloak of the common interests of the whole society. In the absence of government policies aimed at abolishing inequality, the result is to favor continued dominance by private capital at the expense of the majority. Note how, during a television interview, President Lyndon Johnson links government to corporate production and foreign involvement in a paean to the United States, thus weaving together what we identify as the three major presidential functions:

> I am so proud of our system of government, of our free enterprise, where our incentive system and our men who head our big industries are willing to get up at daylight and get to bed at midnight to offer employment and create new jobs for people, where our men working there will try to get decent wages but will sit across the table and not act like cannibals, but will negotiate and reason things out together. . . . We have one thing they [the USSR] don't have and that is our system of private enterprise, free enterprise, where the employer, hoping to make a little profit, the laborer, hoping to justify his wages, can get together and make a better mousetrap. They have developed this into the most powerful and leading nation in the world, and I want to see it preserved.[17]

This chapter examines how the president carries out the three broad functions of defending the corporate complex abroad, assisting corporate capitalism at home, and maintaining social control.

---

[16]Neustadt, chapter 3.
[17]Hirschfield, pp. 147–48.

THE IMPERIAL PRESIDENT
AND THE IMPERIAL REPUBLIC

The rise of the modern presidency has been inseparable from the rise of the United States as an imperial power. Presidential power has thrived on foreign involvement, crisis, and war. The titles of two books published a few months apart—*The Imperial Presidency* by historian Arthur Schlesinger, Jr., and *The Imperial Republic* by French scholar Raymond Aron—evoke the parallel expansion of the presidency within the government and the United States in the world.[18] Presidential power has taken a quantum leap each time the United States has expanded abroad or been involved in a military, diplomatic, or commercial crisis.

One of the chief pegs on which increased presidential prerogative has been hung is the president's role in foreign affairs, including the constitutional power to negotiate treaties, receive ambassadors from foreign countries (which implies the right to recognize or refuse to recognize the regime of a particular country), and, above all, command the armed forces. The framers intended the president's power as commander in chief to be confined to the limited authority of a military leader to issue orders once hostilities exist. The Constitution granted Congress, not the president, the power to declare war and appropriate funds for military expenditures.

Early presidents soon expanded their power as commander in chief—and thereby the power of the presidency as a whole—by deploying American troops in pursuance of their foreign policies. James K. Polk, for example, provoked war with Mexico in 1846 by sending American troops into disputed land between Texas and Mexico. When the troops were fired upon by Mexican forces, Polk quickly extracted from Congress a declaration of war. Polk's actions brought forth an angry reaction from a young Illinois congressman, "Allow the President to invade a neighboring nation, whenever *he* shall deem it necessary to repel an invasion . . . and you allow him to make war at pleasure. Study to see if you can fix *any limit* to his power in this respect."[19]

---

[18]Schlesinger, *The Imperial Presidency;* Raymond Aron, *The Imperial Republic* (Englewood Cliffs, N.J., 1974), first published in France in 1973.
[19]Schlesinger, p. 42, italics in original.

Abraham Lincoln's words proved prescient. The scenario was repeated over a century later when, in 1964, President Johnson ordered naval destroyers deployed close to the coast of North Vietnam, in the Gulf of Tonkin, and provoked an encounter with North Vietnamese forces. The incident was quickly used to obtain from Congress a resolution drafted by the executive (ostensibly in the heat of the crisis—it was later revealed that the resolution had been prepared long in advance) authorizing the president "to take all necessary measures" to pursue the war. The Gulf of Tonkin resolution paved the way to American aerial bombardment of North Vietnam the following year.

Lincoln himself, when president, used presidential war powers during the Civil War in a drastically expanded manner. During the first months after the war broke out, Lincoln refused to call Congress into special session. Among the unauthorized measures he took were the blockading of Southern ports, suspending constitutional rights in judicial proceedings, expanding the armed forces beyond their congressionally prescribed size, and spending money for purposes not approved by Congress. During the course of the war, Lincoln took additional measures without congressional approval: he proclaimed martial law behind the lines, arrested people without following judicial procedures, seized property, suppressed newspapers, and laid out a plan for reconstruction.[20] Edward Corwin, a scholar of constitutional law, notes that Lincoln's actions "assert for the President for the first time in our history, an initiative of indefinite scope . . . in meeting the domestic aspects of a war emergency."[21]

Woodrow Wilson was prophetic when, as a professor, he wrote of the president's new position arising from American power internationally:

> The President can never again be the mere domestic figure he has been throughout so large a part of our history. The nation has risen to the first rank in power and resources. . . . Our President must always, henceforth, be one of the great powers of the world, whether he acts greatly and wisely or not. . . . We can never hide our President again as a mere domestic officer. . . . He must stand always at

[20]*Ibid.*, p. 58.
[21]Edward S. Corwin, *The President: Office and Powers, 1787–1957* (New York, 1957), p. 232.

the front of our affairs, and the office will be as big and as influential as the man who occupies it.[22]

Chapter 10 describes how presidents in the twentieth century have promoted expansion of American power abroad. Following a policy of "gunboat diplomacy" in the early part of the century, presidents ordered American forces to Latin America to "collect debts for American banks and enforce the will of American sugar, fruit, and other interests."[23] President Wilson during the First World War and President Roosevelt during the Second World War exercised wide-ranging powers as military leaders. Through the destroyer deal with Great Britain, in which (by executive agreement) Roosevelt exchanged United States destroyers for the use of British naval bases, the president circumvented Congress to accelerate military preparations. During the war he relocated the entire Japanese-American population (70,000 people) living on the West Coast to makeshift intern camps in California and elsewhere; he created wartime agencies on his authority to regulate prices, rents, and raw materials; and he seized 60 strike-bound plants to force workers to return to their jobs. After the Second World War, President Truman enunciated the Truman Doctrine on his own authority; its pledge to intervene militarily anywhere in the world represented a basic shift in American foreign policy.

Presidents nowadays justify their increased power by reference to the litany of the cold war, the threat of nuclear destruction, the requirements of national security, and the need for speed and secrecy. In Neustadt's words, "Technology has modified the Constitution. The President . . . becomes the only . . . man in the system capable of exercising judgment under the extraordinary limits now imposed by secrecy, complexity, and time."[24]

Presidents frequently defend their actions on the basis of their unique access to secret information. "If you knew what I know,"

---

[22]Woodrow Wilson, *Constitutional Government in the United States* (New York, 1908), pp. 78–79.

[23]I. F. Stone, "Can Congress Stop the President?" *New York Review of Books,* April 19, 1973, p. 23.

[24]Richard Neustadt, "Testimony of Richard Neustadt Before the Senate Subcommittee on National Security Staffing and Operations," in Aaron Wildavsky, ed., *The Presidency* (Boston, 1969), p. 516.

asserted Lyndon Johnson, "then you would be acting in the same way."[25] Yet "backstage" glimpses of workings of the presidency, such as those provided by the Pentagon Papers and the transcription of the White House tapes in the Watergate affair, reveal the limited role of superior information. Moreover, Johnson's argument has a suspiciously self-serving ring. First, presidents do their utmost to withhold information (the top-heavy security-classification system is an example)—and thus try to prevent citizens from knowing what presidents know. Further, the quality of this inside information can be questioned: "I used to imagine when the government took actions I found inexplicable that it had information I didn't have," relates Charles Frankel, who served as an assistant secretary of state under President Johnson. "But after I had served in the government for some months, I found that the information was often false!"[26] In 1983, the state department issued a white paper seeking to document its charge that the Sandinista government of Nicaragua was receiving large quantities of military supplies from Cuba and the Soviet Union. Although the report was used to justify illegal United States intervention in Nicaragua, it failed to provide adequate evidence and was discredited by an international commission of jurists, among other groups. George Reedy, press secretary to President Johnson, notes, "The most easily observable fact about 'secret diplomacy' is that it has not worked very well."[27]

The major consequence of the presumed need for secrecy and the secret information presidents possess is to shield presidential activity from public scrutiny. An extreme illustration is the secret air wars President Nixon conducted in Cambodia during 1969–70 and 1973. (When announcing an American ground invasion of Cambodia in April 1970, Nixon stated that until then the United States had "scrupulously respect[ed] the neutrality of the Cambodian people," and had done nothing "to violate the territory of a neutral nation.") So expansive had the president's war power become that the House Judiciary Committee investigating possible

[25]Robert T. Nakamura, "Congress Confronts the Presidency," in Robert Paul Wolff, ed., *1984 Revisited: Prospects for American Politics* (New York, 1973), p. 82.
[26]Charles Frankel, *High on Foggy Bottom* (New York, 1969), p. 78.
[27]George E. Reedy, "On the Isolation of Presidents," in Tugwell and Cronin, p. 130.

grounds for presidential impeachment in 1974 decided that Nixon's duplicity regarding Cambodia did not constitute grounds for impeachment.

The need for speed as a justification for presidential power is also open to doubt. Presidential decisions rarely need to be made in a hurry. The usual process is policy making by accretion, in the words of former Senator William Fulbright. Foreign engagements such as Vietnam occur through a slow process of escalation, not as the result of a crisis demanding a rapid decision. The image of the finger on the nuclear button has been unjustifiably extended to the entire range of presidential activity. The president's expanded powers in the exceptional conditions of wartime have become standard in an era where the economy is permanently mobilized, American corporations routinely operate throughout the world, and the armed forces are stationed in every continent and are on the brink of war twenty-four hours a day. Presidential power is given an awesome boost by the fact that the United States is a militarized economy.

As commander in chief and chief of the executive branch, the president is in overall control of the military-industrial complex; the president's reach is extended through staff members in the Executive Office of the President, notably the National Security Council, whose members include the secretaries of state and defense, the director of the CIA, and the president's personal national security adviser. The president must contend with conflicting interests among the army, navy, and air force as well as the entrenched power of the service chiefs, key members of Congress, and corporate military producers. Nonetheless, the president is at the apex of the most powerful military machine in history.

Although national security is usually invoked to justify this vast enterprise, the heavy dependence of American corporations on foreign operations means that presidential policies are formulated with an eye to the overseas interests of corporate capitalism. Foreign-investment policies, tariffs, and decisions about currency and other economic matters aim to strengthen American multinational corporations in their worldwide activities. Anticommunism and foreign economic penetration were intertwined as twin justifications for international expansion. The president manages the vast foreign policy and military establishment that has been developed to achieve these goals.

Acting as protector of America's national security strengthens the president at home. "Don't bother the president," presidential adviser Sherman Adams was fond of telling visitors who wanted to see Eisenhower. "He's busy trying to keep us out of war." But national security and international tensions may be invoked for reasons having more to do with presidential interests than with the survival of the United States. The Watergate affair provides a good illustration. In a speech minimizing the gravity of the events, President Nixon mentioned national security thirty-one times.[28]

James Oliver, a student of presidential foreign policy making, observes, "Authoritarian and totalitarian governments are often accused of trying to divert the attention of their populations from domestic difficulties by means of wars or fabricated international crises. It seems, however, that American presidents faced with their own domestic pressures are no less susceptible to [this temptation]."[29]

Whereas after the Second World War presidents had a relatively free hand in foreign policy, since the Vietnam War they have been forced to contend with continual opposition in many areas of foreign policy. As described in the next chapter, Congress now scrutinizes presidential foreign policy more closely and has resisted the scale of military spending increases proposed by President Reagan. Congressional opposition to the president on foreign policy has been associated with other changes in Congress, including the fragmentation of congressional leadership and the development of increased staff expertise.

Opposition to the president on foreign policy has partly been a response to the increasing integration of the United States in the international capitalist system, which affects various sectors of business differently. For example, steel and automobile producers demand quotas on foreign imports whereas agribusiness and some high technology sectors want protectionism reduced.

An important source of pressure on Congress to resist presidential foreign policy making has been the development of strong grass-roots movements. Current examples include the nuclear freeze movement and groups opposing United States intervention

[28]Charles M. Hardin, *Presidential Power and Accountability: Toward a New Constitution* (Chicago, 1974), p. 24.
[29]James K. Oliver, "Presidents as National Security Policymakers," in Thomas E. Cronin, ed., *Rethinking the Presidency* (Boston, 1982), p. 397.

in Central America. As a result of earlier grass-roots efforts, Congress passed a series of measures in the 1970s that structurally altered the balance of presidential-congressional relations in foreign policy. The most influential was the War Powers Act, passed over President Nixon's veto in 1973. The law requires congressional approval of the use of American forces in hostilities beyond a certain period.

Congress has also intervened frequently to cut presidential military budget proposals, for example, after President Reagan proposed a further military buildup in 1985. Conflicts concerned overall spending levels as well as specific weapons programs, for example, the MX missile and the Strategic Defense Initiative ("star wars" research). Another area of presidential-congressional controversy in the 1980s was United States military intervention in Central America.

Congressional and popular resistance to presidential militarist actions has had a significant impact. Yet the president has retained immense power and initiative in foreign affairs. Congressional opposition is limited for four reasons. First, the president has vastly more power by virtue of commanding the military establishment, enjoying unique access to information, and controlling the deployment of nuclear weapons. These are both enormous powers in themselves and also have important symbolic value: they contribute to the awesome, even religious, aspect of the presidency. Moreover, the president has the staff resources of the entire defense establishment and unique access to the media to defend foreign policy positions.

Second, the president can evade a congressional injunction by invoking a crisis or an emergency. Congress would not dare question a president's judgment during the heat of a crisis. Third, the most significant feature of presidential power in foreign affairs is not a sudden and dramatic resort to military force. Instead, presidential activity is part of an institutionalized process directed to the defense of corporate and governmental interests abroad. There are few dramatic acts in this vast domain comparable to the escalation of the Vietnam War. Fourth, debates about whether Congress or the president should exercise greater power in foreign affairs overlook the substantial measure of agreement between the two branches of government on the broad aims of America's actions abroad.

MANAGING THE MANAGED ECONOMY:
DEFENDING CORPORATE CAPITALISM AT HOME

The modern presidency has been pictured as a series of concentric circles, with the president at the center. Surrounding the president are trusted personal advisers in the presidential agency—the White House staff. Close to these advisers are agencies in the Executive Office of the President (EOP). The contemporary presidency is not one person but the several thousand who make up the EOP. Another ring is constituted by the cabinet: the secretaries of the executive departments. They are followed by the "permanent government": the over two million civil servants who work in the bureaus and other agencies within the executive departments.

The sprawling, diverse bureaucracies in the executive give to the government its proverbial character of being slow to act, internally divided, and formless. Yet one agency within the executive does seek to represent the interest of the whole system of established arrangements: the presidency.

Whereas the agencies comprising the executive branch carry out government programs, overall planning is mostly centered in the institutionalized presidency. Sociologist Daniel Bell notes, "In the long run, it is not the growth of personal powers and prestige of the President that is important, but the institutionalization of such crucial control and directing functions—as are now carried out by the Budget Bureau and the Council of Economic Advisers—in the executive."[30]

The Constitution provides ample latitude for the expansive exercise of presidential power. Executive power is vested in the president as well as the power to nominate high officials in the executive and judiciary. The president is instructed to deliver an annual state-of-the-union address and is given a qualified veto over congressional legislation. (For a bill to pass over a presidential veto, a two-thirds vote is required by both the House and the Senate.) An elastic provision empowers the president to take care that laws are faithfully executed and represents an open-ended invitation to presidential discretion. Nonetheless, it would be diffi-

[30]Daniel Bell, *Toward a Post-Industrial Society* (New York, 1973), p. 312. The Budget Bureau has been renamed the Office of Management and Budget—OMB.

cult to explain, on the basis of a careful reading of the Constitution, how the presidency ever came to assume such extensive powers.

Congress has played an important role in expanding presidential policy planning and management of the economy. Numerous laws make the president responsible for wide-ranging planning functions. The Budget and Accounting Act of 1921 instructs the president to prepare the annual budget and created the Bureau of the Budget (since renamed the Office of Management and Budget—OMB) to assist in its preparation. Preparing the budget is important because the budget signifies government in action: what government will do. With 600 staff members, the OMB is among the most powerful agencies in the executive, and it exercises surveillance and control over the entire federal establishment.

Another landmark piece of legislation contributing to the transformation of the presidency into an agency responsible for overall direction of the economy is the Employment Act of 1946, which instructs the president to take steps to maintain high employment and production, combat inflation, and satisfy economic needs. The act created the Council of Economic Advisers (CEA), a group of three professional economists with staff assistance, within the Executive Office of the President. Other congressional legislation that delegates responsibility for economic planning includes the Trade Expansion Act of 1962, which empowers the president to negotiate tariffs with other nations, and the Economic Stabilization Act of 1970, which grants the president broad authority to "issue rules and regulations as he may deem appropriate to stabilize prices, rents, wages, and salaries."

Legislative texts alone cannot explain the development of the modern presidency. The most important factor underlying its enormous growth of power is the rise of corporate capitalism. In an earlier era, when the political economy was quite decentralized, it would have been hard to imagine the kind of presidency that has developed since the 1930s. Since then, it would be hard to imagine the present highly concentrated, interdependent political economy functioning without a central planning agency; and the only one that presently exists is the presidential office. The president has flourished thanks to the growth of corporate capitalism and corporate capitalism could not flourish without a powerful presidency. Presidential planning has become an essential feature of modern

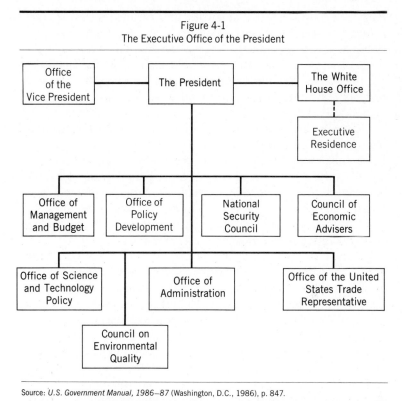

Figure 4-1
The Executive Office of the President

Source: *U.S. Government Manual, 1986–87* (Washington, D.C., 1986), p. 847.

capitalism, no less under a laissez faire ideologue like Ronald Reagan than under earlier, liberal presidents.

Annual presidential messages concerning the state of the union, the budget, and the economy provide an opportunity for the president to present a coherent program. The result of these developments is that the presidency has become the nerve center of corporate capitalism. Independent corporations, even "umbrella" business organizations like the Chamber of Commerce, have the narrow focus of what's best for business. Although recent presidents have pursued quite dissimilar social and economic policies—compare Presidents Kennedy and Johnson with Reagan—all presidents have sought broadly similar overall goals. Presidential planning aims to provide a framework that reconciles the divergent demands of capital accumulation and procedural democracy, the system we have designated as capitalist democracy. Of course, they do not always succeed. But there is no comparable mechanism to the presidency for policy planning, mobilizing political support, and implementing policies to stabilize and strengthen capitalist democracy.

Outside the EOP, but partially subject to control by the president and agencies within the EOP, is the group of department heads collectively known as the cabinet. Most departments represented in the cabinet administer government programs concerned with aspects of the economy: agriculture, energy, commerce, labor, housing and urban development, treasury, transportation, and so on. Partial exceptions are the departments of state and defense, whose bailiwick is American interests abroad.

Cabinet members are appointed and can be removed by the president. Although the departments are formally equal, there is an informal division between the most powerful cabinet departments—state, defense, treasury, and justice—and the rest. A few powerful department heads consult with the president quite frequently and advise him on broad political issues. Most cabinet heads, however, rarely see the president, and they have separate interests that derive from their administrative positions as heads of large departments. A cabinet secretary's day-to-day work consists of supervising the thousands of civil servants within his or her department. The full cabinet is too large for policy making, especially since department secretaries are preoccupied with affairs of their own department. Presidents reserve discussions of important policy decisions for meetings with their personal advisers on the White House staff.

Presidents tailor the structure of the White House staff to suit their particular approach, and they may alter the table of organization as advisers change. In his first term, President Reagan chose three roughly coequal chief advisers, each with full access to the president and with separate but overlapping responsibilities.

In his second term, President Reagan changed the organization of his staff. Donald Regan, formerly secretary of the treasury, switched with James Baker, one of the original top three advisers; the other two top advisers left their White House posts and Regan became chief of the White House staff and the sole domestic adviser with full access to the president. In its issue of January 21, 1985, *Newsweek* commented, "Nothing better signifies the growing allure of the White House staff than Regan's decision to forsake the second-ranking cabinet job (fifth in the line of succession to the presidency) to move into the White House. Imagine Alexander Hamilton resigning to become George Washington's chief clerk."

In the Reagan administration, important policy proposals were often developed in five cabinet councils for commerce and trade, economic affairs, food and agriculture, human resources, and natural resources and environment. (In the field of foreign policy, the president's top aides include the national security adviser, who is a key member of the White House staff, the secretaries of state and defense, and the director of the Central Intelligence Agency—CIA.) Each council had a staff headed by an executive secretary from the White House Office of Policy Development; members of the council included cabinet secretaries in the relevant fields and presidential aides. Council proposals were usually reviewed by an informal legislative strategy group composed of the president's top aides, congressional liaison officer, director of OMB, and secretary of the treasury.[31] Another way that the Reagan presidency concentrated power at the top was that the OMB was given increased powers of surveillance and supervision over administrative agencies. OMB gained responsibility for reviewing the entire gamut of federal programs and deciding where drastic cutbacks would be proposed. The agency was also given power to veto all new government regulations, in order to curtail social regulation.

A discussion of the presidency needs to include mention of the vice president for one reason alone: because of the cliché that the vice president is a heart beat away from the president. Vice presidents are chosen to balance the ticket and garner additional votes in the presidential election, not because of their capabilities as a potential president. Only Walter Mondale, vice president under Jimmy Carter, exercised substantial power. (An outsider to Washington, Carter trusted Mondale's judgment as a long-time senator and respected member of Washington's political class.) Nonethe-

---

[31]Richard A. Watson and Norman C. Thomas, *The Politics of the Presidency* (New York, 1983), pp. 253 ff; and Dom Bonafede, "A Day in a Cabinet Officer's Life— Trying to Touch All of the Bases," *National Journal,* October 17, 1981.

less, according to a study of the vice presidency, one president in two has either "left office prematurely or completed his term only after surviving some threat to his incumbency."[32]

Although Mr. Reagan was not an able administrator, and he was utterly unconcerned with the details of policy or management, his administration displayed an amazing ability to formulate policies and gain sufficient political support to get them approved and implemented. One reason was superb legislative tactics; another was President Reagan's personal capacity to build enthusiasm and support for his policies without descending from the level of generalities to discuss specific detail.

The fact that planning occurs does not mean that it will be effective. Among the factors that affect the success of presidential planning are the president's own personality and the abilities of the presidential staff, the general state of the economy (success is easier to achieve during periods of economic growth), and America's position internationally. We focus here on two key features closely related to the presidential office: the federal bureaucracy and the arena of interest-group lobbying.

OF CLIENTELISM, IRON TRIANGLES, AND POLICY NETWORKS

The federal bureaucracy is a patchwork of agencies, commissions, and departments that reflect, in imperfect form, the varied interests of American society. The enormous size, diversity, and fragmentation of the bureaucracy means that it is a lumbering giant. Commands issuing from the top have a curious way of being distorted or ignored at the bottom. For example, one study of the Carter presidency (and the findings are doubtless valid for earlier and later periods as well) found that, two years after Carter issued an order on a topic in which 75 administrative agencies were required to issue their own implementing regulations, only 15 had done so.[33]

---

[32]Joel K. Goldstein, *The Modern American Vice Presidency: The Transformation of a Political Institution* (Princeton, 1982).
[33]Ron Duhl, "Carter Issues an Order, But Is Anybody Listening?" *National Journal,* July 14, 1979.

So powerful is the bureaucracy that it has been aptly described as the "fourth branch of government." In the twentieth century, the federal executive expanded enormously and replaced courts and political parties as the dominant institution integrating American political life.[34] All contemporary presidents have both relied on yet sought to subdue and rationalize the bureaucracy to make it a more efficient instrument for achieving the three general goals of presidential power that are being described here. But the president's efforts encounter deep-rooted sources of resistance in American politics and administration. Thousands of groups have achieved special protection and help from government through "their" particular government agency. Often this is under the guise of government regulation, as with the railroads and truckers, who fall under the jurisdiction of the Interstate Commerce Commission. One form of linkage between a government agency and its constituency is called clientelism. Clientelism enables groups to make their voice heard within the corridors of power and to gain special help from government, such as tax breaks, subsidies, and protection from competition. The flow of benefits is also in the opposite direction: the government agency receives political support from its private "client" on such matters as intrabureaucratic struggles over "turf" (jurisdiction), OMB budgeting, and congressional appropriations.

A consequence of clientelism is to farm government out to those groups powerful enough to appropriate a government agency. Consequently, clientelist relationships have also been described as "subgovernments," because the clientelist alliance within a policy area gains substantial autonomy and legal authority. Subgovernments benefit participants and seek to exclude outsiders, including rival agencies and industries, workers, and consumers.

Closely related to these notions is the concept of the "iron triangle"; it suggests that typically a third partner is involved in addition to the administrative agency and its private client: the congressional subcommittee with jurisdiction over the agency. While, in principle, Congress is supposed to exercise oversight, in practice the congressional subcommittee concerned usually joins

---

[34]The growth of the federal bureaucracy in a key period has been ably described by Stephen Skowronek, *Building a New American State: The Expansion of National Administrative Capacities, 1877–1920* (Cambridge, England, 1982).

with the agency and private interest in attempting to ward off outside interference.[35]

Although this description of the federal executive and governmental authority divided into a series of subgovernments or iron triangles continues to be partially valid, the situation has become more complex. The stable, closed worlds enclosed by iron triangles have in many cases been jostled or replaced by other patterns. First, new participants have forced their way into the administrative game, and their goals often conflict with those of the established players. In particular, a host of grass-roots activist groups and movements—including organizations associated with Ralph Nader, environmental groups, civil rights advocates, and women's groups—have used political pressure and legal skill to force open the closed doors of subgovernments. The older participants shared the goal of mutual protection and benefits—producer groups using government to enhance profitable activity, government agencies using producer groups to safeguard their organizational interests. The new participants seek employment opportunities for women and minorities, safe working conditions, and environmental protection—all of which collide with the earlier goals.

Second, much recent governmental activity cuts across established industry lines, thus ending the cozy isolation and autonomy of subgovernments. Examples of the new issues and regulations include environmental and consumer protection, occupational health and safety, and energy. (Much of the new activity loosely fits under the general heading of social regulation, analyzed in Chapter 9.)

Third, since many of the new issues are extremely complex, independent policy experts play a key role in policy formulation and implementation. These are no mere technical experts; policy analyst Hugh Heclo calls them policy activists.[36] They cannot be counted to know their place and, because their views are respected, they cannot be put in their place.

Finally, the subgovernment has been jostled from above. As described earlier, the presidency now engages in overall economic and bureaucratic management; it has the capacity to penetrate the

[35]For perhaps the most important instance, see Gordon Adams, *The Iron Triangle: The Politics of Defense Contracting* (New York, 1981).
[36]Hugh Heclo, "Issue Networks and the Executive Establishment," in King, *The New American Political System*.

formerly closed world of subgovernments and has the legal authority and financial resources to provide oversight and direction.

Subgovernments continue to flourish in certain spheres. "Subgovernments are especially influential in affecting low-visibility, noncontroversial, routine policy making."[37] But Heclo suggests that the typical new situation is, what he calls "issue networks": there are more participants, they often conflict, knowledgeable policy activists play an important role, and the boundary between the network and its external environment is less sharp than was true for subgovernments. (This is because of the importance of cross-cutting issues like social regulation, which draw in new participants.)

Until now, we have been analyzing changing patterns in fairly stable and specific policy areas. But the actions of business firms, trade associations and interest groups, and citizens' organizations cut across the whole range of government. The term *lobbying* describes the more general process by which groups seek to gain formal or informal access to government. Whereas clientelism, subgovernments, and issue networks are terms describing linkages among participants in a given field, lobbying consists of pressing claims throughout government, either to seek favorable action or prevent action from being taken. Lobbyists rarely concentrate on broad issues (although we shall see that business groups did in the early 1980s). More typically, lobbyists aim to get an administrative regulation rewritten or a bill modified or withdrawn. Given the enormous power of government, rewording a clause can spell prosperity for a corporation or a whole industry.

Lobbying has increased enormously in the past decade. One directory of interest groups has over 14,000 listings.[38] Whereas the Ford Motor Company had a Washington staff of three in the 1960s, this increased to over 40 by 1980. The main reason for the vast increase in lobbying is the growth in the size, power, and complexity of governmental regulation. The result is an important change in the entire character of American political economy.

In an earlier period, as described in Chapter 3, certain industries, like trucking and airlines, were regulated by independent

[37]Pika, p. 303.
[38]Margaret Fisk, ed., *Encyclopedia of Associations* (Detroit, 1980); cited in Benjamin I. Page and Mark I. Petracca, *The American Presidency* (New York, 1983), p. 143.

regulatory commissions (IRCs). An IRC would license firms to operate in a given industry and prescribe conditions of activity. These were industries in which public opposition to industry practices created a movement for government regulation and industry itself often sought government protection.

Nowadays, the environment movement has succeeded in subjecting all industries to social regulations, including standards for occupational safety and health, employment opportunities for women and minorities, and the like. Since these regulations cut across industrial lines and apply to all firms, the distinction between regulated and unregulated industries has lost meaning. Further, several of the regulated industries, including airlines, trucking, and banking, have been partially deregulated. The Civil Aeronautics Board, one of the IRCs, was abolished in 1985 and several of its residual functions transferred to other administrative agencies.

A study of the "politics of regulation" under the supervision of political scientist James Q. Wilson found that, nowadays, no single pattern characterizes the relationship between the various IRCs and regulated industries.[39] In the past, the regulated industries were the field of subgovernment par excellence. Regulated industries were carefully nurtured by their governmental patrons, for good reason since the industry typically captured the IRC and bent it to its own purposes. Indeed, the very line between regulator and regulated was often hazy since members of the IRCs were usually recruited from the ranks of the regulated industry; and they returned to a comfortable and well-earned position with the industry after having served it while in government. (Political analyst William Domhoff calls them "revolving directors.")[40] For example, one study found that 21 of 33 commissioners of the Federal Communications Commission (FCC) returned to the communications industry after leaving the FCC. (Most of the rest had reached retirement age.)[41]

For a brief period, grass-roots mobilization made a difference. The new social movements pressured government in the 1970s to transform the existing IRCs so as to protect workers' and con-

---

[39]James Q. Wilson, ed., *The Politics of Regulation* (New York, 1980).

[40]G. William Domhoff, *Who Rules America Now? A View for the '80s* (Englewood Cliffs, 1983), p. 43.

[41]Cited in Edward S. Herman, *Corporate Power, Corporate Control* (Cambridge, England, 1981), p. 179.

sumers' interests, rather than exclusively corporate interests, and they succeeded in getting new regulatory agencies created. Thanks to some audacious appointments, several of the older IRCs and the new agencies developed a quite adversarial relationship with the regulated industry.[42] (This was especially true of the Occupational Safety and Health Administration—OSHA; the Environmental Protection Agency—EPA; the Federal Trade Commission—FTC; and the FCC.) Moreover, the economic crisis led Presidents Carter and Ford to deregulate several formerly protected industries in order to foster greater competition and lower prices.

However, the major thrust of regulation under President Reagan has been to undermine social regulation, in order to increase corporate freedom and dominance and achieve economic growth, regardless of social costs. In the process, the social regulatory agencies were underfunded or abolished, restraints on industry were scrapped, and administrators appointed to head the agencies were hostile to the agency's mandate.

Capital as an interest group

Lobbying, clientelism, and the other patterns analyzed previously are forms of linkage between government and private interest groups. There is a comforting picture of American politics in which the society is composed of a mosaic of relatively equal interests, each one pursuing its own activities and occasionally making demands on government, with government responding in an even-handed way.[43] This picture is false. In a capitalist society, groups are inherently unequal: the fact that the society depends on an adequate level of production for its material survival means that business has a favored place; conversely, workers in factories and offices are forced to work at others' direction.

Capital's position of structural primacy is translated into a concrete capacity to influence the president, Congress, and administrative agencies through political activity. Lobbying occupies a key role. For example, business executives are the largest group ap-

[42]Paul J. Quirk, *Industry Influence in Regulatory Agencies* (Princeton, 1981).
[43]Mark Kesselman, "The Conflictual Evolution of American Political Science: From Apologetic Pluralism to Trilateralism and Marxism," in J. David Greenstone, ed., *Public Values of Private Power in American Democracy* (Chicago, 1982), pp. 34–67.

pointed to the many advisory commissions associated with federal agencies. Advisory commissions are an important mechanism by which private groups' demands are transmitted to the agency. Further, business executives are appointed in large numbers to independent regulatory commissions and managerial positions in the federal executive, from the president's cabinet on down. Even after the rise of grass-roots social movements in the 1960s and 1970s (indeed, partly because of the opposition that such movements provoked within industry), business organizations remain the best-financed and organized interest groups in Washington and throughout the country.

In addition, capital has unmatched political and financial resources at its disposal, including think tanks, trade associations, and umbrella business organizations. Indeed, every individual business firm can be considered a pressure group, since it seeks specific benefits from government, takes stands on wider policy disputes, and joins with other business firms in broad alliances. When large corporations have been threatened with collapse, as occurred in recent years for Lockheed, Chrysler, and Continental Illinois Bank of Chicago, they have been highly successful in extracting lavish benefits from government in order to survive.

The typical pattern in the past was for business to enjoy unchallenged preeminence but, partly for that reason, not to intervene actively and visibly in the electoral and administrative arenas. However, following what business interpreted as a threat to its position by social movements in the 1960s and 1970s, it organized far more aggressively. Among the recent trends:

1. Corporations have stepped up their political contributions (through Political Action Committee—PACs, described in Chapter 8), actively supported the Republican party, and engaged in advocacy advertising—which delivers an ideological message. (See one such ad in Figure 4-2.)

2. Corporations have become their own political lobbyists through increased activity in Washington. (The number of corporations with Washington offices increased from 100 to 500 within a decade.) Corporations have also organized "grass-roots" lobbying efforts—directed from the firm's Washington office. Thanks to computerized lists of its suppliers, subcontractors, customers, stockholders, and employees, a corporation can quickly contact constituents in selected congressional districts to mobilize support

for a key vote. (A similar process can be organized to lobby an administrative agency.) Within days, a member of Congress can be bombarded by a deluge of letters, telephone calls, and delegations of constituents, including officials of labor unions from the company's local plant, and political donors (who can dangle the possibility of future support).

Edwin Epstein, a student of business political activity, finds that corporate executives are now mobilizing the internal resources of the corporation for political ends, including the corporation's specialists in finance, law, and advertising. In Epstein's phrase, the corporation has become a "political weapon."[44]

3. Business organizations, which group firms on an industry-wide, regional, or national basis, have increased their grass-roots and Washington-based lobbying efforts. The United States Chamber of Commerce is probably the largest and most effective umbrella business organization.[45] With over 500,000 member firms, the Chamber of Commerce is formidable. Its $68 million budget in 1980 for research and lobbying was many times larger than the largest "public interest" lobbying group; and five times larger than the budget of the Democratic National Committee in that election year.

The Chamber rarely takes a position on pending legislation since its member firms have diverse and often conflicting interests. But on issues that unite the interests of capital, the Chamber goes into action. Such a case occurred in 1981 with President Reagan's tax and budget proposals (reviewed in Chapter 3). The Chamber's all-out effort on the president's behalf has been credited with passage of the controversial plan. According to a grateful White House aide, "Different groups may match the Chamber in a specific area, but with their media programs, Hill contacts, and grass-roots organization, nobody can match them in overall effectiveness. They're simply in a class by themselves."[46]

Alongside the Chamber of Commerce are thousands of trade associations and a variety of other "peak" associations, including

[44]Edwin M. Epstein, "Business and Labor under the Federal Election Campaign Act of 1971," in Michael J. Malbin, ed., *Parties, Interest Groups, and Campaign Finance* (Washington, D.C., 1980), pp. 107–51.
[45]Richard I. Kirkland, Jr., "Fat Days for the Chamber of Commerce," *Fortune*, September 21, 1981.
[46]*Ibid.*, p. 456.

the National Association of Manufacturers, Business Roundtable, and Business Council, which represent the largest corporations. (The Chamber groups all size firms.) The high-powered lobbying efforts of the more prestigious organizations are directed at the top ranks of the political establishment, beginning with the White House itself.

4. Business finances a range of think tanks, PACs, foundations, university programs and professorships whose mission is to defend business interests. For example, immediately following President Reagan's election, the Heritage Foundation, an ultraconservative think tank funded by wealthy Colorado brewer Joseph Coors, issued a massive study, *Mandate for Leadership*, which contained over 1,000 policy proposals for the incoming administration.[47] The preface to the study carried an enthusiastic endorsement from none other than the president-elect. Many of the study's proposals shaped the Republican administration's policies; the project was such a success that the Heritage Foundation published a second study after President Reagan's reelection.

5. Although not a new trend, it is worthy of mention that business has excellent access to every government agency. Environmental, labor, and minority groups have shaky standing with most agencies; the few presumably sympathetic to their concerns, for example, the Department of Labor, are among the weaker in the administrative firmament. (Moreover, to pursue the example of labor, the administrator appointed to head the agency will not necessarily be sympathetic to labor's concerns; President Reagan's choice for secretary of labor was a business executive who was no friend of labor.)

In the case of business, not only is there automatic entry to any government agency but some of the most powerful departments and agencies, such as the Department of the Treasury and the Federal Reserve Board, can be considered an extension of business. For example, the Federal Reserve Board, which regulates the banking industry and sets interest rates charged to banks (thereby influencing the money supply and general economic conditions), is closely tied to banks. Private bankers choose most members of the Fed's powerful regional boards.

---

[47]Dom Bonafede, "Issue-Oriented Heritage Foundation Hitches its Wagon to Reagan's Star," *National Journal,* March 20, 1982.

Business does not win every battle and on many or even most issues segments of business conflict. A variety of social movements contest aspects of business activity. And the president and the institutionalized presidency seek to define broad policies that sectors of business or even, in rare cases, business as a whole may oppose. (The wave of social regulation again provides a good example.) Yet corporate capitalism is so vast, its power so great, its function so central to the entire society, that business is often not regarded as a "special interest" at all.

The president as lobbyist

The president has emerged as a powerful "lobbyist" with interests that may diverge from those of business. More generally, in an attempt to establish direct links with specific constituencies, recent presidents have created an Office of Public Liaison in the White House. President Reagan chose assistants for liaison with business—yet another link between business and the president—labor, Jews, consumers, blacks, Hispanics, women, and the elderly. Why these groups? Probably because they are well organized and politically active. But it should not be thought that they have equal influence.

Communication flowed in both directions: whereas the liaison mechanism permits groups to communicate their positions to the White House, the president's staff often uses the channel to mobilize support among these groups for the president's policies. More generally, in the face of increased lobbying efforts by other groups, the presidency now organizes its own lobbying efforts. As mentioned at the beginning of this chapter, the decline of the political party as a mechanism for building stable support has led to the "single issue presidency," in which presidents organize ad hoc coalitions from issue to issue.[48]

The present situation evolved from the social protest of the 1960s: the street protests of that decade were transformed into the political activism of the 1970s and 1980s. Further, whereas community activism was initially of a progressive variety, and sought to increase the rights and resources of blacks, workers, women, and the poor, a social backlash developed in the middle 1970s in which

[48]Pika, p. 320.

a "new right" of religious fundamentalists and populist conservatives organized to promote reactionary movements. What probably tipped the scales in the conservative direction by the early 1980s was the massive support of business. And, it is no coincidence that the most pro-business president since Herbert Hoover was elected soon after business mobilized.

The shift to the right sponsored by the Republican administration in the 1980s required more than responsiveness to business interests. It was no mean feat, in a period of economic crisis and social discontent, to mobilize electoral and congressional majorities in favor of policies that harmed millions of Americans. Presidential leadership of public opinion was key.

SOCIAL CONTROL: MANAGING DISCONTENT AND PACKAGING THE PRESIDENT

Capitalist production systematically generates dislocations, inequality, and discontent. However reform-minded presidents have been, they find it in their personal interest and that of the government to foster capital accumulation (capitalist-sponsored economic growth). This provides the structural context for the third arena of presidential activity: containing the discontents generated by capitalist production. Thomas Cronin suggests that "calibration and management of conflict is the core of presidential leadership."[49] The president's concern in this arena is to keep conflict from threatening structural stability and is centered on those who do not control corporate capital: small-capital business, wage earners, women, racial minorities, the unemployed, and consumers.

The legitimacy of American corporate capitalism depends on the periodic ratification of existing arrangements by electoral majorities and by popular acceptance of presidential policies. When discontented groups express grievances, the president often takes to the media. In a public address, sympathetic symbolic gestures

---

[49]Thomas E. Cronin, "'Everybody Believes in Democracy Until He Gets to the White House . . .': An Examination of White House-Departmental Relations," *Law and Contemporary Problems* 35 (Summer 1970): 575.

are made on behalf of the aggrieved group. When groups are strong, angry, and determined, they may succeed in wresting real benefits from government: the president may develop new policies, programs, and institutions to deal with the crisis. Illustrations are provided by presidential reactions to the urban crisis, poverty, and civil rights.

Often, however, threats can be overcome by symbolic means or repression. Consider, as an illustration, the issue of black insurgency in Northern cities during the 1960s. The "urban crisis" was viewed by several presidents less as the impoverished and disadvantaged conditions in which a large proportion of blacks lived than as the political challenge posed by black militancy. By a combination of government aid, institutional innovation, and police repression, presidents Kennedy, Johnson, and Nixon managed to get confrontation out of the streets while providing real if limited benefits to the black community, and without substantially altering the conditions that caused the challenge. In 1972, President Nixon declared that the "urban crisis has passed" and that the "ship of state is no longer in danger." Given the fact that the social, economic, and political situation of black and Hispanic urban groups had declined, not improved, since the late 1960s, the president's declaration represented an exercise in public relations. But the kernel of truth contained in his statement—that black insurgency had been overcome—is revealing of how presidents define crisis.

The president attempts to reassure Americans (and the world) that established arrangements are basically sound—and whatever problems do exist will be solved if his proposals are accepted. Whether he claims that America's invasion of Vietnam has ended in "peace with honor," or that reducing federal subsidies to the poor will increase their freedom and self-reliance, the president's aim is to legitimize and strengthen established arrangements. When the president calls on all Americans to work together to support the country, this means asking them to support the capitalist system and its associated inequalities. The president has unique opportunities to provide an authoritative interpretation of the political and economic situation through reports and recommendations to Congress, ceremonial duties as chief of state, and instant access to the media.

A president's staff contains specialists in legitimizing established arrangements and packaging the president. Speechwriters, press secretaries, and media consultants strive to present the president and his policies in a favorable light. The methods used to sell the president are not fundamentally different from those used to sell toothpaste. Much presidential action represents an exercise in public relations. Presidential use of the media, especially television, is particularly important. In the electronic age, presidents can reach out to millions of homes to present the presidential message. No other person in the world can command comparable access to the media. Prime-time speeches, presidential press conferences, and other public appearances all provide occasions for packaging the president.

An illustration of packaging techniques was the manner in which Richard Nixon nominated Gerald Ford to succeed Spiro Agnew as vice president in October 1973. During the speech announcing his choice of Ford, carried live by the three major television networks, Nixon never mentioned that Agnew was the first vice president in American history to resign from office because of criminal misconduct. (Agnew pleaded no contest to a criminal charge involving nonpayment of income taxes, amid extensive evidence of accepting bribes.) Instead, the president turned the occasion into a celebration—a "fiesta" in the words of a television correspondent.

The president can draw upon the salience and pomp of the presidential office and thereby link up with the secular rituals of patriotic America, for example, by issuing a national proclamation on Thanksgiving, the Fourth of July, and New Year's Day. In a country without a state religion, patriotism has taken its place— with the president as high priest.[50] Another analogy, with which we opened the chapter, is to an elected monarch. One account of White House personnel enumerates

seventy-five retainers, including forty-two mechanical and maintenance workers, thirty domestic employes, and three civil servants on loan from other Federal agencies. Among the seventy-five are: a head butler and four butlers; a chief floral designer; four doormen; a foreman of housemen and six housemen; six maids, a pantryman and a pantrywoman; a *maître d'hôtel*; a chef, an assistant chef, a second cook, a pastry chef, and two kitchen stewards; a head laun-

[50]Henry Fairlie develops the point in *The Kennedy Promise: The Politics of Expectation* (New York, 1973).

dress, an assistant laundress, and a combined porter and laundry-man. There are also a transportation specialist, a film projectionist, three operating engineers, and someone with the title of "principal foreman operating engineer."

Not included are extra waiters and other help recruited for special events, U.S. military personnel assigned to the White House, Secret Service agents, Navy cooks for the White House staff mess, fifteen gardeners, Executive Protection Service officers, General Service Administration employes who handle the West Wing business office area, and the President's executive staff.[51]

Scholarly writing on the president from Franklin D. Roosevelt until the early 1970s was close to unanimous in its celebration of strong presidents. For a generation, political scientists equated strong presidents with good and wise presidents. Theodore Sorensen, staff aide to Presidents Kennedy and Johnson, notes, "A president cannot afford to be modest. No one else sits where he sits or knows all that he knows. No one else has the power to lead, to inspire, or to restrain the Congress and country. If he fails to lead, no one leads."[52] According to Richard Neustadt:

> The more determinedly a president seeks power, the more he will be likely to bring vigor to his clerkship. As he does so he contributes to the energy of government. . . . The contributions that a President can make to government are indispensable. . . . In a relative but real sense one can say of a President what Eisenhower's first Secretary of Defense once said of General Motors: what is good for the country is good for the President, and vice versa.[53]

Clinton Rossiter marvels that the presidency is "one of the few truly successful institutions created by men in their endless quest for the blessing of free government."[54] One scholar laments that the American president's power "is seldom fully available or appropriate for the worst problems he must cope with."[55] Another declares, "Measured against the opportunities, the responsibilities, and the resources of others in our political system and in other nations, the powers of the Presidency are enormous. It is only when

[51]Dom Bonafede, "The Keeping of the President," *The Progressive,* February 1974, p. 45.
[52]Theodore E. Sorensen, *Decision-Making in the White House* (New York, 1963), p. 83.
[53]Neustadt, *Presidential Power,* p. 185.
[54]Rossiter, p. 13.
[55]Louis W. Koenig, *The Chief Executive* (New York, 1968), p. 1.

we measure these same powers against the problems of our age that they seem puny and inadequate."[56]

Thomas Cronin has questioned the picture of the president presented in most textbook accounts. He finds that textbooks present

> inflated and unrealistic interpretations of presidential competence and beneficence. . . . What is needed, most texts imply, is a man of foresight to anticipate the future and the personal strength to unite us, to steel our moral will, to move the country forward and to make this country governable. The vision, and perhaps the illusion, is that if only we can identify and elect the *right* man—our loftiest aspirations can and will be accomplished.[57]

One reason many textbooks present the president in such a light, according to Cronin, is that political science courses train citizens as well as communicate truth. In unvarnished language, this amounts to deceiving students by exaggerating the merits of presidents and concealing the deficiencies of American politics.

The mass media (especially TV) play a crucial role in magnifying presidential power, narrowing the scope of American politics to presidential activity, and thereby contributing to what political analyst Theodore Lowi has called "the plebiscitary presidency."[58] In general, the media tend to personalize politics, that is, reduce complex issues and collective struggles to disputes among individuals. And there is no politican who comes close to vying with the president as a source of media coverage. For example, compare coverage of the presidency with that of Congress. One study found that, in two randomly selected years, well over half the lead stories in *Time* and *Newsweek* dealt with presidential activities.[59] Under these circumstances, it becomes more understandable that "for most Americans, the presidency has come to be nearly all there is to democratic politics. The president's monopoly over the public space reduces the incentives for political action for most citizens."[60]

[56]Nelson Polsby, *Congress and the President* (Englewood Cliffs, N.J., 1964), p. 30.
[57]Thomas E. Cronin, "The Textbook Presidency and Political Science," *Congressional Record*, October 5, 1970, S17102-03.
[58]Theodore J. Lowi, *The Personal President: Power Invested, Promise Unfulfilled* (Ithaca, 1985), chapter 5.
[59]Bruce Miroff, "Monopolizing the Public Space: The President as a Problem for Democratic Politics," in Cronin, ed., *Rethinking the Presidency,* p. 221.
[60]*Ibid.,* p. 219.

By commanding media attention and the ability to dominate the political agenda,

> the president gains an unparalleled advantage in defining political reality for most Americans. . . . Press or partisan criticism may challenge a president on the form or details of his actions, but the outline of reality that he has sketched is usually left intact.[61]

Even when the president's specific policy pronouncements are criticized, the president as a person and the presidential office are treated with respect bordering on reverence. A study of the president's relations with the media comments, "Since each side can inflict considerable damage on the other, cooperation suits the needs of both better than an adversary relationship."[62]

The media president

No president has ever matched Ronald Reagan's appreciation of the media's importance or his ability to use the media to promote support for administration policies. Even more than his predecessors in this age of the "selling of the president," Reagan and his advisers focused their efforts on achieving maximum media impact.[63] Whereas other presidents accorded high priority to the media during election campaigns but downgraded its importance at other times, the Reagan administration was a meticulously crafted nonstop media event. In concentrating on image over content (not that the Reagan administration ignored policies: it simply talked less in public about the specifics), the president was in tune with the times. One estimate is that President Reagan devoted 20 percent of his work time to shaping policy and 80 percent to selling it. According to the *New York Times* White House correspondent, "To an unprecedented extent, Mr. Reagan and his staff have made television a major organizing principle of his Presidency. His day is planned around opportunities for TV coverage. Every effort is made to assure a constant flow of positive visual images and symbols from the White House."[64]

[61] *Ibid.*, p. 220.
[62] Michael Baruch Grossman and Martha Joynt Kumar, *Portraying the President: the White House and the News Media* (Baltimore, 1981), p. 15.
[63] Joe McGinnis, *The Selling of the President, 1968* (New York, 1969).
[64] Steven R. Weisman, "Can the Magic Prevail?" *New York Times Magazine*, April 29, 1984, p. 39.

A good example of how the use of the president's time was planned to maximize "photo opportunities" was President Reagan's busy foreign travel schedule in the spring of 1984—not coincidentally shortly before the start of the 1984 election campaign. A trip to China in April produced superb footage of President and Nancy Reagan admiring the Great Wall of China—but little discernible business was conducted during the Reagans stay. In June, the president was off again, this time to visit his highly photogenic ancestral village of Ballyoreen in Ireland, a visit the president's advisers doubtless hoped that the 40 million Irish-Americans would recall on election day. From there, President Reagan again set off, reaching the Normandy coast of France to participate in ceremonies marking the fortieth anniversary of D-Day (the allied landing on the European mainland during the Second World War). It was no accident that the ceremonies were timed for the TV networks' morning news.

President Reagan's campaign style exhibited a dual aspect. On the one hand, his approach was upbeat, optimistic, and buoyant— if somewhat corny. For example, his TV ads portrayed "scenes from a sunlit land in which no one was sick, sad, fat, infirm or afflicted by ring around the collar."[65] On the other hand, there was a grimmer aspect to the celebration of American greatness: an enormous military buildup and occasional references to the possibility of "winning" a nuclear war. With respect to electioneering, his entire campaign strategy, according to one observer, was to persuade voters that "an attack on Reagan is tantamount to an attack on America's idealized image of itself—*where a vote against Reagan is, in some subliminal sense, a vote against a mythic 'America.'* "[66] This was not the jaundiced view of an embittered critic; it is a quotation from a memo by Richard Darman, one of Reagan's chief White House aides, and it helped to shape the entire 1984 campaign.

A related aspect was a calculated attempt to discredit Walter Mondale and the Democratic party. Mr. Reagan said in a campaign speech that the Democrats had moved "so far left they've left America." *Newsweek* commented that the core of the campaign

[65] *Newsweek Election Extra,* November/December 1984, p. 77.
[66] *Ibid.,* p. 76, italics in original.

"was to make a vote for Mondale almost seem unpatriotic. Issues had little to do with [Republican] strategic design. . . ."[67]

Reagan's success did not derive from a capacity for hard work or mastery of complex details. His confusion and ignorance about matters ranging from trivial to momentous were legendary. A trivial example: while in Brazil on a Latin American tour, he mistakenly toasted the people of Bolivia. Infinitely more consequential: he apparently did not grasp why the Soviet Union rejected out of hand his proposal to reduce both the American and Soviet land-based intercontinental ballistic missiles (ICBMs) by a large and equal number: the Soviet Union is far more dependent on its land-based ICBMs. (Its strategic missiles are 70 percent land-based, compared to only 30 percent of the U.S. ICBM force. For both nations, the remaining missiles are based in nuclear-powered submarines and bomber aircraft.) And yet Reagan's appalling ignorance never harmed him politically.

> He has committed untold public bloopers and been caught in dozens of factual mistakes and misrepresentations. He has presided over the worst recession since the Great Depression. The abortive mission in Beirut cost 265 American lives, and there has been a sharp escalation in United States military involvement in Central America. An extraordinary number of Mr. Reagan's political appointees have come under fire, with many forced to resign, because of ethical or legal conflicts. Yet he is The Man in the Teflon Suit; nothing sticks to him.[68]

Under Ronald Reagan, America had come a long way since the time when political analyst Jonathan Schell could write, "In the years of the Vietnam War, the United States experienced a systemic crisis, which reached its final stages when, under the Nixon Administration, the American Constitutional democracy was almost destroyed by its President."[69]

On the one hand, Watergate was an isolated scandal, the result of blunders, misconduct, and treachery of President Richard Nixon. Yet on the other hand, Watergate cannot be isolated from the context of the increasing centralization of power in the presidency, the arbitrary power exercised by recent presidents, and,

[67]*Ibid.*
[68]Weisman, p. 39.
[69]Jonathan Schell, *The Times of Illusion* (New York, 1976), p. 337.

above all, the deep divisions engendered by war, economic crisis, and political conflict.

There is a close connection between the disgrace of Richard Nixon and the triumph of Ronald Reagan, both conservative Republicans but of a very different kind. Reagan symbolically represents an attempt to efface from the historical record the painful memories of Vietnam, Watergate, and divisions in America during that period. Although separated in years, Reagan's presidency is closely linked to Watergate. It represents an attempt to reaffirm the values of conservative middle America that Nixon betrayed. What is not yet clear is whether media wizardry is sufficient to build stable support for limiting the democratic sphere in favor of private power, as well as for using government to extract resources from the most vulnerable members of society for the benefit of the most privileged. Nor is it clear what will occur after the Great Communicator, a lame duck president at the moment of his reelection in 1984, is mute. The most likely prospect is that the 1980s will prove a temporary lull before the economic crisis deepens. No matter how skillfully presidential "photo opportunities" are exploited, it is doubtful that they can obscure the growing dimensions of the crisis.

5
congressional representation

Because the United States is a sprawling, complex society, it is not possible for all citizens to participate directly in political decision making. Instead, political democracy depends on representative institutions. The House of Representatives and the Senate are the basic formal representative links between the American people and the national government. Congress makes laws, shapes and constrains the actions of the president and the federal bureaucracy, conducts investigations, certifies appointments, and can remove officials from office.

The United States Congress must be understood in two dimensions. It is, first, a complicated organization, with a structure of rules, values, and procedures that allocate power within the Congress and help determine the size of government, the priorities of its budget, and which legislation is likely to pass into law. It is, second, the key link in the United States between government and society. Members of Congress are elected. They are lobbied by a myriad of interest groups, and pressured by government officials, including the president. In turn, what the members do helps shape the nature of the society in which we live: how unequal it will be, how clean the environment, how secure the prospects for peace.

Because the Congress is a hinge between government and society, and because it is a complex organization, we should not be surprised that it has changed a great deal in this century. The causes, features, and implications of these changes are terribly important, not only because they are crucial to the state of American democracy, but because Congress is the institution that determines most directly the degree to which the political system functions as an open, responsive democracy.

One of the most common, but too simple, complaints about Congress in the past two decades has been a lament about its decay as a representative institution. In the early 1970s a *Time* magazine account noted, "That branch of government that most closely represents the people is not yet broken, but it is bent and in danger of snapping." Some fifteen years later, a comprehensive journalistic assessment in *The Atlantic Monthly* argued that Congress is out of control: "Only once in the past six years has Congress finished the budget appropriations before the beginning of the fiscal year; many spending bills have not been completed until months after the spending they supposedly control has begun. Long periods of legislative stalling are followed by spasms in which bills are passed with wild abandon, and these often contain 'unprinted amendments' whose contents Congressmen have never had an opportunity to read."[1]

The problem with such assessments is that they can be found in every generation of American history. Congress has long been attacked for irresponsibility, cowardice, and chaos. It is impossible to evaluate such charges—just as it is impossible to evaluate the claim that the Congress is the world's most successful democratic legislature and deliberative institution—without understanding how the place of Congress has changed both in the long sweep of the past two centuries, and in the period between the assessment of *Time* and the conclusions in *The Atlantic Monthly*. In this chapter, we examine both.

---

[1] *Time*, January 15, 1973, p. 12; Gregg Easterbrook, "What's Wrong With Congress?" *The Atlantic Monthly*, December 1984, p. 57.

THE PLACE OF CONGRESS

The Constitutional Convention of 1787 raised and resolved basic institutional questions of representation. It was widely assumed at the Convention, political scientist Robert Dahl has written, that a popularly elected House of Representatives "would be the driving force in the system; that the people's representatives would be turbulent and insistent; that they would represent majorities and would be indifferent to the rights of [elite] minorities; that the people would be the winds driving the ship of state and their representatives would be the sails, swelling with every gust."[2]

The delegates were divided on the questions of whether, and how, this popular force should be modified and checked. James Madison, in particular, pointed to the dangers of class conflict and popular sovereignty in a strikingly modern statement that put issues of social control on the delegates' agenda:

> In all civilized Countries the people fall into different classes having a real or supposed difference of interests. There will be creditors and debtors, farmers, merchants, and manufacturers. There will be particularly the distinction of rich and poor. . . An increase in population will of necessity increase the proportion of those who labour under all the hardships of life and secretly sigh for a more equal distribution of its blessings. These may in time outnumber those who are placed above the feelings of indigence. According to the equal laws of suffrage, the power will slide into the hands of the former. . . . How is the danger in all cases of interested coalitions to oppress the minority to be guarded against?[3]

The Convention's answer was a Senate whose principle of representation was very different from that of the House. There were to be two senators from each state, irrespective of its size, and they were to be chosen by the state legislatures, which were presumed to be more favorable to mercantile, financial, and business interests than the electorate as a whole.[4]

---

[2]Robert Dahl, *Democracy in the United States: Promise and Performance,* 2nd ed. (Chicago, 1972), p. 151.

[3]Charles Tansill, ed., *Documents Illustrative of the Formation of the Union of the American States* (Washington, 1927), pp. 180–81.

[4]Senators were not popularly elected until the passage of the 17th Amendment to the Constitution in 1912.

Together, the House and the Senate were given substantial responsibilities by the Constitution. Article I, section 8 enumerates Congress' power to levy taxes, borrow and spend money, regulate interstate and foreign commerce, declare war, support the armed forces, create courts inferior to the Supreme Court, and, most generally, "to make all laws which shall be necessary and proper for carrying into execution the foregoing powers, and all other powers vested by this Constitution in the government of the United States, or in any department or officer thereof." In addition, the House of Representatives was granted the power to impeach—that is, to bring charges against—members of the executive and judiciary branches; and the Senate, the power to try all impeachments (conviction requires a two-thirds majority of those voting).

In the early nineteenth century, the Convention's conception of the House as the popular driving force of government was borne out. Under the leadership of Henry Clay, the House of Representatives dominated the government. When President Madison called for a declaration of war in 1812 (which was approved by both houses), he was largely bowing to pressure from the House. Supreme Court Justice Storey aptly remarked in 1818, "The House of Representatives has absorbed all the popular feelings and all the effective power of the country."

A transition that heralded future changes in the position of Congress was the presidency of Andrew Jackson (1828 to 1836) who claimed to represent *all* the people—an assertion echoed by most twentieth-century presidents—and attempted to place the presidency at the center of national decision making. In spite of his success in augmenting the power of the executive branch, Congress remained preeminent. Even the nineteenth century's most domineering president, Abraham Lincoln, conceded that "Congress should originate as well as perfect its measures without external bias." If anything, the position of Congress was strengthened after the Civil War. In the late nineteenth century, the House, in particular, increased its power under the leadership of strong Speakers who centralized the powers of the chamber in their hands.

Congress reached the height of its powers in the early years of this century. In the opinion of some observers at the time, the Speaker of the House from 1903 to 1911, Joe Cannon, was even more powerful than the president. Like other strong Speakers before him, Cannon made skillful use of his wide congressional powers as presiding member: to make committee assignments; to control floor debates by recognizing only those members he wished to allow to speak; and to chair the Rules Committee, which determined which legislation would be allowed to come up for debate on the House floor. In the utilization of these powers, Cannon and his late nineteenth-century predecessors functioned much like a British prime minister; they led the party caucuses that adopted formal legislative agendas, which were passed by disciplined party majorities.

Under Cannon, the power of the Speaker and the House grew tremendously, but the power of the individual representative was reduced to near impotence. In 1910, the rank and file of the House rebelled. Cannon was disqualified from serving on the Rules Committee; he lost his absolute power to make committee appointments and his arbitrary authority to decide who should speak. No subsequent Speaker has regained these powers.

Paradoxically, the strengthening of the individual representative's hand vis-à-vis the Speaker weakened the power of the House and made it easier for the president to exercise legislative authority. After his election in 1912, Woodrow Wilson fundamentally transformed the president's legislative role. The shift in the congressional-presidential balance in his administration "was to alter permanently the relationship between Congress and the President." Whereas formerly, strong Speakers like Joe Cannon had been able to function like a British prime minister, now it was the president who assumed the role of party leader and legislative initiator:

> Wilson laid out to Congress a fully formulated legislative program and then used the full powers of his office to induce Congress to enact it. He signalled this major political alteration of the President's role in American politics by dramatically going before Congress in person to address the members. It was the first such appearance of a President before Congress since Jefferson gave up the practice in 1801.[5]

With ups and downs to be sure, the relationship between Congress and the executive has remained much the same since Wilson's presidency. And the most basic changes and crises in twentieth-

[5]Neil McNeil, *Forge of Democracy* (New York, 1963), p. 32.

century American society have further widened the gap in power between these two branches of government. During the depression, Franklin Roosevelt called Congress into special session, presented a presidential program to meet the crisis, and virtually ran over Congress as the Senate and House passed legislation they barely had time to read. In his administrations, the leaders of both houses became the president's men on Capitol Hill. And when Congress balked at presidential legislation, Roosevelt went over the head of Congress and appealed directly to the general public through press conferences and radio "fireside chats." Much of the legislation he proposed, and many bills proposed since then by presidents Truman, Eisenhower, Kennedy, Johnson, Nixon, Ford, Carter, and Reagan have been rejected by Congress. Yet the shift in the initiation of domestic legislation to the executive has gone unchallenged.

The president proposes, Congress disposes, has become the most common pattern, but not the only one. Congress almost always makes alterations to the president's policies, and he rarely gets them through intact. Congressional innovation in policy making is a fact that has never gone away. We need to understand its limits and its possibilities.

If Congress is not merely decorative, the long-term trend has in fact been one of a decline in its ability to *initiate* large-scale policy initiatives. We think the basic reason for this trend is one the United States shares with other western democracies: the growth of a vast corporate complex, in which a powerful executive government and powerful economic interests act in concert. The turning point in the history of the policy-making relationship between Congress and the executive branch took place at the end of the formative period of the corporate complex, when President Wilson assumed the role of party leader and legislative initiator. Political scientist Lawrence Chamberlain has noted that between 1882 and 1909 Congress was responsible for initially drafting 55 percent of the major laws passed in that period. After 1910, that percentage declined to a low of 8 percent during the New Deal years (between 1933 and 1940).[6]

---

[6]Lawrence Chamberlain, *The President, Congress, and Legislation* (New York, 1946), pp. 450–52.

The new political and economic configurations of the corporate complex required long-term investment planning, political and administrative stability, and the rationalization of bureaucratic administration. From the vantage point of those who directed the complex, congressional initiative and intervention in these matters were potentially threatening. A far safer solution was provided by the creation of a bureaucracy of regulatory agencies. These agencies, not Congress, set the ground rules for future interactions between corporate capitalism and government, and in so doing, they also presaged and contributed to the changing place of Congress.

The alterations in the position of the Congress have not all pointed in the direction of a decline in importance. The *constitutional* autonomy of Congress is unique in the West, and it guarantees that Congress will remain more capable of independent action than Parliament in England or even in France. This capacity, however, rarely takes the form of the initiation of new public policies, though there are uncommon instances, as in the Clean Air Act of 1970, of congressional initiative. More often it takes the form of saying "no"—no to a program, no to appropriations and spending, no to excessive presidential behavior. Precisely because of the vast growth of government and the corporate complex—the very cause of Congress' loss of ability to initiate policy—Congress has more opportunities to say "no," and in this way its veto has become more important. Indeed, before the late nineteenth century, when Congress was relatively important within the national government, it was less significant a body than most state legislatures, since the federal government itself was relatively weak. The decline of the Congress is thus not absolute, but rather a relative decline within a growing government in Washington.

This growth has given members of Congress more to do. As more and more legislation has been proposed by the president who sets the basic policy agenda, more and more legislation must be disposed of by Congress. Such headlines as "A Coming Logjam for Congress," "Time Pressures on the Senate," and the like have become increasingly common. Members of Congress have more to do because the growth of the corporate complex has made their activities as providers of access to the bureaucracy and of tangible services to constituents more important. As political scientist Morris Fiorina notes, "the growth of an activist federal government has stimulated a change in the mix of congressional activities. Specifically, a lesser proportion of congressional effort is now going into programmatic activities and a growing proportion into pork-barrel and casework activities."[7]

How Congress carries out these functions depends in large measure on the nature of congressional representation. Given the enhanced and changing scope of congressional action (in volume if not in importance), one might ask *whose* legislature is the Congress of the United States. The answer can be approached best by applying the four criteria of representation discussed in Chapter 1. There, we distinguished between procedures, especially elections, by which representatives are selected; personnel, or the social-background characteristics of representatives; consciousness, their substantive orientations; and effectiveness, the ability of representatives to produce the results they desire. Let us examine each in turn.

Senators and representatives have desirable jobs. They participate in affairs of state, and they have a chance to mould public policy. They are respected and visible members of their local communities. In some cases, they become national media figures. In Washington, they interact with interesting and intelligent people, both in and out of government. Their calendars are full; the work is varied and stimulating.

Other occupations, such as corporate management and the practice of law in national law firms, offer talented local figures high remuneration and prestige. But the perquisites of office continue to attract the ambitious. In addition to their annual salary of $72,600 members of the House and Senate receive generous pensions (if they last at least five years in office), inexpensive life insurance, tax breaks if they own two homes, a stationery allowance, a large telephone allowance, almost unlimited mailing privileges, nearly free medical care, free underground parking, and command over a large staff. Each year many members of Congress travel abroad at government expense, sometimes with little apparent government purpose. Congress also functions as a full-service club for its members. The Senate alone has a dozen restaurants and a barbershop where the senators may get their hair cut for nothing. There are two swimming pools, steam baths, and a shop that sells

[7]Morris Fiorina, *Congress: Keystone of the Washington Establishment* (New Haven, Conn., 1977), p. 46.

stationery supplies at discount prices. The total package of salary, benefits, and services has been estimated to be worth from $150,000 to $350,000 a year. All this is joined to the more intangible importance of ease of contact with the powerful both in and out of government, access to a hectic social life, and continual deference. The "most seductive part of it," a congressman from the Midwest observed, "is the deference. My God, it's amazing how many people can never seem to do enough for you, here or when you go home. . . . Maybe I could and maybe I couldn't make more money in private business, but I do know this: I'd never have have my ego fed half so grandly."[8]

Not surprisingly, most members of Congress spend a great deal of time getting reelected. Indeed, some political scientists argue that most of the behavior of members of Congress follows from their principal goal—the desire for reelection. By getting favorable publicity, by claiming credit for government actions, by delivering benefits to specific constituents, and by taking broad policy positions calculated not to offend too many people, they work hard to please their constituents.[9] "This is a business, and like any business you have to make time and motion studies," one member told Richard Fenno when he studied the activities of representatives in their constituencies. Since the first order of business is to stay in business by getting votes, representatives develop what Fenno calls a "home style" calculated to make the member appear qualified, as a person who identifies with constituents, and as a person who empathizes with their feelings and needs.[10] This need to construct such a relationship inevitably makes Congress the most representative of our national institutions.

But, increasingly, the electoral connection builds ties between members of Congress and those they represent that are based more on the delivery, or claim of delivery of specific services (getting a dam built, finding a lost social security check), and on matters of style (appearing to be above politics or to be trustworthy) than on coherent and consistent positions on political issues. Indeed, Fiorina argues that there is a connection between how safe a represen-

---

[8]James Wooten, "Washington Journal: A 'Mighty Nice' Life," *New York Times*, May 30, 1978.

[9]David Mayhew, *Congress: The Electoral Connection* (New Haven, Conn., 1974).

[10]Richard Fenno, "U.S. House Members in Their Constituencies," *The American Political Science Review* LXX (September 1977): 883–917.

tative is and how openly he or she talks about issues. So long as districts

> are represented by congressmen who function as national policy-makers. . . . reasonably close congressional elections will naturally result. For every voter a congressman pleases by a policy stand he will displease someone else. The consequence is a marginal district. But if we have incumbents who deemphasize controversial policy positions and instead place heavy emphasis on nonpartisan, nonpro-grammatic constituency service (for which demand grows as govern-ment expands), the resulting blurring of political friends and enemies is sufficient to shift the district out of the marginal camp.

More and more members of Congress have come to understand this reality, and come to prefer to be "reelected as an errand boy than not be reelected at all."[11]

As all candidates, but especially those running without the advantages of incumbency, find it harder to command public atten-tion, they must spend more in an effort to get it. Some of the expenditures are staggering. When Abraham Lincoln ran for Con-gress in 1846, he had one campaign expense—a barrel of cider. Today, a typical House race will cost more than $300,000, a sixfold increase in the past decade alone. Those running for senator spend an average of over $2 million. Candidates for office do not spend so much money because they want to, but because they are afraid not to. Most of these funds are spent for television campaigns and on advertisements that seek to enhance name recognition and im-age rather more than provide discussions of substantive issues.

The sheer cost of running for office has many consequences. Members of Congress organize their offices as money machines. Since expenses rise so quickly, they must devote a good deal of their own time, and that of their staffs, to insure that they have adequate funds to spend on the next campaign. Most of the funds they raise come from Political Action Committees, individuals who give at the behest of PACs, and from direct mail solicitation. A decade ago, most money was raised from the representative's home district. Today, the sums are too large for traditional sources to suffice. Thus, much time is spent at Washington fund raisers: cock-tail parties or dinners where lobbyists and members of PACs come

[11]Fiorina, pp. 36–37.

to donate money. There are nearly one hundred such events each week in Washington.

Funds are targeted to members on key committees. Journalist Elizabeth Drew has observed that "serving on some congressional committees is more lucrative—the term is actually used on Capitol Hill—than it is on others, the most lucrative being the House Ways and Means and the Senate Finance Committees, which have jurisdiction over tax legislation, and the House Energy and Commerce Committee and the Senate Committee on Commerce, Science, and Transportation. The Commerce Committees have jurisdiction over, among other things, regulatory policy affecting business."[12]

Individuals, like Representative Dan Rostenkowski of Illinois, the chair of the House Ways and Means Committee, who are in positions to do specific favors for specific groups and industries, have little trouble raising funds. In 1982, he raised $519,000 (and another $168,000 the next year, when there was no election), even though he had only token opposition (he won with 84 percent of the vote). When he holds a fund raiser every important Washington lobbyist shows up. He uses his funds not only to win big at election time, but to donate money to colleagues in the Congress who are in need. The result is an immense power base in the House of Representatives.

Rostenkowski is not alone in this practice. Another example is that of Representative Henry Waxman of California, who won the contested chairmanship of the Health and Environment Subcommittee of the Commerce Committee in 1979 after donating election funds to eight colleagues who served on the Committee. Seven later voted for him.

The list of congressional donors is very long, and it reflects national more than local interests. Thus, members of the House Energy and Commerce Committee receive donations from the milk industry, commodity exchanges, poultry and livestock producers, the automobile, chemical, and computer industries, real estate and construction, hospitals, gun groups, hotel industries, and unions, among others. Most of these sources of funds are invisible to voters; and most buy access to the Congress on behalf of issues that are of narrow concern to a particular group. If an issue is not very

[12]Elizabeth Drew, "Politics and Money," *The New Yorker*, December 6, 1982, p. 123.

visible and thus does not affect an important group in the representative's constituency, the member of Congress is open to persuasion; and the group that gains access is most likely to persuade.

The high cost of politics not only affects how members of Congress spend their time and how open they are to lobbying and influence. Expensive campaigns confer advantages to incumbents who are more likely to be able to raise money to stay in office than opponents are likely to be able to raise money to get elected for the first time. An important recent study, Gary Jacobsen's *Money in Congressional Elections,* has shown that incumbency has the most decisive impact on campaign finance. As a result, most elections are not really competitive.[13]

Elections are meant to be the mechanism for insuring the substantive representativeness of the Congress. In 1787, George Washington endorsed the two-year term for congressmen. Power, he wrote, "is entrusted for certain defined purposes, and for a certain limited period . . . and, whenever it is executed contrary to [the public] interest, or not agreeable to their wishes, their servants can and undoubtedly will be recalled." The House would rapidly turn over in membership, it was expected, thereby giving the people a hold on the actions of their representatives.

This expectation has not been borne out. In the nineteenth century, congressional turnover was very high; in 1870, more than half of the representatives sent to the House were newly elected. By 1900, fewer than one-third; today, over 85 percent of the members of the House of Representatives have been elected to office more than once. The average representative has served for over seven two-year terms; the average senator for over ten years.[14]

No district is ever completely safe. In their careers, about one in three members is eventually thrown out of office by voters either in a primary or in a general election.[15] Yet fewer and fewer seats today can be classified as "marginal," where winning percentages are from 50 to 55 percent. Once a person is elected there is an

---

[13]Gary C. Jacobsen, *Money in Congressional Elections,* (New Haven, 1980).
[14]Samuel Huntington, "Congressional Responses to the Twentieth Century," in David Truman, ed., *The Congress and America's Future* (Englewood Cliffs, N.J., 1965), pp. 8–9; Mark Green, James Fallows, and David Zwick, *Who Runs Congress?* (New York, 1972), pp. 226–27.
[15]Robert S. Erikson, "Is There Such a Thing as a Safe Seat?" *Polity 8* (Summer 1976): 623 ff.

excellent chance that he or she will stay in the seat for a long time. Since the Second World War, nine in ten of all members of the House, and three in four of senators have won reelection. The average member of Congress has been in office for about a decade.

This change reflects the decline in the number of marginal seats. Political scientist David Mayhew has found that fewer and fewer districts are competitive. More and more are safe for incumbents. The vast majority of incumbents win by securing more than 60 percent of the vote.[16] Elections, as a consequence, have come to have less and less of a capacity to keep Congress representative. Rather, Fiorina argues, as marginal districts disappear, and therefore as dissatisfied voters have increasingly limited chances to defeat incumbents, "we face the possibility of a Congress composed of professional officeholders oblivious to the changing political sentiments of the country."[17] Who are these representatives? Whom do they represent?

The representatives

In the representative ideal, a representative body mirrors the population as a whole. But no legislature in the world measures up to this standard. It can be argued, moreover, that not only is perfect symmetry between representatives and represented unlikely but that even without it the interests of the population as a whole can be substantively represented. Fair enough—but a disproportionately unrepresentative legislature on the other hand is likely to leave many members of the population without representatives who even minimally comprehend their life situations and needs; while others, who are overrepresented, are likely to have their views taken into account as a matter of course, sometimes without the representatives even being aware of their own predispositions.

These considerations are important in the case of Congress, since the average social background of representatives differs so strikingly from the population as a whole. In the words of a recent comprehensive study:

> Against the background of the great cultural, religious and ethnic diversity that is America, a close focus upon the Congress reveals it

[16]David Mayhew, "The Case of the Declining Marginals," *Polity 6* (Winter 1973): 295–317.
[17]Fiorina, p. 14.

as predominantly an elite club for aging, white Protestant men from the upper levels of the income ladder. Those who represent America in its national legislative bodies are, as a group, a narrow slice of the American pie. Large segments of the population—especially women, working people, and non-whites—are minimally, if at all, represented in Congress.[18]

More than half of Americans are female. In 1982 of the 435 House members, 21 were women (up from 9 in 1942); and of 100 senators, 2 were women. One in nine Americans is black. No member of the Senate and only 21 members of the House were black.

Class patterns of representation are even more skewed. A student of Congress, Richard Zweigenhaft, found that "the fathers of Congressmen are likely to be businessmen or professionals as are the fathers of corporate executives, corporate lawyers, or Ivy League college professors. Apparently the 10 percent of the male population engaged in business or professional careers are highly overrepresented in the number of sons they have who assume leadership in several arenas of American society," including the Congress.[19] Just over half of House members, and two-thirds of senators have been trained as lawyers. Other frequent occupations are business, teaching, banking, and farming. One American in three thousand is a millionaire; one in three senators is a millionaire. A few members of Congress come from working-class backgrounds. But there are former manual workers in the Senate, and only a handful of former union officials in the House.

The social backgrounds of members of Congress separate them from direct contact with and understanding of the relatively subordinate. Congress as an institution further isolates representatives from the general public by providing a comfortable clublike setting for the interaction of members with each other and with noncongressional political participants.

Like most clubs, Congress has an elaborate set of norms to regulate the interpersonal behavior of its members. Collectively, these norms dampen conflict among members, restrict their scope of action, and reinforce their general parochialism.

In December 1956, newly elected Senator Joseph Clark of

[18]Richard Zweigenhaft, "Who Represents America?" *The Insurgent Sociologist* V (Spring 1975): 121.
[19]Zweigenhaft, p. 122.

Pennsylvania had lunch with an old friend, Senator Hubert Humphrey. Clark reports that he asked Humphrey, "Tell me how to behave when I get to the Senate."

> He did—for an hour and a half. I left the luncheon I hope a wiser man, as well briefed as a neophyte seeking admission to a new order can be. In essence he said, "Keep your mouth shut and your eyes open. It's a friendly, courteous place. You will have no trouble getting along. . . . You will clash on the filibuster rule with Dick Russell and the Southerners as soon as you take the oath of office. Don't let your ideology embitter your personal relationships. It won't if you behave with maturity. . . . And above all keep your mouth shut for awhile."[20]

This advice, given a quarter century ago, summarized some of the most important unwritten rules of the Senate at that time: members were expected to work at their legislative tasks, to concentrate attention on a specialized set of manners connected to his or her constituency or committee assignment, to be courteous and avoid personal conflicts, to help colleagues when possible and to keep bargains, and to serve a period of apprenticeship.[21] All but the last of these norms still operate today (although the norm of specialization has less of a hold on members than in the past). At present, "not only do junior members not want or feel the need of an apprenticeship, but also the senior members do not expect them to do so."[22] With this exception, Senator Humphrey's advice to Senator Clark would still hold.

In addition, members of Congress take pride in their institution and are expected to defend it against detractors. Members often feel that whatever differences they have are largely internal matters; to the outside world they present a largely united front. In this enclosed world, those who raise nettlesome issues do so at the cost of influence, friendship, and esteem. When Congressman Michael Harrington revealed CIA activity in Chile in 1974, for example, many members thought "he had acted inappropriately in violating committee's rules in making the information public."[23]

[20]Joseph Clark, *Congress: The Sapless Branch* (New York, 1964), p. 2.
[21]Donald Matthews, *U.S. Senators and Their World* (New York, 1960).
[22]Norman J. Ornstein, Robert L. Peabody, and David Rohde, "The Changing Senate, From the 1950's to the 1970's," in Lawrence C. Dodd and Bruce I. Oppenheimer, eds., *Congress Reconsidered* (New York, 1977), p. 8.
[23]Philip Brenner, "Notes," Workshop on 'Congress and U.S. Foreign Policy,' Con-

These personal characteristics and congressional norms make it difficult for representatives to understand some interests and views, and make them more comfortable with others. But more important, in our view, for the shaping of the nature of representation, are the ways in which Congress is organized, the rules that govern its practices, and the nature of its relationships both with the executive branch (and the president in particular) and the wider society.

The framework for representation is provided by the pathway of legislation before it can become a law. For a bill to become a law, it must pass through a labyrinth of procedural hurdles.

Although a bill must be formally introduced by a representative or senator, major legislation is rarely the work of an individual or even initiated in the Congress. Proposals that lack presidential support usually are doomed. Most major bills are drafted in the executive agencies and are put on the president's legislative program, which becomes the basic legislative agenda. Major legislation is almost always introduced by a leading member, often the chairman, of the standing committee to which the bill is referred. Once the bill is introduced, its fate is largely in the hands of senior committee members, who guard their committee's prerogatives.

Committee procedures in the Senate and the House are essentially similar. Most of the bills referred to committees are never taken up. After they have been introduced on the floor—often by representatives seeking to build political capital with their constituency—they die a quick death. Public hearings are held on the majority of bills that survive. At their conclusion, the real legislative work begins. The committee goes into session, where the bill is read line by line. This is called the mark-up stage. At this critical point, the bill is amended, rewritten, or, if no version can be worked out that is acceptable to the majority of the committee, the legislative process ends and the proposal dies. The relatively few bills that emerge successfully from this procedure have the support of a large majority of committee members and are the product of a committee process that puts a premium on interpersonal relationships and a broad substantive consensus. Thus, controversial proposals rarely survive.

ference on the United States, U.S. Foreign Policy, and Latin American and Caribbean Regimes, March 1978.

Once a bill is passed by the relevant committee in the House or the Senate, it is placed on the chamber's calendar. In the Senate, major bills are usually taken up for consideration from the calendar by the majority leader. In the House, bills must be reported out by the Rules Committee, which schedules House business, before they can reach the floor. As one of the more traditionally conservative committees, the Rules Committee has been a major barrier to the consideration of legislation that challenges patterns of dominance.

By now, before the legislation is debated on the Senate and House floors, the bill's substance and possibilities for passage have largely been determined. Though the floor debates seem to the observer to be the most important phase of the legislative process, in fact, the debates rarely influence any votes.

When the House Rules Committee schedules debate on legislation, the representatives meet as a Committee of the Whole House (identical to the membership of the House of Representatives) to consider the bill and proposed amendments. At this stage, no recorded votes are taken, debating procedures are relaxed, and a quorum of only 100, instead of the usual 218, is required for business. Like the mark-up, this procedure takes place behind closed doors. The Committee of the Whole then reports the bill to the House with any new amendments that have been added. These changes may be voted on again. Then the entire bill as amended is put to a vote.

By contrast to the House, where the Rules Committee usually sets time limits to the floor discussion, debate in the Senate is unlimited. More frequently than not, the majority leader, in agreement with the minority leader, fixes time limits for debate. But this schedule requires unanimous consent. Should one senator object, debate continues.

The Senate provision for unlimited debate can lead to a filibuster, in which one or a group of senators attempt to defeat a measure by holding the floor for hours, or even days, and thus preventing the bill from coming to a vote. If they succeed in holding up Senate business for a long period, the bill is usually dropped. This tactic has been used successfully in the past, principally by Southerners opposed to civil rights legislation. Cloture, a vote to limit debate, needs support by three-fifths of those voting, not just a majority. Many senators who support a bill are reluctant to vote for cloture for fear of weakening a device that they might wish to use in the future. Like the House Rules Committee barrier, the filibuster is another device used to quash controversial legislation.

If a bill is one of the lucky few to be approved by both the House and Senate, it has still not become law. If, as in most cases, there are differences between the versions passed by the House and the Senate, the bills are sent to a conference committee charged to iron out the discrepancies. Usually composed of five or six members from each house, these *ad hoc* bodies may alter provisions, insert new amendments, or even write a whole new bill.

The members, or managers, of these committees are not selected at random from the House and Senate. Rather, the conference committee's membership is chosen on the recommendation of the chairman of the standing committee that had jurisdiction over the bill in the first place. Normally, the chairman proposes senior members from his or her own committee. In this way, the legislative process comes full circle, as the same senior committee specialists who marked-up the bill in private once again have a critical private task—producing the final legislation.

Conference committee reports are the privileged business of each house, since other floor business must be put aside to consider the reports. They may be approved, voted down, or returned to the conference committee. Typically, they are approved, and the bill, now passed in identical form by the Senate and House of Representatives, goes to the president for his approval or veto. Should he sign the bill, it becomes law; should he veto, a vote of two-thirds of the House and Senate is needed to override the president's action and pass the bill into law.

Let us linger on each of these steps of the legislative process to see what they reveal about the character of congressional representation.

The great majority of bills introduced in Congress do not fare well. About 15,000 bills are presented on the clerk's desk of the House of Representatives each year, but fewer than 1,000 become the law of the land. Most are introduced without any expectation of success as a way of going on record in support of a particular position or goal.

The bills with the greatest chance of success that define the main agenda of Congress are those proposed by the president. Most modern presidents have proposed between 200 and 500 pieces of legislation each year. Depending on the year and the administration, anywhere from one in four to three in five of these bills is likely to become law, much higher odds of success than most legislative proposals.

In pursuit of these legislative objectives the president has many resources to call on in drafting proposals, in providing testimony to congressional committees, and in lobbying on their behalf. For these reasons, the most important legislative items tend to be introduced by presidents, in accord with the general goals they sketch in state-of-the-union messages and in numerous messages sent to Congress on a variety of topics.

With regard to legislation that goes to the core of the president's agenda, he may call on a host of advantages in the legislative process. The Office of Management and Budget (OMB) together with the congressional liaison staff in the White House coordinate the executive's legislative efforts. The OMB acts as a clearinghouse to centralize public policy from a presidential perspective by reviewing all executive branch requests for legislation; and the White House staff coordinates presidential lobbying.

Presidents have a variety of tools at their command to win votes in Congress. These range from symbolic ones like photo opportunities with the president to the doling out of project grants for local buildings, roads, and dams, and appointments to federal agencies and to judgeships. President Eisenhower was the first to institutionalize these efforts in the White House. Since his administration, legislative liaison staff have grown in number and in the assertiveness of their activity.

In a recent study, Benjamin Page and Mark Petracca have taken note of how the president can influence each stage of the legislative process. He can work to see that his bills get referred to the most friendly committees; that testimony is scheduled in a timely way; that mark-up sessions go well; that members know how important the bill is to him when it comes up for a vote on the Senate or House floor; that the "right" members are assigned to a conference committee; and that compromises go in the preferred direction. Even for a president this is difficult terrain to traverse, but it is easier for him to navigate than for any other political actor.[24]

[24]Benjamin I. Page and Mark Petracca, *The American Presidency* (New York, 1983), chapter 10.

The president, of course, also has blocking power. He can veto bills the Congress passes that he does not like. When Congress is out of session the president can pocket veto a bill by failing to sign it. When Congress is in session a bill becomes law if he signs it, or even if he does not within ten days of its passage. If within ten days he sends a veto message to Congress the two houses can override him if they both can muster a two-thirds vote. This is not an easy task. The great majority of vetoes are sustained.

The relationship between the president and the Congress is not just one in which the president gets his way. There is conflict built in to their relationship. The presidency is centralized, and proposes legislation with a four-year electoral timetable in mind based on an attempt to create a centralized and coherent program. The Congress is decentralized, is more likely to be influenced by interest groups, and moves to a different electoral cycle.

Members of Congress and the president are elected separately, and, in part, at different times. One-third of the Senate runs for office every two years, for six year terms. All the members of the House are elected every two years. As the intensity of loyalty to a specific political party has declined in past decades, there has been more split voting, so that the president and the members of Congress appeal to voters in different ways and on different terms. No member of Congress can afford to forget local interests and local voters.

Although party loyalties and ideologies help determine the votes of the members of Congress, they are above all political entrepreneurs who must act to secure their local political bases and win elections in their districts. Much of a representative's efforts are devoted to claiming credit for projects in their districts, and in service to individual constituents who must deal with such federal agencies as the Social Security Administration. Where a president may wish to control spending, a representative may have as a higher priority the preservation of a construction project or a defense contract in his or her district.

There are formal organizations of the political parties in the Congress (the Speaker and majority and minority leaders and whips, and their staffs), but their capacities are more limited today than in the past. They depend on persuasion and on a likemindedness of views, but it is hard to enforce party loyalty. Indeed, as numerous students of Congress have observed, the institution is characterized by weak parties and strong committees. It is in the committees that the main legislative action takes place.

Committees are the places where legislation is shaped, promoted, or buried. In his study of the Senate, Donald Matthews found that if a proposal was supported by over 80 percent of the members of the relevant committee, it passed on the floor every time; if from 60 to 79 percent supported the bill in committee, it passed 90 percent of the time. In accordance with the norms of reciprocity and courtesy, most legislators will follow the decision of the committees unless they have a basic reason to doubt it. For almost all legislation, the committee actions are the decisive factor.

Congressional committees work on specialized subject areas, such as labor, education, defense, and agriculture. In theory, they are major battlegrounds where different interests compete in the making of public policy. Individuals and groups who are affected by proposed legislation are usually granted the chance in public hearings to argue their positions, transmit information, and attempt to generate congressional and public support for their point of view. In practice, the routine operation of congressional committees *limits* controversy and buttresses prevailing patterns of dominance in the following ways.[25]

Limited participation and close interaction   The number of people who work on bills in congressional committees is small. Much of the day-to-day work is accomplished in subcommittees of about five legislators. The largest committees are those dealing with appropriations. Yet even their membership totals only 13 percent of the House and 26 percent of the Senate. "Limited participation in a conflict," political scientist Philip Brenner observes, "engenders quick resolution because there are fewer positions to reconcile." Further limiting the range of options explored is the fact that small committees engender close interaction and friendships.

> Over many years members do come to see each other as friends with common problems, rather than as representatives of a position. . . . Close interaction thus encourages members to avoid intense conflict in order to maintain cordial relations with their "friends." It further discourages the congressman who might fight for a position which is antagonistic to prevailing interests from continuing his fight, because

[25]Philip Brenner, "Committee Conflict in the Congressional Arena," *The Annals* 411 (January 1974): 98–100.

in doing so he tends to alienate himself from the people with whom he works closely.[26]

Thus, committees duplicate the clublike atmosphere of Congress as a whole and take on an integrated life of their own that often cuts across party lines. Richard Fenno's study of the House Appropriations Committee, for example, found a deeply rooted committee consensus on goals. Members were recruited to produce "a group of individuals with an orientation especially conducive to Committee integration. . . . Key selectors speak of wanting, for the Appropriations Committee, 'the kind of man you can deal with,' or 'a fellow who is well-balanced and won't go off half-cocked on things.'"[27]

Limited scrutiny Given the wide range of specialization and the sheer number of subcommittees, they cannot adequately be covered by the press. In the Senate in 1968, according to the *Congressional Quarterly Almanac,* 93 percent of the hearings of the Rules and Administration Committee were held behind closed doors; 46 percent of the Foreign Relations Committee meetings; 30 percent of the Public Works Committee sessions; 67 percent of the Armed Services Committee hearings; and 47 percent of the hearings of the Labor and Public Welfare Committee. In the House, *all* of the Appropriations Committee hearings were conducted in secret. The overall figure for committee hearings held in secret was 43 percent.[28] Although the 1970 Legislative Reorganization Act required that all committee sessions be opened to the public unless a majority of the committee voted for a closed session, approximately 30 percent are still secret. As a consequence, not only is the general public excluded, but most members of Congress must depend on the judgment of the members of the relevant committee. When a bill reaches the Senate and the House for debate, only the committee members have a detailed acquaintance with the legislation, and they usually remain in control of the floor debate.

Seniority Power within the committee system is determined principally by seniority. The chairmanship of a committee is allo-

[26]*Ibid.,* p. 99.
[27]Richard Fenno, Jr., "The Appropriations Committee as a Political System," in Robert Peabody and Nelson Polsby, eds., *New Perspectives on the House of Representatives* (Chicago, 1963), p. 85.
[28]*Congressional Quarterly Almanac* (Washington, 1968), pp. 798–99.

cated traditionally, though no longer automatically, to the member of the majority party who has served longest on the committee, thereby preventing a potential cause of conflict. Further, as Philip Brenner notes, seniority procedures "take away a focal point for outsiders [who] . . . would be encouraged to pressure members, and for candidates [who] might be 'encouraged' to campaign on the basis of their positions on upcoming issues."[29]

The seniority system puts a premium on specialization. It is widely agreed that effective legislators are those who focus their energy only on matters that either affect their districts directly or come before their committees. The most senior people on the committees have been there a long time. They have been enmeshed in a mutually beneficial relationship with special-interest groups for decades; and they tend to identify with and share the defensive interests of the most powerful lobbies. As a result, the committee structure based on seniority is substantively biased for the status quo and against fundamental change.

Congressional committees changed in basic ways in the 1970s. Under rules adopted first by the House Democratic Caucus in 1971, which were exercised initially in 1975, committee chairmanships were no longer awarded, as they had been, solely by seniority. From roughly the turn of the century until then, chairs of committees who attained their positions by the longevity of their service exercised total control over the creation of subcommittees, the appointment of their chairs, the scheduling of hearings, and the hiring of all staff. Approximately 50 senators and representatives wielded this power.

Today, power is much more widely dispersed. There are 326 committees and subcommittees, held by 202 of Congress' 535 members. More than one in three members is in charge of some committee. These committees have staffs, and lives, of their own.

Members of Congress usually try to get committee assignments appropriate to their districts. Representatives from districts with strong unions try to get seats on Education and Labor committees, and farm representatives prefer seats on the Agriculture committees. Sometimes personal interest is the basis of committee assignments. Members of the Banking, Finance, and Urban Affairs committees tend to own much stock in banks, for example.

[29]Brenner, p. 100.

The result of this sorting out is a fragmented congress, one of subcommittee government, that is hard for the leadership to control, and permeable to interest groups at every stage of the legislative process.

The committee-agency nexus   We saw earlier in this volume how corporate capitalism and the executive branch of the federal government have formed the relationship we call the corporate complex. Congress is at the periphery of this complex. Congressional committees, however, pose the key legislative hurdle for corporate-complex policies. Committees can oversee the practices of government agencies and regulatory commissions, fail to pass legislation initiated by the executive branch, and modify the president's proposed budget.

These checks are not routinely applied. Individual standing committees have fashioned close and stable relationships with their companion executive agencies. The Department of Agriculture and the agriculture committees, the Pentagon and armed services committees, and the Department of Labor and the education and labor committees have become mutually supportive. The agencies are attentive to the wishes of the committees that formally supervise them, and within Congress the agencies are regarded as the substantive property of the relevant committees.

The support of powerful corporate-sector interest groups for members of Congress in strategic locations and the close interaction, secrecy, and seniority system of the committees facilitate the development of an enduring committee-agency nexus that functions in the interests of the corporate complex. Most issues "tend to be decided in accord with agreements reached in close cooperation between key members of Congress (usually senior committee and subcommittee members), key representatives of interest groups, and key bureaucrats."[30] In this way, Congress, though not an integral part of the corporate complex, becomes its predictable ally.

Consider the operation of what political scientist Gordon Adams calls "the military subgovernment," consisting of the Pentagon, defense contractors, and the military committees in Congress. "The natural congressional inclination to delegate authority for expenditure review to subunits," he writes, "created a powerful

[30]Lowi and Ripley, p. 161.

committee that came to consider the military as its client. Committee hearings provided a forum insulated from outside criticism of military assumptions about foreign policy and from competing social programs." As a result, Congress has largely abdicated its responsibility to review the Pentagon budget. Only very rarely do executive-branch defense recommendations get cut.[31]

The committee-agency nexus has been mitigated to a minor degree by the Budget and Impoundment Control Act of 1974, which established new Budget Committees in each chamber. These new committees specify target ceilings for fourteen categories of federal spending by May 15 of each year. All spending bills must be approved by the appropriations committees by Labor Day, and both houses must reconcile their spending differences by September 25. Programs authorized by the Senate and House in specific appropriations bills are considered in relationship to each other, thus giving the Congress the means to shape priorities as a whole. Although this new procedure has imposed some discipline on spending, and in isolated instances has forced a rollback of recommendations by appropriations committees, it is important to realize that the new procedure was overlaid on the old, more entrenched committee system. The Budget Committees, as general committees, usually are no match for the specialized substantive committees and their staffs.[32]

Lobbying and interest groups

Most members of Congress believe that lobbyists are indispensable to the legislative process. A Brookings Institution study argued that "because of the publicity given to early, blatantly improper attempts to influence legislators, the general public views with suspicion anyone classified as a lobbyist. The constructive services that are provided by today's professionals are often little known." A representative whose views were typical had this to say:

> A lot of people seem to think that lobbying is a bad thing. I think that is one misconception which still needs to be corrected as far as the general public is concerned. Lobbying is an essential part of

[31]Gordon M. Adams, "Disarming the Military Subgovernment," *Harvard Journal on Legislation* 14 (April 1977): 461.
[32]Louis Fisher, "Congressional Budget Reform," in *ibid.*; John Ellwood and James Thurber, "The New Congressional Budget Process," in Dodd and Oppenheimer.

representative government, and it needs to be encouraged and appreciated. Lobbyists are frequently a source of information. If they come to your offices and explain a program or factors contributing to the need for legislation, you get a better understanding of the problems and answers to them. If you have our independence, and I think we all do, they can teach you what an issue is all about, and you can make your own decision.[33]

But what this perspective fails to see is that lobbying activity systematically injects a powerful bias into the legislative system on behalf of those who command specialized information (such information is never neutral), staff, and money, and who ensnare representatives in a web of favors ranging from an early evening drink to substantial campaign contributions.

The attention of interest groups is focused on the specific committees and their members who handle relevant legislation. In addition to their access to individual representatives, there are two moments when they have the greatest opportunity for leverage: when hearings are held and at the mark-up stage of a given bill. Interest groups provide the bulk of testimony at the hundreds of days of committee hearings held by each committee each year. They provide committees with information, argumentation, and a sense of public pressure. When bills are "marked up" after these hearings, interest groups monitor how individuals act.

Before the middle 1970s, these sessions were held in closed, executive sessions. No longer. They are now open, public affairs. The result has not been the intended one of the reformers to give more influence to the broad public. Rather, these meetings are attended mainly by lobbyists who try to ensure that those they support get continuing pressure to maintain the preferred policy position.

In the past decade, with these shifts in procedures as well as in the cost of politics, interest groups have become more sophisticated, talented, persistent, and successful. The number of registered lobbyists has doubled to about 7,500 in just the past ten years. Another group of equal size participates in lobbying efforts but does not register because of vague features of federal disclosure laws. Registered lobbyists reported spending $42 million in 1984,

[33]Charles Clapp, *The Congressman* (New York, 1964), pp. 183, 184.

but the *U.S. News and World Report* believes that true spending may reach over a billion dollars a year.[34]

Without access there can be no success. Thus, many groups hire former members of Congress or former government officials to lobby for them. Some of these individuals with specialized access organize their own lucrative firms. Bob Gray, for example, who cochaired President Reagan's first inaugural and who was a communications advisor to his 1980 campaign, has a firm with a staff of 100. Another large firm is headed by William Timmons, a former aide to two Republican presidents; one of the newest is led by Michael Deaver, one of President Reagan's top White House assistants in his first term and a personal friend of the Reagan family.

The services of such firms do not come cheap. They demand annual retainers of $250,000, and charge up to $400 each hour. For this, they utilize computerized banks of information to monitor bills and legislative action and to stoke up grass-roots support through targeted direct mailings.

It should be obvious that these resources are not distributed evenly across the range of interests and views in the United States. The combination of weak parties, strong but decentralized committees, and active lobbying create strong incentives for members of Congress to maintain the basic contours of the corporate complex and to assist its most powerful members.

Potentially, the electorate should be a counterweight to such intense pressures. In fact, the electorate provides little oversight. The ability of voters to influence representatives is predicated on an electorate that is politically interested, informed, and involved, and the evidence is increasingly to the contrary. In a classic article on constituents' awareness of congressional candidates, political scientists Donald Stokes and Warren Miller found that the public's knowledge about those competing for office was meager: "Of the people who lived in districts where the House seat was contested in 1958, 59 percent—well over half—said they had neither read nor heard anything about either candidate for Congress, and less than 1 in 5 felt they knew something about both candidates."[35]

[34]Jeffrey Sheler *et al.*, "Lobbyists Go for It," *U.S. News and World Reports*, June 17, 1985, pp. 30–34.
[35]Donald Stokes and Warren Miller, "Party Government and the Saliency of Congress," in Theodore Lowi and Randall Ripley, eds., *Legislative Politics USA* (Boston, 1973), p. 170.

More recent findings not only confirm the general lack of public awareness but also indicate that the indifference of constituents to their representatives is on the increase. A Gallup poll conducted in 1970 found that 53 percent of Americans did not know their representative's name; 75 percent had no idea how he or she had voted on even one bill in the past year; 76 percent admitted knowing nothing about the activities of their representative on behalf of the district; 67 percent had given little or no thought to the coming congressional elections; 38 percent did not even know whether their representative was a Republican or Democrat.[36] There has been virtually no change since that poll was taken.

As a result, in spite of the need for representatives and senators to renew their electoral mandate with regularity (every two and six years, respectively), the typical member of Congress is remarkably free on most matters from broad constituency pressures, or even from constituency knowledge. This near absence of a give-and-take relationship between members of Congress and the public may be thought somewhat surprising since enormous sums are spent on election campaigns, and a very large proportion of a member's time is spent on cultivating ties to constituents. It is often said—especially about members of the House—that they must begin to run for reelection the day they are elected. What accounts for the failure of congressional elections to develop a reciprocal interchange between representatives and represented?

One part of the explanation has to do with the changing role of the member of Congress within his or her district. As one student of politics argued in 1959:

> Fifty years ago, in his district or state, the campaigning Congressman did not have to compete in a world of synthetic celebrities with the mass means of entertainment and distraction. The politician making a speech was looked to for an hour's talk about what was going on in a larger world, and in debates he had neither occasion nor opportunity to consult a ghost writer. He was, after all, one of the best paid men in his locality, and a big man there.[37]

Today, by contrast, there are a multitude of diversions competing for the public's attention, the television set has supplanted the pub-

[36] *Gallup Opinion Index* 64 (October 1970): 9–14.
[37] C. Wright Mills, *The Power Elite* (New York, 1959), p. 250.

lic meeting as a means of campaigning, and the member of Congress is no longer a leading celebrity in the community.

Thus, in practice, the six-year and two-year terms have become a device to hold members of Congress accountable to the wealthier segment of capital that finances elections and that, unlike many voters, not only knows the representative's name but how he or she acts in minute detail. A reciprocal relationship has developed between powerful interests and members of Congress.

Senators and representatives do not make the fundamental decisions about the organization or running of the corporate complex. They are, however, in a position to delay, block, or veto policies the corporate complex wishes to implement. As a result, corporate capital attempts to establish working relationships with those members of Congress who occupy strategic locations in the congressional hierarchy. As a representative or senator gets reelected, he or she becomes less dependent on local capital for campaign financing and more able to hinder or facilitate the passage of legislation favored by national corporate interests. The most obvious of these strategic locations that members of Congress with seniority come to occupy "include elective leadership posts, memberships on party policy (agenda) and steering (committee assignment) committees, committee chairmanships (or in the case of the minority, 'shadow' chairmanships), chairmanships of subcommittees, membership on more than two regular legislative committees, and membership on the Appropriations Committee."[38]

Perhaps the close connection between corporate interests and members of Congress in strategic locations, and the narrow nature of the substantive representation members provide, are most apparent in the area of military spending. The Pentagon budget is regularly approved with relatively little examination. Given the lack of pressure from the electorate in general, the most tangible publicly funded project a representative can get for his or her district is a military installation or a defense contract for local firms. Hence the defense budget is characterized by a great deal of logrolling; it is implicitly understood that Representative A will not question defense spending in Representative B's district so long as the favor is reciprocated. Not surprisingly, the most vigorous ad-

[38]Nelson Polsby, *Congress and the Presidency* (Englewood Cliffs, N.J., 1964), pp. 38–39.

vocates of military retrenchment come from areas with no military installations or defense contractors. Congressman Jamie Whitten, a Mississippi Democrat who chaired the House Appropriations Committee, Subcommittee on Defense, was candid on this point:

> I am convinced that defense is only one of the factors that enter into our determinations for defense spending. The others are pump priming, spreading the immediate benefits of defense spending, taking care of all services, giving military bases to include all sections. . . . There is no state in the Union, and hardly a district in a state which doesn't have defense spending, contracting, or a defense establishment.[39]

Given the shift in the locus of national political power in this century from the Congress to the executive branch, most of the efforts of corporate interests to influence Congress are essentially *defensive*. As David Truman, a leading analyst of Congress, has noted, organized interest-group activity does not seek to convince members of Congress to initiate new policies. Rather, most such activity, especially that of lobbyists in the corporate sector, is "dedicated to preventing any change in the existing order of things. Where there are groups whose claims involve a change, there are as likely to be others . . . vigorously defending the *status quo*."[40] After studying the relative success or failure of congressional interest-group activity, he concluded that "the business corporation has been such a favored group in the United States . . . it normally enjoys defensive advantages."

TRENDS AND PROSPECTS

No institution is a 'constant.' Buffeted by internal and external pressures, institutions change, often in incoherent and partially contradictory ways. Such has been the case for Congress in the 1970s and 1980s. These two decades constitute a period of major alterations in the way Congress conducts its business. While these

[39]Testimony before the Joint Economic Committee's Defense Procurement Subcommittee, January 29, 1960.
[40]David Truman, *The Governmental Process* (New York, 1951), p. 353.

shifts do not all point in one direction, overall a general tendency may be discerned.

Some reforms have made Congress more of a centralized legislature and have highlighted the role of the two political parties. During the Nixon presidency, and again in the Reagan years, Democrats in Congress sought to develop the means to assert their influence against the Republican administration. Moves to increase the power of the Speaker of the House was one result. In 1973, the Speaker was placed on the Committee on Committees, thus giving him a major role in the selection of committee members and chairmen. In the same year, a new Steering and Policy Committee was founded. Its members included the Speaker, the chairman of the party caucus, the majority whip, the chief deputy whip, the three deputy whips, four members selected by the Speaker, and twelve representatives elected by regional party caucuses. This committee became the principal instrument of shaping party policy. Since it was chaired by the Speaker and its membership was determined principally by him, it augmented his abilities to shape the activities of Democrats in important ways. Further, in 1974, this committee was given the responsibilities of the Committee on Committees. And in that year, the Speaker was given new control over the scheduling of legislative business by the power to appoint the chair and the Democratic members of the House Rules Committee, which oversees such scheduling. Finally, the prerogatives of the Speaker were increased by more staff being added to the office of the whip, whose job it is to try to impose party discipline on members. In the Senate, under majority leaders Mansfield and Byrd, the Democratic Conference has become a significant forum for Democrats, and the place where many reforms concerning the filibuster (reducing the number required to break one from two-thirds to three-fifths of voting members), open committee hearings, and staffing have been initiated.

During the Reagan administration, the tendency toward party voting and discipline has grown further. The administration succeeded in its early years in office in unifying the Republican party in support of the program of a popular sitting president. Much of this program for higher defense spending, lower marginal rates on income taxes, some cuts in welfare state domestic spending, and fewer regulatory restraints on business passed the Congress based on such unified Republican support, joined to a group of conservative Democrats from the South and Southwest. Overall, though, the Democratic senators and representatives voted together in opposition to many of the key elements of the President's program.

But these centralizing trends concerning the leadership and party life of each house have been crosscut by even more powerful trends of decentralization. The most important of these developments has been the dramatic increase in the size of congressional staffs and in the number and scope of subcommittees. In 1966 the Senate and House had a combined total of about 6,000 staff. In two decades, this total has tripled. This dramatic growth in numbers has allowed each member of the Senate and House to be more autonomous, as he or she develops sources of expertise and service independently of the parties, the leadership, and the institution as a whole.

This autonomy has been augmented by the growth of the subcommittee structure. The number of subcommittees has nearly doubled in the past quarter century. In 1971 a committee of the Democratic Caucus on reform, chaired by Representative Julia Butler Hansen, limited subcommittee chairs to one per member and specified that each subcommittee chair could select a staff member for the group. These changes not only made more chairs available to more representatives, but they added to subcommittee activity. "It provided sixteen members with new policy forums" and "it recognized that subcommittees would remain ineffective without minimal staff support."[41]

The next round of reform of the Hansen Committee, in 1973, was even more important. The "Subcommittee Bill of Rights" gave subcommittees a budget, an enlarged staff, clear jurisdiction over specific areas of legislation, and other incentives for subcommittee chairs to be active in this role. Subsequent Hansen reforms reinforced this "Bill of Rights" by requiring all committees with more than fifteen members to have at least four subcommittees. The main concomitant of this rise in the importance of subcommittees and their chairs has been a matching decline in the power of committee chairmen. These fragmenting trends have been accompanied by provisions to make the legislative process more open by requiring roll-call votes in committee in many cases, by making

---

[41]Dodd and Oppenheimer, p. 35. Also see, Philip Brenner, "Congressional Reform," *Harvard Journal of Legislation* 14 (April 1977).

committee hearings—and even conference committee sessions—open to the press and public, and by modifying the previously automatic operation of seniority.

On balance, these recent changes have had the following principal effects. They have made the job of a member of Congress—even a junior member—more desirable. They have given members a larger "piece of the action." They have allowed members to allocate more staff to district offices and to service constituents from Washington. They have made it more likely that a member will serve on a committee or a subcommittee that relates to constituency interests directly. And they have provided more forums for the construction of cooperative ties between agencies, relevant industries, and congressional committees and subcommittees. Overall, they have reinforced local interests, and have provided for a plurality of access points by organized interests, including bureaucrats, to the Congress. The outcome is a Congress capable of being led by a strong and ideologically committed president, but one composed of individual 'political businesspeople' better informed and more capable in many ways than members in the past, but less concerned with coherent policy formulations and less automatically disciplined by party organizations and loyalties.

6
the quality of justice

The American justice system of the police, prisons and courts is the largest in the world. One in three men in America is arrested for a crime other than a driving offense before the age of thirty. Some 2 million Americans are confined in jails run by local governments each year. Over 600,000 Americans are lawyers. Roughly one of every 200 citizens in the country's largest cities is a police officer or court officer. Each state has dozens of different kinds of courts that conduct trials, hear lawsuits, and provide chances to appeal decisions. Federal courts also hear both criminal and civil cases. Further, the law is routinely used to promote such goals as environmental and consumer protection, civil rights, and other aims of reformers. What tasks does this immense justice system perform? How does it manage these activities? With what results?

THE DEVELOPMENT OF FORMAL LEGALISM

Formally, the justice system is a system of written laws, legal procedures, and institutions that are the means of securing justice for all Americans. In appearances, trappings, and stated principles and procedures, the justice system is committed to upholding the equality of all citizens before the law. Police officers wear uniforms and judges robes to signify that they are performing their duties in the interest of justice, not for their personal gain. Police officers are protected from partisan political pressures by civil service regulations; judges, by long tenures of office. And all participants in the courtroom process are bound by deference to the authority of the law.

The development of a formally nonpolitical legal system was intimately bound up with the development of capitalism in Western Europe. The assertion of parliamentary prerogatives in England after 1688 and the toppling of the Old Regime by the French Revolution of 1789 paved the way for the elaboration of modern legal codes and institutions that adhered to predictable, publicly articulated sets of regulations and procedures. The new capitalist enterprises in these countries were not based on the traditional authority of the lord-serf relationship, and they needed the new legal systems to legitimize their existence and to provide a calculable context within which capitalists could make contracts and exchange goods for money. The law thus provided capitalist enterprises with the legal stability and security they required.

America's legal system, from the colonial period to the present, has had its roots in British law. After the American Revolution, however, key legal questions remained unresolved, the most important being the relationship between the individual states and the national government. The Articles of Confederation, the country's first constitution that went into effect in 1781, allowed each state to retain "its sovereignty, freedom and independence" and declared that every power not "expressly delegated" to the national government was reserved to the states. In the national Congress, each state had one vote.

The new national government could neither tax nor regulate commerce. As a result, it failed to prevent costly economic disputes between states and provide the kind of stable climate necessary for economic development. The Constitutional Convention of 1787 was largely the result of the dissatisfaction of financial and commercial groups with existing legal arrangements.

The Founding Fathers drafted a Constitution that provided for truly revolutionary democratic procedures and liberties. The Constitution of 1787 was expressly concerned with securing three types of citizenship rights. The first cluster are those necessary to the creation of a republican form of government; that is, to the popular control of government by the people through their representatives. Such rights include elections, freedom of speech and press, and the right of citizens to gather in assembly and to petition the government. The second cluster of rights guards the private lives of citizens from unreasonable intrusion by the state. These include freedom of religion and the separation of church and state; the right to be secure from unreasonable search and seizure. The third cluster of rights is procedural, concerned with due process: rights to speedy trial, *habeas corpus,* and protection against *ex post facto* laws and bills of attainder. In short, these rights provide for the rule of law, which is the central feature of the Constitution as a whole.

This profound democratic advance was consistent with, and motivated in part by, the economic interests of the Founders. Many provisions of the Constitution were drafted to protect property rights. By creating a national government that had powers of taxation, sole control over a national monetary system, and the right to regulate interstate and foreign commerce, the Constitution provided an overarching legal framework that facilitated the growth of American capitalism in the nineteenth and twentieth centuries.

American law was transformed in the period from the Revolution to the Civil War. The law became increasingly formal in appearance as it simultaneously facilitated economic growth and development. The most basic change was what legal scholar Morton Horwitz calls "the emergence of an instrumental conception of law." In the late eighteenth-century republic, law was still conceived of as a set of principles that were eternal, "expressed in custom and derived from natural law." The law was primarily a guide to achieve justice in individual cases. By the Civil War, this conception had been eroded. Instead, the law came to be seen as an instrument to promote desirable policies and social ends, most notably those of the growth of the market and rapid industrial development.[1]

These changes, Horwitz shows, entailed basic alterations in conceptions of property and contract. Before the nineteenth century, the law recognized a static, basically rural, understanding of

---

[1]Morton J. Horwitz, *The Transformation of American Law, 1780–1860* (Cambridge, Mass., 1977), chapter 1.

property that entitled its owner to undisturbed enjoyment. As the tempo of economic growth altered after the turn of the century, property came to be seen in more instrumental terms that stressed the virtues of productive use and development. In the case of *Palmer v. Mulligan* (1805), the New York State Supreme Court reversed traditional common-law understandings by holding that a landowner could obstruct the flow of water downstream in the interest of supplying a mill on his property. This obstruction, of course, hurt others downstream, but in this case and in subsequent cases the courts held that the possession of property implies above all the right to develop it for business purposes. Indeed, throughout the period of early industrialization, the common law was often used to give property owners protection from legal liabilities when they undertook programs of economic development.[2]

The early nineteenth century also witnessed basic changes in the law of contracts, changes that were basic to the development of a modern capitalist economy. Before this period, judges had regularly held that the inherent fairness, or justice, of a contract determined its legality. Contracts were void when they were substantively inequitable. This traditional practice was replaced by the "will theory of contract," which held that the validity of contracts depended not on their equity but on the willingness of the parties to make the contract.[3]

This shift prepared the way for the coexistence of formal justice and substantive inequalities. Unlike feudal relationships, which tied serfs to particular fiefs, capitalist relationships are contractual. Workers sell their labor for a wage to those who contract to buy it. This exchange relationship is an exchange among legal equals: wages for work. Yet, of course, these legal equals are not substantively equal. But the premise of a contract now was that of equal bargaining power among the parties. Since the only measure of justice was the contractual agreement between the parties— between unequals assumed to be equal—"the law had come simply to ratify those forms of inequality that the market system produced. . . . Law, once conceived of as protective, regulative, paternalistic, and, above all, a paramount expression of the moral sense of the community, had come to be thought of as facilitative

---

[2]*Ibid.*, chapter 2.
[3]*Ibid.*, chapter 6.

of individual desires and as simply reflective of the existing organization of economic and political power."[4]

Ever since the mid-nineteenth century, the contrast between formal legal equality and substantive inequality has been mirrored in the routine operation of the American justice system. The law is formal and technical. It has no official political or economic ends or goals. Once understandings of property and contract had been "modernized" to function in harmony with the new market economy, the law certified as "legal," and by implication just and fair, the rules and patterns of the new industrial capitalism. While serving these interests, the justice system acts in a way that is based on an objective, apolitical, and professional conception of the law. The distributive and political functions of law are thus masked.

Legal formalism, however, is not simply a hidden system of domination. For formal legal equality has also considerably widened the average citizen's freedom by granting and protecting basic rights, including free speech, freedom from unreasonable search and seizure, and religious choice. Even political elites may be penalized for violating the norms and procedures of the justice system—at least, as in the case of Watergate, when the violations are so flagrant as to arouse public indignation. Thus the justice system does not simply protect the social order; it also sets a formal framework of rights and procedures that gives citizens tangible resources and acts to restrain the power of dominant authorities. The justice system routinely upholds the equality and rights of citizens as it perpetuates inequalities. It enlarges and protects freedom at the same time that it acts as an instrument of social order.

THE ROLE AND POWERS OF THE SUPREME COURT

The United States Supreme Court bestrides the entire justice system. It is the court of last resort; there is none higher. Indeed it is the only court mentioned in the Constitution: "The Judicial power of the United States shall be vested in one Supreme Court, and in such inferior courts as the Congress may from time to time ordain and establish."

[4]*Ibid.*, pp. 209–10.

Historically, the Supreme Court has performed four basic functions:

First, with the exception of transitional periods like the mid-nineteenth century and the 1930s, the Court almost without fail has supported the policies of the dominant national, as opposed to regional, interests of the time.

Second, the Court has provided an arena where conflicts can be settled between those in positions of economic and political power: between unions and corporations, state and federal governments, Congress and the executive branch. The Court thus provides an extrapolitical means of resolving intraelite conflicts.

The third function of the Supreme Court has been to issue decisions that may be too difficult or unpopular for the president or Congress to take. The May 1954 *Brown* v. *Board of Education* decision, which held segregation in public schools unconstitutional, was fundamental in challenging the quasi-feudal, precapitalist pattern of social relations in the South. But at the time, neither the president nor Congress would have been prepared to take this step because of the electoral perils involved. Thus, through the Court, elites can satisfy some of the needs and demands of subordinates without taking responsibility for these actions.

Fourth, the Court, more than any other part of the justice system, has acted to protect and extend the system's formal legal protections. Hence the Supreme Court has been the pivotal arena for the expansion of the rights of criminal defendants and the protection of civil liberties and civil rights. In this respect, the Court has at least partial institutional autonomy, since it makes these decisions according to the logic of formal legal justice, often over the opposition of important members of the corporate and political elite. Let us examine how the Court has carried out these four functions.

The United States has a dual court system. Both the states and the federal government maintain trial courts. State courts far outnumber federal courts: there are only 89 federal district courts for the entire country (with 333 federal district court judges in all), but there are thousands of state courts, reaching into every governmental jurisdiction. Federal courts hear criminal matters that concern federal law; they hear noncriminal, or civil, matters that involve either citizens of more than one state or complaints filed by the federal government. State courts hear the rest.

Today, both state and federal courts have their own appeals procedures. Decisions of city, county, and state trial courts may be appealed to state appellate courts; decisions of United States district courts may be appealed to one of eleven federal courts of appeal, and then to the Supreme Court. In a few cases, decisions of district courts may be appealed directly to the Supreme Court.

This dual structure dates only from 1891. For the first century of American independence, the basic structure of the federal courts was a subject of struggle between competing regional and national interests. By mentioning only the Supreme Court, the Constitution left two basic issues unresolved: "(1) Should lower federal courts be created at all, or should adjudication of claims of a federal nature be adjudicated in the first instance by state courts? and (2) if lower federal courts were created, what limitations should Congress place over this jurisdiction?"[5]

The Judiciary Act of 1789 represented a compromise between those who saw federal courts as a threat to state interests and those who viewed a system of state courts as inevitably parochial, and thus unable to dispense justice fairly to out-of-state citizens. The act established lower federal courts, but limited them to a state focus: their jurisdictions were drawn along state lines, the federal district judge was required to be a resident of his district, and the major task of the new lower federal courts was the preparation of materials for Supreme Court justices who traveled to the localities to hear cases.

Institutional federal supremacy was finally established with the creation of a federal court of appeals in 1891. The new court detached the appeals procedure from the pressures of the states and districts, diminished the possibilities of interpretations of the law varying too widely from area to area, and freed the Supreme Court from routine duties so that it could concentrate on more substantive matters.

The Supreme Court caps the dual court system, whose basic organization has remained virtually unchanged since 1891. The Court receives the vast majority of its cases from the federal district and appellate courts and from the state courts. Whereas review of lower federal court decisions has been widely accepted as logical

---

[5]Richard Richardson and Kenneth Vines, *The Politics of Federal Courts* (Boston, 1970), p. 19.

and necessary, the Court's power to review state court decisions, as we shall see, has been the source of much dispute.

In addition, in a very small number of cases involving foreign diplomats or a state as a party, the Court has original jurisdiction and gets the cases directly. These cases are usually extremely important and politically controversial. Examples have included disputes between the federal government and California, Louisiana, Texas, and Florida concerning title to rich oil deposits just off the coast; and *South Carolina* v. *Katzenbach* (1966), in which the Court sustained the constitutionality of the 1965 Voting Rights Act, whose purpose was to guarantee Southern blacks the right to vote in the face of restrictive state practices.

Many more cases are filed with the Court each year than it has time or inclination to hear. Hence the Court carefully chooses which cases to hear, following principles expressed by Justice Fred Vinson in 1949:

> The Supreme Court is not, and never has been, primarily concerned with the correction of errors in lower court decisions. In almost all cases within the Court's appellate jurisdiction, the petitioner has already received an appellate review of his case. . . . The function of the Supreme Court is, therefore, to resolve conflicts of opinion on federal questions that have arisen among lower courts, to pass upon questions of wide import under the Constitution, laws and treaties of the United States, and to exercise supervisory power over lower federal courts. If we took every case in which an interesting legal question is raised, or our *prima facie* impression is that the decision below is erroneous, we could not fill the Constitutional and statutory responsibilities placed upon the Court. To remain effective, *the Supreme Court must continue to decide only those cases which present questions whose resolution will have immediate importance far beyond the particular facts and parties involved.*[6]

Supreme Court decisions have frequently been the result of legal battles that mirrored the basic cleavages between different economic and political interests expressed in different periods of American history. Broadly, the Court has passed through four ideological periods: until the Civil War it was preeminently concerned with protecting national economic and political interests at the ex-

---

[6]Fred Vinson, "Work of the Federal Courts," *Supreme Court Reporter,* 1949, cited in Emmette S. Redford et al., *Politics and Government in the United States* (New York, 1968), p. 474. Emphasis added.

pense of state and regional interests (there were important countercurrents within the Court to be sure). It advanced the legal doctrines of national supremacy, judicial power, and the protection of an emerging market system. After a period of decline, before and after the Civil War, the Court, in the late nineteenth century to the New Deal of the 1930s promoted the interests of industrial capitalism, and validated the largely, but not exclusively, laissez-faire economic programs of the Republican party, which governed for all but eight of these years. From the New Deal, especially after 1937, to the late 1960s the Court upheld the new partnership between government and large business, which we have called the corporate complex, and took decisions in the areas of civil rights and liberties that could not have been taken easily by the president or Congress. The fourth period, inaugurated by the confirmation of Warren Burger to succeed Earl Warren as Chief Justice of the United States, has been marked both by a consolidation of decisions taken in the post–New Deal era, and by a shift in nuance and substance toward a more "strict constructionist" view of the role of the Court in interpreting the Constitution.

The Marshall Court: two landmark decisions

Up to the Civil War, the basic issues to confront the Court concerned the scope of national, as opposed to state, powers. The earliest broad cleavage in the country was that between the largely Southern and Western agrarian, planter, and small landowning interests in the Republican party led by Thomas Jefferson; and the largely Northern manufacturing, finance, and mercantile interests who dominated the Federalist party led by Alexander Hamilton. Two key decisions taken by the Supreme Court in this period under the leadership of Chief Justice John Marshall (who served from 1801 to 1835) established the national supremacy of the federal government and the principle of judicial review by the Supreme Court of acts of Congress. Each marked the triumph of national, industrial interests over agrarian, local interests.

In 1791, the Congress established a United States Bank. The issue found Hamilton and Jefferson sharply divided. Hamilton argued that the bank was necessary for the national fiscal well-being of the country and that the authorization of the bank was constitutional because Congress had the power "to make all laws necessary and proper for carrying into execution" the powers of the national government (Article I, Section 8). Jefferson, who hoped America's future would be one of a small landowning agrarian democracy, opposed the bank. He argued that Congress did not have the power to establish a national bank: Congress had the right to pass only those laws that were *indispensably* necessary to carry out governmental powers. By passing the bank bill, the Federalist-dominated Congress opted for the more liberal interpretation of its powers.

The issue came to the Supreme Court in 1819, after the state of Maryland had taxed the bank and the bank had refused to pay. In a far-reaching decision in the case of *McCulloch* v. *Maryland*, the Court supported the bank. "Let the end be legitimate, let it be within the scope of the Constitution," Marshall wrote, "and all means which are appropriate, which are plainly adapted to that end, which are not prohibited, but consist within the letter and spirit of the Constitution, are Constitutional."

The decision not only supported Hamilton's broad reading of the "implied powers" clause of the Constitution but it made clear that where state and national laws conflicted, the state law would be declared unconstitutional by the Court. The court has never wavered from this principle since, but it has been a recurring point of controversy as many state regulations and programs, including provisions for racial segregation, have been struck down.

Earlier, in the case of *Marbury* v. *Madison* (1803), the Marshall Court first asserted the Supreme Court's right to declare acts of Congress or the president unconstitutional. This power, called *judicial review,* authorizes the Court "to hold unconstitutional and hence unenforceable any law, any official action based upon it, and any illegal action by a public official that it deems to be in conflict with the Basic Law, in the United States its Constitution."[7]

The case itself is fascinating. Thomas Jefferson defeated President John Adams' reelection bid in 1800. Adams feared for the survival of his Federalist party and decided before leaving office to pack the federal judiciary with as many Federalists as possible. Early in 1801, at Adams' suggestion, the outgoing Federalist-dominated Congress passed two court acts providing for the appointment of 48 new federal judges. Adams also appointed his secretary of state, John Marshall, chief justice of the Supreme Court.

[7]Henry J. Abraham, *The Judicial Process* (New York, 1965), p. 251.

As secretary of state, Marshall was given the task of delivering the commissions to the new judges. But on the eve of the inauguration of Thomas Jefferson, and of his own assumption of the duties of chief justice, Marshall ran out of time and was unable to deliver seventeen of the commissions. He left them to be delivered by his successor as secretary of state, James Madison.

Jefferson and Madison decided not to carry out Adams' appointments. A number of the disappointed prospective judges hired Adams' former attorney general, Charles Lee, to seek redress in the courts. Lee petitioned to the Supreme Court on behalf of William Marbury, basing his case on an article of the Judiciary Act of 1789 that gave the Supreme Court the power to issue a writ (called a *writ of mandamus*) ordering public officials to perform their official duties.

It was probably expected that Marshall would rule on behalf of Marbury in order to get more Federalists on the bench and to use the full powers granted to the Court by Congress. Indeed, in his opinion, Marshall stated that he thought Marbury had a just complaint based on the law. But instead of upholding Marbury's case, he used the opportunity to make a landmark decision that widened the power of the Court more than any other before or since.

He argued that the article of the Judiciary Act of 1789 was *unconstitutional* because Congress had by law added to the original constitutional jurisdiction of the Supreme Court, something that the Constitution does not permit. By rejecting the claims of a Federalist petitioner and overturning a law passed by a Federalist Congress, Marshall succeeded in securing a basic Federalist objective— the doctrine of judicial review, which at the time was seen as a protection to the propertied against the dangers of congressional democracy.[8] He wrote, echoing almost exactly Alexander Hamilton's arguments in *The Federalist* No. 78: "It is emphatically the province and duty of the judicial department to say what the law is. . . . A law repugnant to the Constitution is void; . . . courts as well as other departments are bound by that instrument." As a result of this decision, Federalist principles triumphed, even though the Federalist party soon disintegrated. The Supreme Court had asserted the right of judicial review and had strongly reinforced

[8]Wallace Mendelson, *Capitalism, Democracy and the Supreme Court* (New York, 1960), p. 20.

the Constitution's declaration that it is the supreme law of the land. This right, though initially asserted with regard to a federal act, applied to state laws as well.

After Marshall's death in 1835, President Andrew Jackson appointed Roger Taney, a Maryland Democrat, to the post of chief justice. In contrast to the Marshall Court, and in the context of growing threats to the integrity of the Union, Taney and his court tended to look more favorably on states' rights and landed interests. As one scholar notes, "Taney, and with him the great majority of his court, demonstrated a faithful attachment to the economic interests of the South and the rapidly developing frontier of the West."[9] Nevertheless, it is possible to overstate the contrast between the Marshall and Taney Courts. In the noted case of *Charles River Bridge* v. *Warren Bridge Co.* (1837), the court ruled on the claim by the owners of a toll bridge in Massachusetts who argued that their state-granted charter implied a promise that the legislature would not authorize a competing bridge; by implication, the owner said the state had granted them a constitutionally guaranteed monopoly. The Court disagreed with the company, holding that the charter did not confer such exclusive rights and that public grants should be interpreted narrowly and strictly. At the time, many thought the Taney Court had reversed Marshall's concern for the sanctity of contracts; but in retrospect it is clear that this was not the case. Rather, as one legal historian has put it, the decision presented "no challenge to the basic principles of Marshall's contract-clause doctrine—that a charter is a contract that binds the state—nor is there evidence in later contract-clause cases that the Taney Court was reckless of property rights."[10] The Court, instead, found a middle way, by giving the states some say in commercial affairs but by also insisting that the state keep the actual promises it contracted for.

The Taney Court might better be seen not as the antithesis of the Marshall Court but as the Court that had to struggle with the tensions between an industrializing North and a slave-owning agrarian South. The Court's balancing act stumbled in its decisions on slavery, presenting judgments that cost the Court both its prestige and its ability to act for some time to come.

[9]Abraham, p. 303.
[10]Robert G. McCloskey, *The American Supreme Court* (Chicago, 1960), pp. 88–89.

In the Taney Court's best-known decision, *Dred Scott* v. *Sanford* (1857), by a 7 to 2 vote, the Court decided that no black could be an American citizen; that a black was "a person of an inferior order"; that no individual of African descent was "a portion of this American people"; and that blacks were slaves and possessions of their owners no matter whether they were in a slave or a free area of the country. This decision, historians agree, hastened the onset of the Civil War.

It also speeded the demise of the Taney Court. Taney continued to serve until 1864, but he was stripped of effective power by the outbreak of the Civil War; during the Civil War (1861 to 1865), President Lincoln acted as a near-dictator, ignoring constitutional niceties where he thought appropriate, and in 1863 Congress increased the size of the court from nine to ten.[11] By 1864, with the appointment of Salmon Chase as chief justice, the Court was securely in the hands of Northern Republicans, who were chiefly concerned with safeguarding property and providing a legal climate for the development of competitive industrial capitalism.

The court as protector of corporate capitalism

The Marshall Court in two landmark cases—*Gibbons* v. *Ogden* (1824) and *Dartmouth College* v. *Woodward* (1819)—had provided the legal framework for the protection of incipient industrialization by ruling in favor of federal control of interstate commerce (thus laying the groundwork for national capitalism) and by declaring that contracts were inviolable. The predominantly Republican-dominated Courts of the late nineteenth and early twentieth century further extended the legal infrastructure of capitalism. Most notably, corporations were given legal status as persons in 1888; they now had a charter of civil liberties, which would be used to declare unconstitutional state and federal laws that restricted their operations as well as labor-union activities of organizing and strikes. In 1895 alone, other Court decisions dismissed prosecutions against the sugar trust, declared the income tax unconstitutional, and upheld the contempt conviction of Eugene Debs, a socialist who was president of the American Railway Union.

---

[11]Congress altered the size of the Court two more times in this decade; from ten to seven in 1866, and from seven to nine in 1869.

After the turn of the century, with the development of an increasingly dominant corporate sector, the Court's continued pro-business orientation was no longer as clear-cut. In attempting to curb attacks on the unbridled power of business by labor unions and Progressive reformers, the Court often struck down or delayed measures that the immense new corporations either wanted or did not oppose. For example, workmen's compensation bills, which the corporations wanted to limit their liability for workers' accidents, were declared unconstitutional by the Supreme Court in 1920 and 1924; it struck down child-labor legislation from 1916 to the late 1930s (unlike small-capital farms and family farms, the larger corporations did not need to employ children).

Yet, on balance, the zealous protection of property, the shackling of unions, and the limitations on corporate legal vulnerability won for the Supreme Court the enthusiastic support of America's capitalists. In 1895, a New York bank president told an audience of businessmen: "I give you, gentlemen, the Supreme Court of the United States—guardian of the dollar, defender of private property, enemy of spoliation, sheet anchor of the Republic!" Sixteen years later, a Standard Oil executive praised a Court decision limiting the scope of the Sherman Antitrust Act: "I am for the Supreme Court every time. For more than a hundred years it has been at work and it has never made a mistake."[12]

This kind of direct, often blatant defense of the capitalist order that the Supreme Court provided, however, stood in the way of the New Deal effort to save corporate capitalism during the depression of the 1930s. The Court continued to rule narrowly on behalf of laissez faire by striking down legislation regulating agriculture, the railroads, and setting minimum wages. In 1937, President Roosevelt sought to smash this roadblock to modernized capitalism by proposing "whenever a Judge or Justice of any Federal Court has reached the age of seventy and does not avail himself of the opportunity to retire on a pension, a new member shall be appointed by the President then in office, and with the approval, as required by the Constitution, of the Senate of the United States."[13] Since six of the nine justices then serving were over seventy, Roosevelt was in

[12]Cited in Redford et al., pp. 498–99.
[13]Theodore Becker and Malcolm Feeley, eds., *The Impact of Supreme Court Decisions* (New York, 1973), p. 41.

effect proposing to add up to six new members to give the New Deal a majority.

Though Congress refused to go along (an alliance of those opposed to the New Deal and those who favored the change but thought it should be done by constitutional amendment, rather than legislation, prevented the bill's passage), two of the justices now began to vote with the New Deal. By 1941, the turnabout was complete. Roosevelt was able to make four new appointments in four years, cementing his majority.

The Warren and Burger Courts

From the late 1930s to the present, the relationship between the Court and the corporate complex has generally been much more indirect than it was before and during the New Deal. Since 1937, the justices have consistently held themselves aloof from the management of the economy. Instead, they have let the corporate complex manage and regulate the economy without Court interference. In this respect, the Court has served the interests of corporate capital, since its hands-off policy has made it possible for the elaborate interpenetration of government and corporate capitalism to continue to develop.

Thus, while almost all of the Court's pre-1937 rulings were in the field of property controls, including taxation, regulation of commerce, antitrust cases, and labor relations, today the Supreme Court's economy-related rulings are largely confined to settling conflicts between authorities: they turn largely on interpretations of actions by federal regulatory commissions, of tax laws, and of the federal regulation of labor relations. In all these areas of decision, however contentious they may be at times, the existence of corporate capitalism is never questioned.

The Court increasingly came to spend the bulk of its time on cases dealing with criminal procedures, civil liberties, and civil rights, especially under Chief Justice Earl Warren, who was appointed by President Eisenhower in 1953 and served through the Eisenhower, Kennedy, and Johnson administrations. The Warren Court consistently acted to protect and extend the legal system's commitment to legal equality. Among its landmark decisions were *Baker* v. *Carr* (1962), in which the Court held that the federal courts could act to ensure that the drawing of election district lines by state legislatures give each vote equal meaning (thus each district had to have roughly the same population); *Miranda* v. *Arizona* (1966), which stated that confessions obtained under interrogation from criminal suspects were not admissable as courtroom evidence unless the accused person had been informed of his or her rights to remain silent and be represented by a lawyer; and *Harper* v. *Virginia State Board of Elections* (1966), in which the Court determined that requiring voters to pay a poll tax (a device to keep blacks from voting) violated the guarantees of equal protection of the Fourteenth Amendment. Desegregation and voting rights have consistently been upheld, defendants' pretrial rights have been made more explicit, and one man, one vote has become the national standard.

It is striking that none of these landmark decisions were in the area of economic relations. When the University of Michigan *Law Review* devoted a special issue to a critical analysis of the Warren Court, its articles focused on desegregation, reapportionment, criminal procedure, religious liberty, and the press. Minor emphasis was paid to labor and antitrust decisions.[14] In these areas, most of the Court's activity reaffirmed preexisting doctrines. The Warren Court was thus devoted, with a passion, to legal equality. Its decisions widened the political community and made more and more citizens legal equals. But issues of substantive economic equality were beyond the purview of the Court.

Overall, the Warren Court's record of judicial activism in the field of civil rights and liberties was the most active in American history. To cite just a few of the less well known examples, in the middle 1950's the Court struck down most state laws against political subversion (*Pennsylvania* v. *Nelson* [1956]); restricted the procedures of legislative investigative committees (*Yates* v. *United States* [1957]); and held that states must provide indigent defendents who wish to appeal the transcripts of their trials (*Griffen* v. *Illinois* [1956]). In the early and middle 1960's, the Warren Court's activist heyday, the Court dramatically extended the right to counsel in state criminal proceedings (*Gideon* v. *Wainwright* [1963]); restricted prayer in the schools (*Engel* v. *Vitale* [1962]); and struck down laws restricting access to birth control devices (*Griswold* v.

[14]Richard Sayler, Barry Boyer, and Robert Gooding, Jr., *The Warren Court: A Critical Analysis* (New York, 1969).

Connecticut [1962]). In short, judicial intervention in public affairs and in shaping the contours of society's liberties dramatically increased, and not without controversy.

Like almost every other president before him, Richard Nixon made appointments to the Court (Chief Justice Burger as well as justices Blackmun, Powell, and Rehnquist) to change its ideological complexion. As a candidate in 1968, Nixon attacked the libertarian decisions of the Warren Court and pledged to rectify the Court's shortcomings by appointing conservative justices. His four appointments in his first term were calculated to win the votes of "middle America" to the Republican party.

The Burger Court has behaved as President Nixon expected only in some respects. It reversed some of the protections the Warren Court extended to criminal defendants, and it ruled in favor of allowing communities to decide their own standards of obscenity (subject to Supreme Court review). The Court also supported the Nixon administration's stand against busing to achieve racial integration of the schools. In July 1974, the Court overturned a lower court ruling that had mandated busing across city lines in the Detroit metropolitan area to integrate the region's public schools. All of Nixon's appointees voted with the majority, and all of the dissenters had served on the Warren Court.

Ironically, the Burger Court played a major role in bringing down the Nixon presidency. Like its predecessors, this Court refused to yield to the president its role as the protector of the legal process. When President Nixon sought to withhold tape-recorded conversations on the grounds of executive privilege that the special prosecutor had requested as evidence for the Watergate trials of the president's closest political allies, the Court ruled unanimously that the tapes had to be turned over. In this case, *United States* v. *Nixon* (1974), the Court reaffirmed the principle laid down by the Marshall Court in the early nineteenth century that the Supreme Court is the ultimate arbiter of the Constitution.

During the Ford and Carter administrations, the Burger Court had not been as conservative as conservatives had hoped or as liberals had feared. By and large it avoided judicial activism. Rather than overturning most of the egalitarian and libertarian gains of the Warren years, the Court refused to extend them. In decision after decision it told would-be litigants to turn to lawmakers or regulatory agencies to solve their problems. "The justices

194 THE QUALITY OF JUSTICE

made it clear," *Business Week* observed, "that they will narrowly read the statutes they are being asked to interpret and will defer to decisions made by administrative agencies."[15] The Nixon appointees have voted together less and less often. In 1976, these four justices voted together 73 percent of the time, but only 36 percent in 1978. Overall, law professor A. E. Dick Howard remarked that the Burger Court had "no overarching doctrine. They're taking cases as they come in pragmatic fashion."[16]

This pragmatism was the Court's most obvious feature in one of the most dramatic cases it has ruled on to date, *Regents of the University of California* v. *Bakke* (1978). After earning a Masters Degree in engineering, Allan Bakke applied to a number of medical schools, none of which accepted him. One of the schools to which he applied, the University of California at Davis, reserved 16 out of 100 places for disadvantaged minority students. Arguing that this affirmative-action program discriminated against himself, Bakke sued and won on appeal in the California Supreme Court. The California Regents appealed. The United States Supreme Court was asked to rule if Bakke should have been admitted, and, therefore, if it was legal for admissions programs to give some preference to blacks over whites in order to remedy the effects of past racial discrimination.

The Court, dividing 5 to 4 each time (with Nixon appointee Justice Powell providing the swing vote), affirmed the lower-court order admitting Bakke to medical school, and ruled that the special-admissions program at the University of California, Davis, violated the Civil Rights Act of 1964. Numerical quotas based entirely on race, where no previous pattern of discrimination was found, were illegal. In the second decision, however, the Court upheld affirmative-action programs, declaring that a university could take race into consideration in admissions, along with other criteria. Universities were thus left with a good deal of discretion; how they use it is entirely up to them. The largest question left open by this decision, which was won in some respects by both sides, "is how far a remedy may go if an institution or industry is found to have excluded minorities itself."[17]

[15] *Business Week,* July 10, 1978, p. 23.
[16] *Time,* July 17, 1978, p. 44.
[17] Anthony Lewis, "'Bakke' May Change a Lot While Changing No Law," *New York Times,* July 2, 1978, section 4, p. 1.

The divisions and fragmentation of the Burger Court on this and other issues yield to a more consistent philosophy in business and labor affairs. Here, unlike the Warren Court on these matters, and unlike its judicial reserve on other questions, the Burger Court consistently supported business in antitrust, regulatory, and labor questions. Since 1969, the *Wall Street Journal* noted, "the court has made it easier for employers to halt strikes that violate no-strike pledges, harder for unions to win employer recognition on the basis of employee-signed cards, and easier for management to press antitrust damage suits against building-trades unions." In other areas too, as those affecting the environment, mergers, the stock market, and pricing, the "imprint is generally pro-business."[18] More often than not, this orientation took the form not of making law by explicit decisions but by making it more difficult for anticorporate groups to bring cases to court.

The election of President Reagan and his appointment of a conservative woman, Sandra Day O'Connor, to the Supreme Court renewed hopes by the political right that the Court would finally move to overturn the initiatives of the Warren years. To date, the overall record has been mixed, but there has been a decided tilt in this direction in the more recent past.

No Supreme Court decision has proved more troubling to the Right than *Roe* v. *Wade* (1973), which gave women the constitutional right to elect to have an abortion any time during the first two trimesters of pregnancy. In spite of a massive political effort to overturn it, the decision still stands. The same can be said for the basic civil-rights decisions of the Warren Court. Indeed, not only has the desegration impulse not been reversed, but the Burger Court upheld the constitutionality of busing as a remedy for school segregation provided that the buses do not cross municipal lines. And the Court extended its understanding of unlawful discrimination to include sex discrimination by state and local governments as a violation.

The Court, however, had decided differences of emphasis with its predecessor in a number of areas. In the domain of criminal procedure, the Burger Court made it possible to introduce some evidence that was illegally seized by police and made it

---

[18]Wayne E. Green, "Supreme Court Shows a Pro-Business Tilt in a Series of Rulings," *Wall Street Journal*, July 1, 1975, pp. 1, 11.

easier for police to stop and search passengers in their cars and in airports without search warrants. In the area of civil rights, it curbed the rights of judges to interfere with seniority systems in order to help minority groups.

Some of the most recent court cases, in the middle 1980s, have been decided in ways that show a sharp conservative tilt in the direction proposed by the Reagan administration. In the term that ended in July 1984, for example, the Court carved out an exception for the first time to the *Miranda* rule that requires the police to advise a suspect in custody of his or her rights against self-incrimination before any questioning may begin. The Court ruled in *New York* v. *Quarles* that "overriding considerations of public safety" may justify immediate questioning without first giving the suspect warnings against self-incrimination. It also held in other decisions that prisoners were not protected in their cells against search and seizure and have no constitutional right to visits from friends and family. And it found that illegally seized evidence may be used in immigration proceedings.[19]

In other areas, in this term the Burger Court supported the federal government's position that it need not consider the environmental concerns of coastal states when it awards oil and gas leases for sale on the outer continental shelf; it reinstated a ban on travel to Cuba; and it weakened the divide between church and state by ruling that a city may include a Nativity scene as part of an official, tax-supported Christmas display.[20]

In 1986, Reagan appointed conservatives William H. Rehnquist, as Chief Justice, and Antonin Scalia to the Court. While the effects of this remain to be seen, Reagan succeeded even more dramatically in recasting the character of the federal judiciary at lower levels. If the current rate of appointments continues, he will have appointed a majority of lower federal court judges by the beginning of 1988, thus completing a shift from a predominantly Democratic to a conservative Republican bench. During his first term alone, President Reagan appointed 130 district court judges, of a total of 506; and he selected 31 of 123 regional appeals court judges.[21]

There is nothing new about presidents trying to shape the

[19] *Hudson* v. *Palmer; Block* v. *Rutherford; INS* v. *Lopez-Mendoza.*
[20] *Secretary of Interior* v. *California: Regan* v. *Wald; Lynch* v. *Donnelly.*
[21] *Congressional Quarterly Almanac,* 98th Congress, 2nd Session, 1984, p. 243.

judiciary by making a significant number of appointments. Fully one in three of currently sitting federal judges were appointed by President Carter. He made his main aim that of adding a significant number of women and minority judges. Blacks accounted for 16 percent of his appointees, and women for 20 percent.

Most of these appointees were political liberals, but many moderate conservatives were also selected by President Carter to serve on the bench. The Reagan administration, by contrast, has used the most systematic ideological screening of judicial candidates in the past half century. The results have been quite dramatic.

Consider the federal appeals court for the District of Columbia. Widely regarded as the country's most important court after the Supreme Court, the D.C. Circuit has undergone a transformation in orientation.

Eleven judges serve on this court. President Carter appointed four: Abner Mikva, a former liberal Democratic member of Congress from Illinois; Harry Edwards, a liberal University of Michigan law professor; Ruth Bader Ginsburg, a politically moderate feminist law professor from Columbia University; and Patricia Wald, a political centrist who had been an assistant attorney general. In his first term, President Reagan selected three conservatives to sit on this bench: Kenneth Starr, a former justice department aide; Antonin Scalia, a University of Chicago law professor; and Robert Bork, who, as President Nixon's solicitor general, fired the Watergate special prosecutor at the behest of the president after two of his superiors had declined to do so.

The new judges have begun to make a considerable difference to the decisions of the court. Even though the full court has a 6 to 5 liberal majority, most of its cases are heard by three-judge panels in which the conservatives often find they have the controlling majority. Such has been the case in a number of important instances. In 1982, for example, Judge Bork ruled that the Food and Drug Administration has broad leeway in evaluating the risks of food additives. Judge Mikva dissented, referring to the FDA's "disgraceful" record. Two years later, the court found that defendents who claim insanity may be examined by court psychiatrists without their lawyers being present. The dissent denounced the court's "failure to protect the rights of defendents." Later that year, Judge Bork wrote a decision that denied the right of privacy to homosexuals serving in the armed forces.

The Court as policymaker

More than two decades ago, political scientist Robert Dahl argued perceptively that the Supreme Court is involved in the making of public policy. It is called upon to select between competing policies in areas of wide disagreement. Who benefits, he asked, from this role of the Court? He concluded, after an examination of cases where federal legislation was found unconstitutional by the Court, that "the main task of the Court is to confer legitimacy on the fundamental policies" of the dominant coalition of groups and interests in control of the national regime:

> Except for short-lived transitional periods when the old alliance is disintegrating and the new one is struggling to take control of political institutions, the Supreme Court is inevitably a part of the dominant national alliance. As an element in the political leadership of the dominant alliance, the Court, of course, supports the major policies of the alliance. By itself, the Court is almost powerless to affect the course of national policy.[22]

In the few instances, such as *Dred Scott* and attempts to reject New Deal legislation, when the Court sought to make policy against the wishes of the dominant governing classes, it paid a heavy price in terms of its autonomy and prestige.

A recent empirical test by political scientist Richard Funston bears out these claims. Examining the 168 laws found to be unconstitutional by the Court within four years of their passage by the Congress in the period from 1801, when Chief Justice Marshall was appointed, to 1969, when Chief Justice Warren retired, he found that the Court's pattern of rejecting legislation was not random. Rather, "over long periods of time, the Supreme Court reflects the will of the dominant political forces." In stable periods of electoral alignments, the Court strikes down national legislation far less frequently than it does during periods of partisan upheaval and electoral realignment, periods which are usually also marked by major social and economic changes in the society. During realignment periods, the Court is about three times as likely to strike down federal legislation; and more of the legislation that it does find unconstitutional had been passed in the four preceding years.[23]

One lesson of this finding is that it is a mistake to equate an activist Court with a liberal Court, and a restrained Court with a conservative one. Rather, as law professor Philip Kurland has suggested, "An 'activist' court is essentially one that is out of step with the legislative or executive branches of the government. It will thus be 'liberal' or 'conservative' depending upon which role its prime antagonist has adopted."[24]

Even in the long periods when the Court is in tune with the policy orientations of the president and the Congress, however, it still helps shape public policy. Above all, it stamps its label of constitutional legitimacy on controversial legislation. The Voting Rights Act of 1965, for example, which struck down barriers to black voting in the South, was quickly brought to the Court for a constitutional test; the Court upheld the act. In economic matters, the Court has provided "nonpolitical" approval and indispensable support for such basic features of the economy as private property, contracts, and the regulatory activities of government. It follows, Dahl wrote,

> that within the somewhat narrow limits set by the basic policy goals of the dominant alliance, the Court *can* make national policy. Its discretion, then, is not unlike that of a powerful committee chairman in Congress who cannot, generally speaking, nullify the basic policies substantively agreed on by the rest of the leadership, but who can, within these limits, often determine important questions of timing, effectiveness, and subordinate policy. Thus the Court is least effective against a current lawmaking majority—and evidently least inclined to act. It is most effective when it sets the bounds of policy for officials, agencies, and state governments or even regions, a task that has come to occupy a very large part of the Court's business.[25]

By constitutionally standing apart from the elected branches, the Supreme Court is cast in the role of the protector of minority

---

[23]Richard Funston, "The Supreme Court and Critical Elections," *The American Political Science Review* LXIX (September 1975): 796, 806.
[24]Philip B. Kurland, *Politics, the Constitution, and the Warren Court* (Chicago, 1970), pp. 17–18.
[25]Dahl, p. 294.

rights and opinions in the face of popular pressures. But here, we shall see in the next section, the Court's record is mixed, as is that of the justice system more generally.

LAW AND SOCIETY

The law and the legal system have an autonomy and logic of their own. Liberal legal systems like our own depend on a conception of citizenship, rights, and predictable, open procedures. Only in a minority of the world's countries may such a legal system be said to exist. In some societies, as in Latin America's Chile or Eastern Europe's Czechoslavakia, formal legal orders exist but they are wholly controlled by the state apparatus for its own purposes. Citizen rights exist only by suffrance of the authorities. In South Africa, liberal legal codes and formalities are used to manipulate a racist society and ensure legal rights for whites only.

Even in a liberal democracy such as England "the police can arrest you on no more than 'reasonable suspicion' that you have committed a crime. If you are arrested, the police officer in charge of your case may deny your request to see a lawyer on the ground that this would impede the progress of the investigation. You may be held incommunicado by the police for interrogation up to thirty-six hours. . . . If you are poor there is no guarantee you will be assigned a lawyer, unless the case is one of some gravity."[26]

By contrast, the American legal system comes much closer to the ideals of rights, fair procedure, and equal protection under the law. The achievements of the American justice system in these central respects make even more striking the moments when the justice system is used to quash political opposition that has operated outside the usual boundaries of party politics, elections, and interest-group competition; and it makes very stark the unequal access to legal protection and rights embedded in the routine operation of the criminal justice system. Let us examine these issues in turn.

[26]Graham Hughes, "We Try Harder," *New York Review of Books,* March 14, 1985, p. 17.

The most important legal basis for recent political prosecutions is conspiracy. Conspiracy laws make it a crime to conspire to commit certain acts, whether or not the acts are carried out. Conspiracy, legal scholar Herbert Packer has noted, is the "shabbiest weapon in the prosecutor's arsenal" because "it is what is referred to as an 'inchoate crime.' It does not require proof that anyone did anything illegal, but only that he intended to commit a crime, or . . . that he 'agreed' to commit a crime."[27]

Throughout the nineteenth century, conspiracy laws were routinely used to prevent workers from organizing unions. In the landmark cases of the *Boot and Shoemakers of Philadelphia* in 1806 and the *Journeymen Cordwainers of New York* in 1811, workers were convicted of the charge of criminal conspiracy for trying to organize a union. Today, most union activity is protected by law. But conspiracy laws are still on the books. In the late 1960s and early 1970s especially, when social unrest was high, antiwar activists and black militants were prosecuted by the government for conspiracy.

To name only some of the more celebrated cases: In 1968, five well-known antiwar spokesmen, including Dr. Benjamin Spock and the Reverend William Sloane Coffin, were tried for conspiracy to counsel, aid, and abet violations of the Selective Service law and to hinder administration of the draft. Only one defendant (Marcus Raskin) was acquitted. In 1969, eight radical activists were tried for conspiracy under an amendment to the Civil Rights Act of 1968 that made it a crime to cross state lines with the *intent* to incite a riot. They were charged with conspiring to create disorder at the 1968 Democratic party convention in Chicago. Six (including Black Panther Bobby Seale, Tom Hayden, and Abbie Hoffman) were convicted. And in 1970, Manhattan's district attorney charged 21 members of the Panthers with conspiracy to blow up department stores, the Statue of Liberty, and other public targets. They were acquitted; eventually the convictions of the draft and Chicago cases were reversed on appeal.

The Justice Department knew that most of its cases were weak. In this respect, the 1973 trial, held in Gainesville, Florida, of seven antiwar veterans (and an eighth supporter) on charges of having conspired to assault the 1972 Republican national convention with automatic weapons, slingshots, and crossbows was typi-

---

[27]Noam Chomsky et al., eds., *Trials of the Resistance* (New York, 1970), p. 173.

cal. After a month-long trial, the jury took only three hours to bring in its verdict of not guilty. "They had nothing on those boys," a juror remarked afterwards.[28] The prosecution of this conspiracy case and others was not aimed primarily at conviction, but at disrupting and harassing radical activity. Conspiracy trials take a long time; they keep radicals away from their activities; they cost a good deal of money; and they provide others with a symbolic warning of what might be in store for them. The cases were brought not to uphold the conspiracy laws, but to crush opposition through legal means.

In virtually all of these trials, moreover, evidence revealed how thoroughly the government had sought to use its police powers to infiltrate radical organizations. The Gainesville veterans' group had been infiltrated by undercover police officers; in one case, where five priests were accused of raiding the offices of a New Jersey draft board, the judge told the jury it could acquit because "of overreaching participation by government agents or informers."[29]

Conspiracy laws and trials, of course, are not the only means of overt political repression. Some laws are explicitly directed at political opposition.[30] In 1940, Congress passed the Alien Registration Act (Smith Act), which made it illegal to teach or advocate the overthrow of the government of the United States by force, or to organize groups or publish materials for that purpose. Conspiring to commit these acts was also made a crime. A decade later, the Internal Security Act (McCarran Act) was passed. This act established a Subversive Activities Control Board that was to hold hearings to determine whether certain organizations were "Communist." If they were found to be, they were required to register with the attorney general, disclose their sources of funding and expenditures, and give the names and addresses of their officers. Members of organizations identified by the board as Communist were forbidden to work in defense plants, apply for or use a passport, or hold nonelective federal jobs. These acts and numerous others passed

[28] *New York Times,* September 9, 1973.
[29] *Ibid.*
[30] Much of the following discussion is drawn from Alan Wolfe, *The Seamy Side of Democracy: Repression in America* (New York, 1973).

by the federal and state governments were aimed to suppress not the actions of individuals or groups, but the expression of their opinions and their ability to organize.

These laws were passed in the heyday of the cold war. Up to the early 1960s, the Supreme Court consistently held that the anti-Communist legislation was constitutional; in 1961, for example, the Court found in favor of the government, which had prosecuted individuals under the Smith Act for "knowing membership" in the Communist party. But as the cold war began to ease, as the Kennedy, Johnson, and Nixon administrations pursued a policy of détente with the Soviet Union, the Supreme Court began to find many aspects of these laws unconstitutional. As one judicial scholar noted, "The dominant lesson of our history in the relation of the judiciary to repression is that courts love liberty most when it is under pressure least."[31]

Very few laws are overtly repressive. But a great many can be used for repressive purposes. For example, immigration and deportation laws, which define the attributes of citizenship, were often used in the past to exclude and deport political activists. In the case of *Fong Yue Ting* v. *The United States* (1893), the Supreme Court found that the federal government's right to expel foreigners who had not become naturalized citizens "is as absolute and unqualified as the right to prohibit their entrance into the country." Leaders of the radical trade union, Industrial Workers of the World, were deported in the early 1920s as undesirables. Deportation has since been used retroactively; people who had joined the Communist party when membership was legal were deported after passage of the Smith Act in 1950.

Indeed, virtually any law, however innocuous, can provide the basis for the repression of political opposition. In the late 1960s, the police in Oakland, California, enforced traffic regulations much more strictly against members of the Black Panthers, a radical nationalist organization, than the general public in order to keep Panthers off the streets and to make them conscious that they were likely to be stopped and searched regularly. A fund-raising party for the Marxist W. E. B. DuBois Club held in Manhattan in

[31]John P. Frank, cited in Redford et al., p. 554.

1966 was raided by narcotics police who claimed to be searching
for drugs:

> All the young people were held for fifteen hours by the police, then
> charged and cleared for arraignment. As there were no narcotics
> present (the DuBois Club, the group's infiltrator must have informed
> the police, was opposed to the use of drugs), the charges were even-
> tually dismissed. No convictions were seriously entertained. The
> purpose of the raid was just one of nuisance.[32]

The existence of many laws prohibiting certain forms of conduct,
in short, makes it possible for police and prosecutors to use their
wide enforcement discretion to establish limits of legitimate political action. As an analysis of legal repression concluded, "Laws exist
in a political context. . . . The existence of a government of laws
and not men is sometimes praised, but when the laws are used by
the men to preserve their own power, the law itself becomes the
problem."[33]

    The leading law enforcement agency in the United States, the
Federal Bureau of Investigation (FBI), became the problem when
it undertook a campaign of harassment and unrelenting surveillance of civil rights leader Martin Luther King, Jr. One month
before King was assassinated, a memo from FBI headquarters to
field offices on March 4, 1968, expressed the fear that King might
become a "black messiah." Stating that one of the goals of its
counterintelligence operation was to prevent the rise of such a
"messiah," the memo went on to say that "King could be a very
real contender for this position should he abandon his supposed
'obedience' to 'white, liberal doctrines' (nonviolence) and embrace
black nationalism."[34]

    The FBI had been watching King since the late 1950s. A few
years later, after FBI Director J. Edgar Hoover wrongly informed
President John Kennedy and Attorney General Robert Kennedy
that King's Southern Christian Leadership Conference had many
communists in its leadership, the attorney general authorized the
bureau to wiretap King's phone conversations. Taps were installed

[32]Wolfe, p. 96.
[33]*Ibid.*, pp. 101–02.
[34]David Wise, "The Campaign to Destroy Martin Luther King," *The New York Review of Books,* November 11, 1976, p. 38.

on King's phones at home, in sixteen hotel rooms where King stayed, and in SCLC headquarters in Atlanta and New York. In fall 1964 the FBI told reporters that it had uncovered evidence that King had had extramarital affairs; the FBI coupled these unsupported claims with the old, equally unsupported, claims that King was under communist control. When this campaign failed to discredit King, Hoover told the press in November 1974 that King is "the most notorious liar in the country." Three days after this attack, the FBI mailed an anonymous letter and a tape of the alleged hotel room bugs to King and to his wife Coretta. The letter read:

> King, there is only one thing left for you to do. You know what it is. You have just 34 days in which to do it. This exact number has been selected for a specific reason. It has definite practical significance. You are done.

The letter was mailed three weeks before King was scheduled to receive the Nobel Peace Prize in Norway. As journalist David Wise observes, "Since it was accompanied by a tape which the FBI considered compromising, the letter could be interpreted as an invitation for King to kill himself."[35] More petty harassment continued until King's assassination.

On some occasions, the justice system may abandon the principle of legal equality altogether. The response of the criminal courts to the ghetto rebellions of the 1960s is a case in point.

The rebellions were seen at the time as profoundly threatening to authorities, since their targets of white-owned property and the police were the most visible symbols of economic legitimacy and public authority. It thus appeared that a *structural* challenge was being mounted against existing patterns of dominance. The justice system reacted by defending those arrangements *at the expense of formal legal protections*.

The police acted to contain and subdue the disorders, often quite ruthlessly and with unnecessary brutality. In New Jersey, the Governor's Select Commission on Civil Disorder, for example, concluded that "the amount of ammunition expended by police forces was out of all proportion to the mission assigned them . . . this reflects a pattern of police action for which there is no possible

[35] *Ibid.*, pp. 39–42.

justification."[36] This behavior was quite consistent with the more routine pattern of police abuses, which, as we have seen, usually stem from what police see as direct threats to their authority. The greater the threat, the greater the likelihood that the police will act without reference to formal legal restraints.

The same proved true of the criminal courts, whose behavior unmistakably betrayed a commitment to civil order first and to formal standards of legality only secondarily.

Jerome Skolnick studied the judicial response to racial violence in Detroit, Newark, Washington, D.C., Baltimore, and Chicago. In all these cities, the "constitutional right to bail was almost invariably replaced by what in effect was a policy of preventive detention." In Detroit, the twelve judges who heard the rebellion cases agreed at a meeting on the second day of the violence to set bonds averaging $10,000, a sum very much higher than most of the defendants could afford. In violation of routine legal procedure, the high bail policy in all of the cities was "applied uniformly— ignoring the nature of the charge, family and job status of those arrested, the prior record, and all other factors usually considered in the setting of bail."[37]

The judges thus deliberately put aside the canons of formal legality to keep their prisoners incarcerated until structural stability was restored. The imperatives of social control overrode their commitment to legality and justice. In reply to a reporter who questioned the constitutionality of high bail, Chicago's chief judge said, "What do you want me to do—cry crocodile tears for people who take advantage of their city?" In Detroit, a criminal-court judge justified his actions by arguing, "We had no way of knowing whether there was a revolution in progress or whether the city was going to be burned down or what."[38]

These examples of the use of the law to uphold the political and social order at the price of suspensions of legal rights and procedures help show that even in a justice system that is as formally autonomous and nonpolitical as any in the world the law is never entirely a world apart from society.

[36]Governor's Select Commission on Civil Disorder of New Jersey, *Report for Action,* in Theodore Becker and Vernon Murray, eds., *Government Lawlessness in America* (New York, 1971), p. 4.

[37]Jerome Skolnick, "Judicial Response in Crisis," in *ibid.,* pp. 161–62.

[38]*Ibid.,* pp. 164, 162.

The intertwined relationships between law and society provide possibilities for political movements that seek social change. Without the National Association for the Advancement of Colored People, there would have been no *Brown* v. *Board of Education;* and without the women's movement there would have been no *Roe* v. *Wade* (1973) and *Doe* v. *Bolton* (1973), which upheld a pregnant woman's right to choose abortion. Indeed, the history litigation by environmental groups and advocates of consumer protection have reshaped the activities of governments and corporations in these areas.

CRIMINAL JUSTICE

Almost all of us are criminals at one time or another. Nine in ten Americans, a presidential crime commission found in the 1960s, had acted in ways which made them liable to receive prison or jail sentences. But most Americans do not go to jail. The criminal justice system pays selective attention to crime, concentrating on the violent crimes of homicide, rape, and assault, and on crimes committed for the purpose of obtaining money or property. Fully seven-eighths of the FBI-Index crimes are robbery and burglary, crimes against property.

There is a greal deal of crime committed in the United States. Each year one in ten Americans is a victim of some crime; and two in ten are the victims of a serious crime. Over the period of a decade, the chances are one in five that any American will be the victim of a serious crime, and most Americans are closely acquainted with serious crime victims. These chances increase dramatically if a person is poor or black.

There is also much less visible white-collar crime. Tax evasion, embezzlement, price fixing, and consumer fraud are often overlooked, but they are much more profitable than crimes that command most police and media attention.

> Illicit gains from white-collar crime far exceed those of all other crime combined. . . . One corporate price-fixing conspiracy criminally converted more money each year than all of the hundreds of thousands of burglaries, larcenies, or thefts in the entire nation dur-

ing those same years. Reported bank embezzlements cost ten times more than bank robberies each year.[39]

The more visible crimes against people and property are the chief business of the criminal justice complex, while, more often than not, white-collar criminals are dealt with by private auspices— "private psychiatric and counseling assistance often supplant prosecution."[40] Even in the "classes of offenses committed by rich and poor equally, it is rarely the rich who end up behind bars."[41]

It is important to recognize that conditions in contemporary America make crime particularly attractive and accessible. Poor blacks confined to the small-capital sector of the economy often find that crime brings higher financial rewards and higher group status than they could ever hope to achieve otherwise and even, as in numbers-running, carries relatively low risks of apprehension and conviction. Many illegal activities run by organized crime— drug traffic, gambling, prostitution—are "consensual crimes . . . desired by the consuming public."[42] The goods and services provided by organized crime are not only desired, they are in great demand; and profits are high. And corporate white-collar crime is consistent with the logic of profit of corporate capitalism.

The basic difference between the kinds of crime people commit is largely due to the opportunities presented them. Ghetto residents do not have easy access to jobs in large corporations, to relatively unobtrusive patterns of communication, or to paper transactions involving large sums of money. Moreover, poor-people's crimes, economist David Gordon notes, are much more apt to be violent because of the selectivity of the criminal justice complex. He notes that it is only natural

> that those who run the highest risks of arrest and conviction may have to rely on the threat or commission of violence in order to protect themselves. . . . Completely in contrast, corporate crime does not require violence because it is ignored by the police; corporate criminals can safely assume that they do not face the threat of

[39]Ramsey Clark, *Crime in America* (New York, 1970), p. 38.

[40]David Gordon, "Class and the Economics of Crime," *Review of Radical Political Economics* 3 (Summer 1971): 54.

[41]Ronald Goldfarb, "Prison: The National Poorhouse," *The New Republic* (November 1969), p. 312.

[42]Clark, p. 68.

jail, and do not therefore have to cover their tracks with the threat of harming those who betray them.[43]

Of course not all white-collar crime is ignored; when the criminal practices of the relatively well-to-do become egregiously offensive in their violation of the law, they must be punished in order to protect the ideological claim that all are equal under the law. But for the most part, the justice system disregards white-collar crime. In the past, much violent and working-class crime was also ignored by the justice system, since those "crimes rarely impinged on the lives of the more affluent. Gambling, prostitution, dope, and robbery seemed to flourish in the slums of the early twentieth century, and the police rarely moved to intervene."[44] As crime has burst out of its traditional slum boundaries, it has become a "crisis." The justice system's concern with crime by subordinates has thus been directly related to the class status of the victims (most crimes, however, are still committed by the poor against the poor).

Indeed, crime and the creation of means to control it have traditionally been problems of boundaries and social control. The origins of modern police forces provide a case in point.

The police

Modern police forces are only just over a century and a half old. They were created quite consciously to protect existing structural arrangements. London's police force, which was the model for American urban police, was the first to be established. Its founding in 1829 was not a response, as sociologist Allan Silver notes, to criminality as such, but to the growth of a destitute underclass in early industrial England that was thought to threaten the social order.

> It was more than a question of annoyance, indignation, or personal insecurity; the social order itself was threatened by an entity whose characteristic name reflects the fears of the time—the "dangerous classes". . . . But even where the term is not explicitly invoked, the image persists—one of an unmanageable, volatile, and convulsively criminal class at the base of society.[45]

[43]Gordon, p. 61.
[44]*Ibid.*, p. 62.
[45]Allan Silver, "The Demand for Order in Civil Society: A Review of Some Themes in the History of Urban Crime, Police, and Riot," in David Bordua, ed., *The Police: Six Sociological Essays* (New York, 1967), p. 3.

Before the creation of the professional, bureaucratic police force, police functions in England were carried out by local property owners who acted as constables. However, as the size of the underclass grew under the impact of industrialization, most large property owners became increasingly vulnerable as direct targets of popular abuse. The agrarian rich responded by attempting to strengthen the private constabulary, but most of the new manufacturers "turned towards a bureaucratic police system that insulated them from popular violence, drew attack and animosity upon itself, and seemed to separate the assertion of 'constitutional' authority from that of social and economic dominance." From the moment of their creation, modern police forces were the officially sanctioned legal enforcers of the prevailing structural arrangements. By their regular presence among all classes, especially the new industrial proletariat, the police permeated society in a way that traditional landed constabularies could not. As one authority noted, "the police penetration of civil society lay not only in its narrow application to crime and violence. In a broader sense, it represented the penetration and continual presence of central political authority throughout daily life."[46]

Individually, the police officer maintains order and tranquility on the beat; collectively, the police act as guardians of the social order as a whole. This structural role is fraught with tension, since, often, the police must *police* a hostile public, and their definition of order and appropriate public behavior may clash with the perspectives of the community. A reporter who spent two years with the Philadelphia police force found that the police interpenetrated poor neighborhoods so completely that they often produced heightened tension, anxiety, and the disruption of neighborhood life:

> The neighborhoods seem to be overflowing with police cars, which give the police an enlarged presence as they pass. Cars are frequently seen whizzing down the street, their sirens blaring and their emergency lights flashing. It is common to see police cars streak down intersections, breaking red lights, running over sidewalks and into alleys. Every day, many times on some days, people walking on the sidewalk see the police converge, jump from their cars with

[46]*Ibid.*, pp. 12–13.

guns drawn, abandoning their cars in the middle of the street, doors open.[47]

In this context, police develop what sociologist Jerome Skolnick calls a working personality. They use a perceptual shorthand of characteristics such as race, dress, language, and gestures to identify in advance those people likely to pose a threat to order on their beat. Thus police often come to see the world as divided between "us" and "them"; anyone identified as one of "them" is likely to be the target of harassment that goes beyond the law. The result is a significant number of what have been called police abuses, a term that is misleading since these "abuses" are an integral part of routine policing.

Police act to preserve their authority even if their actions violate the formal rules under which they operate. After conducting an extensive study into abuses by the New York City police, attorney Paul Chevigny concluded that challenges to police authority are consistently met by "anger and one or more weapons out of the arsenal of legal sanctions from a summons up through summary corporal punishment. Criminal charges, beginning with disorderly conduct and ranging up to felonious assault, are commonly laid to cover the actions of the policeman and to punish the offender." Chevigny found that for most police officers, arrest was equivalent to guilt; hence many arrests are followed by false or misleading testimony by officers in court. "Distortion of the facts becomes the most pervasive and the most significant of abuses. The police ethic justifies any action which is intended to maintain order or to convict any wrongdoer (that is, anyone actually or potentially guilty of a crime)."[48]

This pattern of routine illegal policing to protect police authority is made possible by the extraordinary discretion police have on the job, by the presumption of innocence their actions carry, and by the protective solidarity of police bureaucracies. The officer on the beat, despite the hierarchical proto-military characteristics of police organization, operates virtually without supervision. Police selectively enforce the law by deciding which people to suspect and which laws to enforce (white-collar crimes, as we have seen, and the wealthy are rarely police targets).

[47]Jonathan Rubenstein, *City Police* (New York, 1973), p. 351.
[48]Paul Chevigny, *Police Power* (New York, 1969), pp. 276–77.

In a police officer's world of "us" and "them," the only completely trustworthy people are fellow officers. Socially and organizationally isolated from the communities in which they work, the police develop a sense of solidarity and exclusiveness. Thus corrupt officers as well as those who violate the legal rights of citizens are usually protected by their colleagues. The overworked, harassed, possibly authoritarian and racist officer may use unnecessary violence, make illegal arrests, lie in court, and be on the take, but is more likely than not to escape detection outside the precinct work group.

Criminal courts

Once arrested, a defendant becomes enmeshed in the other two institutions of the formal justice complex—criminal courts and prisons. Bail is the first step in the process beyond arrest, and bail practices weigh heavily on the poor. Early Anglo-Saxon law provided for bail because the wait between arrest and trial was often lengthy, and the cost of detention to the sheriff was high. When defendants posted collateral security, they were free pending trial. Virtually the same system operates today, at least in theory.

The Constitution prohibits "excessive bail," yet does not give defendants an absolute right to bail. But it is widely agreed among jurists that since those arrested are formally presumed innocent until proven guilty, defendants should ordinarily be allowed freedom until they are tried. In practice, however, bail is often set at levels higher than defendants can afford. A study in New York found that of all defendants charged with criminal assault, burglary, forgery, larceny, narcotics possession, robbery, and sex crimes, 29 percent were denied bail, and fewer than one-third were granted bail under $1,000.[49] Of those whose bail exceeded $1,000, only about half were able to post bond. As a result of such practices, of the prisoners in local and county jails in the United States *fully half have not been convicted of a crime*. Most are poor and black.[50] The wide discretion available to judges in setting bail is thus routinely

[49]Charles Ares et al., "The Manhattan Bail Project: An Interim Report on the Use of Pre-Trial Parole," in James Klonoski et al., eds., *The Politics of Local Justice* (Boston, 1970), pp. 79, 80, 86.
[50]Herbert Jacob, *Urban Justice* (Englewood Cliffs, N.J., 1973), p. 103.

used to segregate and punish those whom the police identified as guilty and who are too poor to raise bail.

Those who are put in jail because they are unable to make bail are treated exactly like convicted prisoners and for no inconsiderable period of time: a wait of up to six months is common. Perhaps most importantly, they are placed at a great disadvantage in terms of their defense, as it is much more difficult to prepare a defense in jail than out. As political scientist Herbert Jacob notes, "Even if one receives assigned counsel or is defended by a public defender, one cannot personally round up witnesses and assist the attorney in interviewing them."[51] As the classic study on bail in New York City revealed, there is a demonstrable relationship between being detained in jail awaiting trial and the likelihood of having to go to prison after the trial. Almost half of those freed pending trial were either found innocent or spared prison sentences, while over 90 percent of those detained while awaiting trial were found guilty and sentenced to prison. The latter group not only were more likely to be convicted but they automatically forfeited their chance of probation after conviction. One of the basic conditions of probation is that the individual be employed; but it was hardly likely that those imprisoned pending trial could have kept their jobs. The class bias of policing procedures is thus reinforced by the administration of bail and parole.

The vast majority of criminal cases never come to trial. In almost all American cities fewer than 10 percent of felony cases go to trial, and in some this figure is under 2 percent. Most of the other cases are resolved by the defendant pleading guilty, often as the outcome of a process known as plea bargaining.

Defendants are often charged with multiple crimes, some involving much more serious penalties than others. As a result, prosecutors have the leeway to negotiate with defendants: in exchange for a plea of guilty on the lesser charge, the others are dropped. Where there is only one charge against the defendant, the prosecutor offers to argue for a reduced sentence in exchange for a guilty plea. The extent of discretion available to prosecutors is not specified by law; hence they are free to act as *de facto* judges who make the critical decisions about innocence, guilt, and length of sentences.

[51]Herbert Jacob, *Justice in America* (Boston, 1972), p. 170.

One spectacular case of plea bargaining involved former Vice President Spiro Agnew. In October 1973, Agnew resigned his office and, in a Baltimore courtroom, pleaded "no contest" to a government charge of income-tax evasion. This plea was the outcome of elaborate bargaining between the vice president and the Justice Department, which had uncovered evidence that Agnew, a former Baltimore County executive and Maryland governor, had extorted bribes from state contractors for almost a decade. Had he been charged and convicted of all the crimes the prosecutors alleged he committed (Agnew has consistently maintained his innocence) he might have gone to prison for many years; instead, in exchange for his plea; the government settled for a sentence of three years of unsupervised probation and a $10,000 fine.

Most defendants are not nearly as well known, of course, and plea bargaining for them is much more routine. Generally, the formal adversary confrontation between prosecutor and the defendant's lawyer is a meeting of unequals. Most defendants in urban criminal courts are represented by court-employed public defenders or lawyers from private agencies like the Legal Aid Society. Many of these lawyers are well intentioned but have little experience in criminal law. They are usually just out of law school and have had virtually no courtroom experience. They lack funds to investigate the police-prosecutor version of events; since most cases do not even get to court, it is this version that serves as the basis for the terms of the bargain. Counsel may be assigned to the defendant many days after the arrest and pretrial imprisonment; by then, the defendant may have made an incriminating statement to the police or prosecutor that may be inadmissible as courtroom evidence but is damaging in the plea-bargaining process. And the public defender's or Legal Aid lawyer's caseload may be so heavy that there is almost no time to prepare for the confrontation with the prosecutor.

Plea bargaining has considerable advantages for the permanent members of the criminal justice system. It permits an extraordinarily high rate of conviction (sometimes even in cases where the evidence would be insufficient for a jury-trial conviction), which enhances prosecutors' law-and-order reelection appeals and helps police officers win promotions. It relieves prosecutors from having to prepare cases for trial, and it lightens and simplifies the judges' workload, since all they need do is ratify decisions reached by prosecutors and defendants' lawyers. In short, although some defendants may gain lighter sentences from the plea-bargaining process, the arrangement is much more likely to benefit the justice establishment.

Without the cooperation of criminal-court judges, plea bargaining could not exist. Judges who are supposed to be neutral arbiters of courtroom proceedings become accomplices in the inequitable dispensation of justice by permitting their courtrooms to be used at critical junctures. They "cooperate by imposing harsher sentences on defendants convicted after a trial than on those who plead guilty, by maintaining predictable decision patterns according to which defense and prosecutor can calculate their own actions, and by supporting requests for delay, plea and sentence made by prosecutors."[52]

It is often rightly observed that the behavior of criminal-court judges is limited by the actions of police, the size of their caseloads, deals worked out between prosecutors and defense lawyers, and administrative procedures beyond their control. Nevertheless, judges are the gatekeepers of the system of formal criminal justice. They not only legitimate plea bargaining but they also have the power to schedule cases, set bail, dismiss charges, admit evidence, influence juries (in the small proportion of cases that come to trial), and sentence with wide discretion.

Criminal-court judges are selected by a wide array of differing procedures. These include a "merit" procedure by which a governor appoints from a list of nominees compiled by a nonpartisan committee and selection by either the state legislature or local city councils. In most states, however, judges are chosen either through judicial elections or by governors and mayors. In both cases, public information is limited, and devotion to a political party is a more important test than legal competence.

Judicial elections rarely evoke much public controversy or attention. Since it is against judicial ethics to campaign with great vigor, the candidates' campaigns usually lack issues or colorful personalities. As a result, the candidate nominated by the area's majority party is overwhelmingly likely to win. Securing the party's nomination is tantamount to election.

Appointment to the bench, likewise, is a procedure that is

[52]Jacob, *Justice in America,* p. 104.

hardly subject to much popular control. Because the population processed by the courts is relatively powerless, and because they are often nonparticipants in the electoral system and thus do not threaten local politicians in any way, criminal-court judgeships give party organizations the opportunity to reward loyal lawyers at almost no political cost. And in return for appointing friends to the bench, local politicians gain privileged access to the courts, opportunities to make more patronage appointments in auxiliary court personnel, and significant sums of money.

The jury   The size of juries differs from state to state. In some, only six people serve in minor cases and twelve in major cases; in other states, twelve jurors are required in all cases. But everywhere, the composition of juries is likely to be unrepresentative. Businessmen and professionals tend to be much overrepresented, workers and minority groups much underrepresented. In Baltimore, for example, a study found that "professionals, managers and proprietors constituted only 18.7 percent of the population but contributed 40.2 percent of the jurors. . . . At the same time 41.4 percent of the population were working-class people but only 13.4 percent of the jurors were blue-collared."[53]

Procedures for the selection of juries make equal representation nearly impossible. In almost all cases, jurors are selected from lists of registered voters; but the poorer a person is, the less likely he or she is to register to vote. Many states excuse women from jury duty. Since jurors get paid for service, commissioners in small localities often use jury duty as a focus of patronage and choose friends and acquaintances to serve. On the other hand, a juror's pay is usually lower than a typical worker can earn in a day's work; hence many blue-collar workers who would lose wages ask to be excused on grounds of financial hardship. White-collar workers, by contrast, often continue to be paid while they serve. Class bias is thus built into the jury system. Finally, those previously convicted of a crime are ineligible for jury duty.

Sentencing   Conviction by a jury may result in vastly different consequences for different defendants, depending on the sentence handed out by the presiding judge. There are wide disparities in the way this discretion is used. During the Vietnam War, for ex-

[53]Edwin S. Mills, "Statistical Study of Occupations of Jurors in a U.S. District Court," *Maryland Law Review* XXII (1962): 205–16, cited in Jacob, *Justice in America*, p. 124.

ample, offenders against Selective Service regulations were usually given probation in Oregon, and five year terms in Texas. In rape cases in Maryland, one study has shown that the average prison sentence for a black convicted of raping a black was about four years; five years when whites raped whites; six years when whites raped blacks; but sixteen years when blacks raped whites. Overall, the average federal prison sentence for whites is eight years; for blacks, eleven.[54] Small drug users of heroin and cocaine are often given long prison terms, but large drug dealers often go free; a state senate committee in New York found that of those "*convicted* (not arrested) for possession of more than one pound of heroin or cocaine 40 percent received no jail sentence at all, and 26 percent received less than one year in jail."[55] Yet the crime of possession of more than one pound of hard drugs in New York carried a maximum penalty of *life imprisonment.* Not surprisingly, many observers have concluded that the temptations open to criminal-court judges because of the discretion they have in sentencing leads some to corruption.

Prisons

A very high proportion of the population of the United States is incarcerated. In 1981, more than 500,000 citizens served time in American federal prisons and in local and county jails, a figure that means of every 100,000 people in the country, 250 were behind bars. Only in South Africa and the Soviet Union is a higher percentage of the population in prison. American rates are three times higher than those in Great Britain or the Federal Republic of Germany.

These jails and prisons house America's most graphic losers. They are dependent on the decisions of others for the basic amenities of their lives and if convicted of a crime, stripped of political rights to vote and hold office. Most have not been convicted of a crime. Many are mentally ill, alcoholic, or addicted to hard drugs. Virtually all are poor, unemployed, ill-educated, and either black or Hispanic. About two-thirds have been in jail before. They are often despised by their fellow citizens.

[54]Calvin J. Larson, *Crime, Justice and Society,* (New York, 1984), p. 275.
[55]Newfield, p. 25.

Their condition of social, economic, and political subordination is reflected in the custodial brutality of American jails. Most rural jails hold inmates convicted of misdemeanors, transients awaiting transfer to other facilities, and people being detained before trial who cannot raise bail. These prisons are usually governed by local county boards and directly controlled by locally elected sheriffs who are also principally responsible for police duties. "The majority of county jails suffer from a perennial lack of funding, from physical neglect, from the absence of any kind of program. Frequently, they fail to meet even the most rudimentary safety and health standards."[56]

At a polar extreme is the large urban jail, such as Rikers Island in New York, Los Angeles' massive jail system, and Chicago's notorious Cook County Jail. More than half of the country's prisoners are held in jails of this type. Most often they are under the control of the chief of police; in some cities they are run by autonomous departments of correction. The overwhelming number of inmates in these jails are pretrial prisoners; 80 percent of the prisoners in Philadelphia have not been convicted of a crime. Without exception, these jails are characterized by overcrowding, brutality, and dehumanizing conditions.

Most jails as well as state and federal prisons in which most convicted felons are housed cage their prisoners in cells. Conditions are unsanitary: many cells lack toilets and sinks and most prisons smell of human excrement. These institutions are understaffed and fail to provide even minimal supervision to guarantee the safety of inmates. Indeed, dormitory conditions in most prisons, overcrowding, and the lack of useful activities and recreational facilities turn prisoners against each other, and inmates develop their own means of control. Robbery, homosexual rape, extortion, and other physical violence are not only tolerated but they are made inevitable by the institution's physical and human organization. For these reasons, when subordinates leave the prisons, they are even more ill-prepared than when they entered to challenge and overcome their subordination effectively. Hence most remain or become criminals. Once arrested, they enter the system of formal criminal justice again, and the cycle comes full circle.

[56]Edith Elizabeth Flynn "Jails and Criminal Justice," in Lloyd Ohlin, ed., *Prisoners in America* (New York, 1973), p. 59.

political participa-tion and represen-tation

after community, the events that occurred in Lowell in the 1840s were replicated. By the end of the nineteenth century, as the Western frontier closed, capitalist class divisions overtook an older America of self-employed merchants, artisans, farmers, professionals, and traders.

The impact of these changes on everyday life was overwhelming. In their study of Muncie, Indiana, between 1890 and 1924, sociologists Helen and Robert Lynd documented the massive shift in social relationships that resulted from the development of industrial capitalism. Traditional craft patterns broke down under the impact of machines and assembly-line techniques in the local factories; skilled labor was now unnecessary for most jobs. As self-employed craftsmen and local entrepreneurs were forced out of business, workers' traditional neighborhoods lost their cohesiveness and autonomy. The city as a whole lost its sense of autonomy as well, since most of the urban economic changes were the result of national forces outside the city's control. The businessman, not the independent craftsman, was now at the top of the town's wealth, status, and power hierarchies.[6] In short, the division between the capitalist class and the working class came into being.

People became divided by class not only at the work place but also in their daily lives in the community and in politics. New institutions, including unions and businessmen's associations, developed that became vehicles for the expression and containment of the new structural antagonisms of interest. Unlike regional or religious distinctions, class distinctions underpinned the experience of living in a total, inescapable way.

Tocqueville and Dickens visited an America of *independent* workers; after the Revolution, four out of five workers (excluding slaves) were farmers, artisans, merchants, doctors, traders, small businessmen, lawyers, and craftsmen. Property was a liberating force. Because property, especially land, was distributed relatively equally, it provided a basis for a more substantive level of democracy than any country had known before. In this respect, the United States was truly a revolutionary society. Thomas Jefferson's dream of a dynamic agrarian democracy has been put into practice for white American men (excluding, however, a politically invis-

---

[6]Robert S. Lynd and Helen Merrell Lynd, *Middletown* (New York, 1929).

ible majority of the population, made up of blacks, women, and Indians).

By 1900, however, the independent middle class had declined in size and was replaced by a growing percentage of Americans who did not own their tools of production but sold their labor for a wage. Whereas in 1780, only 20 percent of the work force were paid employees, in 1900, 68 percent were wage earners; the independent middle class had shrunk to less than one-third of all workers.[7]

Today, the demise of the independent property-owning middle class is virtually complete. Fewer than 3 percent of Americans are farm owners, and fewer than 7 percent are self-employed. Thus, with the development of industrial capitalism, ownership of the tools of production has come to divide Americans rather than unite them. As a result of the dual trend of the decline of the independent middlc class and the development of a working-class majority, almost all Americans, excepting those who own and control the means of production, work for a wage. Of course, their conditions of work, the size of their pay packets, and their life chances differ enormously. But their shared condition as wage earners makes them dependent on the opportunities made available to them in their local labor markets, and it makes the skilled engineer as well as the dishwasher vulnerable to the threat and actuality of unemployment.

The decline of the independent middle class was no accident. Rather, it was required by the development of industrial capitalism. Mass production had two effects: one was to force independent craftsmen and entrepreneurs out of business; the second was to standardize the labor force. As factories grew rapidly in size at the turn of the century, working conditions became more uniform and impersonal. Technological innovations mechanized work and undermined the need for skilled craftsmen. In the automobile industry, for example, skilled mechanics and work gangs were replaced by semiskilled assembly-line workers. The skills needed in one industry became similar to those needed in others. As a result, workers no longer needed to have very specialized skills that took

---

[7]Michael Reich, "The Evolution of the United States Labor Force," in Richard C. Edwards, Michael Reich, Thomas E. Weisskopf, eds., *The Capitalist System: A Radical Analysis of American Society* (Englewood Cliffs, N.J., 1972), p. 175.

a long time to learn. Instead, they could be trained on the job in a short period to perform the tasks required in one or another factory or work site. Working people more and more became an indistinguishable mass, people who were units of labor.

WORK

In the past half century, changes in the character of work have been characterized by two main trends: the growth of white-collar (professional, clerical, and sales) employment and the transition to a situation in which most workers produce services rather than goods.

As American industry has continued to mechanize and automate, fewer workers are needed to produce increasing amounts of goods. In 1985, for example, it took fewer than half the Chrysler workers it took just a decade earlier to produce each automobile that rolled off the assembly line. At the same time, the number of white-collar workers within manufacturing corporations has continued to increase. Economist Michael Reich tells us why:

> With the development of far-flung corporate sales and distribution networks and corporate divisions specializing in research and development and overall corporate coordination, more white collar workers—managerial, professional, technical, clerical and sales—are needed.[8]

In high-technology industries—particularly in electronics—scientists, technicians, and engineers comprise the majority of employees. Indeed, two very different fields of white-collar jobs have developed since the Second World War: clerical jobs (two-thirds of which are held by women) and technical and professional jobs. The increase in both types of white-collar employment is linked to the shift in the economy from manufacturing to service occupations.

The word *services* applies to a number of distinct kinds of employment, all of which are expanding. As sociologist Daniel Bell notes, "in the very development of industry there is a necessary

---

[8]Reich, in Edwards, Reich, and Weisskopf, p. 178.

expansion of transportation and of public utilities as auxiliary services in the movement of goods and the increasing use of energy, and an increase in the non-manufacturing but still blue collar force."[9] Thus the first kind of service employment is an integral part of the industrial process. This is not a new service sector.

With the growth of the population and mass consumption of goods, more and more people are involved in the distribution of goods and in the fields of insurance, real estate, and finance. This cluster of activities provides the supportive services needed to keep goods circulating and to provide capital for industrial expansion.

Personal services have also expanded numerically, but their organization has changed. Chains of restaurants, hotels, and automobile garages as well as the entertainment and sports industries carry out functions that were once fulfilled by independent entrepreneurs. Today, the production and distribution of personal services is increasingly in impersonal corporate hands.

The fourth major area of services are those provided by government, including education, health care, and welfare. Government service employment grew more rapidly than work in any other sector between 1945 and 1980; in this decade, in a climate of austerity, the rate of governmental employment growth has slowed.

In the past decade, the shift away from manufacturing to services has accelerated; and the working possibilities of Americans have been affected in a fundamental way by three broad sets of trends:

First, the world economy has been restructured by an information revolution based on high technology. The introduction of computers on a large scale has affected the factory floor through the introduction of the robotization of production, and it has affected the office by changes in the ways in which numbers and words are processed and communicated.

Second, the American economy has experienced a basic regional rearrangement. Especially in the period 1981 to 1984, much of the East and Midwest "deindustrialized." Manufacturing plants closed down in large numbers, some moving to the South and West where there were fewer unions and lower wage rates. This trend was reinforced by an oil boom in Texas, Oklahoma, and Louisiana and by the massive increases in military spending in the first Reagan

---

[9]Daniel Bell, *The Coming of Post-Industrial Society* (New York, 1973), p. 127.

administration whose impact was felt disproportionately in the Sun Belt.

Third, there had developed a large and growing "underground" economy, accounting for about 15 percent of the gross national product. It involves both illegal activities like drug traffic and various cash transactions not reported to tax authorities, as well as low-wage manufacturing, often employing illegal immigrants who provide cheap labor for employers.

These shifts in work and the economy, taken together, have produced a highly differentiated work force, whose members have very different conditions and rewards of work. Moreover, as we will see, the conditions of different groups—blacks, women, union members—have special characteristics. And yet, we would do well not to overstress the differentiation of the work force.

Some observers argue that the class division between capital and labor has been superseded by a more complex, stratified, occupational order in which there are numerous gradings of material rewards, status, and power. A related proposition is that the shift in employment from the production of goods to the production of services has fundamentally transformed American capitalism. Daniel Bell, for one, has suggested that we have entered a new age in which the basic antagonism is not between capitalist and worker in the context of the factory but between the white-collar professional expert and the rest of the population. These views are only partial truths at best. Perhaps most importantly, they overstate the distinctiveness of white-collar and service occupations.

In 1870, there were only 82,200 clerical workers in the whole country (less than 1 percent of the work force). These bookkeepers, secretaries, bank tellers, payroll and postal clerks, and stenographers more often than not had the status of craftsmen and were very well paid. In 1900, economist Harry Braverman reports, "clerical employees of steam railroads and in manufacturing had average annual earnings of $1,011; in the same year the average annual earnings of [blue-collar] workers in these industries was $435 for manufacturing and $548 for steam railroads."[10] The division between the large mass of blue-collar workers and the tiny number of white-collar workers was great. If this gap had continued, the rapid

---

[10]Harry Braverman, "Labor and Monopoly Capital," *Monthly Review* 26 (July–August 1974): 51.

expansion of white-collar clerical work would have been significant indeed.

But the very process of clerical expansion has made office work more and more like blue-collar work. Indeed, according to the Bureau of Labor Statistics, weekly clerical wages today are lower than those for every type of blue-collar work, including unskilled labor. Moreover, clerical work is now depersonalized. It has been stripped of its craft status, routinized, and systematized. The tasks of most clerical workers have come to resemble those of shopfloor workers. Common office tasks have been precisely quantified so that corporate offices may be run as large, efficient machines. The Systems and Procedures Association of America, for example, has published a guide based on information provided by General Electric, the General Tire and Rubber Company, and other enterprises, which presents a standard for office performance: "File drawer, open and close; no selection, .04 minutes; . . . desk drawer, open side drawer of standard desk, .014 minutes," and so on.[11] As sociologist C. Wright Mills concluded in his study of office work, except for hard physical labor, there are few characteristics of blue-collar work that are not also true for at least some white-collar work. "For here, too, the human traits of the individual, from his physique to his psychic disposition, become units in the functionally rational calculations of managers."[12]

Even skilled and professional white-collar work has changed. Engineers, scientists, and technicians have lost their traditional independent craft status. Like manual laborers, they work for others who control the aims and conditions of their labor. Lawyers and doctors—the best-paid and most respected white-collar workers— have also lost a significant amount of their traditional independence. Year after year, a diminishing proportion of lawyers are engaged in their own practices, as a larger number work for big law firms or are employed directly by government or corporations on a salary basis. Similarly, an increasing proportion of doctors work for a salary in large urban research centers, clinics, and hospitals.

Undeniably, the rapid growth in the production and distribution of services has changed American capitalism. But it has not eliminated or transformed the most fundamental distinction be-

[11] *Ibid.,* p. 74.
[12] C. Wright Mills, *White Collar* (New York, 1954), pp. 226–27.

tween capital and labor. Although the content of production has changed, its class character has not. Like factory workers, service workers (both blue and white collar) remain wage earners without control over the means of production or the work process.

THREE HISTORIES

Americans are not a homogeneous lot. In particular, today's working class of wage earners consists of three broad groups, each with its own distinct history, each having entered the industrial work force at different periods of American economic development, and each of which today plays an economic role different from the others. These three groups are blacks and other non-European minorities, white Europeans, and women.

Blacks and other non-European minorities

The experience of America's non-European minorities—blacks, Indians, Asians, and Hispanics—has been considerably different from that of other Americans, including European immigrants. With the notable exception of Indians and some Chicanos, minorities came to the United States for the same reason as European immigrants: to work. But the answers to where and under what circumstances they worked were quite different for the two groups.

The native North American Indian tribes, many of whom were mobile hunters, withstood the attempts made by the New World colonists to force them into dependent labor relationships, including slavery. They resisted agricultural peonage and fought for their lands. South of the Rio Grande, where Indian settlements were dense, the Spanish succeeded in subjugating the Indians economically and in capturing their labor. By contrast, in the territories that eventually became the United States, Indian settlements were sparse and thus difficult to colonize for labor. Instead, a process of genocide drove Indians off their lands to make room for European settlements.

Today, the surviving remnant live on reservations and, increasingly, in middle-size and large cities. Their living conditions are more depressed than those of any other American minority group. Indian unemployment is over 40 percent, and an overwhelming number of those who work have low-paid menial jobs.

In the American South, neither Indian nor white labor was sufficient to meet the demands of large-scale plantation agriculture. Slaves were imported to meet that need. There, as in other parts of the continent, property ownership was largely restricted to whites. "White men, even if from lowly origins and serf-like pasts, were able to own land, property and sell their labor in the free market."[13] Even the most degrading "free labor" jobs of the developing capitalist sectors of the economy were for whites only. Blacks and the other racial minorities were channelled into a secondary labor market that was both noncapitalist and unfree. The correlation between color and "free" work was nearly exact.

After the Civil War, as America rapidly industrialized, the manpower needs of the factories were not filled by newly freed blacks but by white ethnics from Europe:

> American captains of industry *and* the native white proletariat preferred the employment of despised, unlettered European peasants to that of the emancipated Negro population of the South. Low as was the condition and income of the factory labor, his status was that of a free worker.[14]

Black Americans became sharecroppers and tenant farmers on Southern plantations, little removed from their former conditions of slavery.

A similar pattern of work relations was created in the Southwest in the nineteenth century. After the Mexican defeats in the Texas war of independence in 1836 and the Mexican War of 1846 to 1848, a new pool of dependent Mexican labor was available to the colonizers. This work force was usually bound to contractors and landowners in a status little above peonage. Asians, too, especially the Chinese, were contract rather than "free" laborers in the Southwest, where they were used in work gangs to build railroads and mines.

In our discussion of class relations, we emphasized the basic distinction between those who own and control capital and those who sell their labor for a wage. The colonized minorities, however,

---

[13]Robert Blauner, *Racial Oppression in America* (New York, 1972), p. 58.
[14]*Ibid.*, p. 59.

at least until well into the twentieth century, were outside of this class dynamic. Workers in capitalist enterprises, including the European immigrants, worked within the wage system, whereas the minorities filled jobs in the least advanced, most industrially backward sectors of the economy. As a result, sociologist Robert Blauner notes:

> In a historical sense, people of color provided much of the hard labor (and also technical skills) that built up the agricultural base and mineral-transport-communication "infrastructure" necessary for industrialization and modernization, whereas the Europeans worked primarily within the industrialized modern sectors. The initial position of European ethnics while low, was therefore strategic for movement up the economic and social pyramid. The placement of nonwhite groups, however, imposed barrier upon barrier on such mobility, freezing them for long periods of time in the last favorable segments of the economy.[15]

A dual labor market, in which whites are distinguished from nonwhites, continues to exist in the United States at present. Although the following discussion examines the particularities of the black experience, the same general trends hold for Indians and Hispanics.

Black and white economic inequality, which declined in the 1960s and in the first half of the 1970s, has been increasing again for the past ten years. According to U.S. census data, the median black family earned two-thirds of the income of the median white family in 1975; by 1983, however, this gap grew. The median black family in that year earned only 56 percent of the income of the median white family; that is, $14,506 as compared to $25,707.[16] The incomes of the top 20 percent of black workers was $29,100, not much above the average earnings for all white families. "Viewed within the context of the white income distribution," social analyst Norman Fainstein concluded, "about 40 percent of blacks are poor, 40 percent working class, and the remainder middle and upper-middle class."[17]

---

[15] *Ibid.*, p. 62.
[16] U.S. Bureau of the Census, *Statistical Abstract of the United States* (Washington, 1985), table 745.
[17] Norman Fainstein, "The Continuing Significance of Race in the Economic Situation of Black Americans," unpublished ms., September 1985.

Moreover, the higher the wage and prestige of an occupation, the lower the percentage of black workers in that occupation. One in four white men are managers or professionals, versus one in eight blacks. One in five white men are laborers; one in three black men. One in a hundred white women is a domestic; seven in one hundred black women work in private households as maids and in similar jobs. Overall, blacks represent only 5 percent of the country's professionals, but half of its domestics.

The majority of blacks work for small business firms, not the big corporations, or are unemployed (the unemployment rate for blacks has been approximately double the rate for whites in the 1980s). And within the relatively depressed sector of the economy in which most blacks work, a significant amount of discrimination limits blacks to the meanest, lowest-paid, most transient work, or to black service firms that sell goods and services to the ghettoes. A recent study of Chicago's labor market found that 70 percent of small firms did not employ any blacks; of the 30 percent that did, virtually all had a majority of black workers.

In the past two decades some of the great class and economic differences between blacks and whites have gradually been eliminated. One of the clearest indicators of this change can be found in the area of education. In 1970, the average white had finished 12.1 years of schooling; the average black 9.8. By 1983, this gap had virtually closed. Whites now finished 12.6 years of school; blacks 12.2. High school dropout rates for blacks and whites are now virtually the same, at 20 percent of the school population. In 1960, by contrast, 80 percent of blacks failed to complete high school. Further, more young blacks in the middle 1980s hold professional and managerial jobs, and fewer were laborers than only ten years before. Much of this was due to gains achieved by the civil rights movement of the 1960s, which broke barriers to black employment in many corporate and government jobs. However, one ironic result has been a widening of the gap between middle- and lower-income blacks, the latter still being the majority confined to semi-skilled and unskilled jobs, unemployment, or welfare. As a *New York Times* survey noticed in the early 1970s:

> The decade produced the most extensive gains for the most favored segments of black America—the middle class and working class blacks. Blacks who entered the decade with educational and mar-

ketable skills were in a better position generally to exploit the newly created opportunities. . . . Those mired in rural poverty and the urban welfare system derived peripheral benefits of food stamps, improved health care and larger dependency payments, but on the whole remained poor, unskilled, and disaffected.

These deepening divisions created a new generation of haves and have-nots in black America. . . . If middle class blacks complained about the widening gap with whites, lower income blacks bitterly pointed to the widening gap between them and the black middle class.[18]

These trends have accelerated. Thirteen years after noticing this development, a *New York Times* reporter surveyed the situation of the black population of Philadelphia. He found that in this period the most successful 30 percent had achieved economic security and influence in many walks of life, symbolized by the election in 1983 of a black mayor, W. Wilson Goode. Blacks now were located in the top management of such firms as R.M.S. Technologies and the First Pennsylvania Bank; Temple University's Law School had a black Dean, and the University had a black vice president; and the black community had a thriving cultural life, represented by such institutions as the New Freedom Theater, Opera Ebony, and the Arthur Hill Dance Ensemble.

Yet the gap between this successful segment of the black community and the majority of blacks was large and growing. The majority lived in segregated ghettoes, with a high poverty rate (one-third of blacks were in poverty, by federal standards), and high unemployment rates, rising to over 40 percent for young men and women.[19]

This gap mirrored national trends. Between 1967 and 1983, the proportion of black households earning over $35,000 (in 1983 dollars) doubled to 11 percent of the total, while a bigger group, earning less than $10,000, rose to 42 percent of all black households, up 2 percent since 1967. At the bottom of the black community there has emerged a growing underclass, trapped in joblessness, broken homes, and substandard living conditions. For a black youngster in 1986 there was a 50 percent chance of living in poverty and of growing up in a household without a father. One in four

[18]*New York Times*, August 26, 1973.
[19]William K. Stevens, "Philadelphia Blacks: More Get to the Top, but Most Are Low on the Ladder," *New York Times*, March 2, 1986, p. 50.

black births is to a teenager, and almost half of teenagers are out of work. Poor blacks are often the victims of violence. A startling 5 percent of young black men die by murder.[20]

If the growing division in the black community is the most significant trend affecting non-European minorities in this decade, the second most important is the dramatic increase in the number of illegal aliens who now live in the United States. Accurate estimates of their numbers are hard to come by, but a recent informed guess placed this population at approximately 8 million. About 60 percent are Mexicans who crossed the border without being seen; the next largest group is Central and South Americans. These immigrants, who generally come from desperately poor situations, work at very low-status, low-paid jobs. These newcomers live in fear of being caught, rarely use public services, and are targets for gross exploitation. As a group, they have replaced blacks at the bottom of the social structure. Language barriers and their illegal status make resistance or protest virtually impossible.[21]

White Europeans

The United States is a nation of immigrants, most of whom have come from Europe. With the exception of American Indians (the country's real native Americans), virtually all Americans came from overseas, or their ancestors did, no earlier than the seventeenth century. Colonial America was largely settled by Protestant English, French, and Dutch settlers. Their descendants today (sometimes referred to as WASPs, for White-Anglo-Saxon Protestants) do not often think of themselves as immigrants or as an ethnic group. Yet, they too have been an integral part of the massive migration of European ethnics to the United States during the past four centuries. Hence they are included in this discussion of white European workers.

Factory capitalism, however, did not develop during a period of mass Protestant European immigration, but during a period of Catholic and Jewish immigration. Thus, while many white Protestants joined the industrial labor force from the farms and smaller cities of rural America, the newer, late nineteenth and early twen-

---

[20]"A Nation Apart," *U.S. News and World Report,* March 17, 1986, p. 18.
[21]Elizabeth Midgley, "Immigrants: Whose Huddled Masses?" *The Atlantic Monthly,* April 1978, pp. 6–26.

tieth century, European immigrants entered the industrial work force directly. In 1850, 11.5 percent of the population was foreign-born; in 1890, 16.6 percent, a figure that remained roughly constant until the passage of restrictive immigration legislation in the early 1920s. Major industrial centers were mosaics of numerous distinct ethnic communities.

In late nineteenth-century America, class and ethnicity inter-penetrated each other. Before 1880, when the large-scale migration from Southern and Eastern Europe began, the members of the newly developing working class consisted of the following basic ethnic elements: (1) native-born white Protestant artisans who continued to work in handicraft industries that predated the American revolution; (2) a small number of white native-born farmers who came to the cities and factories of the Northeast instead of joining the larger migration westward to new agricultural lands; (3) skilled Northern European immigrants—German, French, English, Welsh, and Scotch-Irish—who had craft occupations in the new factories; and (4) Irish and Chinese peasants who "were propertyless in the historical sense of possessing neither capital nor land, as well as in the modern sense of possessing no skills that would give them status within the industrial system."[22] Most were employed in railway construction, which required large numbers of unskilled laborers.

As the economy developed in the late nineteenth century, work that had been done by skilled mining, textile, and steel workers could now be done by unskilled workers tending machines. The massive migration from Southern and Eastern Europe brought the millions of unskilled workers needed to staff the developing corporate industries. In 1880, only 4 percent of the miners in the coal fields of eastern Pennsylvania were from Southern or Eastern Europe; but as the coal industry was mechanized and skill levels were reduced, immigrant workers poured into the mines from Italy, Poland, Russia, Czechoslovakia, Austria, Hungary, and Lithuania. Similar changes in the work force occurred in textile, iron, and steel plants. By 1900, the new ethnic immigrants provided the core of productive factory labor.

As more and more factory jobs became unskilled and were filled by the white-ethnic immigrants from Southern and Eastern

[22]Stanley Aronowitz, *False Promises* (New York, 1973), p. 146.

Europe, native-born and Northern European skilled workers established formidable craft-union barriers to protect their jobs from incursion by the rest of the labor force. Especially by the use of separate seniority lists, unskilled workers were barred from skilled jobs even when they accumulated company seniority. Until the 1930s, in many industries only the skilled workers were represented by trade unions; the unskilled remained without union protection.

Hence, at least until the late 1930s, there was little occupational mobility available to the newer ethnic immigrants who had joined the industrial work force at the bottom rungs. There were exceptions—mainly Jewish and Greek—who had arrived with experience as artisans and proprietors that facilitated their entry into small business as owners. The great bulk of Catholic immigrants, on the other hand, had no such entrepreneurial preparation.

Most of the newer ethnic immigrants were peasants from societies that were sharply stratified along hierarchical, semifeudal lines. The inheritance of semifeudal social relations was a major factor in fragmenting the developing industrial working class and in dividing workers from each other. As sociologist Stanley Aronowitz has noted:

> Contrary to the commonly held belief that the success of our economic development has been due, in large measure, to the absence of a feudal past, it is evident that the genius of American capital consisted in its ability to incorporate the institutions of rank and obligation, the separation of mental and physical labor, the distinction between town and country, and the authority relations that marked feudalism. Feudalism was not denied, but transformed and used by employers in the development of capitalism.[23]

Today, children and grandchildren of the newer European immigrants provide the bulk of the work force for the country's largest industrial corporations. Indeed, with the development of industrial unionism in the 1930s and the relative prosperity of the corporate sector of the economy, these white ethnics as a group are better off economically than women workers and racial minorities. Although ethnic categories are an important basis for the organization of the daily lives of many Americans (ethnic schools, churches, neighborhoods, and shops continue to provide a sense of solidarity and identity), the distinctions between old and new ethnics no longer

[23] *Ibid.,* p. 183.

differentiate workers from each other in terms of either their wages or their occupations. With minor exceptions, the Southern and Eastern European ethnics have achieved an occupational profile remarkably like that of the society as a whole. Proportionately, roughly as many ethnics are managers, white-collar workers, blue-collar workers, and farmers as the American population as a whole.

Women

In his report on manufacturers in 1796, Alexander Hamilton proposed that women and children be put to work in developing industries to save them from the "curse of idleness." In Lowell, Massachusetts, and in other New England mill towns, unmarried women were recruited to meet the labor needs of the new factories. But it was assumed that married women would stay in the home. As the country industrialized in the middle and late nineteenth century and the economic world of the independent middle class was shattered, an increasing number of men began to work in impersonal factory surroundings beyond the immediate embrace of home and community. Ideas about women conformed to his new reality:

> With men removed from contact with children during the lengthy and exhausting day, women had to fill the breach. Simultaneously, [capitalist] economic policies which emphasized individualism, success and competition replaced the old puritan ethic which emphasized morality, hard work and community. Men who worked hard and strove for success required wives who could competently super- ·vise the household and exercise supportive roles as well. . . . In what Bernard Wishy calls a reappraisal of family life that took place after 1830, motherhood rose to new heights, and children became the focus of womanly activity.[24]

But this new ethos applied almost exclusively to white, native-born American women. Immigrant and black women were driven into the labor force by need and, from 1850 on, took jobs in the burgeoning industries. The prevailing feminine ideal of domesticity, however, "provided employers with a docile labor force of women who, for the most part, were convinced that their real call-

[24]Alice Kessler Harris, "Women, Work, and the Social Order," unpublished manuscript.

ing lay in marriage and child-rearing, and had only a transient interest in their jobs."[25] In complementary fashion, since women "really" belonged at home, employers were permitted to treat them as if their earnings were not necessary for family survival. Thus, from the very entry of women into the mainstream work force to the present, women's wages have been considerably lower than men's (a tendency that has been reinforced by consistently lower rates of union membership by women).

During the last decades of the nineteenth century, the place of women in the labor force began to undergo considerable change. Before then, most clerical workers were men. But with the growing concentration of American industry and the expansion of corporate capitalism, the demand for clerical workers rose rapidly, and the number of available literate men was inadequate. A large pool of educated women was tapped.

In this century, the entry of women into office work has increased at such a rate that clerical labor has become feminized: many jobs are labeled "women's work" and entail services of a sex-stereotyped nature. Indeed, as sociologist Margery Davies points out, the work of a secretary came to be compared functionally with the role of a wife:

> Secretaries began to be expected to remind their bosses of birthdays and other social occasions, go out to buy sandwiches or coffee, and even run such personal errands as buying Christmas presents. All clerical workers were expected to dress nicely and be personable to visitors to the office; in other words, to be conscious and careful of their female roles as decorative sex objects and practitioners of the social graces.[26]

Women have thus come to occupy low-wage white- and blue-collar jobs. Collectively, they make up a marginal, exploited labor force. Only just over one-third of women work full time; the many women who work on a part-time or temporary basis never achieve seniority or fringe benefits. Women are readily fired in periods of economic recession and rehired when employers need them. Because many must stop working to look after their families, they have high turnover rates in the work force and are more exposed

---

[25] *Ibid.*

[26] Margery Davies, "Woman's Place Is at the Typewriter: The Feminization of the Clerical Labor Force," *Radical America* 8 (July–August 1974): 19.

than men to the risks of unemployment. They are discriminated against in being promoted to supervisory jobs. And they are paid significantly less than men.

In 1939, the median income of men was $1,419, as compared to $863 for women, or 60.8 percent of men's wages. Even comparing workers of the same age and education, women are still paid about a third less than men. And as more and more women enter the labor force with higher educational qualifications, the outlook for improvements in the relative standing of women workers is not good. Overall, in 1981, the median salary for women who worked full time was $12,001, about 59 percent of the median male salary of $20,260. The next decade, a report of the National Academy of Sciences concluded in 1985, will produce few professional and even more low skill jobs for women. In part this is the result of a combination of sex stereotyping, segregation, and discrimination. Of the 503 occupations listed by the U.S. census, 275 were greater than 80 percent male or female, and the occupations where women are most likely to be found—nurses, bookkeepers, secretaries—were most likely to be segregated by sex.[27]

EARLY UNION STRUGGLES AND REPRESSION

July 16, 1877 is a landmark date in American labor history. On that date, the Baltimore and Ohio railroad cut wages by 10 percent. In protest of the move, the crew of a cattle train in Martinsberg, West Virginia, abandoned the train, and other trainmen refused to replace them. By the end of the month, the first mass strike in America had spread across the country. "Strikers stopped and seized the nation's most important industry, the railroads, and crowds defeated or won over first the police, then the state militias, and in some cases even the Federal troops" who were called out to deal with the class insurrection. In a dozen major cities, all industrial activity was stopped by general strikes. The strikes were eventually put down by employers with the help of police and military authorities, but the Great Upheaval, as the event came to be known, was

[27]Kenneth B. Noble, "Low-Paying Jobs Foreseen for Most Working Women," *New York Times*, December 12, 1985, p. A 20.

profoundly important in two respects. First, it reflected the workers' sense of their new structural position in American society in face of the decline of the independent middle class. ("There was no concert of action at the start," the *Labor Standard* wrote. "It spread because the workmen of Pittsburgh felt the same oppression that was felt by the workmen of West Virginia and so with the workmen of Chicago and St. Louis.") Second, the strikes highlighted the need for workers to organize if they were to successfully resist the repression of workers' movements by employers and the government.[28]

By the middle 1880s, the Knights of Labor, the most important national union organization of the period, was growing at a phenomenal rate. In July 1884, it had just over 71,000 members; two years later it had over 729,000. The Knights sought to link all workers, skilled and unskilled, black and white, men and women. But the Knights' leadership was opposed to the strike weapon and to the wage system as a whole. Instead, they developed a fundamentalist religious perspective that eschewed wage struggles and promoted a cooperative fellowship among workers. The Knights' opposition to strikes proved to be the cause of their undoing, because strikes were the only weapon workers had to resist collectively the hardships inflicted by the developing factory economy. Hence, by the turn of the century, much strike action was spontaneously organized, outside of the formal structure of unions.

By the First World War, two very different kinds of unions had emerged. The American Federation of Labor (AFL), which had been founded in 1881 and was led by Samuel Gompers, organized skilled craft workers, the most well paid of the new proletariat. The AFL was a conservative union force. It did not challenge the developing distribution of resources or the basic structure of industrial capitalism. Rather, the AFL sought to defend the relatively privileged position of the craftsmen it represented and limited its demands to higher wages and shorter working hours. By contrast, the Industrial Workers of the World (IWW), which was founded in 1905, appealed to the interests of all workers, especially those who were most exploited. By the end of the First World War, the IWW had been smashed, and the AFL was gaining in strength. What accounts for the difference in their relative success?

[28]Jeremy Brecher, *Strike!* (San Francisco, 1972), pp. 1–21.

The key factor was the response of management and government authorities to the two unions: The AFL was tolerated and even welcomed by some employers because, by representing only skilled craft workers, it divided workers from one another. But the IWW, which sought to articulate the interests of all workers as a class and which posed socialist alternatives to prevailing economic arrangements, presented a far greater threat both to capitalist industry and the social order as a whole. Thus, between 1905 and the outbreak of the First World War, IWW activities were systematically countered by government action:

> In Pennsylvania, the state police, which had been originally created by reformers "anxious to abolish the use of private police forces during industrial conflicts" constantly worked for the employers, not for the strikers. In San Diego, Washington State, and Arizona vigilante mobs . . . took direct repressive action against the IWW. Contacts between the mobs and leading state figures made such actions official government policy. . . . Vigilante action was frowned on, however, by some state officials who felt that there were "cleaner" ways to repress the organization. A public safety committee in Minnesota, a council of defense in Washington State, and a Commission on Immigration and Housing in California became official bodies seeking official solutions for the elimination of the IWW.[29]

Many of these local organizations urged the Wilson administration to take federal action to repress the IWW. There followed a campaign of federal action that included the deportation of many IWW leaders who were aliens and the trial of hundreds on conspiracy charges (conspiracy against industrial production). In one instance, after deliberating less than an hour, a Chicago jury found more than one hundred defendants guilty of four counts of conspiracy each.[30]

The demise of the IWW was also closely linked to the legitimization of the AFL. In particular, Gompers, Felix Frankfurter (who was later to become a justice of the Supreme Court), and Ralph Easley of the National Civic Federation campaigned actively for recognition of the AFL as a "safe" alternative to more threatening workers' organizations. One manufacturer urged that workers

---

[29]Alan Wolfe, *The Seamy Side of Democracy* (New York, 1973), pp. 26–27.
[30]*Ibid.*, p. 29.

should be granted the "shadow of industrial democracy without the substance" to keep them "contented and productive."[31]

The repression of the IWW, of course, was not the only response of capitalists and the government to the militancy of the new industrial working class. Ideological propaganda, the reliance on state militias to protect strike-breakers, and the fostering of antiunion violence were among the common techniques of the day. And among these strategies were the manipulation of existing ethnic, racial, and sexual divisions in the work force and the creation of new divisions between kinds of workers (clerical versus managerial, white collar versus blue collar). Indeed, these strategies were related, since the antagonisms based on personal characteristics were exacerbated in order to legitimize new divisions between levels of work in the firm. As two historians have noted:

> Within the shop immigrants and Negroes did almost all unskilled and some semiskilled work, whereas the skilled jobs and minor administrative positions were reserved for native white Americans. "That job is not a hunky's job, and you can't have it," was the answer given to intelligent foreigners who aspired to rise above the ranks of common labor. Thus a wedge of racial discrimination was driven into the labor force.[32]

And as white-collar work increased, discrimination against women was used to solidify emerging lines of division within the office between jobs with and without managerial career potential. "In the office as well as the plant, organizing internal segments around externally sanctioned divisions—white over black, men over women, native American over immigrant—apparently reinforced the emergent lines of authority within the industrial hierarchy."[33]

UNIONS JOIN THE CORPORATE ECONOMY

Until the 1930s, as a result of the divisions in the work force and in the union movement, the vast majority of American workers were without union protection or representation. Between 1930 and

[31]*Ibid.*
[32]Thomas Cochran and William Miller, *The Age of Enterprise: A Social History of Industrial America* (New York, 1961), pp. 230–31.
[33]Gordon, Edwards, and Reich, "Labor Segmentation in American Capitalism."

1940, however, the number of unionized workers more than doubled from 3.1 million to 7 million. In that decade, unions affiliated with the Congress of Industrial Organizations (CIO), founded in 1935, succeeded in unionizing the most important mass-production industries in the country, including steel and automobiles.

But their success came only after bitter, protracted struggles, in which class antagonisms were raw and palpable. "Four men were killed and eighty-four persons went to hospitals with gunshot wounds, cracked heads, broken limbs or other injuries received in a battle late this afternoon between police and steel strikers at the gates of the Republic Steel Corporation plant in South Chicago" as the United Steel Workers of America successfully sought recognition, the *New York Times* reported in May 1937.[34] In January 1936, automobile workers demanding recognition of the United Automobile Workers (UAW) stated sit-ins and took control of General Motors automobile plants in Flint, Michigan; Atlanta, Georgia; Anderson, Indiana; Norwood, Ohio; and Kansas City, Missouri. On the forty-fourth day of the sit-in and strike at Flint, General Motors gave in and recognized the UAW, but only after massive police violence and cooperative attempts between the governor and the company had failed to dislodge the workers.

Thus in the late 1930s, workers, through union-led mass actions, seemed to be moving rapidly to achieve a significant amount of substantive representation and fundamental structural change.

In 1973, however, thirty-six years after the Flint sit-in, *Business Week* editorialized:

> the unions have become an established institution, well financed and run by highly professional managers. These officers are paid on much the same basis as businessmen. . . . And they deal with many of the same problems—budgets, investments, taxes, even bargaining with staff and office worker unions.[35]

The editorial also noted that the unions were "acting responsibly" and that strike figures had reached "the lowest level in years." In the same year, the steelworkers (led by a president who earned an annual salary of $70,000) signed a contract that pledged the union to fight wildcat strikes by its members. They also agreed—in ad-

---

[34]Melvyn Dubofsky, ed., *American Labor Since the New Deal* (Chicago, 1971), p. 113.
[35]*Business Week,* August 18, 1973, p. 88.

vance of a wage settlement—not to strike, but to settle all wage disputes by arbitration. A major study of the UAW concluded:

> The relationship between the General Motors corporation and the United Automobile Workers has altered—they are not enemies, nor, in any large sense, adversaries. It is true . . . that the two, General Motors and the UAW, have *a greater community of interest than of conflict.*[36]

What had happened to produce the shift in less than four decades from militant class organization and confrontation to "responsible" routinized cooperation?

The development of a relatively conservative AFL-CIO (they merged in 1955) was made possible by the growing divisions between the corporate and small-capital sectors of the American economy. Unlike small-capital industries, whose major costs are wages and who have to absorb wage increases at the expense of profits, the corporate-sector industries were largely able to pass along wage increases in the form of higher prices. In the corporate sector, wages, prices, and profits were not determined by the operation of a traditional competitive market but are planned by the corporations and government. Hence corporate-sector companies, whose major expenses relate to technology, not men and women, were able to accept the emergence of mass industrial unionism as one more element among many to be planned for in advance. Indeed, corporate-sector firms gained tangible benefits from the existence of a unionized work force because the unions guarantee that, outside of strike periods, the companies would have a predictably available work force at predictable wages.

By the end of the Second World War, most industrial unions had entered into permanent collective bargaining agreements with the largest corporations in the corporate sector. The unions succeeded in obtaining higher wages for their members, but not without relinquishing much in return. In addition to agreeing to increased productivity, union leaders began to collaborate with company managements to introduce technologically advanced production methods, which usually are resisted by the rank and file. Overall, from the standpoint of those who own and control corporate capital, "the main function of unions was (and is) to inhibit

[36]William Serrin, *The Company and the Union* (New York, 1972), pp. 305–06.

disruptive spontaneous rank and file activity (e.g., wildcat strikes and slowdowns) and to maintain labor discipline in general. In other words, *unions were (and are) the guarantors of managerial prerogatives.*"[37]

The union movement, to be sure, has supported progressive welfare-state legislation; in particular, unions have vigorously promoted the expansion of the social security system, unemployment and disability insurance, and other protections against economic insecurity (national health insurance is a present important target). But as we will see in Chapter 9, none of these programs threaten major corporate firms; indeed, to the extent that they make workers more secure and provide them with state, rather than corporate, benefits, the corporations stand to gain a more contented, productive work force. For this reason most major advances in social insurance since the New Deal have been supported by large industrial employers.

Thus, in terms of their economic welfare, the growth of industrial unionism has made a very real difference to corporate-sector workers. But the costs of these gains have been high. In particular, the union movement has left workers without the ability to control decisions that affect them at the work place. Political scientist David Greenstone notes, "the crucial fact is that the workers neither own nor control—*that they exercise no substantial economic authority over*—the firms in which they work."[38] In fact, the growth of industrial unionization, by conceding management prerogatives, has often made the conditions of work much more difficult. As companies introduce new technological innovations, individual workers have to bear the brunt of the speed-up of the work process.

For example, in 1966, General Motors opened a new Chevrolet plant at Lordstown, Ohio, that turned out 60 cars per hour, the company's usual production rate. In late summer 1971, the company brought in a new management team that introduced production methods aimed at increasing the number of cars produced to 110 per hour. The pace of work, which traditionally had been rapid, became maddening. A worker whose assembly-line job was the installation of front seats was now expected to perform eight differ-

[37]James O'Connor, *The Fiscal Crisis of the State* (New York, 1973), p. 23. Emphasis added.
[38]J. David Greenstone, in *The Nation*, September 8, 1969, p. 214.

ent operations—walking about 20 feet to a conveyor belt that transported the seats, lifting the seat and hauling it to the car, lifting the car's carpet, bending to fasten the bolts by hand, fastening them with an air gun, replacing the carpet, and putting a sticker on the hood signifying that the job had been properly done—in a total period of 36 seconds.

In the winter and spring of 1971–72, plant workers, mainly high-school graduates in their twenties, began to sabotage the work process. The workers began to pass many cars down the production line with bolts and parts missing. Unassembled engines were passed along, covered by their outer shells. More than half the cars that came off the production line had to be returned for major repairs.

This situation was threatening both to General Motors and to the leadership of the workers' union, the United Automobile Workers (UAW). The company's production and profits were jeopardized; even more importantly, the command authority of the plant's management to regulate the work process was directly challenged by the workers' in-plant protests. Similarly, the UAW had much to lose, since the workers' sabotage bypassed the union completely and implicitly raised issues of worker control that transcended the routine pattern of wage bargaining between the company and the nation.

Thus, it was in the interests of both the company and the union officials to regain control over the workers. When 350 workers were dismissed for "efficiency" reasons in February, the UAW stepped in to call for a strike vote. In March, Lordstown's workers walked off the job. The strike did not revolve around the issue of the debilitating work process, but concentrated instead on wages, layoffs, and back pay for those who had been fired. The spring strike ended with a proclaimed victory by the union. The real victory belonged not to the strikers but to company and union officials who had succeeded in restoring normal patterns of bargaining and in cooling the workers' discontent by channeling it in traditional directions. The union bargained *for* wages and job security; control of the work process was bargained *away* in return. Working conditions were unchanged.

Although the union leadership claimed "total victory" at the end of the strike, some workers were not so sure. One bitterly complained, "Before the strike the union was in favor of not working faster than you could. Now people are afraid not to work. The company and the union say everything is settled, we had a strike. But what did we achieve for it?"[39]

The growth of industrial unionism has been achieved at a high cost for nonunionized workers as well. Although unions are seen as the representatives of workers, most workers are not represented by unions and do not receive the benefits of collective bargaining. Yet they have to pay the higher prices companies charge to offset wage increases. Nonunionized labor literally pays the price of unionized workers' gains. Thus, by representing only a portion of the working class, unions splinter workers into opposing groups that are more conscious of antagonisms that divide them than of long-range interests that bind them together.

LABOR'S DECLINE

In 1955, the United Steel Workers had 980,000 members; in 1985, 572,000. In the same period, the membership rolls of the International Ladies Garment Workers Union declined from 383,000 to 210,000; the International Typographical Union from 78,000 to 38,000; and the United Automobile Workers from 1,260,000 to 974,000. Unions in 1985 represented only 18.8 percent of the labor force, a level not much higher than that of the period of the Great Depression *before* the massive organizing campaigns of the CIO. In 1950, more than 30 percent of American workers were organized in unions, and as late as 1979 the numbers were over 24 percent. If not for the large growth of service and governmental workers in the union movement, the decline would have been even more steep. Today, unions win only about 46 percent of their organizational elections. Many new plants come into operation without unions.

Unions also strike for higher wages and working conditions less often. In 1970, there were nearly 400 work stoppages involving over 1,000 people, but in 1985, there were fewer than 40. This number represented the lowest level of strikes in the four decades

[39]Aronowitz, p. 43.

that the federal government has been collecting this information. What accounts for the accelerating decline of the labor movement in numbers and in militancy in the Reagan years?

Following the penetrating interpretation of sociologist Rob Wrenn, five basic causes can be identified: "(1) the recent recession and the cumulative effect of high unemployment in the past decade; (2) the international domestic non-union competition confronting unionized firms and plants; (3) the corporate 'counterattack' and managements new hard-line anti-union stance; (4) changes in government policy; and (5) organized labor's own failure to maintain and expand its membership."[40] Let us consider each of these factors in turn.

Throughout the period of the mid- and late 1970s, the American labor force experienced unemployment at a rate over 6 percent, a higher fraction of the working class than had experienced unemployment in the previous decade. In 1982, unemployment zoomed to over 12 percent, the highest rate since the Great Depression. More people were out of work for longer periods than had been the case for over four decades. The threat of plant closings and job losses put a brake on union demands and expectations, and they weakened the bargaining power of unions vis à vis their employers.

But the end of the recession and the subsequent vigorous period of economic growth has not seen the recovery of the trade union movement. In part this is the result of a continuing, even intensifying competition for unionized workers from nonunion American workers and from inexpensive overseas labor and international competition in such industries as steel, automobiles, textiles, and shoes. Further, union membership tends to be concentrated in older industries begun before 1960. Most industries that have developed since then, as those in high-technology fields like computers, have tended to be nonunion. As a result, the dynamics of growth and decline in the economy even in a period of expansion tend to contract the number of workers in the unionized as compared to the nonunionized sector.

These trends have been reinforced by an effort by business firms to undermine the power of organized labor. A number of recent studies have estimated that up to half of the recent union

[40]Rob Wrenn, "The Decline of American Labor," *Socialist Review,* no.82/83 (July–October 1985).

decline is the result of a stiffening resistance by employers to the organization of unions and to their effective campaigns to persuade workers to vote against union representation. And where unions have long existed, businesses are demanding that workers make wage concessions and agree to changes in work rules in order to keep plants open and competitive. In 1982 and 1983, businesses succeeded in winning such concessionary "give-backs" from over half of the contract talks in mining, transportation, furniture manufacturing, textiles, rubber, and leather goods. At the extreme margin, there has been an increasing use of tactics as the hiring of thugs, the discharge of union activists, and blacklisting of union organizers.[41]

Some aspects of government policy have also made it harder for unions to organize workers. The Reagan administration has made fighting unemployment a lower priority than fighting inflation, thus creating something of a surplus of labor. The administration's appointments to the National Labor Relations Board have been very conservative, creating a tilt against the union movement. And reductions in social benefits, discussed in Chapter 9, make the pain of unemployment even greater than it was.

Finally, labor itself has been very defensive, willing to try its best to protect its traditional terrain, rather than fight to organize new workers. Many unions grew comfortable as partners in corporate capitalism, and they have found it difficult to readjust to a more difficult environment. Today, in part as a result of these internal shortcomings, the union movement is weaker than at any time since the Second World War. In part, this declining influence is the result of the failure of workers to fashion a working-class political party of the kind commonly found in Western Europe. It is to the nature of the country's political parties and mechanisms of political participation, therefore, that we now turn.

[41] *Ibid.*

8

competition without representation: political parties and elections

Justin Dart, founder of Dart Industries and a large contributor and fundraiser for the Republican party and conservative interest groups, once said that dialogue with politicians "is a fine thing, but with a little money they hear you better."[1] According to the guidelines of procedural democracy, the appropriate arena for citizen participation and for exercising citizen sovereignty is political parties and elections. Moreover, the fact that citizens can vote freely serves to justify existing arrangements, notably, that system of private control of the economy and rule by professional politicans and administrators that we have termed capitalist democracy. Yet the

[1]Quoted in Elizabeth Drew, *Politics and Money: The New Road to Corruption* (New York, 1983), p. 78.

extent of democratic choice depends on the alternatives citizens are offered. Elections are rightly held up to scorn when, as in some nations, only a single political party is permitted to present candidates or there is fraud in counting ballots.

Yet, parties and elections in the United States are not an accurate mirror of citizen preferences either. If they were, the shape of the political economy would be quite different. For example, the United States would have long since had a system of free public medical care and government-guaranteed employment—both of which according to public opinion polls, have been favored by majorities of Americans for years.

The party system does not accurately reflect citizen preferences, but it does channel and restrict citizen participation. For most Americans, politics is a spectator sport. By structuring participation as they do, moreover, the two major parties obscure alternative approaches to American politics. In the process, parties serve to shape citizens' expectations and attitudes even as they narrow the available choices. Although the two parties disagree on specific and occasionally even broad policies, they agree on the most fundamental question regarding the character of the political economy: the desirability of preserving and perfecting capitalist democracy. Although appearing self-evident, this agreement is probably the most important feature of the American party system. Nor is it typical: every other capitalist democracy has a large socialist or social democratic party that advocates reducing capitalist control in key domains.

A cynical reaction to the observation that American political parties agree far more than they differ might be that parties and elections therefore don't matter very much. Yet, in fact, partly because of the narrow range of choice available in the party system—along with the illusion that choice is fully free—the party and electoral arena are very important indeed. The party system obscures citizens' lack of representation by the fig leaf of competition.

WHY PARTIES AND ELECTIONS MATTER

In a capitalist democracy, it is legitimate for citizens to participate in politics. However, according to the dominant ideology, participation is supposed to take the limited, passive form of voting for a political party candidate or, at most, donating funds to a candidate and working in a political campaign. Political scientist Benjamin Ginsberg describes the two-side process: elections both expand and democratize

> mass political involvement. At the same time, however, elections help to preserve governmental stability by containing and channeling away potentially more disruptive or dangerous forms of mass political activity. By establishing formal avenues for mass participation and habituating citizens to their use, governments reduce the threat that mass involvement in politics can pose to the established order.[2]

Elections thus have a conservatizing impact even when a reform-minded party is elected. Except in rare instances, which party is elected matters less than the fact that the electoral process provides an aura of legitimacy to the status quo and deters citizens from seeking change directly rather than through their representatives. Further, by voting for and electing pro-system parties, citizens signify their assent to the entire political system, in which they are passive spectators, and the economic system which they do not control.

Why do many citizens vote contrary to their interests? To begin with, two groups do not: relatively affluent citizens, who have good reason to vote for representatives committed to strengthening capitalist democracy; and the many citizens, nearly half the entire electorate, who do not vote at all.

As described in earlier chapters, there is a fundamental class cleavage in American society. But this cleavage is not reflected within the party system. Only about half the adult population goes to the polls in a typical presidential election. Even fewer vote in off-year elections, when there is no presidential contest. Among the ranks of nonvoters are found a disproportionate number of blacks, unemployed, elderly, uneducated, and poor. Political scientist Walter Dean Burnham suggests that "our whole electoral politics rests upon a huge and growing political vacuum at the bottom of the social structure."[3] Political scientist E. E. Schattschneider has called nonvoting

---

[2]Benjamin Ginsberg, *The Consequences of Consent: Elections, Citizen Control and Popular Acquiescence* (Reading, Mass., 1982), p. 6.
[3]Walter Dean Burnham, "The 1980 Earthquake: Realignment, Reaction, or What?" in Thomas Ferguson and Joel Rogers, eds., *The Hidden Election: Politics and Economics in the 1980 Presidential Campaign* (New York, 1981), pp. 126–27.

by a wide margin the most important feature of the whole system, the key to understanding the composition of American politics. . . . It is profoundly characteristic of the behavior of the more fortunate strata of the community that responsibility for widespread nonparticipation is attributed wholly to the ignorance, indifference and shiftlessness of the people. This has always been the rationalization used to justify the exclusion of the lower classes from any political system. There is a better explanation. Abstention reflects the suppression of the options and alternatives that reflect the needs of the nonparticipants.[4]

In order to understand the largest significance of American political parties, one needs to broaden the focus beyond day to day partisan disputes or even the quadrennial presidential elections. Viewed from the perspective of their overall impact on the political system, American political parties and elections reflect and thereby reinforce the existing distribution of political and economic power. Although they differ somewhat in terms of their electoral constituencies and policy preferences, both major parties are conservative forces that blur cleavages and strengthen the status quo.

More concretely, this means that political parties reinforce the dominance of business. As political scientist Andrew Martin puts it, "In the absence of any political party independent of business . . . , American business elites remain effectively insulated from political challenge through the democratic process."[5]

By not voting, many citizens have in effect opted out of the political system. Although political withdrawal is far from the most rational or effective way to challenge inequality, this response is understandable given the obstacles to voting and the absence of viable alternatives. But one may also ask why so many citizens *do* continue to support a system biased against them. One harsh possibility is that they are brainwashed: $1.8 billion was spent in 1984 on political parties and elections. An additional $2 billion was spent by business in grass-roots lobbying and advocacy advertising. A unifying theme of this activity was that the system is democratic, fair, and responsive; it is your civic duty to vote and support the existing party system.

[4]E. E. Schattschneider, *The Semi-Sovereign People* (New York, 1960), pp. 103–105.
[5]Andrew Martin, *The Politics of Economic Policy in the United States: A Tentative View from a Comparative Perspective* (Beverly Hills, Cal., 1973), p. 31.

Yet citizens are not sheep. Support for the existing system has a rational basis in that participation does, at least partially, serve citizens' needs and interests—especially those needs that the system defines as valuable. A capitalist system is fairly effective at satisfying short-term material needs, the very ones that the system emphasizes are worth having in the first place. With an economy producing about $3 trillion worth of goods and services annually, most citizens have a material stake to protect. It makes sense for them to vote for that party which offers the best chance of delivering material benefits in the short run as well as promoting economic health and growth. This means that citizens will be likely to choose political parties that seek piecemeal reforms to improve the status quo rather than advocating long-term, especially anticapitalist, changes.[6]

All citizens are hostage to capitalist prosperity: when the economy is flourishing, most citizens benefit because wages are higher and jobs more plentiful; when the economy stagnates, most people suffer. And the dilemma is precisely here: if a political party is elected that advocates reducing capital's privileges, the result is likely to be economic difficulties at least in the short run. Anticapitalist reforms are not the best recipe to create "business confidence," quite the contrary. When, in other capitalist democracies, governments have been elected that pursued anticapitalist policies, for example, Chile in 1970 and France in 1981, capitalists in these nations and abroad mounted an investment strike and an economic boycott. Their governments were soon weakened and discredited.

This does not mean that socialist parties that propose anticapitalist reforms never arise or gain extensive support within capitalist democracies. As previously stated, the United States is exceptional compared to other capitalist democracies in lacking a large socialist party. But for citizens to support such a party usually involves membership in a movement that seeks collective changes in the future as much as individual, material gains in the present. The key to following this longer-term logic is the existence of a labor movement seeking substantial reforms. As we analyzed in Chapter 7, the

---

[6]For excellent analyses of this issue, see Adam Przeworski, "Social Democracy as a Historical Phenomenon," *New Left Review,* no. 122 (July/August 1980): 27–58; and Przeworski and Michael Wallerstein, "The Structure of Class Conflict in Democratic Capitalist Societies," *American Political Science Review* 76 (June 1982): 215–38.

character of the American labor movement is an important reason for the conservativism of American politics. Hence, the American party system matters because it serves to confine the available choices offered Americans to pro-system parties committed to preserving capital's privileges.

Yet, secondly, elections matter because, despite their agreement on fundamentals, rival parties often *do* differ, especially during transitional periods. Thus, important consequences flow from which party gets elected. Within the United States, each party represents a broad and distinctive coalition of interests. How such coalitions get formed and how they evolve constitutes a major element in American politics. Yet, beneath the public clash of interests, there is a covert process in which the key economic interests participate. Social scientists Thomas Ferguson and Joel Rogers, term this process "the hidden election":

> Any presidential race can be usefully thought of as consisting of two campaigns. One is public, and unfolds through the primaries and party conventions, speeches and debates, and final polls and voting results. The other is more obscure, and features the complex process by which pivotal interest groups like oil companies, international banks, weapons producers, labor unions, and even foreign countries coalesce behind particular candidates to advance their own ends.[7]

Elections are thus a mechanism for facilitating peaceful changes in the ruling constellation of power and interests. During most periods in American history, a single party has stably dominated national elections. As time passes, however, the majority coalition of regional, economic, and ideological interests organized within the leading party begins to unravel. In a fashion that parallels the long historical waves of technological and social change described in Chapter 3, a political party that reaches power well equipped to address leading issues in one period is poorly equipped to handle new issues that arise in the course of that period.

The transition to a new majority coalition is often signalled by increased party competition, changing party alignments, and especially the replacement of the formerly dominant party by the opposition party.

While American party competition in the twentieth century has been played out within the overarching framework of the two

[7]Ferguson and Rogers, p. 6.

parties' mutual quest to improve capitalist democracy, they have generally differed on whether to extend the democratic or the capitalist features of the system. Since the New Deal, the Democratic party has sponsored an expansion of welfare-state programs, civil rights, and other elements within procedural democracy. (This did not mean the Democrats were anticapitalist, since they argued that these measures would promote capitalist economic expansion.) Until the 1980s, the Republican party either opposed Democratic programs in favor of a no-frills defense of free enterprise and limited government; or it echoed the Democrats without contributing distinctive elements.

For decades, the Democratic party's approach seemed responsible for promoting economic growth and prosperity, and the party was rewarded electorally by grateful voters. (For example, the Democratic party controlled the presidency for all but eight years between 1932 and 1968.) By the same token, however, the Democratic party was penalized when it proved unable to deliver an ever-greater stream of benefits. In the 1960s and 1970s, there was a surge of grass-roots participation expressing multiple grievances and demands, most directed against the Democratic program. Moreover, in the 1970s, the entire party system was buffeted, as neither party succeeded in capturing the loyalties of the new participants.

As the dominant party since the 1930s, the Democratic party was the principal target, while the Republican party served as a vehicle for many groups discontented with the status quo. In 1980, Republican candidate Ronald Reagan fashioned a new majority coalition on a platform of capitalist revitalization with a populist flavor. Although the Republican program has had quite mixed success, Reagan was resoundingly reelected in 1984. Yet, for reasons explored in this and other chapters, it is unlikely that the current attempt to champion capitalist virtues will succeed and the Republican party will enjoy stable dominance.

The present era represents a period either of party *realignment,* with the Republicans replacing the Democrats as the dominant party; party *decay,* with neither party able to organize a stable majority; or a combination of the two, as the Republicans increase their support in a period of party decomposition. The possible decay of the party system provides a third reason why elections matter. The major thrust of the 1980s has been to reverse progressive gains of the New Deal through the 1970s in the fields of social programs, civil rights, and environmental protection. The Republican approach represents new challenges and opportunities. As its policies demonstrate what it means to strengthen the capitalist elements within capitalist democracy, the space increases for new alternatives challenging capitalist democracy and seeking to promote a progressive alternative.

POLITICAL PARTIES AS DEMOCRATIC FORCES

Parties were once a democratizing force in the United States. During the late eighteenth century, when other nations were governed by narrowly based oligarchies, political parties originated in the United States and contributed four democratizing elements that leavened traditional political arrangements.

American political parties expanded political *participation,* both in the choosing of government officials and in the ruling process itself. Parties first mobilized eligible voters in the period before the Civil War, when restrictions on the suffrage were (compared to other countries) few; and they helped break down the deferential system of politics in which only the socially privileged and wealthy could participate.

This does not mean to suggest that America started out as a pure democracy. For several decades after the Constitution was ratified, the suffrage extended only to white male landowners. In most states, white propertyless men were excluded from participation by a property qualification until the 1820s, and slaves, Indians, and women were excluded even longer. Moreover, the sphere of electoral politics was limited. Within the federal government, the only officials chosen by popular elections were members of the House of Representatives. Senators and the president were indirectly elected: senators, by state legislatures, which were themselves chosen by popular election; the president, by members of the electoral college, who were also chosen by state legislatures.

And yet, despite numerous qualifications, the United States had the first popular government in the world, and citizen interest in politics ran high.[8] In the presidential election of 1840, 80 percent

---

[8]The French Revolution of 1789 ushered in universal manhood suffrage earlier than in the United States. But Napoleon's coup d'état and the Restoration ended France's brief democratic experiment.

of the eligible voters turned out to vote, a figure far above current turnout rates.[9]

Political parties represented *contending social and political forces.* By linking groups that were geographically separated, parties made it possible for people to organize and defend their interests within the national arena. This did not happen overnight. The first national governments were physically and functionally remote from popular forces. It was not until political parties extended their organization to the grass roots—beginning in Andrew Jackson's time (1820s to 1840s)—that one can begin to speak of a national constituency.

American political parties institutionalized *opposition* to the government. In other countries, the men holding public office might organize themselves into a group. But what made the American party system unique was that officeholders were organized into *several* groups, that these groups developed links to popular forces outside the government, and that one of these early groups (the Republicans under Jefferson's leadership) represented an open, organized opposition to the government's policies.

However, neither of the first two party groupings accepted the legitimacy of opposing parties. As historian Richard Hofstadter notes, "the creators of the first American party system on both sides, Federalists and Republicans, were men who looked upon parties as sores on the body politic."[10] In fact, the Federalists, the first party to rule, tried to destroy Republican opposition by passing the Alien and Sedition laws. The Sedition Act made it a crime to express criticism of the government, and the Federalists used it to indict the editors or publishers of fourteen major Republican newspapers. (Their humorless approach can be inferred from their indicting, convicting, and fining one editor "for expressing the wish that the wad of a cannon discharged as a salute to President Adams had hit the broadest part of the President's breeches."[11] The Federalists not only failed to destroy the Republicans, however, but the attempt cost them office—they were turned out in 1800 when

[9]William Nisbet Chambers, "Party Development and the American Mainstream," in William Nisbet Chambers and Walter Dean Burnham, eds., *The American Party Systems: Stages of Political Development,* 2nd ed. (New York, 1975), p. 12.

[10]Richard Hofstadter, *The Idea of a Party System: The Rise of Legitimate Opposition in the United States, 1780–1840* (Berkeley, 1969), p. 2.

[11]Henry Jones Ford, *The Rise and Growth of American Politics* (New York, 1898), p. 112, cited in V. O. Key, Jr., *Politics, Parties, & Pressure Groups* (New York, 1964), p. 205.

Jefferson was elected president—and was influential in leading to their ultimate disappearance from the political scene.

Parties facilitated *alternation* in office. The replacement of Federalist President John Adams by Thomas Jefferson, a Republican, was the first case of peaceful transference of power from one party to another as a result of election returns. Parties thus made it possible for the principle of majority rule to determine the composition of the government.

On the whole, American political parties and elections in the early years represented a substantial advance in democratic practice over other countries. But what was a democratic—and even influential—system in one epoch may not be equally so in another. During the last century, political parties became both less democratic and less influential as forces affecting the course of American politics.

THE DOMINANT LIBERAL TRADITION

During the course of American history, the party system has rarely been the only forum for the expression of political conflict, nor has it always been the major forum. As political scientist Robert Dahl points out, "From the very first years under the new Constitution American political life has undergone, about once every generation, a conflict over national politics of extreme severity."[12] In addition to the Civil War, when there was outright warfare between opponents, conflict in the United States has found expression through protest activity, political violence, demonstrations, and strikes. Clashes have occurred among organized agencies, such as interest groups, business organizations, and labor unions; and among regional, ideological, and ethnic groups. A more violent form of conflict has been the official destruction of Indians, enslavement of blacks, and repression of women, Orientals, Hispanics, and other minorities.

Yet, with the important exception of the Civil War, the extremes of conflict that characterize other countries have been less

[12]Robert A. Dahl, *Political Oppositions in Western Democracies* (New Haven, 1966), p. 50.

apparent in the United States. In contrast to Europe, conditions in early America fostered relative equality, discouraged class consciousness, reduced the need for violent disruptions, and provided a framework for a democratic party system. Foremost was the lack of a powerful hereditary aristocracy. Alexis de Tocqueville, who visited the United States in the 1830s, observed in *Democracy in America* that Americans were born equal rather than having to fight a revolution to achieve equality. According to sociologist Seymour M. Lipset, in *The First New Nation,* the leading cultural values in America came to be individualism, equality, and achievement. A second condition that differentiated the United States from Europe was the pluralism of American society, which embraced a gamut of occupational, regional, ethnic, and religious subcultures; encouraged toleration; and splintered power. Third, unlike most Europeans, Americans had a way of escaping from the old life and finding a new one: they could move. Land was plentiful and cheap, and the lure of the frontier was strong. Moreover, the demand for labor in the thinly populated nation increased workers' bargaining power and social status.

Lastly was the fact that suffrage requirements were minimal. In eighteenth-century Europe, workers, merchants, and entrepreneurs were legally excluded from political power. As a result, they organized their own political parties, which were illegal and revolutionary, operating against (not within) the political system. In America, where universal white male suffrage was achieved before the industrial revolution, political parties were less class oriented and represented coalitions of social, economic, and regional interests. Groups did not have to struggle to gain admission to the system: they were already inside the political arena. However, as class divisions hardened after the industrial revolution, American parties became less and less representative of the existing social structure.

The same conditions that acted to moderate conflict in the United States contributed to the acceptance of a basic ideology, which political theorist Louis Hartz has called the liberal tradition.[13] This ideology was based on the views of English philosopher John Locke, who believed that individual freedom flourished through

[13]Louis Hartz, *The Liberal Tradition in America* (New York, 1955).

private property and limited government—a view ideally suited to the simple conditions of early America.

Capitalism was not seriously challenged in the United States, as it was by socialists and anarchists in Europe and Chartists in England. Nor—again in contrast to Europe—was there a powerful preexisting conservative establishment consisting of the Church, the army, and the aristocracy to oppose the rise of capitalism.

Procedural democracy came early in the United States in part because of the triumph of capitalism. The framers of the Constitution used procedural democracy to protect the interests of private property. In contrast to the feudal system of fixed status and obligations, capitalism required legal equality and freedom: the freedom of citizens to acquire private property, choose an occupation, and sell their labor for a wage; to enter the market, produce whatever was demanded, and buy and sell the commodities thereby produced.

So long as agriculture predominated, manufacturing was rudimentary, and there were relatively few extremes of wealth, capitalism and procedural democracy could be defended as having expanded freedom in comparison with the feudal system. But when conditions changed toward the end of the nineteenth century—the end of the frontier, an increase in population, technological innovations, and the development of harsh industrial production sponsored by corporate capitalism—procedural democracy and capitalism paved the way to a new oppression.

The evolution of political cleavages

As the United States changed, one can distinguish several periods, each characterized by the dominance of a particular cluster of economic and regional forces. Such forces are usually grouped within a ruling political party and opposed by a minority party containing groups and regions on the defensive. The cleavage between parties both shaped and reflected the major conflicts within the society at that time.

The degree to which American political parties have been able to attract stable electoral followings seems to follow a cyclical pattern. Political scientist Walter Dean Burnham has described contrasts in the party system during stable and unstable periods. American parties thrive during stable periods, when they can count on a large loyal constituency and when they can express (and at the same time blur) important political differences of the time. During such periods, one party is usually dominant, able to unite leading economic, social, and regional interests in a broad majority consensus on important issues.

But, Burnham points out, "'Politics as usual' in the United States is not politics as always."[14] At periodic intervals, when economic and social crisis looms, parties become unable to adapt to the new conditions. As a crisis gathers momentum, issues develop that cut across existing party lines, alienating voters, heightening their attention to issues and their discontent with the alternatives offered them by the existing parties. At these times, voters begin to seek answers outside the existing party system, and the parties are ripe for realignment. It is during these periods of crisis that new political movements and leaders have arisen outside the two-party system (third parties, popular movements, protests, and strikes). Their success leads the existing parties to seek ways to adjust to the situation. The result has been a shifting of parties—in terms of the issues they emphasize and positions they take—as well as a shuffling of the parties' constituencies, as voters (especially younger voters without long-standing partisan attachments) gravitate to the party whose position they favor. A new party may emerge to replace one of the leading parties (as the Republican party replaced the Whigs in the 1850s), or the minority party may become the majority party (as the Democratic party did in the 1930s), or the majority party may capitalize on the new issues to regain its dominance (as the Republican party did in 1896). During past crises, at some point a new alignment crystallized and a new period of stability began, issues sank into the background, and voters again relied on partisan identification rather than the parties' policies to guide their voting choice.

This model provides a useful way to describe changing political cleavages in the United States, if one keeps in mind that the American party system overrepresents dominant social groups and underrepresents subordinate groups. The history of the American party system consists of the early defeat of the Federalists, followed

[14]Walter Dean Burnham, "The End of American Party Politics," in Joseph Fiszman and Gene S. Poschman, eds., *The American Political Arena: Selected Readings,* 3rd ed. (Boston, 1972), p. 250.

by the dominance of Jefferson's Republican party (the forerunner of today's Democratic party), whose support rested on Southern and agrarian interests. Following the Civil War, control shifted back to the North and, with greater velocity during the industrial revolution at the end of the nineteenth century, to commercial and then corporate power. The Republican party (as it is still known today) held office nearly without interruption from the Civil War to the New Deal by making itself the spokesman for ascendant industrialism and corporate capitalism.

The New Deal represented another major shift, with the formation of a majority coalition within the Democratic party consisting of organized labor, ethnic and urban groups, and the South. Currently, this coalition has been torn by new social tensions; there is evidence of a general decline in the parties' control over the electorate, and the Republican party has at least temporarily organized a majority coalition resting on the newly ascendant Sunbelt, business, white Protestants, and populist conservatives. The recent course of the American party system and its future prospects will be analyzed after reviewing the key role that money plays in shaping the party system.

MONEY AND POLITICS

If political parties accurately represented the interests of voters, elections would promise the possibility of greater change. Given the large number of Americans whose interest lies in democratic change, one party or the other would find it electorally profitable to propose substantial reforms. An important reason why parties are so conservative is that they need more than votes to succeed: they also need money, vast quantities of it.

Many splinter parties in the United States do advocate far-reaching changes. However, for a political party to be heard requires enormous funds, far beyond what "third parties" can command. The two parties spent over $500 million in the 1976 elections for president, Congress, state, and local offices. This doubled in 1980 to $1 billion and nearly doubled once again in 1984, when the total reached $1.8 billion. (Campaign spending is about equally divided among the presidential, congressional, state, and local elections.) Election costs are high in nonpresidential years as well: about $340 million was spent in 1982. Nearly all contributions go to Democratic or Republican candidates. In effect, political contributions ensure that electoral competition is restricted to two parties. A key to the character of the American party system is to trace the sources of political funds. Four can be identified.

By far the largest and indeed the overwhelming proportion of all political funds is contributed by business interests, including wealthy business executives, professionals, and stockholders, as well as by political action committees (PACs), which in turn raise funds from business donations.

What leads private citizens, who provide the bulk of these funds, to give so generously? Some people contribute from a sense of civic duty or idealistic commitment. However, a California politician may have gotten nearer to the truth when he remarked, "Most people who put money into political campaigns aren't contributors—they're investors."[15] As explored next, most business contributions now go to the Republican party, although the Democratic party raises a substantial share of its (far smaller total) funds from the affluent.

A second source of political money is gifts from rank and file citizens raised by direct mail campaigns. Here again the Republican party comes out far ahead, mainly because it has the funds to purchase the technology needed for a direct mail pitch, including computerized mailing lists and the like. One should not assume that the contributions from direct mail appeals derive from middle and lower income groups. Well over half the citizens sending in political contributions in response to these campaigns are in the wealthiest tenth of the income pyramid.[16]

Labor unions provide a third source of funds, a major one for the Democratic party. Yet labor's campaign contributions are puny compared to business', and labor does not begin to command the political influence that business has the funds to purchase.

As a result of widespread public outrage following revelations of corporate and political corruption in the 1970s, culminating in

[15]Quoted from a TV interview in Frank B. Feigert and M. Margaret Conway, *Parties and Politics in America* (Boston, 1976), p. 262; cited in Samuel J. Eldersverld, *Political Parties in American Society* (New York, 1982), p. 304.
[16]Thomas Byrne Edsall, *The New Politics of Inequality* (New York, 1984), p. 198.

the Watergate scandal, a series of federal election campaign reforms were adopted whose stated purpose was to minimize the
influence of private contributions in federal elections. (In addition,
most states have passed similar laws to regulate campaign finance
for state and local elections.) Public finance of parties and elections
now constitutes the fourth source of party finance.

The 1971 federal Election Campaign Act as amended later in
the 1970s, provides for

(1) Public disclosures of campaign contributions. Candidates
and political parties must make public the names of all donors who
contribute $50 or more.

(2) Spending limits. No individual can contribute more than
$1,000 to a candidate each year. Candidates, PACs, and parties are
also limited in how much they can spend in both the primary- and
general-election campaigns for congressional and presidential
races. However, no limit is placed on the amount that candidates
can spend from their personal funds.

(3) Public financing of presidential elections. Qualified candidates for the presidency are given public funds for their campaign
(to qualify, candidates must obtain $5,000 in small gifts in each of
twenty states); qualified political parties are given money to finance
their nominating conventions. Candidates who receive public funds
for their general-election campaigns are prohibited from raising
additional money from private sources.

In 1980, the two parties' presidential candidates each received
$29.4 million in public funds. While substantial, it was far less than
private groups spent on the presidential election, usually with funds
from business sources. PACs spent an additional $12 million on
Ronald Reagan's campaign and the Republican national party organizations spent $65 million. This represents more than double
what Reagan received in public funds.[17]

Since the legal spending limits do not apply to contributions
that candidates make to their own campaigns, wealthy candidates
are given a substantial edge.

Lavish campaign spending does not guarantee nomination or
electoral victory. There are numerous examples of losing candidates who outspend their rivals. However, having access to ample
funds is a necessity if a candidate is to have a serious prospect of

[17]Drew, p. 107.

winning. As humorist Will Rogers remarked, "It takes a lot of money to even get beat with."[18] Nor is it a coincidence that winners usually spend more. For example, in the 1982 senatorial elections, winning candidates outspent losers in 27 out of the 33 Senate seats.[19]

Furthermore, campaign finance reforms have not only failed to diminish the importance of private funds, but the political influence of business has not been greater in over half a century. At the same time that the campaign finance reforms set limits on individual contributions, authorization was eased for corporate PACs to solicit contributions from their executives, workers, and stockholders. Since then, business and the Republican party have forged closer ties and derived mutual benefits from the PAC revolution.

The PAC phenomenon

Campaign finance has been revolutionized by the eruption of PACs within the past decade.[20] In the 1950s and 1960s, many labor unions and a few trade and professional associations (for example, the American Medical Association) sponsored PACs. Now, however, the number of PACs has skyrocketed and the vast majority are tied to business interests and favor conservative (nearly always Republican) candidates. Business groups have organized PACs as part of their more general political and economic offensive, described in Chapter 4. Whereas in 1974 there were 201 labor PACs and 89 corporate PACs, by 1976 corporate PACs outnumbered labor PACs. In 1980, there were over 1,100 corporate PACs compared to fewer than 300 labor PACs, and in 1982 corporate PACs had zoomed to 1,500 (along with 600 additional trade association PACs) while there were less than 400 labor PACs.[21]

The spending limit on individual donors does not hinder PAC operations; while a single donor can give no more than $1,000 to a single PAC, there is no limit on the number of PACs to which one

[18]Congressional Quarterly, *Dollar Politics* (Washington, D.C., 1971), p. 3.
[19]Drew, p. 25.
[20]For analyses of PACs, see Michael J. Malbin, ed., *Parties, Interest Groups, and Campaign Finance Laws* (Washington, D.C., 1980).
[21]Michael Useem, "Business and Politics in the United States and United Kingdom: The Origins of Heightened Political Activity of Large Corporations during the 1970s and Early 1980s," *Theory & Society* 12 (May 1983): 281–308; and Edsall, p. 131.

can contribute. Thus, affluent donors simply write checks of $1,000 each to the many PACs that will favor their cause. And, while PACs are limited to contributing a maximum of $5,000 to a candidate's primary campaign and $5,000 to the general election campaign, this further encourages the proliferation of PACs, each giving the legal limit to a given candidate. Moreover, PACs can spend unlimited amounts for a candidate's campaign if they do not coordinate their spending with the candidate. A host of other provisions provide ample leeway for PACs to spend large sums.

Business PACs, as well as conservative single-issue PACs favoring causes like anti-abortion and school prayer, have helped move American politics to the right in two respects. First, they favor conservative causes and candidates regardless of party. In the past, most PACs supported incumbents in Congress and at other levels, regardless of party or (in most cases) ideological outlook, on the pragmatic ground that this would secure access in the future. In the 1980s many PACs began supporting conservative candidates even when they were challengers. (There was a modest rise of liberal PACs, for example, environmental PACs, but their influence is far more limited.) In one study of corporate PAC contributions in those congressional races where a clear choice existed between a very conservative and very liberal candidate, over three-fourths of all PAC contributions went to the conservative. Among the PACs giving virtually all their funds to conservatives were major corporations who present themselves as moderate, including McDonald's, Whirlpool, B.F. Goodrich, and Dow Chemical.[22]

Second, the new breed of PACs favor the Republican party by a wide margin. Through the 1970s, the two parties raised about the same amount. However, when business mounted a sharp counterattack to the expansion of the welfare state in the late 1970s, it used the Republican party as its political spearhead. Since then, thanks to the vastly greater funds that capital commands compared to any other private group, the competition for funds between the two parties has turned into a rout. The result is to end any semblance of fair party competition in the current period.

For example, for the 1982 congressional elections, Democratic party committees raised $39 million; Republican committees raised

[22]Dan Clawson, Marvin J. Karson, and Allen Kaufman, "The Corporate PACs Donations in the 1980 Congressional Elections," unpublished manuscript, 1984.

$215 million—more than five times as much. In the first half of 1984, the National Republican Senatorial Committee had raised $58 million; its Democratic counterpart raised $6 million.[23]

What difference does it make that, in 1983, the Republican National Committee's expenditures on stamps alone were about equal to the Democratic National Committee's entire budget? With its ample resources, the Republican party can contribute to state party organizations, recruit promising candidates and provide them with funds, and conduct research and support campaigns using the costly technology of polls, campaign specialists, computerized mailing lists, and computer analysis. In brief, the Republican party can engage far more effectively in the sophisticated political marketing that passes for electoral competition in the United States.

PRESIDENTIAL ELECTIONS

Among the thousands of electoral contests held in the United States, the presidential election held every four years captures the bulk of media and popular attention. A study of presidential elections illuminates the pressures buffeting the party system in this era of political transition.

Space does not permit analyzing state and local electoral contests. (Congressional elections were described in Chapter 5.) However, elections for local office are an important subject in their own right; the outcome of state and local elections has an important impact on the character of daily life throughout America. Further, the influence of political money may be even greater for these elections.

The closest that American parties come to the annual or biannual congresses of major European parties is the Democratic and Republican national conventions held every four years to nominate candidates for president and vice president and to draft a party platform. Since Jackson's time, the national convention has represented the sovereign party, meeting in all its majesty. That picture is changing, however; the convention as a television special has

[23]Edsall, p. 78; and *National Journal*, September 1, 1984, p. 1618.

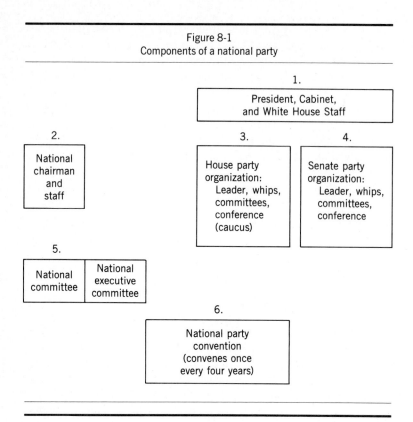

Figure 8-1
Components of a national party

1.

President, Cabinet,
and White House Staff

2.

National
chairman
and
staff

3.

House party
organization:
Leader, whips,
committees,
conference
(caucus)

4.

Senate party
organization:
Leader, whips,
committees,
conference

5.

National
committee

National
executive
committee

6.

National party
convention
(convenes once
every four years)

supplanted the convention as a decision-making body. The use of public opinion polls competes with the expert judgment of local politicians and convention delegates regarding the grass-roots popularity of different candidates. The candidates themselves have begun to develop elaborate preconvention campaigns, such as those of John F. Kennedy in 1960, Barry Goldwater in 1964, Richard M. Nixon in 1968, George McGovern in 1972, Jimmy Carter in 1976, Ronald Reagan in 1980, and Walter Mondale in 1984. (In fact, campaigning for the nomination now operates on a nonstop basis.) The result is that the choice of a candidate has usually been made even before the convention meets. The convention merely ratifies the results of the informal preconvention selection process, puts on a show for television (the convention is staged to have the maximum nationwide impact on prime time), and disperses. In every presidential convention from 1956 to 1976, both parties nominated a presidential candidate on the first ballot; in previous years, except when there was an incumbent president, a first-ballot nomination was a rarity.

Yet bruising battles still occur for the presidential nomination. In 1984, Walter Mondale's meticulously organized nomination drive was disrupted when Gary Hart and Jesse Jackson, seeking support from other elements in the Democratic coalition, were quite successful in the primaries.

The rules used to choose convention delegates affect the kind of candidate who gets nominated. Until 1968, most delegates came from the ranks of the two parties' public officeholders and organizational leaders at the state and local level. Nearly all delegates were white, male, professional politicians; their views were centrist. As a result of severe criticism of the procedures for delegate selection in 1968, the Democratic party sponsored a number of commissions that recommended drastic changes in the manner in which convention delegates are selected. The preferred methods are now state conventions of party members and especially state primaries. (Three-quarters of all states hold primaries for both parties.) The party also committed itself to recruiting women and minority-group delegates. (The Republican party has also somewhat liberalized recruitment of its convention delegates.) For the 1984 Democratic Convention, the party partially reversed itself by reserving a bloc of seats for Democratic elected and organization officials. The result was to favor the prospects of party insider Walter Mondale. However, his crushing defeat suggested that the Democrats' major problem was not the rules used to select a presidential candidate but the lack of funds, organizational strength, and program to develop majority support.

Who gets nominated? An analysis of the candidates illuminates the general significance of political parties and elections. To begin with, potential nominees are usually confined to the vice president, senators, and governors; and all but one major candidate in the past half century have been white, male, Protestant, and relatively affluent. (The exception was John F. Kennedy, a Catholic.) Put another way, any one of the following characteristics has (until now) been sufficient to disqualify one from consideration: female, black, Jewish, known to have had psychiatric treat-

Figure 8-2
A fictitious image of American national party organization

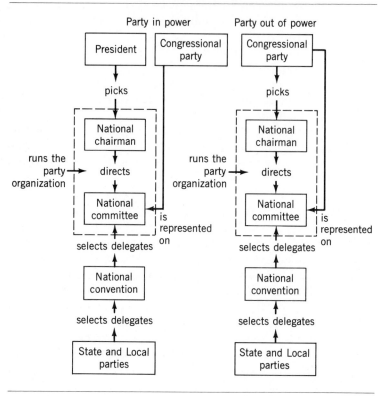

ment, poor, or atheist. The list could be extended but the point is clear: presidential candidates are chosen out of a small pool from which the vast majority of Americans are excluded.

In 1984, the Democrats took the unprecedented step of nominating a woman, Geraldine Ferraro, for vice president. Another important development was the attempt of Jesse Jackson, a black candidate, to gain the Democratic presidential nomination. While both of these steps have helped to stretch the traditional limits of electoral politics, their impact was quite small. However dramatic was Ferraro's candidacy, the position of vice president (and even

more the nominee for vice president) is of relatively minor importance. As for Jackson, only a tiny proportion of whites voted for
him in primaries; despite his call for a "rainbow coalition" of
women, workers, blacks, Hispanics, and other minorities, his support was nearly exclusively from the black community.

The technology of political campaigns

Political parties have generally been declining as independent
forces in American politics. Their loss of power can be seen from
their diminished role in the campaign itself. Three mechanisms
have replaced parties as the dominant instruments in election campaigns: the candidate's own campaign organization, the media, and
professional consulting firms.

Candidates for offices at all levels—from president to town
alderman—prefer to develop their own campaign organizations,
staffed by their personal supporters, separate from the official party
and working in uneasy alliance with it. A bewildering array of
groups may be formed to work for the candidate's election (there
were 222 national-level committees in the 1968 presidential race—
many created simply to evade campaign-finance laws).[24] Within the
overall campaign organization, the regular party apparatus ranks
low, for candidates have more trust in, and control over, organizations staffed by their personal associates.

Since the late 1970s, however, and thanks to a massive infusion
of corporate cash, the Republican party has become thoroughly
revitalized. The Republican National Committee's large permanent staff and sophisticated campaign technology, as well as its cash
contributions, provide Republican candidates with a substantial
edge over their Democratic opponents.

The media, especially radio and television now play a fundamental role in political campaigning. It has become commonplace
that a candidate can reach more people in one television "spot"
than in weeks of arduous campaigning. Reliance on the media
reduces the need for elaborate grass-roots party machinery. Assuming the candidate has the money—no small matter as we have
seen—the media make possible a campaign blitz, and under con-

[24]Herbert E. Alexander, *Financing the 1968 Election* (Lexington, Mass., 1971),
p. 117.

ditions of the candidate's own choosing. Television makes the "selling of the president" possible as no other medium can.[25]

The rise of television has led to an emphasis on image over issues. Ronald Reagan excelled at the new style of campaigning. One reporter observed about his campaign, "Issues take a back seat to invoking such themes as leadership and opportunity, to creating visual images, communicating shared values and stimulating moods and feelings in the audience." Reagan's campaign, the reporter commented, "creates the sensation of being immersed in the manufactured happiness of an infinitely extended television commercial."[26]

Another recent development further weakening the party organization is professional campaign consultants. According to political scientist Frank Sorauf, the parties' "fairly primitive campaign skills have been superseded by a new campaign technology, and more and more they are finding themselves among the technologically unemployed."[27] There have always been specialists in the art of political organizing; people who knew how to get a press conference scheduled, prepare campaign literature, set up a public rally, and resolve the numerous crises that arise in a political campaign. In the past, these people were connected with a party organization and they always worked with only one party.

But in recent years, there has developed whole campaign organizations for hire: the rent-a-car principle applied to politics. Political scientist Samuel Eldersveld suggests, "These firms apply the basic principles of merchandising to political campaigns. They are selling a product (a candidate) and they therefore will use whatever many persuasion techniques of a manipulative nature to do the job."[28]

The new industry of professional campaign consulting has boomed. In contrast to the former free-lance campaign specialist, the consulting firm handles the entire political campaign: speechwriting, polling, data processing, organizing rallies, campaign literature, and on and on. Consultants have become the new gurus of

[25]Joe McGinnis, *The Selling of the President, 1968* (New York, 1969).
[26]Howell Raines, "Reagan Appears to Succeed by Avoiding Specific Issues," *New York Times,* September 23, 1984.
[27]Frank J. Sorauf, *Party Politics in America,* 2nd ed. (Boston, 1972), p. 411.
[28]Eldersveld, p. 286.

politics. They are well paid for their services: a top consultant can command $200,000 in a statewide election, far more for a national election.[29]

What kind of wizardry does the consultant provide? One example, from a highly regarded consultant: "It used to be you'd take a poll, set up a media plan, and six months later find out how it worked. Nowadays, you can send out your media, check out how it worked by the very next day and fine-tune the message accordingly."[30] The use of tracking polls, the process of continuous polling, is effective—and costly.

The new technology increasingly shapes the whole campaign, as the following example illustrates: "Using computers, campaign technicians can combine census data, postal zip codes, previous voting preferences, economic incomes and other information to define voter life-style profiles that can be used effectively to determine media buys, guide the content of direct-mail fundraising drives and dictate the selection of issues for the candidate to emphasize."[31]

What is the message that the expensive campaign gadgetry produces for the candidate? The new-style campaigning carries even further the past tendency to downplay issues and concentrate on simple, popular themes.

Public opinion polls repeatedly show that the broad electorate is unable to distinguish between the policy stands of opposing candidates. Yet responsibility for the electorate's ignorance lies in good measure with the candidates themselves, who take pains to minimize their policy differences and maximize ambiguity. For example, in 1968 the country was wracked by the Vietnam war. To what extent did the Democratic and Republican presidential candidates offer alternative policies toward the war? Not much, according to political scientists Benjamin Page and Richard Brody.

> It is possible for scholars, after reading all their [the candidates'] speeches and statements, to arrive at judgments about what their "real" positions were; but the ordinary citizen may be forgiven if he

---

[29]Dom Bonafede, "Costly Campaigns: Consultants Cash In As Candidates Spend What They Must," *National Journal,* April 16, 1983.

[30]Ron Susskind, "The Power of Political Consultants," *New York Times Magazine,* August 12, 1984, p. 57.

[31]Dom Bonafede, "Strides in Technology are Changing the Face of Political Campaigning," *National Journal,* April 7, 1984, p. 657.

failed to penetrate the haze of vague hints which alternated with total silence about Vietnam in most of the candidates' rhetoric.[32]

In a later study, Page finds that "the most striking feature of a candidate's rhetoric about policy is its extreme vagueness. . . . In short, policy statements are infrequent, inconspicuous, and unspecific. Presidential candidates are skilled at appearing to say much while actually saying very little."[33]

Decline of the parties' electoral reach

Possibly because parties have become quite ineffective in developing distinctive programs, they are becoming less able to mobilize and control the electorate. Reviewing shifts in voter alignments since the 1960s, Walter Dean Burnham sees "a change of revolutionary scope" in progress.[34] Whereas previous electoral realignments strengthened the party system, the present shift is apparently away from political parties altogether as voters choose candidates without much regard for party labels.

With some early exceptions, the first major studies of the American electorate that relied on public opinion poll data were carried out in the 1950s, a period of unusual political quiescence. In these circumstances, it is not surprising that election studies found voters to be relatively uninvolved in politics, hazy about differences between the parties, more clear about their partisan affiliation than their stand on political issues, and trustful toward government. During this period, voters paid little attention to issues, changed their position frequently, but voted with great regularity for the same political party. In retrospect, the 1950s represent a digression from the polarized conflicts that came before and after.

As the New Deal coalition began to erode in the 1960s under the double strain of an unpopular war abroad and domestic tensions, candidates began to put forward sharper ideological alternatives. Barry Goldwater's conservative candidacy in 1964

---

[32]Benjamin I. Page and Richard A. Brody, "The Vietnam War Issue," *The American Political Science Review* 66 (December 1972): 987.

[33]Benjamin I. Page, *Choices and Echoes in Presidential Elections: Rational Man and Electoral Democracy* (Chicago, 1978), p. 153.

[34]Walter Dean Burnham, "American Politics in the 1970's: Beyond Party?" in Chambers and Burnham, p. 308. Also see Martin P. Wattenberg, *The Decline of American Political Parties, 1952–1980* (Cambridge, Mass., 1984).

Table 8-1
Partisan loyalties of particular groups
of the American public (1980 Presidential Election)
(as a percentage)

Group	Democratic Identifiers	Independents	Republican Identifiers
Age			
18–29	31	45	19
30–54	41	35	22
55–69	47	30	22
70 and over	48	22	29
Race—Blacks	72	19	5
Religion			
Catholics	43	37	19
Jewish	73	23	2
Protestants	41	32	25
Education			
Grade school	54	25	17
High school	42	36	19
College	34	36	30

Source: Samuel J. Eldersveld, *Political Parties in American Society* (New York: Basic Books, 1982), p. 56. Sources listed in original. Copyright © 1982 by Basic Books, Inc., Publishers. Reprinted by permission of the publisher.

prompted ideological self-examination and divided opinion. Reform programs sponsored by Democratic presidents in the 1960s further polarized politics and increased public awareness of issues and alternatives. Responses to questions about political beliefs changed drastically between the 1950s and the 1970s; the proportion of those who regarded themselves as centrists declined and those who regarded themselves as leftists or rightists increased.

Younger voters (those in their twenties) were especially affected by the turbulent conflicts of the 1960s. They did not judge these events from the perspective of a stable partisan attachment. Instead, their formative political years occurred as the present crisis began to emerge. When political parties provided little help in understanding or coping with the crisis, young voters saw no reason to give their allegiance to one party or the other—or, for that matter, the whole party system. Thus, in contrast to 1952, when

Table 8-2
Measures of the Public's Interest and Confidence in Parties (as a percentage)

Interest	1952	1956	1960	1964	1968	1972	1976	1980
Use of "party" in evaluating candidates (all citizens)	46	41	41	34	40	24		
Use of "party" in evaluating candidates (identifiers)	52	46	47	37	44	27		
Positive evaluation of own or both parties	74	72	74	64	59	49	49	50
Feel parties "help a good deal in making the government pay attention" to the public				41	36	26	17	28
Do not mention one or the other of the parties as doing the best job on a problem the respondent considers most important (that is, the percentage who are neutral or indifferent)			38	34	48	51	54	50

Source: Samuel J. Eldersveld, *Political Parties in American Society* (New York: Basic Books, 1982), p. 418. Sources listed in original. Copyright © 1982 by Basic Books, Inc., Publishers. Reprinted by permission of the publisher.

only one-quarter of the youngest voters considered themselves independents, in 1974, more than half of the youngest voters considered themselves independents.[35]

Young voters displayed a new kind of political stance in the 1970s: more independent of political parties, skeptical of government, and involved and coherent in their approach to political issues. For these voters—and those youth who came of voting age in the early 1980s and gravitated to the Republican party—the search for an attractive ideological alternative now rivals or exceeds traditional partisan loyalty as a guide to voting choice. The new-style voters tend to split their votes between candidates of different

[35]Norman H. Nie, Sidney Verba, and John R. Petrocik, *The Changing American Voter* (Cambridge, Mass., 1976), p. 60.

parties, switch from one party to the next in successive elections, and may not vote at all, given the unsatisfactory alternatives that parties offer.

If young educated voters led the way in the issue-oriented politics of the present period, voters of all ages and social groups have joined in. Political scientists Norman Nie, Sidney Verba, and John Petrocik comment, "Perhaps the most dramatic political change in the American public in the past two decades has been the decline of partisanship."[36]

The result has left parties floundering as they are no longer able to count on a large stable following. Factional divisions within the parties have increased and candidates often abandon reliance on the party altogether once they gain its nomination, preferring to mount their own campaign and downplay their party affiliation.

Decline of the party system

The decline of the party system can be documented by several related phenomena. First, voter turnout is falling. Through the end of the nineteenth century, voting turnout sometimes exceeded 80 percent of the eligible voters. About 53 percent of the eligible electorate voted in 1984, roughly the same historic low as voted in 1980. And turnout in off-years, without a presidential election to bring out voters, does not exceed 40 percent. Turnout rates in Great Britain, the Netherlands, Austria and other nations of Western Europe rarely fall below 70 percent, a result of more attractive alternatives as well as the fact that working-class movements have succeeded in eliminating the barriers to voting that exist in the United States.

One reason for the sharp drop in voting turnout after the turn of the century was a Progressive reform requiring people to register in order to vote, defended by the Progressives as a way to end election malpractices and improve the quality of the electorate. However, the emergence of personal registration requirements "coincided with the mass immigration of foreign-born newcomers in American cities and the move to disenfranchise Blacks in the South."[37]

[36]*Ibid.*, p. 47.
[37]Penn Kimball, *The Disconnected* (New York, 1972), p. 4.

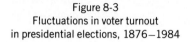

Figure 8-3
Fluctuations in voter turnout
in presidential elections, 1876–1984

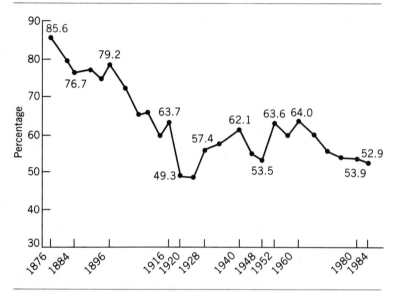

Source: Samuel J. Eldersveld, *Political Parties in American Society* (New York: Basic Books, 1982), p. 336, and *New York Times*, November 8, 1984.

Political scientists William Crotty and Gary Jacobson observe that "the biggest structural barrier to the vote continues to be registration requirements."[38] Even when political activists mount local voter registration campaigns, as occurred on a wide scale for the 1984 elections, the results are usually meager. It takes extensive resources to organize such a campaign. Further, local voting registrars and other government officials often seek to block these efforts on the grounds that the "wrong" kind of people are being registered. In other capitalist democracies, government is responsible for registering voters; this explains why most citizens are registered and voting rates are high. Restrictions on registration are

[38]William J. Crotty and Gary C. Jacobsen, *American Parties in Decline* (Boston, 1980), p. 21. For a study that reaches similar conclusions, see G. Bingham Powell, Jr., "American Voter Turnout in Comparative Perspective," *American Political Science Review* 80 (March 1986): 17–43.

class biased. Professor of journalism Penn Kimball observes that registration "discriminates most particularly against the poor. . . . Voter registration operates as an effective system of political control."[39]

Political scientist Benjamin Ginsberg compared differences in voting turnout among different income groups. Affluent citizens vote in high proportions (over 80 percent) regardless of the complexity of registration procedures. However, turnout among lower-income groups is heavily influenced by registration procedures.[40] In states with complex registration requirements, low-income citizens have a 50 percent turnout rate; in states with simple registration procedures, they vote at a 67 percent rate.

Class-related differences in turnout rates provide the Republican party with a solid bonus, since its major strength is among higher income groups. In 1980, voters with incomes under $10,000 supported Democrats over Republicans in elections to the House of Representatives by 64 to 36 percent. Voters with incomes over $30,000 supported Republicans by a margin of 55 to 44 percent. Yet because the more affluent voters had a 34 percent higher turnout rate, their voting preferences counted far more heavily.[41]

More generally, low turnout means that both parties are more conservative. Political scientist Frank Sorauf suggests that "the parties find it easier to be moderate and pragmatic because the electorate to which they respond is largely settled in and committed to the present basic social arrangements."[42] Low turnout means that party competition plays to a half-empty house. If the full audience participated, the chances are that more would change than a shift from one party as presently constituted to the other. The entire party system—as well as the government—would doubtless be more responsive to the wishes and interests of that half of the electorate presently underrepresented.

The lessening importance of the party as a guide to candidate selection is another reason for the decline of the party system. In 1952, nearly half the citizens interviewed by the Survey Research Center of the University of Michigan mentioned the party affiliation of the presidential candidates as a reason for liking or disliking

[39]Kimball, pp. 3–4.
[40]Ginsberg, p. 37.
[41]Edsall, p. 62.
[42]Frank J. Sorauf, *Party Politics in America,* 2nd ed. (Boston, 1972), p. 203.

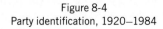

Figure 8-4
Party identification, 1920–1984

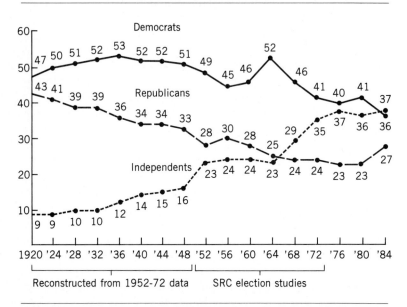

Source: Norman H. Nie, Sidney Verba, and John P. Petrocik, *The Changing American Voter* (Cambridge, Mass., Harvard University Press, 1976). p. 83; Samuel J. Eldersveld, *Political Parties in American Society* (New York: Basic Books, 1982), p. 76; and *New York Times*, October 7, 1984.

them; since 1972, only one-fourth of voters interviewed have mentioned the candidates' party affiliation in explaining their evaluations.[43] Reviewing recent developments, two analysts observe, "The clearest trend . . . is the general rise of the neutrals—individuals who saw neither party as doing what they wanted."[44]

The rise of vote switching and ticket splitting is also important to an understanding of the parties' decline. As voters judge on bases other than the candidates' party label, there is increased switching from one party to the other. This is true even among citizens who identify with one political party or the other: whereas only one-quarter of party identifiers in 1952 reported having voted

[43]Nie, Verba, and Petrocik, p. 68.
[44]Mule Black and George B. Rabinowitz, "American Electoral Change, 1952–1972," in William Crotty, ed., *The Party Symbol* (San Francisco, 1980), p. 241.

at some point for the opposite party's presidential candidate, in 1980 over half reported they had bolted their party's presidential ticket.[45] There has also been an increase in the number of citizens who vote a split ticket, casting their ballot for the presidential candidate of one party and the congressional candidate of the other party. The party label seems to have lost its unifying force. Professor Burnham calls this a four-party system in which voters remain loyal to congressional candidates in election after election but shift their vote in presidential elections.[46]

Finally, there is the rise of independents. In the 1950s, most citizens identified themselves as followers of one of the two major parties. Partisan identification was stable through time and was transmitted from one generation to the next. Starting in the early 1960s, the number of voters identifying themselves as independents began to rise sharply. In 1984, independents pulled close to the Democrats as the largest "party," ahead of the Republicans! (Republican identifiers increased and independents declined in 1985). Further, younger voters are especially apt to be independents, thus presaging a possible further decline in the parties' reach in the future.

Since the early 1980s, there has been a partial reversal of party decline. Thanks to the massive funds it has received from business, the Republican party has been especially fortunate. Further, through effective direct-mail methods, the Republican party succeeded in increasing the number of donors from 35,000 in the early 1970s to over 2 million by 1980. Political contributing not only provides cash but strengthens the donors' party identification. "For the first time in American political history, there exists a substantial number of citizens who consider themselves to be *members* of a national party; they can carry cards in their wallets to prove it!"[47] The Republican National Committee assists candidates and party organizations from the presidential down to the local level. Because it lacks money, the Democratic party lags far behind in these domains. Republican revitalization raises anew the question of whether the party system is undergoing realignment or decay.

---

[45]Eldersveld, p. 77.
[46]Burnham, "American Politics," in Chambers and Burnham, pp. 317–40.
[47]F. Cristopher Arterton, "Political Money and Party Strength," in Joel L. Fleishman, eds., *The Future of American Political Parties: The Challenge of Governance* (Englewood Cliffs, N.J., 1982), p. 105.

REALIGNMENT AND/OR DECAY OF POLITICAL PARTIES?

A political party represents an informal coalition of sectional, class, gender, economic, and racial groups.[48] Within a stable historical period, a party's electoral following tends to remain loyal through time. For example, Franklin Delano Roosevelt ushered in a long period of stable Democratic dominance during the 1930s by welding together a coalition of organized labor, the poor, white Southerners (whose Democratic sympathies dated back a century), blacks, Jews, and Catholic immigrants from Southern and Eastern Europe who were concentrated in industrialized, urban centers of the Northeast and Midwest.

A key partner in the New Deal coalition, in influence if not numbers, was a group of pragmatic international bankers, corporate executives, and financiers in the Northeast, like Averill Harriman. They helped Roosevelt develop policies that favored internationally oriented corporate capital and ensured that his domestic approach would not be unduly influenced by advocates of central planning and extensive redistribution.

The Democratic party developed a conservative form of Keynesianism to sponsor decades of economic expansion. (See Chapter 3.) The federal government helped facilitate American corporate expansion within the United States and abroad, and used the "growth dividend" for welfare programs that consolidated the support of its working-class constituency.

However, the New Deal coalition began to splinter in the 1960s, a result of socioeconomic changes that differentially affected the various member groups. When the economic crisis vastly reduced the growth dividend, and the Democratic party could not find an effective way to restore growth, its dominance waned.

Whereas the Democratic party leadership had been able to reconcile the various elements in its coalition in the 1940s and 1950s, this became increasingly difficult thereafter. Take the movement of Southern blacks northward, for example. Between 1940

---

[48]Members of a given group rarely are unanimous in their support for a party, although the one-party (Democratic) South prior to the 1960s, and blacks in the 1980s (about 90 percent of whom voted for Jimmy Carter and Walter Mondale), did display this tendency.

and 1970, 5 million blacks moved to Northern cities, a result of being forced off the land through the commercialization of Southern agriculture. The consequence was to force into the open the racial issue that the Democratic party had submerged during the New Deal. Before the 1960s, Southern Democrats had succeeded in preventing outside interference with the system of racial injustice in the South. But after a sizeable number of blacks achieved the vote in Northern cities and a wave of black insurgency erupted there in the 1960s, President Kennedy and Johnson sponsored far-reaching civil rights legislation. For the first time in recent American history, the federal government sought to end racial discrimination in education, voting, and public accommodations. Johnson's Great Society program was another response to black militance and provided particular benefits to blacks. These policies set in motion white Southerners' swing away from the Democratic party (and eventually a swing by white Northerners as well). During the Johnson landslide of 1964, the South abandoned its historic Democratic affiliation, and conservative Southern whites proved a major source of support for Barry Goldwater. The trend continued under Presidents Nixon and Ford, whose opposition to school busing and general conservatism contributed to the Southern shift toward the Republican party.

In the years between 1964 and the early 1970s, the percentage of native white Southerners identifying themselves as Democrats declined from 71 percent to 47 percent. It has fallen further since then, and the South has become a Republican stronghold at the presidential and congressional level. On the other hand, black Americans gave increasing support to the Democrats; blacks made up about one-fourth of Walter Mondale's voting base in 1984: more than 90 percent of blacks who voted in 1984 supported Mondale, compared to 30 percent of whites.

The Democratic party was severely split by the Vietnam War and new social issues developing in the 1960s, including drugs, crime, abortion, gun control, and the like. Youthful voters on the left held the Democratic party responsible for the American invasion of Indo-China; at the same time, many Catholic, working-class Democrats blamed the party for being too "permissive" on social issues. Although increasing numbers of women were attracted to the Democratic party, in part on the basis of its stands on social and economic issues—which created a "gender gap," with women more pro-Democratic than men—white males deserted the Democratic party in droves.

The Democratic party was the victim of its own success: since the 1930s, the party of out-groups struggling for entry into the political system, the Democratic constituency became eroded in part thanks to Democratic success in fostering economic growth. Yet the biggest strains developed within the party as growth gave way to stagflation from the mid-1970s. Those groups that had benefited from New Deal welfare policies and the expansion of the welfare state shifted to defending their gains in face of further expansion. Political analyst Thomas Edsall suggests that stagflation

> eroded the fragile consensus behind Democratic domestic spending programs. . . . The Democratic party had permitted a situation to evolve that encouraged hostility between its taxpaying constituents and its nontaxpaying, poor constituents, hostility guaranteed to become directed against the party itself.[49]

By the 1980s, the Democratic party was criticized for supposedly being soft on the Soviet Union, soft on crime, and champions of big government and high taxes. Moreover, the party was severely divided about its future direction, symbolized by a conflict for the Democratic nomination in 1984 among three of the party's warring factions. Walter Mondale attempted to revive the battered New Deal growth coalition but failed to explain why the same policies that had produced stagflation in the 1970s would produce growth in the 1980s. Gary Hart sought to appeal to the "Yuppies" (young, urban, upwardly mobile professionals) but his "new ideas," which implied abandoning basic industries in favor of high-tech, infuriated organized labor. Jesse Jackson attempted to fashion a progressive "rainbow coalition" of "out-groups" in the Democratic party and American society. Yet the fact that he failed to attract significant white support was in part sad testimony to the persistence of racism in the United States.

Given the Democratic party's lack of an attractive new approach, young voters not socialized into the New Deal coalition have flocked to the Republican party. Ronald Reagan got his strongest support from this group. The decades-old trend in which young voters tend to identify with the Democratic party has been

[49]Edsall, pp. 40, 213.

reversed in the 1980s. If the stream of younger voters just entering the electorate continue to support the Republican party, the Republicans will consolidate their position as the new dominant party.

Whichever of the two parties, as they are presently constituted, succeeds in gaining stable majority support, a substantial conservative swing has occurred in American politics in the last decade. Both parties have contributed to the change. Democratic president Jimmy Carter shifted during his presidency from expanding environmental protection and welfare-state programs to curtailing them in a vain attempt to woo business. And this is how a business reporter described the field of candidates for the 1984 Democratic presidential nomination: "Close your eyes, listen to what they're saying and you'd think it was the G.O.P."[50]

As for the Republican party, Edsall comments, "In 1964, the Republican presidential nominee, Senator Barry Goldwater, was decisively defeated while advocating a major reduction in domestic fiscal spending and a sharp increase in military spending; sixteen years later, Ronald Reagan was elected to the presidency on a platform remarkably similar to Goldwater's. . . ."[51]

But there were important differences between the parties. The Republican party under Ronald Reagan's leadership more aggressively promoted extensive redistribution of power and resources from the poor to the rich, a policy which has provided enormous benefits to the Republican constituency. Whereas in the 1980s the Democratic party became internally divided and unsure of its identity, the Republican party was experiencing an extraordinary resurgence. Although cleavages among Republicans increased as lame duck President Ronald Reagan was less able to unite the party, a host of diverse groups, causes, and organizations have found the Republican party useful to press their demands.

Five sources of Republican support can be identified in addition to the party's traditional base among white Protestants. First, many youthful voters, already mentioned, regard the Democratic party as backward-looking and irrelevant. Second, male workers, who formerly voted in high proportions for the Democrats, came

---

[50]Peter K. Kilborn, "Democrats Search for a Winning Issue," *New York Times*, February 26, 1984. (G.O.P. stands for Grand Old Party, the Republicans' informal name.)
[51]Edsall, p. 15.

to resent its high spending, high tax policies and supposed permissiveness on social issues. Third, what political analyst Kevin Phillips calls radical populist post-conservatives, including religious fundamentalists, reactionary single-issue groups like opponents of gun control and abortion, and embittered critics of "big government," gravitated to the Republican party.[52]

Fourth, and related to the third point, the newly ascendant and fast-growing Sunbelt, in which a majority of Americans now live, is highly receptive to the Republican program. Phillips suggests, "The Sun Belt epitomizes the moods and forces resurgent in the United States of the early 1980s: nationalism, fundamentalist religion, but also high technology and 'can do' entrepreneurialism."[53] (The Sunbelt's nationalist values have a solid basis in self-interest, since military spending is highly concentrated in the region.) Fifth and finally, mention has already been made of the massive support that business has provided to the Republican party since the mid-1970s. In Chapter 3, we described the rightward shift by business in the 1970s in opposition to environmental regulation. This was nourished by the growth of a new maverick breed of multimillionaire entrepreneurs (for example, independent oil producers) based in the Sunbelt and ferociously opposed to government regulation; this group has been the major source of funds for far-right causes and think tanks. It has been a bridge between the corporate elite of the Northeast and populist conservative groups.[54] In the process, the traditional meaning of conservatism has been altered.

Phillips points out that conservatives have traditionally wanted to *conserve* the existing system, for the sensible reason that they controlled it. However, this changed in the 1960s and 1970s with the decline of United States power abroad, coupled with an expanded welfare state, more permissive social and cultural values, and the rise of the new left, environmental, women's and black movements. Conservatives came to believe that they had lost political control; consequently, rather than attempting to preserve the existing system, they sought to change it.[55]

[52]Kevin P. Phillips, *Post-Conservative America: People, Politics and Ideology in a Time of Crisis* (New York, 1982).
[53]*Ibid.*, p. 237.
[54]See Edsall.
[55]Phillips, chapter 3.

Despite Republican successes in the early 1980s, however, the party remains divided between its traditional conservative wing and the new, grass-roots populists on the far right. Former Republican governor of Delaware Russell W. Peterson observed, "Moderate Republicans believe in living within our income, while the current [Reagan] leadership is the most reckless by far that we have ever had in office. . . ."[56]

For their part, populist conservative ideologues remain hostile toward traditional corporate capital. Richard Viguerie, who pioneered the use of direct mail appeals for far-right and Republican causes, asserts, "I've come to realize in the past few years that the big business community . . . has its hooks so solidly into the Republican party that I'm not sure you can really make the Republican Party a vehicle that will be responsive to the populist people at the grass roots level. . . ."[57]

These differences were temporarily submerged in the Republican resurgence of the early 1980s. Reagan was handily reelected in 1984 thanks to his extraordinary powers of political persuasion and ability to evade responsibility (the "Teflon effect"), the temporarily favorable economic situation, Mondale's lackluster appeal, and the Democratic party's decline. Mondale was never able to counter the way Reagan posed the choice, in his acceptance speech at the 1984 Republican convention: "their government of pessimism, fear and limits, or ours of hope, confidence and growth." Reagan's popular vote share of 59 percent was exceeded in the twentieth century only by FDR in 1936 and Lyndon Johnson in 1964; Reagan's sweep of the Electoral College (he won all votes save those of Mondale's native Minnesota and the District of Columbia) was even more one-sided.

Along the way, Reagan received majorities from most groups in the United States, save for union members (57 percent for Mondale), big city residents (62 percent Mondale), Hispanic voters (65 percent Mondale), the unemployed (68 percent Mondale), Jews (70 percent Mondale), blacks (90 percent Mondale), and a large majority of low-income voters. Reagan did especially well among men (64 percent, compared to 55 percent among women), the

---

[56]*National Journal,* August 18, 1984.
[57]Rob Gurwick, "Left & Right Compete for Populist Mantle," *Congressional Quarterly,* April 21, 1984, p. 915.

Figure 8-5
The National Vote in 1984

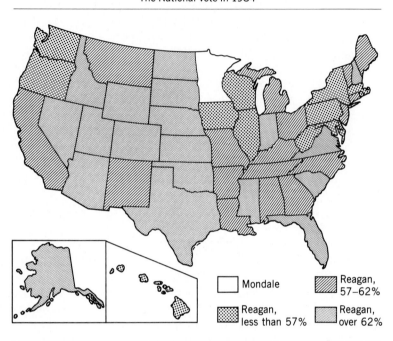

Mondale

Reagan, less than 57%

Reagan, 57–62%

Reagan, over 62%

Source: Gerald M. Pomper et al., *The Election of 1984: Reports and Interpretations* (Chatham, N.J.: Chatham House, 1985), p. 61.

wealthy (68 percent of those with over $50,000 annual incomes), and young voters (67 percent of the 18–24 age group).[58]

However, Reagan's personal triumph did not necessarily signify a new era of Republican dominance. The same voters who were reelecting Reagan were also reelecting a Democratic-controlled House of Representatives, sending additional Democrats to the Senate, and electing a large majority of Democrats to state offices. The Democratic party remains more popular among those voters identifying with one of the two parties.

In the 1970s and 1980s, political analyst Everett Ladd discerns the existence of a "two-tier electoral system" that exhibits what he

[58]*Newsweek Election Extra,* November/December 1984; *Time,* November 19, 1984.

describes as a "split personality": whereas the Republican party has controlled the presidency for all but four years between 1968 and 1988, the Democratic party has controlled at least one house of Congress and the bulk of state and local offices throughout the period.[59] (The tendency toward divided control of the presidency and Congress was reinforced by the 1986 congressional elections. The Democrats regained control of the Senate and thereby dominated both houses of Congress in the last years of the Reagan administration.) Ladd suggests that this situation reflects the ambivalence of American voters regarding partisan and policy choices. Moreover, he contends, the partial realignment of the political system that results from this evolution does not preclude— indeed, it may accompany—further tendencies toward party dealignment and decay.

It remains an open question whether the future holds a realignment resulting in Republican party dominance, a Democratic party revival, a two-tier arrangement, or further decay of the entire party system. The Reagan administration and the Republican party generally were rocked in late 1986 by revelations of massive secret U.S. arms shipments to Iran in violation of official American policy as well as by the news that funds from the Iranian arms sales had been covertly channeled to the Nicaraguan Contras. The scandal, which involved high administration officials, further dimmed prospects for the Republican party to gain dominance within a realigned party system. The failure of the Republican attempt at constructing a procapitalist coalition seeking conservative, populist social goals would create new possibilities for broadening the ideological and-political agenda. Rather than lamenting the present situation, thoughtful political participants may be in a better position to shape the future.

[59]Everett Carll Ladd, "On Mandates, Realignments, and the 1984 Presidential Election," *Political Science Quarterly* 100 (Spring 1985): 1–25.

political
processes

9

the welfare state

In the past century, governments in all the western societies have
assumed responsibility for providing their citizens with a variety of
programs to protect against the possibilities of unemployment, in-
jury, and sickness and to insure a decent standard of living in old
age. Other cash benefits and services are aimed at those who are
most poor and vulnerable and provide a minimum standard of
subsistence for all members of society.

In the United States, as in other western countries, the welfare
state is divided into two categories of welfare-state expenditures,
both quite different, though related. The first takes the form of
social insurance. Old-Age and Survivors and Disability Insurance
under Social Security are the best known and most inclusive. They
are universal programs, providing coverage for all individuals in a
specific category (such as retired workers over the age of 65, or
people who lose their jobs by being laid off by their employers).
The second category, commonly referred to as welfare, consists of
programs mainly directed toward poor people, including Food
Stamps, Medicaid, and, most important, Aid to Families with Dependent Children (AFDC). These programs are selective, in that
they are available only to Americans whose income or wealth is
below a level set by law.

Spending on welfare-state programs of both kinds has dramatically expanded in the twentieth century, and especially since the

295

end of the Second World War. In some countries of Western Europe, social-welfare expenditures and their costs of administration absorb as much as half of their annual gross national products (GNP).

In the United States, too, such expenditures have grown substantially, even though, in contrast to many countries in Europe, no major political party is committed to the growth of government. Indeed, most politicians, most of the time, talk of cutting out unnecessary programs, eliminating waste and controlling the share of GNP taken by the welfare state. And yet, such spending has continued to increase under both Democratic and Republican administrations. At the close of the Eisenhower administration about 10 percent of GNP was used for welfare-state spending. Five years later, when President Johnson was in office, the proportion was up to 12 percent of GNP. Under President Nixon in 1970, 15 percent of GNP went for such programs; 18 percent, under President Ford; and when President Carter left office, just over 23 percent.

Ronald Reagan entered the presidency with the explicit goal of cutting this overall percentage to 19 percent, and he pledged a major overhaul aimed not at a retrenchment of the welfare state, but at a fundamental overhaul of it. After six years of effort, President Reagan had succeeded not in reducing the welfare state's share of GNP, but in stabilizing it at 23.5 percent. More important, very few programs have been entirely eliminated, although many were pared back, at least for a time. Yet, overall, as two critical observers have noted, "Welfare state structures, programs, and funding remain largely intact, at least so far."[1]

So, too, some of the key features of the American welfare state that distinguish it from that of other countries have remained intact. The welfare state in the United States lacks many programs that are familiar elsewhere, especially in health, family allowances, and employment policy. And more than any other, the American welfare state distinguishes very starkly between social insurance and means-tested welfare programs. And it remains comparatively small in size, capturing a more limited share of tax revenues and national wealth than in other countries.

This history poses three key questions: Why is the American welfare state qualitatively different than that of other countries?

---

[1] Frances Fox Piven and Richard A. Cloward, "The Future of the Welfare State in an Age of Industrial Working Class Decline," Unpublished paper, April 1985.

Within the United States, how are we to understand the long history of growth in the size and scope of governmental social-welfare programs? Last, how has the Reagan administration fared in its attacks on the welfare state, and in its attempt to stop the pattern of welfare state expansion that had prevailed for so long?

HISTORICAL FOUNDATIONS

The history of state involvement in social welfare can be variously interpreted. On the one hand, it can be seen as an account of the growing liberalization of provisions for the poor and of developing attempts to address the causes of poverty. Before 1935, the United States lacked even a basic social-security program of the sort that had long been adopted in the capitalist countries of Western Europe. By 1964, the government's involvement in social welfare had expanded to such an extent that an American president declared unconditional war on poverty; five years later, a conservative president proposed a guaranteed minimum income for all Americans. But, on the other hand, the growth of the welfare state can be seen as the continuation of basic historical traditions that "include repression, local financing and administration, a minimization of the amount of money spent on the poor, an emphasis on the work ethic, a distinction between the deserving and the undeserving poor, and a stigma attached to those who are dependent on relief."[2] As a result, the major innovations in public-welfare policy in this century have consistently been paternalistic at best, and often punitive to the poor.

Twentieth-century American welfare programs are rooted in the assumptions and practices of the English Poor Law of 1598. The act was passed in response to the social problems created by the shift from feudal to early capitalist patterns of agriculture, which drove many agricultural laborers off the land. Under the provisions of earlier laws, wandering paupers were punished with whipping, branding, enslavement, and even death. Yet these repressive measures became inadequate in controlling the rapidly increasing numbers of dispossessed workers. A British historian captured the

[2]Bruno Stein, *On Relief* (New York, 1971), p. 43.

mood of the period, which is remarkably similar to that of contemporary America in many respects:

> Wanderers were feared in the sixteenth century as likely to be thieves and rogues, and if in any number to cause more serious trouble, perhaps even political disturbances. . . . [M]obility of labour was to be feared. As Tawney has said, the sixteenth century lived in terror of the tramp. . . . The combination of fear and feeling can be detected in the preamble to the Elizabethan statute of 1598:
>
> *whereas a good part of the strength of this realm consisteth in the number of good and able subjects . . . and of late years more than in time past there have been sundry towns, parishes and houses of husbandry destroyed and become desolate, whereof a great number of poor people are become wanderers, idle and loose, which is the cause of infinite inconvenience . . .*[3]

The Poor Law attempted to deal with this breakdown of social control by mandating that local governments maintain their *own* poor at the smallest level of government, the parish. Local officials were given wide latitude in determining the level of benefits and how they would be disbursed. All able-bodied people, including children, were compelled to·work. A refusal to work was a punishable crime.

The principles of the Poor Law, and of the subsequent amendments to it that usually followed periods of mass unrest in Britain, were transplanted to the American colonies and became the basis of American social welfare. The autonomy of localities produced widely different eighteenth- and nineteenth-century welfare policies for the poor. It also enabled localities to reduce their tax burdens by making nonresidents ineligible for welfare (such residency requirements were only ruled unconstitutional by the Supreme Courty in 1969). Regulations that made work compulsory provided an ample low-paid work force for developing capitalist enterprises. And like English Poor Law practices, which often segregated the poor in workhouses and poorhouses, American social-welfare policies were administered in such a way as to stigmatize the poor and distinguish between the deserving and undeserving poor.

Local welfare systems could not survive the ravages of the depression, nor were they compatible with the basic shift in the

---

[3]Maurice Bruce, *The Coming of the Welfare State* (New York, 1966), pp. 24, 26.

economy from small-scale, largely local or regional cpaital to corporate capital. As more and more Americans became poor (most of whom had little experience with hard-core poverty), the federal government nationalized welfare policy by funding and setting standards for traditionally autonomous local welfare programs. Nevertheless, many of the system's basic characteristics continued to prevail.

The Social Security Act of 1935 created a countrywide framework for a dual welfare state. It established the basic programs of social insurance and social welfare. The social-insurance expenditures included Social Security and a federal/state system of unemployment compensation. The bill's most significant program of social welfare was Aid to Dependent Children (ADC), which has developed into today's AFDC. Augmented by programs of public health, food stamps, public housing, and other services, it remains the core of the welfare state for the poor.

SOCIAL WELFARE AND THE NEW DEAL

The Social Security Act was not passed in an economic or political vacuum. With the election of Franklin D. Roosevelt in 1932, the federal government began to respond more actively to the massive economic upheaval of the depression. The first response of the New Deal to soaring unemployment rates was the substitution of work relief for direct cash relief. By mid-January 1934 the Civil Works Administration (CWA) had put four million Americans to work, thus making the federal government the largest employer in the country.

But by the spring of 1934 the CWA was closed down. It had drawn the widespread opposition of the corporate community, whose members feared the CWA threatened the private-enterprise system. "Work relief raised the specter of government activity in areas hitherto reserved for private enterprise, and CWA minimum wage scales raised the specter of government interference in the conduct of private enterprise."[4] The abolition of the CWA signified

---

[4]Frances Fox Piven and Richard Cloward, *Regulating the Poor: The Functions of Public Welfare* (New York, 1971), p. 82.

that Roosevelt sought to win support from businessmen (albeit unsuccessfully) in the first year of the New Deal and to restore their confidence in American capitalism.

By the congressional elections of 1934, growing business opposition to the Roosevelt regime made it necessary for the president to seek to save capitalism and members of the corporate order in spite of themselves. As *Fortune* magazine noted in 1935, it was "fairly evident to most disinterested critics" that the New Deal had "the preservation of capitalism at all times in view." A small minority of the corporate community agreed with this assessment and played a major role in the administration, but in the main Roosevelt had to build his political constituency of farmers, workers, and homeowners without overt business support.

The defection of much of his minority business support from Roosevelt's political coalition eliminated political cross-pressures in the administration and freed it to deal with mass discontent more directly than might otherwise have been possible. With the end of the CWA in 1934, millions of Americans who had been given jobs now found themselves again dependent on the largesse of private, local, or state relief agencies. Their restiveness was palpable. Many, at the time, thought the United States was in a prerevolutionary situation:

> For discontent had not evaporated with the elections of 1932; rather, it was stilled for a moment by the promise of a new regime, the confidence a new leader inspired. However, as the Depression wore on, with conditions showing little improvement, unrest surfaced. By 1934, various dissident leaders were drawing upon this unrest, giving it organizational form and coherence, aspiring to build political movements that would change the face of America.[5]

Roosevelt responded by promoting social-welfare legislation that undercut these growing dissident movements and acted to restore stability. In his January 4, 1935, State of the Union message, Roosevelt proposed sweeping reforms, including redistributive tax laws, new labor legislation, the restoration of national work relief, and programs of social insurance. The proposals were largely gutted by the Congress, but the passage of diluted versions had a larger symbolic importance: it convinced many of the discontented that the federal government was acting vigorously on their behalf.

[5]*Ibid.*, p. 85.

The measure that had the most direct impact on the unemployed was the restoration of massive publicly funded employment under the Works Progress Administration (WPA). Millions of Americans were once more put to work, a fact that more than anything else eased the threat of civil disorder. But after 1936, as the most important dissident movements of the period (including the Townsend Old People's Movement, the Workers Alliance, and other populist organizations of the left and right) declined in membership and influence, the New Deal quickly reduced its concessions to the poor, and the number of federally paid jobs was sharply cut. Once the threat of a civil uprising had passed, the government withdrew from the employment picture in order to restore the traditional prerogatives of private capital.

Hence the most enduring welfare innovation of the depression was not work relief but the Social Security Act. It provided the basic framework for the modern American welfare state, and its provisions meshed with, rather than challenged, the dominant corporate system. Unemployment insurance, social security pensions, and categorical aid to mothers and families with dependent children have been with us ever since. These programs have continued to grow in size, and, over the years, were joined by such new government undertakings as Food Stamps, Medicare, and Medicaid. What accounts for both the growth and limitations of these programs?

The post-New Deal development of the welfare state has been shaped in fundamental ways by what Franklin Roosevelt's policies did and did not accomplish. The most important of these legacies was the development of the distinction between social security and welfare. The former is identified by most Americans as a basic obligation of government; the latter, as a series of frequently resented handouts to the poor. The reformers who wrote and later administered the Social Security Act of 1935 were committed to this distinction and worked hard to promote it. In the early years of the program, most old people were assisted at least as much by public assistance as by social security. But, over time, as more and more older Americans had paid taxes into the social security system and were eligible to receive benefits, public assistance came to be identified almost exclusively with younger poor mothers and their children. And, over time, most Americans have come to support the expansion of social-security benefits while being prepared to hold back on increases in social spending for the poor.

The uneasy relationship between social insurance and public assistance that is at the heart of the American welfare state was reinforced after the creation of these programs in 1935 by the ways in which officials in Washington chose to administer and develop them.

Social Security and AFDC were the responsibility of the Social Security Board. The members of the Board fought successfully against using social security as a vehicle to achieve more equality in society. Instead, they insisted that social security be tied very closely to work and the labor market. Recipients would 'earn' their benefits by paying payroll taxes into the system in their working years, and these benefits would be linked to preretirement wages, so that the maximum benefit a family could earn would not exceed 80 percent of their average former wages, even in the case of people who had been in poverty.

In the early years of the program, the Social Security Board fought successfully against proposals to tie social insurance and public assistance more closely together, as well as proposals to equalize benefits or to fund social security out of general tax revenues.

At the same time, the Board was given responsibility for administering public assistance. This program was the joint responsibility of the states and the federal government, but the Board had, and used, the authority to force states to impose strict limits on eligibility and to create a climate in which it was demeaning to seek and receive assistance.

THE DUAL WELFARE SYSTEM: TIES TO THE ECONOMY

There can be no question that the development of the modern welfare state represented a great popular victory. The existence of the various protections and supports it provides makes it possible for most people to live with a modicum of security and dignity. Rather than being dependent only on the ups and downs of the performance of the economy and its provision of jobs, citizens have certain basic assurances about their ability to meet basic needs.

At the same time, the welfare state and its development has been tightly integrated into the routine operation of the economy, and has come to be an important factor in ensuring the persistence of market capitalism and in controlling popular discontent. We have already seen how the major innovations in America's welfare-state policies were utilized to defuse mass protest in the period of the Great Depression. But the welfare state also has economic and political functions in more quiet times. Because the welfare state is not an undifferentiated whole, however, it is necessary to explore these functions with reference to the different sectors of the population and to different sectors of the economy.

Social-insurance programs of all kinds have become tightly integrated into the economy, especially the part of the economy dominated by large corporate firms. Put most provocatively, in economist James O'Connor's terms, one of the main effects of social insurance has been "to expand productivity, production, and profits. *Seen in this way, social insurance is not primarily insurance for workers but a kind of insurance for capitalists and corporations.*"[6] What does this statement mean?

Most corporate leaders would probably agree that the relatively better-off workers in large-capital firms will work harder if they are more secure economically. Thus, many industries instituted systems of workmen's compensation well before such insurance was mandated by law. Although the passage of most landmark pieces of social legislation was primarily the result of political activity by powerful organized workers, corporate leaders of the largest, most economically advanced industries have often been in the vanguard of those demanding the expansion of the social-insurance system.

Today, social-insurance programs enjoy the enthusiastic support of both business and labor. A look at Social Security indicates the reasons. Retired workers in the 1980s share about $250 billion each year in Social Security payments, up from $37 billion in 1970.[7] Workers are taxed to pay for these benefits at the rate of 7.15 percent of the first $43,800 they earn each year. An identical tax is paid by the employer. But most economists believe that, in the case of corporations, the employer's share is passed along to the worker in the form of lower wages. Thus, while corporate employers largely

---

[6]O'Connor, p. 138.
[7]Joseph Pechman, ed., *Setting National Priorities: The 1984 Budget* (Washington, D.C., 1983), p. 82.

escape having to make a real contribution to the social-security system, corporate workers in effect pay a tax (both direct and indirect) of more than 10 percent of their income.

In turn, however, corporate-sector workers gain at the expense of the lower-paid workers in small-capital industries. Although all workers are taxed equally up to the first $35,700 they earn (income over this figure is exempt), the more an individual earns while working, the higher his or her retirement payments. Moreover, millions of people who have been unemployed for long periods do not accumulate the required work-time and receive no benefits at all when they retire, even though they paid taxes when they worked.

In spite of the fact that the social-security tax is America's most regressive tax (exempting interest, profit, rent, capital gains, and all payroll income over $35,700), this and other programs of social insurance, like unemployment insurance and workmen's compensation, favor the corporate worker and thus are supported by organized labor as well as by corporate management. The corporations are enabled to keep wage costs down, and corporate-sector workers gain by what economist Milton Friedman has called "the poor man's welfare payment to the middle class."[8] As O'Connor noted:

> Organized labor is more or less satisfied because the system redistributes income in its favor. Monopoly capital is also relatively happy because the system insures comparative harmony with labor. If monopoly sector workers were compelled to contribute as much as they receive upon retirement, current money wages would have to be slashed sharply. But if retired workers received what they actually paid in, retirement benefits would be impossibly low. In either event, monopoly sector labor-management relations would be seriously impaired. Workers would bitterly resist technological and other changes that threatened their jobs, the ability of unions to maintain discipline would be undermined, and in most industries management would be faced with more uncertainty.[9]

---

[8]Milton Friedman, "The Poor Man's Welfare Payment to the Middle Class," *The Washington Monthly* (May 1972): 16.
[9]O'Connor, pp. 139–40. Also see, "Congress Clears Social Security Tax Increase," *Congressional Quarterly,* December 17, 1977, pp. 2621–24.

Moreover, as rank-and-file workers have come to agitate for better pensions, labor leaders and corporate managements have moved to resolve their shared dilemma by pressuring the federal government for more liberated social-insurance programs. The ritual pattern was set in 1949 when Walter Reuther, the president of the United Automobile Workers (UAW), successfully prodded the automobile companies to pressure for liberalized social security by negotiating a contract that included an expensive pension plan. "The effect of the 'Reuther system' is that corporations socialize . . . costs . . . and thus defend their profits, union leaders conserve their hegemony over the rank and file, and labor discipline and morale are maintained."[10]

In the early 1980s the social security system faced a serious crisis of vulnerability, as a result of the combination of a number of factors. The first was the growth of the aged population who were collecting benefits at a faster rate than the increase in the number of employed people who were contributing to the system through payroll taxes. In the period 1970–85, the number of beneficiaries increased by over 50 percent, but the number of employed Americans grew by only 33 percent. The second was the sluggish performance of the economy after 1973. In the 1970s, there was relatively little economic growth, but there was high inflation. Because social security benefits are tied to the cost of living, these price increases drove up the costs of the system at a time when real wages were not rising. The third concerns the maturation of the system. In its early decades most workers were paying into the trust funds, but few Americans were entitled to benefits. As recently as 1950, fewer than one in six over age 65 received social security. Those who did, received benefits, on average, of about 40 percent of their preretirement earnings. Today, over nine in ten retired people receive benefits, and these are roughly at the rate of 70 percent of preretirement earnings. These developments put pressure on the social security system; in 1983, it faced deficits of over $200 billion for the rest of the decade. Proposals to cut benefits proved politically unfeasible, and, instead, taxes were raised to maintain the solvency of the system.

[10]O'Connor, p. 141.

WELFARE IN THE WELFARE STATE

Before the passage of the Social Security Act in 1935 the provision of public assistance to the poor was principally the responsibility of the state and local governments. At the beginning of the Great Depression national relief programs were created, but these too were supplanted in 1935 by the creation of a *federal* network of arrangements to aid the poor: Aid to Dependent Children, which subsequently became Aid to Families with Dependent Children.

Ever since, welfare programs have been jointly operated by the national, state, and local governments. Within the broad national framework of AFDC, states and cities have been permitted a wide degree of discretion in determining who should be eligible for welfare and how much they should receive. As a result, there have grown up enormous differentials between the payments to families. Thus, whereas a poor woman and her children would have received over $500 per month in New York, she would have been given less than $160 in Arkansas. Benefits have come to depend more on where a person lives than on the person's actual need.

The first phase, 1945–65

Broadly speaking, the history of AFDC may be divided into three phases since the conclusion of the Second World War. From 1945 to 1965, there was a tight link between local labor markets, unemployment rates, and the utilization of AFDC. In these 20 years, the number of new welfare cases rose and fell with the monthly rise and fall of male unemployment.

Overall, the operation of AFDC reinforced the harsh employment market, especially outside of the sector of corporate capital. Whereas corporate workers share somewhat in the gains of corporate growth and technical progress, small-capital workers do not; on the contrary, the wage gap between the two sectors has widened considerably in the past quarter century.

As a result, an increasing proportion of the small-capital–sector population has become dependent on welfare programs for subsistence. With the continuing decline in the economic position of small-capital–sector workers, the traditional correlation between unemployment and AFDC welfare rates no longer held by the middle 1960s. "With the onset of the 1960s the relationship weakened abruptly, and by 1963 vanished altogether. Or rather, reversed itself. For the next five years the nonwhite male unemployment rate declined steadily and the number of AFDC cases rose steadily."[11]

This shift reflected the growing gap between corporate- and small-capital–sector wages. At the end of the Second World War, small-capital–sector workers earned roughly 75 percent of the wages of corporate-sector workers; in the 1960s, their relative earnings declined to 60 percent.[12] Thus even those in the small-capital sector who had jobs were increasingly unable to adequately support their families. Men deserted their wives and children either out of a sense of shame or because their families would be better off with AFDC payments. The welfare rolls skyrocketed as more and more families became dependent on the state. Low wages and underemployment, as well as unemployment, now contributed directly to the growth of the welfare state. Throughout the 1960s, the number of welfare recipients grew by almost 10 percent per year.[13]

The welfare system operated to compel people into low-paid, menial work by following the principle of "less eligibility" proclaimed in England in 1834, which declared that welfare payments should provide a standard of living less desirable than "the situation of the independent laborer of the lowest class." The traditional workhouses that underpinned this principle in England were

> designed to spur men to contrive ways of supporting themselves by their own industry, *to offer themselves to any employer on any terms.* It did this by making pariahs of those who could not support themselves; they served as an object lesson, a means of celebrating the virtues of work by the terrible example of their agony.[14]

This principle makes it possible to understand the ritual degradation of the welfare client often considered a degradation that was no accident. In contrast to social insurance programs in this period, one of the main functions of the welfare system is to de-

---

[11]Daniel P. Moynihan, *The Politics of a Guaranteed Income* (New York, 1973), p. 82.

[12]Barry Bluestone, "Economic Crisis and the Law of Uneven Development," *Politics and Society* 3 (Fall 1972): 68.

[13]*Wall Street Journal,* April 24, 1969.

[14]Piven and Cloward, pp. 34, 35.

marcate a boundary between the "deserving" and "undeserving" poor. The boundary was made clear as soon as a person applied for welfare. Then, as now, AFDC welfare centers were dingy, forbidding places; long waits for attention and a clinical atmosphere set a dehumanizing tone. Once applicants were called to meet a caseworker, their lives were probed in intimate, exhaustive detail—work, family, and finances were all grist for the welfare workers' mill. One prospective welfare recipient described an early experience with the system:

> At the Welfare they got this man they call him the Resources man and sometimes he is also a woman. Whenever you apply for welfare, you must be sent to him because he must ask you a lot of questions. All kinds of questions. Like he may ask you if you belong to a union or are in the Army. Then he will try to do something about that to keep you off welfare.

Finally, after being shunted between four caseworkers who refused to put him on the rolls, "I go away from the welfare center as rich as when I came there." He found a subsistence wage job, but the factory was unionized and the workers went out on strike.

> I have no savings yet, so I must go again to welfare, but this man wants to know when I got my last check. Then he says he can't help me because it is not so long ago that I shouldn't have some money. And he tells me to come back in another week if the strike isn't settled, but today when I went to see him he said, 'Look for work and come back again in another week.' I just don't think he wants to give me the welfare. So that's the way it is again. I have moved out of my room and I am staying with my uncle. . . . If the strike ends soon maybe I will save my money and go to another city. I have friends in Philadelphia. They say it is not so cruel about the welfare.[15]

Once they succeeded in getting on the welfare rolls, recipients were subjected to further degradation. Routinely they were kept under surveillance, exhorted by welfare workers to "rehabilitate" themselves, and asked to prove that they were not welfare chiselers or frauds. They were underbudgeted by welfare workers who are given incentives to keep costs down. They were defined as useless in a society that values work and production; and from time to time, they were denounced as such by politicians in search of headlines.

[15]Richard M. Elman, *The Poorhouse State* (New York, 1966), pp. 94–96.

Most importantly, they were treated as, and became, functionally powerless, dependent on the decisions of others over whom they exercised virtually no control. They came to share the society's image of them as unworthy, and to collaborate in the system that perpetuated their subordination. There were almost no appeals made by welfare recipients on grounds of deprivation either of money or of civil liberties, which are their due under the Social Security Act.[16] This process of systematic degradation also worked to discourage *potential* welfare clients, who accepted subsistence wages rather than suffer the consequences of being on welfare.

The second phase, 1965–70

The second phase lasted roughly from 1965 to 1970. Then, as a part of a broader movement for social change, especially among American blacks, the welfare system was put under great pressure. In this period the connection between AFDC and unemployment rates was severed. In this period, "the nonwhite male unemployment rate declined steadily and the number of AFDC cases rose steadily."[17]

In an influential explanation, Frances Fox Piven and Richard Cloward argued that the explosion of AFDC rolls in the middle 1960s was an attempt to control rebellious turmoil and preserve social order. Many social scientists have debated this position, but there seems to be some evidence that increases in welfare caseloads in fact were associated with urban rioting by poor, unemployed blacks.

States with large black populations where liberal Democrats were in power as a result of forging an electoral coalition between liberal whites and central-city blacks proved to be the places where politicians were most ready to expand both the eligiblity for welfare and the size of grants recipients received. Further, as a result of various technical legislative changes, it became possible for politicians in such states as California, Massachusetts, New York, and Delaware to shift some of the cost of these expenditures to the federal government.

---

[16]Piven and Cloward, p. 173.
[17]Barry Bluestone, "Economic Crisis and the Law of Uneven Development," *Politics and Society* 3 (Fall 1972): 68.

Thus, the most compelling explanation of the welfare explosion from 1965 to 1970 combines an emphasis on mass insurgency with an analysis of why politicians in some states were prepared to change the rules to permit an expansion of AFDC. In one of the best treatments of these issues, Sanford Schramm and Patrick Turbett argue that in the states where rioting was most severe AFDC caseloads increased the most, but only after changes in national and state public policy facilitated this growth.[18]

The end of the second phase was symbolized by the fate of the Family Assistance Plan (FAP) proposed by President Nixon in April 1969. If it had passed, this legislation would have guaranteed a minimum income to every American family with children and would have supplemented the earnings of the working poor. Every family of four, for instance, would have received a minimum of $1,600 per year and would have had its income supplemented as long as family earnings were under $4,000. It was estimated that the plan would have cost $4 billion in its first year of operation.

Coming from a conservative Republican president who had campaigned against welfare, for the work ethic, for "law and order," and who had been elected without direct black support, this proposal to give federal funds directly to the poor seemed remarkable. *Newsweek* called the proposal "so sweeping that even some of his own Republican Cabinet Officers were left gasping for conservative breath." The liberal Detroit *Free Press* found FAP "more radical than anything done by the Johnson administration," whose actions had included the creation of an Office of Economic Opportunity (OEO) to supervise a multimillion-dollar War on Poverty.[19]

Such comments stressed the apparently radical content of FAP without adequately coming to terms with the program's intent, which was to stabilize the structure of society, not to change it. From the perspective of those who governed the United States in the late 1960s, the social order gave every impression of crumbling. Daniel Moynihan, who served in subcabinet and cabinet-level positions under Presidents Kennedy, Johnson, and Nixon, and who

[18]Sanford F. Schram and J. Patrick Turbett, "Civil Disorder and the Welfare Explosion: A Two-Step Process," *American Sociological Review* 48, no. 3 (June 1983): 408–44.
[19]Moynihan, *The Politics of a Guaranteed Income*, pp. 252–53.

was the architect of the welfare reform bill, captured the mood of near panic at the top:

> Nixon shared the anxiety . . . that the spiral of increasing urban racial violence . . . had not ceased. In 1965 there had been four major riots and civil disturbances in the country. In 1966 there were twenty-one major riots and civil disorders. In 1967 there were eighty-three major riots and disturbances. In the first seven months of 1968 there were fifty-seven major riots and disturbances. . . . In retrospect the domestic turbulence of the United States in the late 1960s may come to appear something less than cataclysmic. But this was not the view of the men then in office. Mayors, governors—presidents— took it as given that things were in a hell of a shape and that something had to be done.[20]

Moynihan rightly argued that Nixon's FAP proposal can only be understood as an attempt to deal with growing mass black discontent. Indeed, the leaders of the corporate community, who had the most to lose in the face of mass insurgency, largely favored the Nixon initiative. The specific features of the Family Assistance Plan were developed from proposals of a conference Governor Nelson Rockefeller of New York called in March 1967 "to help plan new approaches to public welfare in the United States." The steering committee consisted of some of the most successful members of the corporate complex, including Joseph Block (chairman of the executive committee of Inland Steel), Albert Nickerson (chief executive officer of Mobil Oil), Gustave Levy (head of the New York Stock Exchange), and Joseph Wilson (chairman of the board and chief executive officer of the Xerox corporation).

The conference collectively recommended that the present welfare system be replaced by a program of income maintenance. It argued for the acceptance of the objective that basic economic support at the federally defined poverty level be provided for all Americans. But any such system, the conference cautioned, "should contain strong incentives to work." Moynihan commented that the "governor's inspiration was to turn to the heads of the large capitalist enterprises of the nation, a community with few ties, certainly, to the Social Security system, having bitterly opposed its establishment, but now including among its members men of gen-

---

[20]*Ibid.*, pp. 101–102.

erous disposition on social issues, *a tendency much accentuated by the onset of urban rioting.*"[21] In other words, rather than the existence of poverty, what concerned many business people was the disruption resulting from poverty.

President Nixon's proposal was not passed into law. Conservative members of Congress, especially those from the South, were adamantly opposed to any extension of welfare benefits. Many liberal Democratic members argued the legislation was not generous enough. But difficult as it might have been for Nixon to forge a majority coalition for the bill, most observers believed he could have had he not lost interest in the legislation. As the urban turmoil of the period receded, the president ceased to lobby for support of FAP. This turning away from his own bill makes sense when we understand that FAP was not meant in the first instance to change the welfare system for the better, but to restore social peace. With that goal accomplished by other means, welfare reform was set aside.

But if FAP was a clear response to riot and unrest, the main causes of the formulation of the social-welfare legislation of President Kennedy's New Frontier and the early proposals of President Johnson's Great Society have puzzled many observers. In 1961, when John F. Kennedy sponsored the appropriation of $10 million for grants to "youth development" under the Juvenile Delinquency and Youth Offenses Control Act; when, two years later, $150 million were authorized for community mental health centers; when, in 1964, Title Two of the Economic Opportunity Act (the antipoverty bill of the War on Poverty) allocated $350 million to community action programs that called for the "maximum feasible participation of residents of the areas and members of the groups served"; and when Congress passed a Model Citizens program to rehabilitate blighted neighborhoods in 1966, there was a marked *absence* of interest groups pressing for the legislation. At the initiative of the White House the bills all passed in an apparent political vacuum. How could this phenomenon be explained?

Moynihan developed a widely accepted explanation that he labeled "the professionalism of reform":

> Increasingly efforts to change the American social system for the better arose from initiatives undertaken by persons whose profes-

[21]*Ibid.*, p. 56. Emphasis added.

sion was to do just that. Whereas previously the role of organized society had been largely passive—the machinery would work if someone made it work—now the process began to acquire a self-starting capacity of its own.[22]

Unlike the New Deal programs, he argued, which were generated by long sustained political pressure and discontent, and which in turn defused discontent, the early New Frontier and Great Society programs of Presidents Kennedy and Johnson originated in a period when "the American poor, black and white, were surprisingly inert. . . . The war on poverty was not declared at the behest of the poor: it was declared in their interest by persons confident of their own judgement in such matters."[23] The development of these programs thus reflected the rise of a technocratic professional elite and the growth of a knowledge industry based on universities and foundations.

While the professionalism of reform played an important part in the expansion of the welfare state in the 1960s, it is not the whole story. It does not account for the *political* appeals of the professionals' proposals and, hence, the reasons for their adoption by politicians, and it tells us little about the impact of the new programs in dealing with the unprecedented black discontent of the middle and late 1960s.

Kennedy's close election victory in 1960 revealed basic weaknesses in the Democratic coalition. The South in particular was no longer a secure party base. In the Northern cities, many Democratic voters were moving to the suburbs, where their political allegiances were more uncertain. In their place were millions of black migrants from the South—a large number of whom did not vote—who had few established links with urban party organizations.

It was this new constituency that the Kennedy and Johnson administrations needed. Hence they welcome the programs proposed by the reform professionals:

> Each program singled out the 'inner city' as its main target; each provided a basketful of services; each channeled some portion of its funds more or less directly to new organizations in the 'inner city,' circumventing the existing municipal agencies which traditionally

[22]Daniel P. Moynihan, *Maximum Feasible Misunderstanding* (New York, 1969), p. 23.
[23]*Ibid.*, pp. 34–35.

controlled services. . . . it was ghetto neighborhoods that these programs were chiefly designed to reach, and by tactics reminiscent of
the traditional political machine.[24]

By creating a direct link between the federal government and the
ghettos, the Democratic administrations not only bypassed existing
service bureaucracies but also left the traditional white ethnic party
organizations relatively undisturbed. In short, the new programs
promised a high electoral payoff at relatively low risk. Blacks were
to be integrated into the predominantly Democratic urban political
system by way of social-welfare programs in traditional machine-
like fashion.

However, this combination of professional proposals and electoral imperatives provided authorities with effective tools to defuse
the black rebellions in the middle years of the decade in two respects. First, the programs created a vehicle for the political integration of the most talented, articulate, militant young blacks of
the period. Militant action was now often directed at winning larger
shares of urban patronage rather than at working for structural
change. In Baltimore, political scientist Peter Bachrach noted that
the federally funded programs "provided black groups with . . .
decision-making arenas in which the struggle for power could be
fought out in the open and within the confines of the political
system." Similarly, urbanist John Strange noted that in Durham
and other North Carolina cities, "community action, with special
emphasis on participation and community organization, has . . .
channeled dissatisfaction and unrest into forms and issues which
can be dealt with."[25]

Secondly, the expansion of the government's welfare role
helped defuse mass discontent by providing tangible, if limited,
benefits, including easier access to AFDC welfare, higher welfare
payments, and new job opportunities. In short, then, black discontent was not caused by the new programs (the causes were structural, not manufactured by government), nor were the programs
originally aimed at defusing discontent (electoral considerations
were of primary importance). Nevertheless, with the outbreak of
massive civil disorder in the middle 1960s, the state used both
traditional welfare programs like AFDC and the newly created
programs like Community Action to absorb and canalize the dis-

[24]Piven and Cloward, pp. 260–61.
[25]Cited in *ibid.*, p. 274.

content. In this respect, the expansion and operation of welfare-state programs in the 1960s bear a striking resemblance to the programs of the New Deal.

Whether or not they were proposed or passed as the result of mass movements and pressures, all the welfare-state programs, from the Social Security Act of 1935 to the most recent, share one basic characteristic: *they are meant to stabilize the social order, not create structural change.* They do not challenge the existence of the corporate complex. Instead, they seek to alleviate—not correct—the basic structural inequalities that are part and parcel of the American corporate-capital system.

This point was stressed by the German sociologist Georg Simmel, who commented at the turn of the century on Bismarck's social-welfare program:

> If we take into consideration this meaning of assistance to the poor, it becomes clear that the fact of taking away from the rich to give to the poor does not aim at equalizing their individual positions, and is not, even in its orientation, directed at suppressing the social difference between the rich and the poor. On the contrary, assistance is based on the structure of society, whatever it may be. . . . The goal of assistance is precisely to mitigate certain extreme manifestations of social differentiation, so that the social structure may continue to be based on this differentiation.

This structure-protecting feature of welfare-state measures, he argued, is apparent because "if assistance were to be based on the interests of the poor person, there would, in principle, be no limit on the transmission of poverty in favor of the poor, a transmission that would lead to the equality of all." But structural transformation is what the dominant want to prevent; as a result, "there is no reason to aid the person more than is required by the maintenance of the *status quo.*"[26]

The third phase, 1970–85

The third phase began in 1970, with the end of the period of urban disorder. Piven and Cloward took note of the fact that "by the mid-1970s all of [the earlier] gains had been substantially eroded," and

---

[26]Georg Simmel, "The Poor," in Chiam I. Waxman, ed., *Poverty: Power and Politics* (New York, 1968), pp. 3–9.

AFDC began a long period of contraction. They explain the shift to this new phase this way:

> There were several reasons. For one, as black protest subsided, federal concessions were withdrawn. With the ascent to the presidency of Richard Nixon, the administration of welfare by states and localities became more restrictive, partly in response to threatening rhetoric and restrictive regulations promulgated by the federal government. At the same time, the Great Society programs that had provided resources and justification for black protest were stifled, their activities curbed, and their funds curtailed or eliminated in favor of new revenue-sharing or block grant programs.[27]

With the decrease in the threat to social peace, and with the loss of federal assistance, locality after locality acted to discourage qualified relief recipients and to make it more difficult to get on the welfare rolls. In New York City, for example, the Bureau of the Budget recommended to the mayor that a case backlog be deliberately created by consolidating the welfare centers and by cutting welfare personnel. Consolidation of the centers began in 1970, and the rise in welfare rolls stopped dramatically.

Since 1970, even states with a history of relatively generous AFDC policies have restricted their access to welfare and the real levels of welfare benefits. These states have been located in those areas of the country that have most experienced economic stagnation and decline and the loss of manufacturing industry and jobs. They have found themselves in competition with states in the South and West for investments by business. As a result, they have tried to cut welfare spending in order to be able to hold down tax rates to make their business climates more alluring.

Thus, in the very same period when social insurance benefits have expanded rapidly, programs aimed at the poor have become less and less generous. The main way in which these benefits have decreased in size has been the failure of the states to make adjustments in benefit levels to take inflation into account. As a result benefit levels fell in real terms by 26 percent between 1970 and 1980. By 1980, the average AFDC payment in the United States was $327 per month for a family of four, a level that was only *one-half* the poverty level established by the federal government.

[27]Frances Fox Piven and Richard Cloward, *Poor People's Movements: Why They Succeed, How They Fail* (New York, 1977), p. 354.

To be fair, a number of new programs, the most important of which were Food Stamps and Medicaid, cushioned this decline in AFDC payments. Yet even after taking these benefits into account, the average welfare family received only three dollars for every four it needed to escape poverty.

If in the first phase of AFDC the private lives of clients was closely supervised and regulated, in the third phase there has been a shift in another direction. Between 1965 and 1970 welfare recipients were successful in winning liberalized patterns of administration of AFDC, characterized by "fewer barriers to eligibility, less intrusion into family behavior patterns, and less investigation of family situations."[28] These changes went hand in hand, of course, with the dramatic growth in AFDC caseloads in that period. When it ended, however, welfare administration did not return to the punitive practices of an earlier era when each client had a social worker who supervised many aspects of her daily life. Instead, a new kind of intrusive system developed, run more by clerks than by social workers, and more concerned with fraud and abuse than with providing therapeutic help to clients. Although, no doubt, the system is more honestly run than before, there is also no question but that tougher welfare administration has also deterred eligible recipients from getting, and staying, on the welfare rolls.

The Reagan administration came to office on a platform pledged to cut the size of government. In practice, the president's leading successes in this regard came in diminishing the size of AFDC and other programs aimed at the poor, such as Food Stamps. The administration had its greatest impact on such spending in its early years. Between 1981 and 1982, expenditures of AFDC fell by 12 percent in real terms, and the AFDC caseload fell by 8 percent despite an increase in unemployment among mothers during the steep recession of 1982.

The results of these expenditure cuts have been felt keenly by less well-off Americans. Today, one in four American children under the age of six—children hardly responsible for their fate—live in poverty. The percentage of all Americans in poverty has risen in the Reagan years to about 15 percent, reversing the decline that began in the 1960s. Overall, the people in the most secure jobs are

[28]Mary Jo Bane, "The Politics and Policies of the Feminization of Poverty," unpublished paper, New York State Department of Social Services, April 1985.

best protected by the welfare state because they benefit most directly from the security and the rewards of social insurance; but those least secure or most disrupted in their lives by shifts in economic fortune, most of which are beyond their own control, are least protected by the "safety net" of vulnerable programs for poor Americans.

A REAGAN REVOLUTION?

President Reagan began his presidency with a vision of the appropriate role for government that was much more broad than that of cutting AFDC. Committed to the idea that with the exception of the military establishment a small government is the best government, the president engaged in an effort to alter the course of American domestic policy. Political scientist High Heclo has recently argued that this effort has been underpinned by a distinctive public philosophy, composed of three main elements. First, President Reagan has combined nationalism with an antigovernment stance. The nation, America, is "number one," with limitless possibilities, which, however, are blocked and impeded by a big and cumbersome government that gets in the way. In this view, the federal government is seen as an alien force (rather than as the product of democratic politics) that imposes its designs on the life of the nation. Defense is an exception, because such spending enhances the role of the nation in a difficult, challenging world.[29]

Second, Reaganism artfully combines ideas of individualism and communalism. Individual Americans must strive for all they can on the playing field of competition. At the same time, the nation's members have a communal obligation to look after each other, one best achieved without intrusive governmental programs. Further, the community should define right from wrong, and thus should oppose abortions, permit prayer in the schools, and so on. Individualism is an attribute of the economic marketplace; communalism, the essence of a society with values. Reaganism has tried to link the two.

[29]Hugh Heclo, "Reaganism and a Search for a Public Philosophy," unpublished paper prepared for the Urban Institute, Washington, D.C., June 1985.

The third element of Reaganism, according to Heclo, is "a kind of free market radicalism." The market is the instrument not just of economic efficiency, the usual claim made for it, but is "the embodiment of an ethically superior moral order" because it promotes individual effort and rewards those who get ahead. The losers in the economy, from this vantage point, are not victims, and to portray them as such is to destroy personal responsibility. President Reagan put the point this way when he addressed distressed farmers on February 23, 1985:

> Yes, we are sympathetic and we will extend support. But American taxpayers must not be asked to bail out every farmer hopelessly in debt . . . or be asked to bail out the banks who also bet on higher inflation. . . . Over the long haul, there's only one sure solution . . . working our way to a free-market economy. What farmers need and we're determined to provide is less dependence on politicians to supply their incomes and greater independence to supply their own incomes.

This perspective had undergirded the Reagan administration's efforts to shrink the size of the federal government. How has the attempt fared? What has become of the welfare state?

Measured against its own ambitions, the Reagan record is a mixed success. In 1981, Budget Director David Stockman predicted that many governmental programs would be "heaved aboard"; instead, most of the programs that existed that year remain in place today. As we have seen, the rate of growth of domestic government spending has been slowed. Spending for domestic fiscal programs in fiscal year 1986 was lower by about $80 billion than it would have been if pre-1981 policies had been followed. But these savings have been achieved by paring programs rather than by heaving them aboard. Some programs have been axed—mostly concerned with public service jobs, and revenue sharing funds directed at state treasuries—but a very large number—including community services block grants, a public corporation providing legal services to poor people, and urban development grants—have survived attempts to eliminate them.

The most important reason the Reagan administration has been unable to cut the size of domestic government is the political support most Americans give to social insurance. In May 1981, the administration did try to cut social security. At that time, David Stockman realized that because of impending tax cuts and increases in military spending more savings would be needed to keep the federal deficit from mushrooming out of control. At the same time, Richard Schweiker, the Secretary of Health and Human Services, was looking for a way to deal with social security's own fiscal problems.

The result was a proposed package of changes that, in part, would have saved money by cutting benefits for people who retire before age 65. This plan was greeted by a huge outcry, and by the unanimous rejection, by vote of 99-0, of the Republican-controlled Senate. President Reagan then withdrew the proposal, and instead appointed a bipartisan commission on the future of social security. Ever since, he has pledged not to cut benefits.

Instead, the only programs to be cut significantly were those that were most vulnerable politically: those providing aid to the poor, especially food stamps and AFDC. Yet, as the Reagan administration draws to a close, these programs are still intact, if diminished, leaving open the possiblity that they will grow again when the political climate changes. The consequence has been a limited amount of change: "A lot has happened, but a lot less than I wish had happened," Senator William Armstrong, a conservative Colorado Republican, has remarked. "The administration's record on the budget so far is one of missed opportunities. Stuart Eisenstadt, President Carter's chief domestic policy adviser, agrees: "We will have gone through eight years of the most conservative presidency we've ever had, and the basic structure of the American welfare state will be significantly intact."[30]

If the Reagan administration has achieved only a mixed record in relation to its goal of cutting the welfare state, it may have achieved an important long-term victory. Its history of mammouth tax cuts, large federal deficits, and the passage of the Graham-Rudman-Hollings legislation mandating deficit reductions through 1991 have made it impossible for the Congress to enact any new programs to deal with current social problems. At the same time, President Reagan, by accepting the basic outlines of the welfare state created in 1935, has consolidated its legitimacy, and thus, paradoxically, has preserved its basic outlines, and its strengths and weaknesses, for future generations of Americans.

[30]Quoted in Paul Blustein, "Recent Budget Battles Leave the Basic Tenets of Welfare State Intact," *The Wall Street Journal,* October 21, 1985, p. 1.

THE WELFARE STATE AND STRUCTURAL CHANGE

Although the welfare state complements, and is in fact necessary for, the country's advanced capitalist economy, its logic of need is diametrically opposed to the economy's logic of profit. Welfare-state programs are publicly fought over, defended, and legitimized on the basis of the deprivation of one group or another. Carried to its conclusion, as Simmel argued, this logic of need would be satisfied only when structural inequalities are overcome.

Yet welfare-state programs and debates about them take place within a context of corporate capitalism, which is driven by goals of growth and profit. For this reason, French commentator André Gorz has argued that *logically* the welfare state is in "antagonism to the capitalist system. . . . Collective needs are . . . objectively in contradiction to the logic of capitalist development . . . since the welfare sector is necessarily outside of the criteria of profit."[31]

Even more importantly, the expansion of the welfare state requires a large surplus of capital for programs that, by themselves, do not turn over a profit and which are not directly productive. For this reason, German political sociologist Claus Offe has argued that "the political-administrative system of late capitalist societies, tailored to satisfy in concrete ways the requirements of maintaining the capitalist order will reveal itself as an alien element."[32] However, where working class parties and movements have been relatively strong, as in Scandinavia, the expansion of the welfare state has made more likely the creation of a socialist alternative. In Sweden, for exaple, the expansion of the welfare state in the past half century, which occurred largely when Social Democratic governments were in power, has given political authorities considerably more control over the economy than is the case in the United States. Moreover, as survey research has found, the experience of an advanced welfare state has made socialism both plausible and desirable to Swedish workers.[33] Workers in the United States, who have not experienced a bountiful and democratic welfare state, are

---

[31]André Gorz, *Strategy for Labor* (Boston, 1968), p. 98.
[32]Claus Offe, "The Abolition of Market Control and the Problem of Legitimacy," *Kapitalistate* 1 (1973): 112.
[33]M. Donald Hancock, "The Swedish Welfare State: Prospects and Contradictions," *The Wilson Quarterly* I (Autumn 1977); Richard Scase, *Social Democracy in Capitalist Society* (London, 1977).

much more skeptical about the possibility of major structural change.

Where strong working-class socialist or social democratic parties compete for power, their very existence pushes the development of the welfare state forward at a pace more rapid than is required for the maintenance of their countries' economies. Even in routine periods of relative social peace, the very existence of a credible electoral alternative and an organized working class severely constrains the actions of government and the dominant classes. Thus, for example, the Conservative British governments of the 1950s had to maintain high employment policies despite the preferences of most businesspeople who wished to give priority to the problems of inflation and balance of payments deficits. The Labour party thus provided a brake on government activity that would be directed against the interests of workers by its very existence as a potential government.[34]

The United States is distinguished from other western capitalist democracies in that it lacks such a regular political instrument for securing progressive expansions in the welfare state that go beyond the minimum needed to keep the economy going and to preserve order. The American welfare state is a cluster of programs without a persistent, coherent organized popular movement that attempts to direct and improve the programs. As a result, the American welfare state has expanded in one of two ways: attempts by elites to solve what appear to be technical problems, as in the case of the Social Security reforms of the early 1980s, and *ad hoc* social movements that in special periods compel concessions as in the case of black urban movements of the 1960s. Although major initiatives in social policy have been the product of such special times, *ad hoc* social movements are very short-lived.

Indeed, the American pattern is strikingly similar to the dynamics of social policy innovation in England in the 1880s, when the resources of the new unionism were only beginning to be available to British workers and those of the Labour party were more than a decade away. The disruptive protests of London's casual workers were marked by the absence of a coherent movement ideology, and by the "co-existence of violence and reformism."[35]

[34]Andrew Martin, *The Politics of Economic Policy in the United States: A Tentative View from a Comparative Perspective* (Beverly Hills, Calif., 1973), p. 44.
[35]Gareth Stedman Jones, *Outcast London* (London, 1971), p. 345.

Writing in February 1886, George Bernard Shaw noted, "Angry as they are, they do not want revolution, they want a job. If they be left too long without it, they may turn out and run amuck through the streets until they are destroyed like so many mad dogs. But a job or even a meal will stop them any time."[36] This expressive radicalism nevertheless provoked panic among politicians and professional reformers. The predominant feeling was not one of guilt, but one of fear. The response to this social crisis did in fact produce advances for the poor, as the collective sphere of the state expanded. But, as historian Gareth Stedman Jones stresses, these new policies can only be understood as part of an effort to reassert order and social control. For every proposal to provide subsidized housing and meals, there were "parallel proposals to segregate the casual poor, to establish detention centers for 'loafers,' to separate pauper children from 'degenerate' parents or to ship the 'residuum' overseas."[37] In the context of the very limited political capacity of the disorganized, pre-social democratic English working class, repression and reform were joined by policymakers in an effort to find a formula for the protection of British capitalism.

This parallel, however, cannot be stretched too far. For the kind of welfare state that the United States has today is far more developed than the English situation of a century ago. And, even in the absence of working-class pressures organized in a political party demanding structural change, the American welfare state has grown as a complement to American capitalism.

But the compatibility of the welfare state and the operation of the economy continues to be an uneasy one. The relationship is characterized by a number of tensions, the most important of which is a changing, but continuing, fiscal crisis.

The massive expansion of welfare-state programs in the 1960s and 1970s produced a significant increase in government expenditures, both in grants and in salaries to a growing number of employees. This wage bill grew rapidly, because more and more government workers joined unions who bargained effectively on their behalf in a period of high inflation. In the 1980s the fiscal squeeze has continued because of pressures of a different sort, the insufficiencies of revenue caused by sharply lower federal tax rates.

---

[36] *Pall Mall Gazette*, 11 February 1886, p. 4; cited in *ibid.*
[37] *Ibid.*, p. 314.

An increase in costs over revenues affects the government differently from the way it affects private industry. Corporations administer their prices to pass along costs to consumers. Government, by contrast, has three ways it can increase its revenues. First, it can try to step up the economy's rate of growth by deficit spending in order to generate more tax revenues. But this strategy is flawed on two counts—it is inflationary (and hence politically risky), and it often exacerbates inequalities between the corporate and small-capital sectors, thus necessitating the further expansion of welfare expenditures.

Secondly, the government can try to increase the productivity of its programs and employees, but this is inherently difficult since, unlike the corporate sector, the government is a "labor intensive," not a "capital intensive" economic arena. Like most new government activities, new welfare programs require more people to a greater extent than they require or use more hardware.

Thirdly, the government can raise taxes. Politically, as Walter Mondale discovered when he proposed it in 1984, this solution is increasingly risky to attempt. President Reagan has successfully persuaded most Americans that high taxes retard economic growth and that the programs they pay for mostly help a minority of poor people. Because the tax system has become more regressive over time, people of middle to low income are very reluctant to have their share of funding social programs increase. As a result, they are skeptical of plans to increase taxes, thus making it difficult to find revenues to solve the fiscal problems of the welfare state.

At the same time, as we point out in our concluding chapter, most Americans support welfare-state programs and are uneasy about the growing inequalities of wealth and income in the United States. As the 1980s draw to a close, it is by no means clear that a politics favoring a reinvigorated, and more egalitarian, welfare state is out of the question.

10

corporate capitalism and government abroad: military and foreign policy

Some statistics provide the context for understanding American foreign policy: with less than 5 percent of the world's population, the United States accounts for one-quarter of the world's gross national product. One-third of all telephones are in the United

States. The United States consumes nearly one-quarter of the world's total energy; the average American uses five times the world average. One-third of all airline passengers each year are American. Nearly half of all Americans between the ages of 20 and 24 are enrolled in an institution of higher education; the comparable proportion for Europe is one-quarter; for Latin America, Asia, and Africa, it does not exceed one-twentieth.[1] Overall, most Americans are wealthier, better-fed, and receive more education, material benefits, and services than most people in the world. Although these figures do not take note of the extensive inequalities *within* the United States, which are the subject of other chapters, they suggest that even greater inequalities exist between the United States (along with the capitalist countries of Western Europe and Japan) and the rest of the world. When American political leaders talk of the need to maintain world order and stability, they are referring to a world based on this inequality. Stability means the persistence of United States privilege.

However, a situation of inequality is not natural or inevitable. Just after the Second World War, the United States rapidly attained a position of unprecedented world power. American dominance has rested on two pillars, described by political scientist Samuel Huntington as "U.S. military superiority over the Communist world and U.S. political-economic hegemony in the noncommunist world."[2] To put it another way, American dominance has consisted of United States corporate penetration of other countries coupled with the use of the government's political and military power abroad. This chapter describes how American corporate capitalism and government function abroad and shape American foreign policy.

A common view holds that after the Second World War the United States did not deliberately seek to extend its power but, "having many obligations and vast responsibilities in the world," was forced to "adopt a policy not dictated by any American material needs and certainly not in response to any American ambition or desire."[3] President Lyndon B. Johnson proudly stated, "History

[1]United Nations, *U.N. Statistical Yearbook, 1976,* pp. 2, 69; *U.S. Statistical Abstract, 1985,* p. 855.
[2]Samuel P. Huntington, "After Containment: The Functions of the Military Establishment," *The Annals* 406 (March 1973): 4.
[3]Charles E. Bohlen, *The Transformation of American Foreign Policy* (New York, 1969), p. 124.

and our own achievements have thrust upon us the principal responsibility for the protection of freedom on Earth."[4] Writing in the fiscal 1975 annual Defense Department report, the secretary of defense observed:

> The United States today, as opposed to the period before 1945, bears the principal burden of maintaining the worldwide military equilibrium which is the foundation for the security and the survival of the free world. This is not a role we have welcomed; it is a role that historical necessity has thrust upon us. . . . There is nobody else to pick up the torch.

Nonetheless, the facts remain that the United States has emerged as the foremost power in the world, has devoted vast resources to maintaining dominance, and has derived rich benefits from its position. American military, diplomatic, and economic influence is visible in virtually every country. However, American dominance was challenged from the beginning and has proved extremely short-lived. "While American military power has declined relative to that of the Soviet Union, American economic strength has declined relative to that of Europe and Japan. . . . The United States remains the strongest power in the world. But the preeminent feature of international politics at the present time is the relative decline in American power."[5] Since those words were written, the United States has embarked on a vast military buildup. But whether the remilitarization of the 1980s has brought greater power and security is doubtful; the United States may be in a more perilous situation since the arms race intensified at the beginning of the decade.

American foreign policy before the second world war

During the eighteenth and nineteenth centuries, the United States was far removed from world power struggles. In his farewell address, George Washington advised the country to profit from the good fortune that geographic accident provided and not to get involved in "entangling alliance." For more than a century, the United States attempted to derive maximum benefit from isolation and refused to ally for long with any European power.

---

[4]Quoted in Richard J. Barnet, *Roots of War* (New York, 1972), p. 19.
[5]Huntington, p. 5.

Until the twentieth century, the United States expanded toward the vast western frontier. Although this differed from the overseas expansion and the search for colonies of European powers during the same period, it represented imperialism none the less—and on a continental scale. Other elements in this expansion were the conquest and extermination of Indians, the enslavement of blacks as a source of cheap labor, and war with Mexico in 1846 (which resulted in the annexation of a substantial portion of that country, including the area that is now California, New Mexico, Utah, Arizona, and Nevada). Other examples of territorial expansion include the taking of Florida from Spain in 1819 and the annexation of Texas in 1845.

Furthermore, isolation from Europe did not mean abstaining from foreign intervention. Uninterested in Europe's struggles, the United States attempted to stake out its own sphere of influence close to home. In 1823, President Monroe issued a proclamation warning European powers not to intervene in Latin America. "But it is not the negatives [in the Monroe Doctrine] that really count. It is the hidden positive to the effect that the United States shall be the only colonizing power and the sole directing power in both North and South America."[6]

In the half century between the Spanish-American War in 1898 and the Second World War, the United States vacillated between a new expansionism overseas and an inward-looking isolationism. War with Spain resulted in United States control over the Philippines, Puerto Rico, and Guam. Gunboat diplomacy in Latin America insured that this area would remain a preserve for United States business interests. The navy and marines overthrew "uncooperative" governments and installed and kept in office puppet regimes. For example, American marines occupied and governed Nicaragua between 1926 and 1932. President Theodore Roosevelt maneuvered to build the Panama Canal by carving up Colombia and creating the client state of Panama, which quickly ceded to the United States sovereignty over the land for the canal.

United States influence was mostly confined to the Western Hemisphere until the two world wars made the United States a global power, although American political leaders had a lively interest in Asia (for example, President McKinley dispatched 5,000

[6]Richard W. Van Alstyne, *The Rising American Empire* (Chicago, 1965), p. 99.

troops to China to help crush the Boxer Rebellion in 1900). The wars resulted in a weakening of the leading European nations; the United States did not enter either war until years after it began, and it was an ocean away from the actual fighting. The Second World War was decisive, for it signified the irrevocable decline of Great Britain, the dominant capitalist power and the hub of world production, commerce, and banking.

The Soviet Union (USSR), Japan, Germany, and France—the other major industrialized countries—all suffered direct damage from the war. The United States was the only country to emerge unscathed. Indeed, in 1945 the United States was far stronger than before the war, partly because the government-sponsored techno-logical innovation and wartime expansion of productive capacity were quickly converted to peacetime production and overseas ex-pansion when the war ended.

After the Second World War, American policymakers initiated a basic reorientation in United States foreign policy by rejecting a return to isolation within the Western Hemisphere. Europe's de-cline, the existence of a political and ideological rival in the Com-munist regime of the Soviet Union, and the fear of American officials that a domestic depression would recur unless the United States expanded outward, produced a transformation of the United States from a powerful, but insular, country to the dominant force shaping the world political and economic system.

Cold war rivalry

In 1945, United States officials hoped to create a peaceful, stable world free for international trade, where there would be formal equality among nations, and where American industry would have easy access to raw materials and markets throughout the world. Like Woodrow Wilson after the First World War, American leaders after the Second World War pressed the colonial powers (Great Britain, France, and the Netherlands) to dismantle their empires. Only one country threatened the vision of an integrated capitalist world order: the USSR.

The Soviet Union opposed a capitalist trading bloc and was perceived as a potential aggressor, bent on territorial conquest in Europe. American foreign policy since the Second World War, which has depended heavily on military power, has usually been interpreted as an attempt to counter the threat of Communist aggression around the world.

Although the Soviet Union played a crucial role in the allied coalition during the Second World War, it was prostrate after the war. "The moment of victory was to find the Soviet Union enfeebled and devastated on a scale unprecedented in the past by countries *defeated* in a major war."[7] Soviet losses far exceeded those of the other allied powers.

> For three years, from June of 1941 to June of 1944, the Soviet Union carried the main burden of the fight against Hitler. . . . Partly because of Russian military successes, the United States Army got through the war with less than half the number of divisions prewar plans had indicated would be necessary for victory. Casualty figures reflect with particular vividness the disproportionate amount of fighting which went on in the east. A conservative estimate places Soviet war deaths—civilian and military—at approximately 16 million. Total Anglo-American losses in all theaters came to less than a million.[8]

In 1945, Soviet industrial output was only 58 percent of the 1940 level, and the country faced famine because of drought and destruction of its agriculture.[9] This contrasted sharply with the United States, whose industrial base had expanded during the war and whose military strength was enhanced by exclusive possession of atomic weapons. Most historians "now generally agree on the limited nature of Stalin's [postwar] objectives."[10] Invaded twice from the West within a generation, Russia aimed to create a buffer zone under her control in Eastern Europe. Regardless of the ethics, legality, or wisdom of this goal, it was far from an attempt to foment global revolution. Indeed, Premier Joseph Stalin restrained Communists in Western Europe, Yugoslavia, and China from seeking power.

In part, American political leaders probably sincerely misjudged Soviet intentions after the Second World War when they

[7]Adam Ulam, *The Rivals: America and Russia Since World War II* (New York, 1971), p. 11.
[8]John Lewis Gaddis, *The United States and the Origins of the Cold War, 1941–1947* (New York, 1972), pp. 79–80.
[9]Joyce Kolko and Gabriel Kolko, *The Limits of Power: The World and United States Foreign Policy, 1945–1954* (New York, 1972), p. 53.
[10]Gaddis, p. 355, fn. 2.

continually alarmed Americans with the prospect of a Soviet invasion of Western Europe.[11] In part, however, the Soviet threat was used to frighten Americans into supporting activist policies. "Scare hell out of the country," Senator Vandenberg advised President Truman. The president heeded the advice and proposed the Truman Doctrine, which symbolized American expansionism. Truman advocated quite specific measures of military aid to the governments of Greece and Turkey. But he justified American assistance in global terms, which constitued a sharp break with past American isolationist doctrine and practice. "I believe that it must be the policy of the United States to support free peoples who are resisting attempted subjugation by outside minorities or by outside pressures."[12] As historian Stephen Ambrose comments:

> The statement was all-encompassing. In a single sentence Truman had defined American policy for the next thirty years. . . . The Truman Doctrine came close to shutting the door against any revolution, since the terms "free peoples" and "anti-Communist" were thought to be synonymous. All the Greek government, or any dictatorship, had to do to get American aid was to claim that its opponents were Communist.[13]

The Truman Doctrine—and the entire American foreign policy to this day—regards indigenous, progressive opposition movements to authoritarian, capitalist regimes as local agents of an expansionist Soviet Union. Justified as an attempt to preserve peace and freedom, United States foreign policy aims to maintain American dominance, oppose progressive change in the Third World, and weaken the Soviet Union. Just three years after the United States and the Soviet Union were wartime allies, the cleavage between the two hardened into what British leader Winston Churchill called an "iron curtain." More important than the question of which country "started" the cold war is the ensuing and

---

[11]Many of those influential in shaping the containment policy have subsequently admitted their error in judgment. See, for example, Dean Acheson, *Present at the Creation* (New York, 1969), p. 753; George Kennan, "'X' plus 25: Interview with George F. Kennan," *Foreign Policy* no. 7 (Summer 1972): 14; and others cited in Ronald Steele, "The Power and the Glory," *New York Review of Books,* May 31, 1973, p. 30, fn 3.

[12]Stephen E. Ambrose, *Rise to Globalism: America's Foreign Policy, 1938–1980,* 2d. ed. (New York, 1980), p. 132.

[13]*Ibid.*

continuing destructive spiral of arms production, which has maintained world tensions at a dangerous pitch. And, since the United States has initiated virtually every new phase of arms escalation, it bears a heavy responsibility for the menace threatening world survival.

Global expansion and the invisible empire

Focusing on the US–USSR cold-war rivalry—important as the issue is—may obscure another key development that occurred following the war. Joyce and Gabriel Kolko have suggested that the most important aspect of American foreign policy during the last thirty years has not been US–USSR hostility but the postwar quest of the United States for worldwide domination.[14] As restated by foreign-policy analyst Graham Allison, "Historians in the year 2000, looking back with detachment on the cold war, are apt to conclude that the main feature of international life in the period 1945–1970 was neither the expansion of the Soviet Union nor Communist China. Instead, it was the global expansion of American influence: military, economic, political and cultural."[15]

In the years after the Second World War, the United States sponsored the creation of a new integrated world order. Its chief elements included easy access for American capital to both the markets of industrialized nations and the raw materials (notably petroleum) of nonindustrialized nations, as well as American government support for stable procapitalist governments throughout the world. (American-Soviet rivalry can be better understood when placed in this context, for the Soviet Union opposed both elements of American foreign policy and erected a rival noncapitalist military and trading bloc in opposition to the American world order.) American efforts were relatively successful and permitted a worldwide economic boom, sparked by American industrial expansion, during the postwar period.

However, the American "empire" was not a traditional form of imperialism or colonialism. With the exception of a few protectorates—Puerto Rico, the Virgin Islands, and some Pacific posses-

---

[14]Kolko and Kolko, *passim.*
[15]Graham Allison, "Cool It: The Foreign Policy of Young America," *Foreign Policy* no. 1 (Winter 1970–71): 144–45.

sions—the United States did not establish legal custody over territory. Although American power is both more global in scope and more far-reaching within individual countries than past imperial situations, it is exercised through informal political, military, and economic influence rather than formal colonial arrangements. What must be examined, then, are the specific new features of American dominance, which are linked to corporate capitalism, rapid communications, and military technology.

Underlying the new expansionism—a process that was already underway when the United States began to pick up the slack left by England, France, and Germany after the First World War—was a fear shared by political officials and corporate leaders that the depression, which had sapped the United States economy in the 1930s and had ended only when war needs created new demand, would recur. "Fully aware that the New Deal had not solved the problem of unemployment in peacetime, Roosevelt and his associates hoped that foreign markets would help absorb the vast quantity of goods which would have to be produced if employment levels were to be maintained after the fighting had stopped."[16]

The search for foreign markets and spheres of influence took several forms.

Replacing Western Europe as a world power   Before the First World War the capitalist countries of England, France, Germany, Belgium, Italy, and the Netherlands were the leading world producers, traders, and colonial powers. All were severely weakened by the two world wars. Within a few years after the end of the Second World War, the United States moved into the vacuum thus created—and used economic aid and political pressure to hasten the process.

The United States set out to replace England, which had been the keystone of the former international capitalist system and the largest trader, banker, and colonial power. This was the price England was forced to pay for American assistance in the desperate years after the Second World War. Historian John Gaddis notes that "blunt pressure from the [American] negotiators eventually forced London to accept most of Washington's plans. Dependent on American aid for both its war effort and postwar reconstruction, Great Britain was in no position to resist."[17] Within a few years, the

---

[16]Gaddis, p. 21.
[17]*Ibid.*, p. 22.

Figure 10-1
Foreign investments of capital-exporting countries

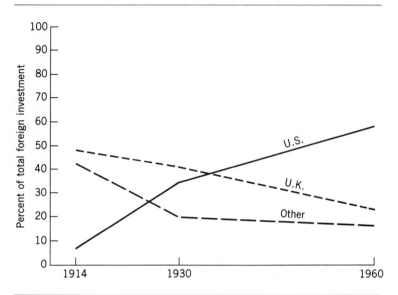

Source: Adapted from William Woodroof, *Impact of Western Man* (New York, 1966), p. 150.

United States succeeded in supplanting England as international trader and banker. By the Bretton Woods agreement of 1944, the dollar replaced the British pound as the international currency, providing the United States with substantial benefits. For example, other countries must maintain reserves in dollars, which results in the equivalent of a several-billion-dollar low-interest loan to the United States each year. Through this means and recurrent United States balance of payments deficits, other countries have helped pay the costs of American takeovers of their economies and American foreign military intervention overseas. Soon the United States replaced European countries as the leading world investor.

The Third World   Since European countries needed all their available resources to rebuild their own economies after the Second World War, American business was uniquely situated to expand into other areas. American aims in the Third World were to open up these areas to investment by American corporations and to prevent local government control by regimes that might challenge foreign (particularly American) interests. (The Third World is usually defined as the rural, poor countries in Asia, Africa, and Latin America, which are aligned with neither the Communist nor Western capitalist bloc. Yet nearly all countries in the Third World are tied—by trade, investment, political, and military links—to the capitalist bloc under United States direction.)

With Latin America already to a large extent under informal American control, the United States expanded into other resource-rich areas. Particularly important was the Middle East, which contained vast petroleum deposits that American petroleum companies soon dominated, as well as countries in Africa and Asia with mineral deposits. In 1940, Great Britain controlled 72 percent of Middle East oil reserves; the United States, 10 percent; and other countries, the rest. By 1967, Great Britain controlled 29 percent; the United States, 59 percent; and other countries, the remainder.[18]

Containment The new expansionism required checking potential challengers. Both because the Communist trading bloc represented an alternative to the Western capitalist trading bloc, and, from a fear of Soviet expansion, American policy aimed to confine Soviet influence to Eastern Europe, reserving the rest of the world for capitalist economic development and political control. The world was thus divided into two areas: the Communist countries of the Soviet Union, Eastern Europe, and (after 1948) China; and the capitalist areas (both industrialized and agricultural).

The United States gave first priority to rebuilding war-torn Europe, militarily, economically, and politically, in order to assure reliable and prosperous allies among the industrialized nations. In 1948, Secretary of State George Marshall proposed a program of American financial and technical aid to Europe. Marshall defended his plan to Congress on the humanitarian ground that famine was sweeping Europe. Moreover, he warned, unless the United States helped other countries to recover, "the cumulative loss of foreign markets and sources of supply would unquestionably have a depressing influence on our domestic economy."[19] The secretary of

[18]Harry Magdoff, *The Age of Imperialism: The Economics of U.S. Foreign Policy* (New York, 1969), p. 43.
[19]William Appleman Williams, *The Tragedy of American Diplomacy* (Cleveland, 1959), p. 177.

the interior also defended the plan as essential to America's continued productivity and prosperity.

The Marshall Plan was further justified as a way to prevent
socialist regimes from taking power in Western Europe and to stop
the spread of communism. Marshall Plan funds were provided to
Germany, America's enemy in the war, but conditions imposed on
funds offered to the Soviet Union, the wartime ally of the United
States, virtually insured the USSR's refusal. At the same time that
the Marshall Plan was launched, two military initiatives were also
taken by the United States, the Truman Doctrine, and the North
Atlantic Treaty Organization (NATO), which linked the United
States and Western Europe in an anti-Soviet military alliance.

American expansion abroad has thus taken two major forms:
economic penetration by multinational corporations, and political
and military influence exercised by the American government. The
two are distinct yet intertwined, and each has contributed to ad-
vancing the other. According to political economist Robert Gilpin,
the income generated by American business investments abroad in
the postwar period was used "to finance America's global political
and military position. The income from foreign investments, in
other words, had become an important factor in American global
hegemony."[20] In the following section, we will discuss economic
penetration and America's political and military influence in the
world.

ECONOMIC PENETRATION AND
MULTINATIONAL CORPORATIONS

American corporate capitalism has expanded outside the United
States in response to three internal dilemmas. Each one has shaped
a different form of American economic expansion.

Dependence on raw materials   The United States is among
the countries best endowed with natural resources. It has some of
the world's largest deposits of coal, copper, natural gas, iron, petro-

---

[20]Robert Gilpin, *U.S. Power and the Multinational Corporation: The Political Economy of Direct Foreign Investment* (New York, 1975), p. 161.

leum, and aluminum. The United States is also among the world's leading food producers; for example, it is the largest producer of corn, soybeans, cotton, and oranges, and the largest exporter of wheat and rice.[21] However, no country is fortunate enough to contain within its borders all the raw materials it needs for modern industrial production—and the United States is no exception. Moreover, the United States has begun to deplete many of the natural resources it once contained in abundance. Both factors produce a growing dependence on other countries for essential raw materials.

The speed with which the United States has come to rely on other countries for raw materials can be seen from the following figures: of the thirteen minerals considered essential for a modern industrial economy, the United States had to import more than half its supplies of only four in 1950; yet by 2000, estimates are that the number will have climbed to twelve. The United States already imports all its natural rubber, over 90 percent of its manganese, cobalt, and chromium, and over half its aluminum, platinum, tin, nickel, antimony, bismuth, mercury, and zinc.[22] Most of these raw materials come from less developed countries in Latin America, Asia, the Middle East, and Africa.

American corporations and government seek to assure a cheap and adequate supply of minerals and other natural resources flowing to the United States. The most effective way in the past has been for American corporations to invest in the Third World and to gain direct control over foreign raw materials. Thus, Kennecott and Anaconda control much of the world's copper deposits, located in Zambia, Chile, and elsewhere. And a handful of American petroleum corporations (along with a few foreign companies) control most of the capitalist world's petroleum supplies, located in the United States, the Middle East, Nigeria, Mexico, and Venezuela.

Foreign trade: export of manufactured products and food In 1983, American business exported $199 billion worth of goods produced in the United States, providing a profitable outlet for surplus agricultural and industrial capacity. Most foreign activity is organized within the sector of corporate capital. Encouraged by govern-

[21] *New York Times,* January 6, 1974; Emma Rothschild, "The Politics of Food," *New York Review of Books,* May 16, 1974, p. 17.
[22] *New York Times,* November 5, 1972; December 22, 1973.

Table 10-1
The growth of U.S. private investment abroad, 1950–1974

| | Value of Direct Investment Assets (billions of dollars at end of year) | | Direct Investment Flows (billions of dollars during year) | |
Year	Total	Capital Outflow from U.S.	Total Inflow* to U.S.	Income from Investment Abroad
1950	11.8	0.6	1.5	1.3
1955	19.4	0.8	2.1	1.9
1960	31.9	1.7	2.9	2.4
1965	49.5	3.5	5.2	4.0
1970	75.5	4.3	7.9	6.0
1974	118.6	7.5	20.7	17.7

*Includes investment income plus royalties and fees.

Source: Richard C. Edwards, Michael Reich, and Thomas E. Weisskopf, eds., *The Capitalist System: A Radical Analysis of American Society,* 2nd ed., © 1978, p. 476. Reprinted by permission of Prentice-Hall, Inc., Englewood Cliffs, N.J. Sources listed in original.

ment help, including tax incentives, technical assistance, insurance against political difficulties, and, most important, a foreign policy that aims at creating conditions throughout the world favorable to American corporations, the expansion of America's foreign trade has been rapid.

Capital export: foreign investment   In recent years, sagging demand in the United States has meant that American corporations now find it more profitable to invest capital in building new factories abroad rather than to expand manufacturing at home. Foreign investments give American corporations direct access to foreign markets and a hold over the economies of other countries. When manufactured products or food are exported, the transaction ends once they are purchased by foreign customers. However, when capital and technology are exported, and an American corporation creates a foreign manufacturing subsidiary, the transaction only *begins* with the initial investment: the foreign subsidiary remains year after year, continuing to produce and sell goods that make a profit for the American home company. American corporations began investing heavily in foreign manufacturing subsidiaries during the 1950s and have substantial investments piled up abroad. Between 1950 and 1977, direct overseas investment by American corporations increased from $12 billion to $149, and new foreign investment was double the rate of domestic investment.

Profits on foreign investments represent a substantial and growing proportion of total American corporate profits. The share of after-tax corporate profits accounted for by foreign investment rose from 7 percent of all corporate profits in 1950 to 25 percent in 1974.[23] The 100 largest corporations obtain about one-third of their profits from overseas investment.[24] About one-third of foreign profits flow back to the United States as corporate income. The rest remain abroad as new foreign investment. Thus, American corporations use the resources extracted from a foreign country to increase the profitability of the corporation and to enrich its American stockholders, as well as to strengthen American corporate control over that nation's economy.

The multinational corporation   The term *multinational corporations* has been coined to describe corporations heavily involved in foreign operations. Multinationals have reshaped the world political economy and are the new Goliaths of the present era. In 1986, about one-third of the world's 100 largest economic units (measured by countries' GNP and corporate sales) were United States multinational corporations. Multinational corporations straddle countries. They make decisions about research, investment, manufacturing, and sales without much regard for national boundaries: decisions are governed by profitability. In an exhaustive study of multinational investment abroad, economist Mira Wilkins concludes that, when a multinational shops around for a location for new foreign investment, the most important factor influencing its decision is the local political climate, that is, which government offers the corporation the biggest tax breaks, shows a willingness to crack down on workers, and the like.[25]

[23]Table 13-B in Richard C. Edwards, Michael Reich, and Thomas E. Weisskopf, eds., *The Capitalist System: A Radical Analysis of American Society,* 2nd ed. (Englewood Cliffs, N.J., 1978), p. 477.
[24]Barry Bluestone and Bennett Harrison, *The Deindustrialization of America: Plant Closings, Community Abandonment, and the Dismantling of Basic Industry* (New York, 1982), p. 42.
[25]Mira Wilkins, *The Maturing of Multinational Enterprise: American Business Abroad from 1914 to 1970* (Cambridge, Mass., 1974), p. 458.

Economist Daniel R. Fusfeld explains that the multinational corporation

> was made possible by advances in the technology of transportation and communication after World War II (jet aircraft and automatic data communication, for example). U.S. corporations were able to take advantage of the new technology much more readily than foreign corporations, in part because much of that technology was developed here, but chiefly because of the predominance of the United States in world trade and international finance.[26]

Multinational corporations can integrate far-flung operations as a result of technological advances in communications and information processing. A multinational corporation may carry out product research in one country, obtain raw materials from another, manufacture parts in a third country, assemble the product in a fourth, and market it in other countries.

Most huge American corporations are multinational and most American investments aborad are carried on by the largest corporations and financial institutions. Seventy-one of the top 100 American manufacturing corporations have over one-third of their payroll employed overseas. Some of the largest American corporations, including Exxon, Mobil Oil, Woolworth, National Cash Register, Burroughs, Colgate-Palmolive, and Singer have larger sales abroad than at home. By the late 1960s, nearly all the largest corporations had over one-quarter of their assets abroad. Foreign investments are heavily concentrated among these large corporations: the top 200 American corporations account for over three-quarters of all foreign investment. The rapid growth of United States banks abroad has kept pace with corporate expansion.

Banks and multinational corporations remain national in their ownership and management: a majority of multinational corporations are based in the United States, and their stockholders and managers are mostly American. Some multinational corporations, including Nestlé, Phillips, Sony, and Royal Dutch Shell, are based in Europe and Japan. However, American corporations predominate among the largest multinationals.

This has important consequences both for the United States and the countries where multinationals invest. Professor Gilpin

[26]Daniel R. Fusfeld, *The Rise of the Corporate State in America* (Andover, Mass., 1973), p. 3.

points out that "the essence of American direct [foreign] investment has been the shift of managerial control over substantial sectors of foreign economies to American nationals."[27] This shift in
control has transformed the United States and other countries. The
United States is becoming a headquarters economy: for many corporations, "the headquarters and staff operations remain in the
United States, as directing and service facilities, while manufacturing operations are extended abroad."[28] When corporations create
jobs abroad, there are fewer jobs in the corporate sector in the
United States; and American workers are forced to take low-paying jobs in the service sector or in the spheres of small-scale capital
or marginal labor, or remain unemployed.

Foreign profits get repatriated but not jobs. As a result, "Production of the traditional industrial goods that have been the main-
stay of the U.S. economy is being transferred from $4-an-hour
factories in New England to 30-cents-an-hour factories in the 'export platforms' of Hong Kong and Taiwan."[29] For this reason,
American trade unions have begun to oppose foreign corporate
expansion.

Trends in corporate trade and investment abroad

In the Third World   In the early years of United States foreign
expansion, most investments were directed toward gaining control
of the mineral resources of Third World countries. In recent years,
however, corporations have also been investing in the manufacturing sector in these countries. Setting up a factory in Indonesia or
Singapore (rather than Ohio, for example) provides attractive advantages, including lower wages paid to workers, low taxes, and
few outlays for pollution control and safety devices.

At the extreme, one can speak of company countries, where
foreign-owned (often United States) corporations monopolize the
country's raw materials and manufacturing sector. An example is
provided by Chile, where a few American mining companies (Anaconda and Kennecott) control half the country's extractive indus-

---

[27]Gilpin, p. 11.
[28]Daniel Bell, *Toward a Post-Industrial Society* (New York, 1973), p. 485.
[29]Richard J. Barnet and Ronald E. Muller, *Global Reach: The Power of Multinational Corporations* (New York, 1974), p. 216.

tries—on which Chile relies for nine-tenths of her exports. ITT owns the Chilean telephone and electric companies, two Sheraton hotels, and a radio station. Most Chilean shipping is controlled by W. R. Grace, an American shipper. Multinational corporations are among the best organized, wealthiest, and most powerful forces within many Third World countries. In addition, through the development of a local capitalist group and government whose interests are tied to the foreign corporate sector, political conditions favorable to multinational corporations are fostered.

As the United States has lagged behind in industrial competition with Western Europe and Japan, it has compensated for large trade deficits with these nations by exports to the Third World. In 1981, the United States exported $89 billion of manufactured goods to the Third World. This represented 40 percent of total United States manufactured exports and exceeded the value of manufactured exports to Japan and Western Europe.

Although Third World nations have increasingly challenged the situation, their economies have largely been shaped to serve the needs of multinational corporations. Their natural resources fall under foreign ownership and control; the multinationals locate low-cost manufacturing in the Third World but not technologically innovative research operations. Multinationals have no clout to obtain the resources from within these countries to finance expansion of their control. For example, in the 1960s, four-fifths of United States manufacturing operations in Latin America were financed by local capital, squeezing out entrepreneurs in these countries. At the same time, American firms in Latin America shipped home half their profits, further draining resources from the area.

Haiti, a small island republic in the Caribbean, illustrates why multinationals flock abroad. The headline of an article in the business section of the *New York Times* suggests the reason: "Haiti's Allure for U.S. Business: The pay is only $2.65 a day, a drawing card for hundreds of new factories."[30] The article explains that "tiny Haiti—jammed with 6 million people, most of them unemployed—is emerging as the low wage capital of the world." American firms locating there include MacGregor and Rawlings,

---

[30]Clyde Farnsworth, "Haiti's Allure for U.S. Business," *New York Times,* June 17, 1984. The quotations in this paragraph are from Farnsworth.

manufacturers of sports equipment, electronics producers TRW and GTE, and the conglomerate Gulf & Western. Haiti's investment climate is "attractive" as a result of its high unemployment and a dictatorial regime that provided lavish tax benefits to foreign firms and used repression to prevent strikes. "Labor unrest is also a rarity in a country that has been ruled for over 30 years by the authoritarian Duvaliers. . . . The tranquility on the labor front appears to rule out any dramatic increase in wages in the next few years." American companies have had to adapt to Haiti's special conditions. In order to assure a healthy work force, United States companies distribute vitamin pills to their employees "as a supplement to the meager diet of most Haitians." In 1986, Haitians revolted against their harsh conditions and overthrew the Duvalier regime. A series of strikes resulted, which led some American businesses in Haiti to reduce their operations. However, in an interview reported in the *International Herald Tribune* of July 14, 1986, the chair of MacGregor Sporting Goods explained why he felt the disturbances would pass quickly:

> If I have a strike in New Jersey, the workers get unemployment, they have a working spouse, there is a strike fund. The strike could last a long time. In Haiti, if you go out on strike, there is none of that. It sounds cruel, but if you don't work, you don't eat.

Why should Haitians, who live in a tropical paradise, be unable to provide for their own subsistence? Haiti is typical of many Third World nations. The crisis of world food production is largely a by-product of the expansion of American and European agribusiness.

Agribusiness transforms patterns of land use in ways that are the opposite of what is needed by the people of these areas. Rather than land being devoted to raising staple foods for local consumption, it is increasingly devoted to raising cash crops for export to the West, with agribusiness taking the profits. Throughout the Third World, local farmers have become hired help for United States and other Western nations' agribusiness or are thrown off the land altogether. In some Third World countries the rate of rural unemployment has reached 40 percent, and the vicious cycle continues when the surplus agricultural population migrates to cities to seek jobs, swelling the ranks of the urban unemployed.

Third World countries may achieve high rates of growth. But these figures are deceptive, for the growth is achieved by local subsidiaries of United States corporations, with profits sent out of the country. Often this is growth achieved at the expense of local living standards. For example, new foreign investment in Mexico between 1961 and 1970 amounted to $1.1 billion, while remittances and payments on interest, royalties, and patents were $1.8 billion. This represented resources "contributed" by Mexicans to the industrialized nations. Thus, Mexico supplied North American and West European stockholders with $700 million during this period.[31]

Third World countries also pile up heavy foreign debt as they are forced to borrow or gain access to western technology. The public debt of Third World countries exceeds $700 billion, a staggering burden for these nations. In many cases, merely repaying foreign debt (both interest and principal) absorbs most of a country's export revenues. For example, in 1984 Mexico paid $13 billion to her western creditors and Brazil paid $11 billion. The need to repay foreign debt shapes these countries' entire economies and imposes heavy costs on their citizens, especially the poor.

In order to repay past debts, many countries are forced to seek new loans. When they borrow, they must agree to pursue conservative economic policies dictated by the foreign lending agency, such as the International Monetary Fund (IMF), foreign banks, or the American government. The IMF is the agency to which nations apply when they cannot obtain loans elsewhere. As a business reporter points out, "Because applicants for I.M.F. credit have no place else to turn, the agency exercises enormous influence over the economies and, by extension, the politics of Third World nations."[32] The austerity policies imposed by the IMF include reductions in government social spending and wage cuts, to generate the funds to pay foreign creditors. Between 1981 and 1984, Mexico and Brazil suffered a 15 percent drop in living standards as a result. The swollen foreign debt of Third World nations represents a weak link in the international capitalist system.

In industrialized nations   The small size of most Third World countries means that American investments have a heavy impact

[31]North American Congress on Latin America (NACLA), *Report on the Americas* 11 (September–October 1977): 15.
[32]Clyde Farnsworth, "A Turbulent Rescue Role for the I.M.F.," *New York Times,* May 4, 1984.

Table 10-2
The distribution of U.S. direct private investment assets abroad by area and sector:
1929–1983

	1929	1950	1959	1969	1974	1983
ALL AREAS	$7.5 b.	$11.8 b.	$29.7 b.	$70.8 b.	$118.6 b.	$226 b.
Center	49%	52%	61%	72%	76%	75%
Canada	27	31	34	30	24	21
Western Europe	18	15	18	31	37	45
Japan	*	*	1	2	3	4
Others[1]	4	6	8	9	12	5
Periphery	51%	48%	39%	28%	24%	23%
Latin America	47	39	30	19	16	13
Middle East	*	1	2	3	2	1
Africa[2]	*	2	3	3	2	2
Asia[3]	4	6	4	3	4	6
Petroleum	15%	29%	35%	38%	26%	26%
Manufacturing	24	33	32	42	43	40
Other sectors	61	38	43	30	31	34

*Denotes less than 0.5%.
[1]Includes South Africa, Australia, and New Zealand.
[2]Excluding South Africa.
[3]Excluding Japan and the Middle East.

Sources: Richard C. Edwards. Michael Reich, and Thomas E. Weisskopf, eds., *The Capitalist System: A Radical Analysis of American Society,* 2nd ed., © 1978, p. 478. Reprinted by permission of Prentice-Hall, Inc., Englewood Cliffs, N.J. Sources listed in original. For 1983, *Survey of Current Business,* August 1984, p. 18 and November 1984, p. 24.

on their economies. But in the past several decades, most new American investments have gone to Europe and Canada rather than the Third World. Industrialized countries offer more attractive investment opportunities, higher consumer demand, and more stable political situations. American multinational corporations have gained an important role in these countries. Some of the most advanced industrial sectors in Western Europe are under American control, including 80 percent of the market for computers, 95 percent of integrated circuits, 50 percent of semiconductors, and an important share in automobiles, electronics, and home appliances. American corporations control 10 percent of England's total pro-

Table 10-3
Earnings on U.S. direct foreign private investment by area, 1959 and 1976

	Reported Earnings (millions of dollars during year)	Value of Investment (millions of dollars at year-end)	Rate of Earnings (%)
1959			
Underdeveloped countries	1,615	11,536	14.0
Developed countries	1,640	18,199	9.0
Total investment	3,255	29,735	11.0
1976			
Underdeveloped countries	5,763	22,925	25.2
Developed countries	5,217	43,838	11.9
Total investment	10,980	76,245	14.4

Source: 1976 figures calculated from United States Department of Commerce, *Survey of Current Business,* August 1977, pp. 39–40. 1959 figures from Thomas E. Weisskopf, "United States Foreign Private Investment," in Richard C. Edwards, Michael Reich, and Thomas E. Weisskopf, eds., *The Capitalist System: A Radical Analysis of American Society,* © 1972, p. 430. Reprinted by permission of Prentice-Hall, Inc., Englewood Cliffs, N.J.

duction. The most extreme case is Canada, where United States corporations control half of the country's manufacturing.[33]

In the Soviet Union, China, and Eastern Europe   The rapid economic growth of Western Europe and Japan has weakened the dominant position of American multinationals. In an attempt to find new outlets, American business has turned to Communist countries, with whom there were few economic ties before the 1970s. American companies have negotiated trade, loans, and investment agreements with the USSR and nations of Eastern Europe. Trade and investment between the United States and communist nations accompanied a reduction of international political tensions in the 1970s—and slowed as the Cold War intensified in the 1980s.

In recent years, the People's Republic of China has become a new location for multinational investment, although the total volume remains low. The People's Republic of China sought economic

[33]Raymond Vernon, *Sovereignty at Bay: The Multinational Spread of U.S. Enterprises* (New York, 1971), p. 20.

ties with capitalist nations when it attempted to gain access to western technology and combine market incentives with socialist organization of the economy.

The significance of American corporate expansion abroad cannot be overestimated. The prosperity of American corporate capitalism has become heavily dependent on overseas operations, whose expansion has been far more rapid than growth within the United States. Between 1957 and 1971, the overseas assets of American manufacturers increased more than 500 percent, compared to a 90 percent rise in domestic assets. Foreign investments are particularly attractive because their rate of profit is about double that of domestic investments.

Thanks to United States dominance after the Second World War and the American government's policy of maximizing worldwide access for multinational investments, the functioning of capitalism internationally has produced an integrated global system of production and consumption shaped by the needs of United States, West European, and Japanese corporations. Much of the multinational takeover has occurred through peaceful, legal means. Multinationals have, however, used their vast resources in illegal ways to further their interests and corrupt the political process of other countries. Arms companies, notably Lockheed, Boeing, and Northrop, have bribed government officials in France, Germany, Japan, Indonesia, Italy, the Philippines, Saudi Arabia, and South Korea in an attempt to secure lucrative arms contracts. As part of its $20 million campaign of political and commercial corruption, Lockheed bribed Prince Bernhard of the Netherlands and the prime ministers of Italy and Japan. Petroleum companies have also bribed lavishly. Exxon, for example, contributed $50 million in secret payments to Italian politicians between 1963 and 1972. Fifty large American industrial corporations reported to the Securities and Exchange Commission in 1976 that they had made questionable payments abroad totalling $100 million over the preceding five years. These practices declined after passage of the Foreign Corrupt Practices Act in 1977.

For multinational expansion to occur, friendly policies are necessary from the American as well as foreign governments. But the alliance between multinationals and the American government has come under strain as resistance to it grows both within the United States and overseas.

THE SEARCH FOR MILITARY
AND POLITICAL SUPREMACY

The United States has a vast military establishment, the largest and most powerful in the world. It maintains nearly 400 major military bases around the globe as well as several thousand smaller ones. Over one-half million troops are stationed abroad; the navy has patrols in every ocean; reconnaissance satellites circle the world. American military missions are stationed in 50 foreign countries.[34] Military treaties link the United States to the regimes of over 40 countries in Europe, Asia, and Latin America. Each year, about $300 billion is spent to support the armed forces and purchase new weapons. (This constitutes half the combined military expenditures of all other nations.)

The arms race with the Soviet Union

About one-fifth of the American military budget has gone to develop sophisticated thermonuclear weapons directed mainly against the Soviet Union. Beginning with the cold war arms race in the 1940s, there has been a never ending search by each country for military advantage. The result has been to create a world permanently poised for war and total devastation. Each country possesses a staggering "overkill" capacity: the United States has a stockpile of 9,200 strategic nuclear warheads (the Soviet Union has 7,500) and several times that number of tactical nuclear weapons. For example, the multiple warhead MIRV missiles from one Poseidon submarine could destroy about one-quarter of Soviet industry; the United States possesses more than 30 Poseidon submarines equipped with MIRVs, along with sufficient air-launched cruise missiles (ALCMs) aboard long-range bombers and land-based intercontinental ballistic missiles (ICBMs) to destroy the Soviet Union many times over. Moreover, military analyst Barry Blechman points out, "The United States has generally been the first to introduce new types of [weapons] systems—from the atomic bomb

---

[34]Adam Yarmolinsky, *The Military Establishment* (New York, 1971), p. 115.

itself to MIRVs."[35] The escalation of the arms race in the 1980s, which conforms to the same pattern, will be described later.

The arms race produces stalemate (what has been called the "balance of terror"), but it is not a static one. As each country develops more dangerous weapons, it drains productive resources for military purposes without increasing security or effective power. As a result of popular and congressional pressure, attempts were initiated in the 1970s to limit new weaponry. Strategic arms limitation talks in 1972 (SALT I), extended by accords concluded in 1974, a second SALT treaty negotiated (but never ratified), and the Antiballistic Missile Treaty of 1972 produced agreements between the United States and the Soviet Union to regulate arms buildups. These agreements were part of a broader process of accommodation between the United States and Soviet Union in the 1970s that was termed détente. Although both nations continued to increase their military arsenals, the trend shifted from military confrontation to limited economic and political accommodation.

However, détente ended abruptly in the late 1970s. After successfully negotiating a second strategic arms limitation treaty (SALT II), President Carter reversed his stance under strong pressure from the right. He thereupon sponsored increases in military spending, developed threatening new military doctrines, and refused to submit SALT II to the Senate for ratification, probably because it would have failed to muster the necessary two-thirds majority needed to be ratified. The process of remilitarization accelerated under President Reagan and the United States embarked on the most substantial peacetime military buildup in history.

Developing compliant regimes

American foreign policy has undergone many shifts since the Second World War. But its basic aim has remained the same: to use American political, military, and economic power to assure "friendly" foreign regimes. Whether a government is friendly or not depends on whether it permits American corporations to operate freely within its borders to obtain raw materials, trade, and

---

[35]Barry M. Blechman et al., "The Defense Budget," in Joseph A. Pechman, ed., *Setting National Priorities: The 1978 Budget* (Washington, D.C., 1977), p. 104.

investment opportunities; and whether it supports the United States position in the international arena. Note that Third World regimes friendly to the United States are reactionary and repressive: democratic governments often cannot easily permit their national resources to be developed on terms favorable to American corporate and governmental interests.

In the strange logic of American foreign policymakers, since the United States represents democracy and protects freedom in the world, nearly any actions are justified. The double standard has been described by historian Henry Steele Commager:

> When the Soviet Union intervenes in Czechoslovakia, that is naked aggression, but when we land 22,000 marines in Santo Domingo, that is peace keeping. When communist countries carry on clandestine activities abroad, that is part of an 'international conspiracy,' but when the CIA operates clandestinely in sixty foreign countries, that is a legitimate function of our foreign policy. When Russia establishes a missile base in Cuba (on the invitation of Cuba), that is an act of war which must be met with all the force at our command, but when we build the largest airbase in the world in Thailand, that is part of our ceaseless search for peace.[36]

However, in the middle 1980s, popular pressures, skillful elites, and in some cases United States support, led to the replacement of dictatorial regimes in Argentina, Brazil, the Philippines, and Haiti by moderate liberal governments. By supporting liberalization, the United States aimed to forestall revolutionary change and protect its own economic and strategic interests in these regions.

Political influence

The government attempts to influence other countries through a variety of institutional mechanisms. Financial agencies, including the Agency for International Development (AID), the Export-Import Bank, and the Overseas Private Investment Corporation, provide aid and loans to foreign governments and technical help and insurance to American businesses in an attempt to facilitate American business operations abroad. The United States uses its

---

[36]Henry Steele Commager, "The Defeat of America," *New York Review of Books,* October 5, 1972, p. 12.

preponderant influence within international financial institutions, including the International Monetary Fund, the Organization for Economic Cooperation and Development, and the International Bank for Reconstruction and Development (commonly known as the World Bank), to regulate an international capitalist order within which American business can prosper. The United States exerts influence through its participation in NATO and other international organizations, including the Organization of American States, the United Nations General Assembly, and the United Nations Security Council. More intensive means of influence include foreign aid and military intervention.

Foreign aid

The foreign aid program of the United States has operated in over 60 countries of Africa, Asia, and Latin America. Since the Second World War, the United States has given $200 billion in grants and loans to foreign regimes. This figure includes Marshall Plan grants to Europe. The purpose is presumably to help poorer nations develop. But foreign aid is often a lever used to extract concessions from other countries to assure cooperation with American corporate and political interests.

Military assistance   This form of foreign aid is given not to help countries industrialize and achieve self-sufficiency, but to build foreign armies who protect multinational corporations and regimes favorable to the United States in these countries. Military aid goes to equip and train foreign military personnel each year. More than 250,000 foreign military officers were trained by the United States between 1950 and 1968. Thus, when regimes friendly to the United States are threatened by internal challenge, foreign armies and police attempt to defend those in power. Military assistance has become the favored form of foreign aid: whereas in 1981, 36 percent of foreign aid was for "security assistance" (that is, military purposes), in 1985 security assistance represented 66 percent of foreign aid.[37]

Economic assistance   It is frequently assumed that foreign aid for economic development is evidence of American altruism. How-

[37]Emma Rothschild, "The Costs of Reaganism," *The New York Review,* March 15, 1984, p. 15.

ever, aid is often given in the form of loans by the government and private banks. Loans must be repaid with interest—and the more loans given, the more interest charges pile up. In 1956, the under-developed countries used about 4 percent of their exports to repay past loans; this figure had risen to 20 percent in 1975. One of the most important effects of foreign aid is to create dependence on the United States.[38] In the 1980s, a debt crisis that threatened the entire international capitalist system erupted when several nations, including Poland, Mexico, and Argentina, were unable to meet repayment schedules. If they had declared bankruptcy and refused to repay their debts, most major United States banks (who are the major creditors of these nations) would also have been jeopardized. Intricate maneuvers by international and American financial agencies narrowly averted economic chaos, but 60 nations have made special arrangements to reschedule their debt payments.

Intervention: the CIA

The routine operation of United States influence can be considered a form of imperialism, in which countries remain legally sovereign in principle but dependent on the United States in fact. When cooperative foreign regimes are threatened or an unfriendly regime takes power, the United States may intervene more actively. United States forces invaded Lebanon in 1958, the Dominican Republic in 1965, and Laos, Cambodia, and Vietnam for fifteen years after the mid-1950s. American-financed forces intervened against civilian regimes in Iran in 1953, Cuba in 1961, the Dominican Republic in 1965, and Indonesia in 1966. In many of these countries, United States intervention subverted democratic processes when democratically chosen governments pursued policies opposed by the American government. Thus, American policymakers (and, as we saw earlier in the chapter, American corporate officials as well) consider democracy in other nations to be less important than pro-capitalist policies.

One of the foremost government agencies used to carry out surveillance, espionage, and subversion abroad is the Central In-

[38]Gabriel Kolko, *The Roots of American Foreign Policy* (Boston, 1969), p. 72; Magdoff, p. 150; and Michael Hudson, *Super-Imperialism: The Economic Strategy of American Empire* (New York, 1972), pp. 118, 166.

telligence Agency (CIA). The CIA has secretly funded pro-American political parties, labor unions, and media in foreign countries. It has sponsored political assassinations. It carried on a secret war in Laos, subverted the government of Guatemala (1954), helped plan the 1961 Bay of Pigs invasion of Cuba, and organized the capture and murder of Ernesto "Che" Guevara in Bolivia (1967). In recent years, the CIA has trained and equipped mercenaries and provided covert aid and equipment in an illegal attempt to overthrow the Sandinista government of Nicaragua. The CIA played an active role in organizing the "Contras" in their armed opposition to the regime. It directed the destruction of Nicaragua's largest petroleum storage facility and mined Managua harbor. (These actions were declared contrary to international law by the International Court of Justice in 1986.)

The CIA intervention in Nicaragua, as well as armed intervention by the United States in Grenada and Lebanon in the early 1980s, marked a return to an expansionary stance following a relative lull of several years. Whereas, between 1946 and 1973, the United States intervened in foreign nations an average of once every three years, in the following decade there was not a single such action.[39] The reason was not the absence of Third World conflicts. One analyst enumerates fourteen struggles in 1974–80, including Ethiopia, Mozambique, Angola, Laos, Iran, and Nicaragua.[40] Why did American intervention decline in the 1970s? A major reason was the development during the Vietnam War of a popular movement in the United States opposing foreign intervention. This situation came to be designated as the Vietnam syndrome. Presidents Carter and Reagan set out to reverse the trend. They were remarkably successful. A high administration official under President Reagan remarked, "When we came into office, one of our primary missions was to get Americans out of the 'Vietnam syndrome' and get them accustomed to the idea that projecting power overseas can help the cause of peace. Well, it's worked."[41] The result has been the remilitarization of the American

---

[39]Andrew Winnick, "Rapid Deployment and Nuclear War: Reagan's New Military Strategies," *Socialist Review* no. 73 (January–February 1984): 11–30.
[40]*Ibid.*
[41]Steven R. Weisman, "Reagan Rides the Crest of an Anti-Soviet Wave," *New York Times,* September 25, 1983.

economy, a bellicose return to cold war tensions, increased American intervention abroad, and a growing danger of nuclear holocaust.

THE MILITARY-INDUSTRIAL COMPLEX

The growth of a powerful domestic military sector is quite recent. Except during wartime, the armed forces were small and few resources were devoted to their maintenance. Planning and preparation for war were relatively easy because military technology was simple, and a wartime economy was quickly demobilized when peace arrived. As recently as the period just before the Second World War, the economy was on a peacetime basis, with little military production. In 1917, it took only several months to mobilize and retool civilian industry for the production of war matériel. And several months after the war ended, the economy returned to peacetime patterns.

The Second World War represented a transition in the history of warfare. Military technology advanced enormously, with such innovations as radar, missiles, mechanized warfare, and, perhaps the greatest advance in the science of destruction, atomic weapons. General Dwight D. Eisenhower, the top-ranking Army officer after the Second World War, understood the fundamental implications of the change in military technology that had occurred as a result of the war. In a memorandum entitled "Scientific and Technological Resources as Military Assets," he wrote:

> The recent conflict has demonstrated more convincingly than ever before the strength our nation can best derive from the integration of all of our national resources in time of war. It is of the utmost importance that the lessons of this experience be not forgotten in the peacetime planning and training of the Army. The future security of the nation demands that all those civilian resources which by conversion or redirection constitute our main support in time of emergency be associated closely with the activities of the Army in time of peace. . . .
>
> This pattern of integration must be translated into a peacetime counterpart which will . . . draw into our planning for national se-

curity all the civilian resources which can contribute to the defense of the country.[42]

The peacetime cooperation among the armed forces, business, and science advocated by General Eisenhower began soon after the Second World War. In the decades since then, the new partnership has become a permanent part of the American political and economic system.

Fifteen years after he had written his memorandum, General Eisenhower returned to the subject. Yet this time, in his farewell address after eight years as president, he expressed alarm about the new trend:

> Our military organization today bears little relation to that known by any of my predecessors in peacetime, or indeed by the fighting men of World War II and Korea.
>
> Until the latest of world conflicts, the United States had no armaments industry. American makers of plowshares could, with time and as required, make swords as well. But now we can no longer risk emergency improvisation of national defense; we have been compelled to create a permanent armaments industry of vast proportions. . . .
>
> The conjunction of an immense Military Establishment and large arms industry is new in the American experience. . . . In the councils of government we must guard against the acquisition of unwarranted influence whether sought or unsought, by the military-industrial complex. The potential for the disastrous rise of misplaced power exists and will persist.

The term *military-industrial complex* (MIC) refers to the alliance of government, business, and science devoted to war preparation. It is a mighty alliance: the annual budget of the Department of Defense (DOD) approaches $300 billion.

Business: military production and profits

Sociologist Daniel Bell lists the development of a mobilized war economy as one of the three major changes in American society in the past 30 years.[43] (The other two are a managed, planned econ-

---

[42]As noted in Seymour Melman, *Pentagon Capitalism* (New York, 1970), pp. 231–32.
[43]Bell, pp. 360–61.

omy described in Chapter 3, and the welfare state, described in Chapter 10). Producing for war is the biggest industry in the United States: over 5 percent of the labor force is engaged in military activity. More than two million Americans serve in the armed forces, one million civilians work for the Pentagon (the Department of Defense), and over two million civilian workers are engaged in military production.

The military sector has close links with corporate capitalism and reaches throughout American society. The Department of Defense is the single largest customer in the world: it purchases 15 percent of American manufactured goods.[44] The Pentagon is the nation's largest landlord, owning $40 billion in property. Through the post-exchange (PX) system, it is the third largest retail distributor, after A&P and Sears, Roebuck. Since the end of the Second World War, over $3 trillion have been spent for missiles, nuclear warheads, radar, submarines, tanks, and military personnel. The magnitude of such an amount is hard to grasp. Written out, it looks like this: $3,000,000,000,000 and represents close to the total value of all homes and business structures in the United States.

Military spending is concentrated in the most technologically advanced sectors. Two-thirds of defense spending in the civilian sector is located in three industries: aircraft and missiles, electronics and communications, and shipbuilding and repairing.[45]

Many large corporations benefit heavily from military contracts. Among the 25 largest corporations, all but 5 were on the list of the top 100 firms receiving DOD contracts. Thus, there is extensive overlap between the largest military firms and the largest firms in the country.

The military industry is concentrated. Most military purchasing occurs through the Defense Department awarding prime contracts for large weapons systems—nuclear-powered submarines, missile launchers, radar equipment, and space stations—to a single firm. The firm receiving the prime contract is responsible for the overall work. Prime contracts can involve up to billions of dollars.

One company with over $6 billion in annual sales is immense; that is the amount General Dynamics received in Pentagon pro-

---

[44]Tom Christoffel, David Finklehor, and Dan Gilbarg, "Corporations and Government," in *Up Against the American Myth* (New York, 1970), p. 101.
[45]*U.S. Statistical Abstract, 1985*, p. 334.

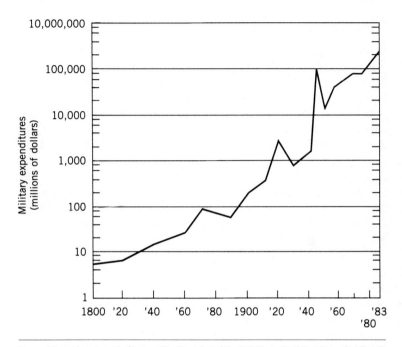

Source: Adapted from James L. Clayton, "The Fiscal Cost of the Cold War to the United States: The First 25 Years, 1947–1971," *Western Political Quarterly* 25 (September 1972): 380; James L. Clayton, "The Fiscal Limits of the Warfare-Welfare State: Defense and Welfare Spending in the U.S. Since 1900," *Western Political Quarterly* 29 (September 1976): 371; and U.S. Statistical Abstract, 1985, p. 334.

curement awards in 1983. Eight other companies each won over $3 billion in Pentagon awards that year; a total of over $40 billion for these nine companies.

Although the largest firms derive immense profits from military production, small companies throughout the United States also benefit, because giant firms subcontract out much of the actual work on prime contracts. Twenty thousand firms throughout the country are engaged in production for the military, integrating communities and small business into the war economy.

Military spending is high in part because it provides jobs and business to corporations and communities all over the country.

Military spending represents subsidies to diverse elements in large- and small-scale capital as well as to corporate labor. Thus, the lobby for militarism includes labor unions, local businesspeople, and local political officials.

The MIC represents the best example of the "iron triangle" of policy influence described in Chapter 4. The three "partners" to the arrangement are the DOD, military contractors, and armed forces congressional committees. They are a mighty and far-flung lobby on behalf of ever-more military spending. In conjunction with local suppliers, trade unions, and veterans organizations, they organize grass-roots lobbying efforts. They are among the largest political contributors. They work closely with the DOD to develop new military technology, invent a mission to justify its deployment, and then sell it to Congress and the nation.[46]

The media also play a role in promoting the notion that the arms race is necessary and inevitable. *Newsweek* solemnly proclaims, "The relentless march of technology now threatens . . . the fragile restraints of existing arms treaties."[47] However, as foreign policy analyst Richard Barnet observes, "The 'technological imperative,' the idea that we are powerless to prevent the development of weapons and strategies of mass murder, is a myth not unlike that of the divine right of kings. It is believed because powerful people have an interest in proclaiming that it is true."[48]

Military production is a lucrative business. This is primarily the result of government generosity. Payments for cost overruns, which total billions of dollars, are the most dramatic example. In recent years, moreover, independent researchers and "whistle-blowers" within the DOD have described countless instances of ludicrously high markups on common hardware purchased by the military. The Air Force paid $180 for a rechargeable flashlight billed as "an emergency lighting system." The Air Force also purchased a ten-cup electric coffeemaker for use aboard the C-5A for $7,600. The coffeemaker was designed to brew coffee "under conditions that would have killed the crew."[49] Even more questionable pur-

---

[46]Gordon Adams, *The Iron Triangle: The Politics of Defense Contracting* (New York, 1981).

[47]*Newsweek*, March 18, 1985, p. 8.

[48]Richard J. Barnet, "Ritual Dance of the Superpowers," *The Nation*, April 9, 1983, p. 453.

[49]*Newsweek*, February 11, 1985, p. 36.

chases have been revealed: General Dynamics sold the Air Force an antenna hexagonal wrench that could be purchased in a hardware store for 12 cents. General Dynamics' price: $9,609. General Dynamics also turned a fine profit with an antenna motor assembly alignment pin, whose hardware store price is two cents. General Dynamics' price to the Air Force: $7,417.[50] As a result of public outrage at revelations of military cost overruns, the Pentagon launched an extensive investigation in 1985. Among the major defense contractors found to have overcharged for military items, produced faulty equipment, and/or engaged in fraudulent practices were Ford Aerospace, General Dynamics, General Electric, Hughes Aircraft Company, Rockwell International, Sperry Corporation, and Texas Instruments.

Focusing on costs, however, misses the major point. Neither the Pentagon nor military producers have an incentive to keep costs low. Quite the contrary. The Pentagon is mainly interested in insuring a steady flow of funds to military producers. These payments can be considered a subsidy to support a constituency for militarism. Both the Pentagon and military contractors share an interest in maximizing the threat of war—which in turn generates support for more military spending.[51]

Military sales abroad

Sales of military equipment abroad have climbed sharply in the 1980s. Thanks to government sponsorship of arms sales, the means of destruction have become one of America's major exports. The United States is by far the world's largest arms exporter, accounting for two-fifths of all international arms exports. (The Soviet Union exports less than half of American arms exports.)[52] Whenever there is an armed conflict anywhere in the world, it is a safe bet that American-made arms will be used—often by both sides. United States military sales have contributed to militarizing the entire world, fuelling regional arms races, increasing the risks of war, and tying up resources that might go for productive purposes.

[50]Lori Comeau, *Nuts and Bolts at the Pentagon: A Spare Parts Catalog* (Washington, D.C., 1984), Section I.
[51]Melman, *Pentagon Capitalism, passim; The Permanent War Economy* (New York, 1974); and *Profits Without Production* (New York, 1983).
[52]*New York Times*, May 14, 1984.

Science: the knowledge industry

As superiority in the science of weaponry has become a major criterion of military power, the arms race has become largely a scramble to develop ever more technologically advanced weapons. Scientists, engineers, and other technical personnel are crucial to the design and production of missiles, sensor devices, unmanned bombers, electronic homing devices, reconnaissance satellites, and antipersonnel weapons.

Social scientists also have an important role in the military-industrial complex. They are called upon to find ways to secure reliable allies among foreign countries by gathering information, analyzing problems, and suggesting alternatives. Anthropologists have developed ways to penetrate Third World cultures and mobilize groups against insurgent movements. Political scientists have elaborated strategic doctrines. And experts in propaganda, linguistics, psychological warfare, cartology, cryptology, and geographic regions have contributed their skills.

The federal government provides about $35 billion annually for research and development (R and D) for military and aerospace research. The intellectuals and scientists who are the major beneficiaries of these funds move back and forth between universities and private industries, think tanks and government. Some statistics suggest the interlocking relationship between science, industry, government, and war. A significant proportion of scientists and engineers work on projects supported with federal funds. Two-thirds of all university research funds are provided by the Defense Department, Atomic Energy Commission, and National Aeronautics and Space Agency. More than two-thirds of federal funds for research and development are spent for military-related research.[53] Between 1981 and 1984, whereas military R and D increased by $18 billion, federal funds for civilian R and D increased by less than $1 billion. Military R and D accounts for one-third of all research and development in the United States, up from one-fourth in 1980.

The United States spends more on research and development than any other country in the world. Western Europe and Japan spend about twice as much per capita as the United States on civilian research and development and half as much per capita

---

[53]Melman, *Pentagon Capitalism*, p. 97; Barber, p. 137; and Bell, p. 253.

on the military. A large share of America's scientific resources are thus geared primarily to nonessential military production. American industry steadily deteriorated partly because American scientists devote their talents to improving weapons rather than improving the production of peacetime goods.

CHALLENGES TO AMERICAN DOMINANCE AND THE REMILITARIZATION OF AMERICA

American policies after the Second World War attempted to create a stable international order in which American corporate and political interests would flourish. In the first years, there was little conflict between the goal of safeguarding the overall framework as well as American interests. Given its predominance after the war, American corporate and political interests were served by whatever contributed to achieving a stable and prosperous world order. For example, American capitalism benefited when Japan and Western Europe recovered from the war. But the costs to the United States of supporting the international framework soon proved to be a heavy burden. Because they are not saddled with heavy arms budgets and can devote their resources to economically productive purposes, Japan and Western Europe have been better able to compete with the United States in the economic realm. For 30 years, American dominance rested on the head start that the United States enjoyed after the Second World War both as a result of the war itself and other advantages the United States possessed: a vast market, a skilled labor force, and abundant natural resources. The United States remains today the most powerful nation in the world. However, since the 1970s there has been a relative decline of American military and economic supremacy. The gap between the United States and other industrialized capitalist nations has shrunk and American dominance has become increasingly more costly and difficult to maintain.

Militarily, the USSR has drawn closer to the United States in recent years. "There was only one global power in 1947; today there are two."[54] In 1964, the United States had five times more

[54]Raymond Aron, *The Imperial Republic: The United States and the World, 1945–1973* (Englewood Cliffs, N.J., 1974), p. 149.

intercontinental missiles than the USSR. Today it has fewer than
the Soviet Union. The SALT I agreement symbolizes United States
acceptance of the narrowing military gap with the USSR rather
than superiority.

The United States has experienced intense economic competition from other major capitalist countries. In 1959, the combined
production of the five other major capitalist countries was less than
half that of United States production; by 1977 their production
exceeded that of the United States, although the trend was reversed
in the 1980s. The United States share of world trade declined from
26 percent in 1956 to 17 percent in 1976. During the same period,
the share of imports into the United States increased from 7 to 14
percent of American GNP.[55]

Another measure of America's declining international economic competitiveness is the balance of imports and exports. The
United States imports 30 percent more than it exports, an indication that foreign goods are more attractive in terms of cost and
quality. Foreign trade deficits exceeded $100 billion annually in the
early 1980s and reached $149 billion in 1985. These deficits, as well
as the federal budget deficit, have been partially financed by foreign
capital entering the United States as a result of the overvalued
dollar, high interest rates, and a conservative government (which
makes the United States a safe refuge for foreign capital). As a
result of the inflow of foreign capital into the United States, the
United States became a debtor nation in 1985 for the first time in
generations: its foreign debt exceeded loans made abroad.

Overall, the United States has been losing its position of international economic dominance that it occupied in the postwar period. Whereas in 1969, only 2 of the world's 20 largest corporations
were non-American, by 1976 there were 8 non-American firms
among the top 20. Between 1950 and 1982, America's share of
world steel production fell from 55 percent to 10 percent, its share
of world automobile production from 82 percent to 19 percent. In
1948, the United States exported twice as much as the original six
countries of the European Economic Community; in 1982, these
countries exported two and one-half times more than the United
States.[56] A dramatic example of economic decline is the success of

[55]Fred Halliday, *The Making of the Second Cold War* (London, 1983), p. 181.
[56]Albert Szymanski, "The Decline and Fall of the U.S. Eagle," *Social Policy*
(March–April 1974): 7–8, and *Handbook of Economic Statistics, 1983*, p. 30.

Table 10-4
Gross domestic product (GDP) as percentage of U.S. GDP

	1950	1960	1969	1972	1977	1982
France	9.7	12.0	15.1	16.5	20.1	17.6
West Germany	8.1	14.1	16.5	22.2	27.2	21.5
Italy	4.9	6.8	8.8	10.1	10.1	11.3
Japan	3.8	8.5	18.0	23.9	36.2	34.2
United Kingdom	12.6	14.0	11.7	13.6	13.0	15.3
All Five	39.1	55.4	70.1	86.3	106.6	99.9

Source: Agency for International Development, *Economic Growth of OECD Countries, 1976–77* (Washington, D.C., 1978); and Albert Szymanski, "The Decline and Fall of the U.S. Eagle," *Social Policy* (March–April 1974): 6 (*Social Policy* published by Social Policy Corporation, New York, New York 10036. Copyright 1974 by Social Policy Corporation); and *The Handbook of Economic Statistics*, 1983, p. 30.

foreign producers in penetrating American markets for basic industrial goods.

A sharp economic recovery occurred in the United States between 1983 and 1986, which improved the country's relative economic position. However, the measures used to stimulate economic growth, including high interest rates and severe budget deficits, damaged the economies of Western Europe and the Third World. Thus, the incipient crisis of American capitalism has been exported to other nations and the world economy remains fragile and prone to periodic crisis tendencies.

The limits of American international dominance were probably reached in the agony of the Vietnam war in the 1960s and early 1970s, with results that persist to the present. At the height of the American invasion in 1968, more than 500,000 American troops fought in South Vietnam. Perhaps even more devastating than the killing and damage resulting from ground combat was the destruction caused by the American aerial bombardment, the most massive in history. The United States dropped over seven million tons of bombs in Indochina—the equivalent tonnage of 350 Hiroshima blasts and more than three times the tonnage of all bombing in the Second World War.[57] In order to destroy the rural strongholds of the Vietcong insurgent forces, the Vietnamese countryside was rav-

[57]*New York Times*, December 26, 1972.

Table 10-5 Import shares of U.S. markets		
	1960	1984
Automobiles	4.1%	22%
Steel	4.2	25.4
Apparel	1.8	30
Machine tools	3.2	42

SOURCE: Mike Davis, "Reaganomics' Magical Mystery Tour," *New Left Review* (January–February 1985), p. 51.

aged: between 1961 and 1970, the United States applied 27 pounds of herbicides, defoliants, and poisons per acre in South Vietnam. Defoliation destroyed 15 percent of South Vietnam's forests and 7 percent of its arable land, as well as over one-third the forests and arable land of North Vietnam.[58]

An even greater cost was paid in human life. One million people were killed in Vietnam, several million were injured, and ten million were made homeless. Yet, despite overwhelming military superiority and the prolongation and brutality of the war, the United States was unable to crush the Vietcong or the Democratic Republic of Vietnam. The war ended soon after the United States withdrew in 1973.

During the remainder of the 1970s, the United States displayed relative restraint in its international stance, remaining somewhat aloof from Third World disputes and reaching limited accommodation with the Soviet Union. (This was the period of détente, described previously.)

However, during the late 1970s the United States shifted toward a more bellicose anti-Soviet stance. The change began in Jimmy Carter's presidency. Although the Soviet Union was building its military arsenal in the 1970s at a faster pace than the United States, it remained behind both quantitatively (in terms of sheer volume of weapons) and qualitatively, for the United States retained and even increased its lead in the technological sophistication of its weapons. The United States led the Soviet Union in

[58]Barry Weisberg, *Beyond Repair: The Ecology of Capitalism* (Boston, 1971), pp. 88–90.

strategic warheads in 1980 by 9,200 to 6,000. And the intercontinental missiles used by the United States to deliver these warheads
were better protected and more accurate. A good indication of
overall strategic capacity is the "lethality" of nuclear firepower,
which measures the destructive potential, accuracy, and reliability
of nuclear weapons. In 1980, *prior* to the substantial American
arms buildup, the United States led the Soviet Union 3 to 1.[59]

Nor can the Soviet invasion of Afghanistan in early 1980, however brutal, explain why the United States reversed course. For the
American arms buildup began before 1980. Moreover, American
aggression in Vietnam, on a far wider scale, had not prevented the
development of détente in the earlier period.

If neither the military balance nor Soviet actions can explain
the American shift toward militarism in the late 1970s, what can?
Two sets of factors have been suggested. Political analyst Fred
Halliday identifies several important changes in the international
arena at this time. First, there was growing economic rivalry between the United States and other major capitalist nations. Second,
there was an upsurge of insurgent activity within the Third World
in the 1970s. Although not directly sponsored by the Soviet Union,
Third World liberation struggles were directed against American-
backed governments and threatened American economic interests.
Halliday suggests that the United States responded to these challenges by returning to a Cold War stance. Through heightening
East-West (Soviet-American) conflicts, the United States government hoped to suppress conflicts within the capitalist West. Furthermore, by reducing Third World struggles to a manifestation of
Cold War tensions, the United States could intervene more easily
to counter Soviet "aggression."[60] Thus, President Reagan was
quick to identify Soviet influence behind such diverse political
forces as the Sandinista government of Nicaragua, the Libyan
leader Muammer el-Qaddafi, the Irish Republican Army, and Middle East terrorist groups. This in turn helped the government justify
such actions as the raid on Libya in April 1986, which killed and
wounded numerous civilians.

Political scientist Alan Wolfe suggests a second explanation
for the resurgence of militarist pressures within the United States.

[59]Halliday, pp. 71, 73.
[60]Halliday, *The Making of the Second Cold War.*

Figure 10-3
Peacetime military build-up in the historical context

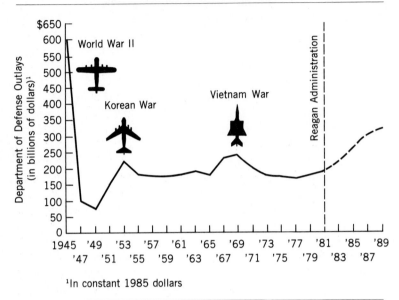

[1] In constant 1985 dollars

Source: Defense Budget Project, Washington, D.C.

According to Wolfe, the peaks of United States hostility toward the Soviet Union have occurred when a Democratic president takes office (Harry Truman in 1945, John F. Kennedy in 1961, Jimmy Carter in 1977):

> During this time, the right wing organizes itself around the notion of a Soviet threat, a politically safe issue for them since they are out of power and need not concern themselves with putting new policies into effect. Pressure from the right makes the newly installed president vulnerable. . . . Without a strong left, Democratic presidents invariably adopt a more aggressive foreign policy as a way of protecting their political base.[61]

Jimmy Carter presided over the new militarism by substantially boosting military expenditures in 1979 and 1980. Carter also

[61] Alan Wolfe, *The Rise and Fall of the 'Soviet Threat': Domestic Sources of the Cold War Consensus* (Washington, D.C., 1979), p. 33.

Figure 10-4
The shift from domestic to military spending in federal outlays

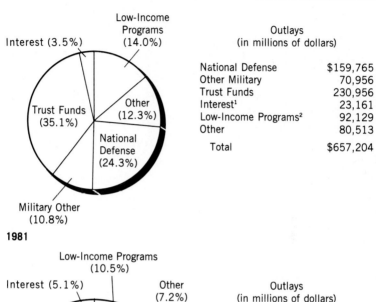

Outlays (in millions of dollars)	
National Defense	$159,765
Other Military	70,956
Trust Funds	230,956
Interest[1]	23,161
Low-Income Programs[2]	92,129
Other	80,513
Total	$657,204

1981

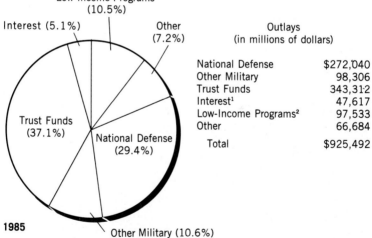

Outlays (in millions of dollars)	
National Defense	$272,040
Other Military	98,306
Trust Funds	343,312
Interest[1]	47,617
Low-Income Programs[2]	97,533
Other	66,684
Total	$925,492

1985

Note:
[1] "Interest" excludes interest on the military-related debt, which is included under "Other Military".
[2] Low Income Programs consist of annual spending for Education, Training, Social Services; Health Care Services; Housing Assistance; Food and Nutrition Assistance; and Other Income Security.

Table 10-6
Guns versus Butter

1. 460 meals for the homeless	= $439	=	One 155-mm. (conventional) high-explosive shell
2. Proposed cut in funds for mass-transit systems	= $2.8 billion	=	Navy (EA6B) airplane program for surveillance and communications jamming
3. Proposed 1986 cuts in guaranteed student loans and in campus-based financial aid for students	= $2.3 billion	=	1986 budget for the M-1 Abrams heavy tank
4. Proposed 1986 cuts in funds for veterans' medical care and housing	= $336 million	=	220 Phoenix air-to-air missiles
5. Proposed 1986 cut in Medicare services	= $4 billion	=	Proposed low-altitude antisatellite weapons
6. Proposed cuts in small-business loans and Job Corps services	= $1.1 billion	=	The Department of Defense's Latin American programs for 1986
7. Proposed Federal cuts in housing for the elderly and handicapped, and the cut in energy assistance for poor people	= $1.5 billion	=	One projected (LHD-1) Marine amphibious assault ship
8. The proposed 1986 cut in Amtrak and in modernization of the Northeastern railway corridor	= $741 million	=	26 Navy air-cushion landing craft

enunciated some of the new doctrine that served to make the unthinkable (nuclear war) thinkable. Presidential Directive 59, signed by Carter in 1980, helped prepare for the new "counter-force" doctrine involving the use of nuclear weapons as an instrument of United States policy.

However, the real shift in American foreign policy occurred with Ronald Reagan. Unlike Republican presidents Dwight Eisenhower, who moderated Truman's aggressive policies, or Richard Nixon, who shifted from Democratic President Johnson's warlike stance toward détente, Ronald Reagan pushed further in the mili-

9. Proposed 1986 cuts in natural-resource and in environmental controls, and in recreational facilities	=	$1.4 billion	=	The Army's 1986 funding for chemical-bacteriological weapons and research, and for rebuilding 48 (CH-47) heavy-lift helicopters
10. Proposed elimination of the Federal share of a 15-year national plan for sewage treatment to meet minimum Clean Water Act standards	=	$30 billion	=	The Navy's Aegis (CG-47) cruiser program
11. Estimated cost of cleaning up 10,000 toxic-waste dumps that contaminate the nation's soil and water	=	$100 billion	=	The Navy's Trident II submarine and F-18 jet fighter programs
12. 1982-85 cuts in Federal income and nutrition programs that left 20 million people hungry among the 35.3 million living in poverty	=	$12.2 billion	=	The Army's Patriot ground-to-air missile system
13. What is needed to abate the growth of hunger: a one-third increase in funding for the Federal school-lunch program, food-stamp program, and Women, Infants and Children (WIC) program	=	$5.3 billion	=	The Army's single-channel ground and airborne radio system

Source: Seymour Melman, "The Butter That's Traded Off for Guns," *New York Times*, April 22, 1985. Copyright © 1985 by The New York Times Company. Reprinted by permission.

tarist direction initiated by Carter. For the first time, a right-wing ideologue gained control of the White House, supported by a political constituency to match (see Chapter 8). Reagan spoke of the Soviet Union as an "evil empire" and launched a crusade to gain even greater military superiority over the USSR. In Reagan's first term in office, the military budget doubled; he proposed that it triple by the end of his second term. Nearly $2 trillion is being spent for the military in 1980–88 (as much as was spent in 1946–80). The annual military budget of $300 billion is more than total spending by nearly every other government throughout the world. Military

spending rose to half of every federal tax dollar and will consume
$.60 by 1988. Moreover, this buildup occurred during a period of
severe retrenchment in domestic programs. The result has been the
remilitarization of the American economy after a period in which
military spending declined in relative terms.[62]

Military spending has increased in virtually every category.
Among the more significant items are the following:

(1) Nuclear warheads. Between 1983 and 1993, the Reagan
administration planned to add 17,000 warheads and retire 11,000
older warheads, a net increase of 6,000. Ths would expand the
American nuclear arsenal to 32,000 nuclear weapons.[63]

(2) Strategic weapons systems. These include 100 B-1B bombers, 100 planned Stealth bombers, hundreds of submarine launched
cruise missiles (SCLMs), 50 MX missiles, 3,400 air-launched cruise
missiles (ALSCMs), the Midgetman missile, Trident II submarines,
and integrated nuclear command, control, communications, and
intelligence systems (C^3I).

(3) Smaller, more accurate nuclear weapons. These are targeted on military installations and command headquarters, not civilian population centers. The implications of this shift will be
discussed later.

(4) An increase in the number, firepower, and sophistication
of "conventional," non-nuclear weapons. These are more powerful, precise, and "smarter" than previous weapons. As military
analyst Michael Klare explains,

> The revolution in conventional weapons is being driven by a variety
> of interrelated technological advances: the introduction of "smart"
> weapons, or precision-guided munitions (PGMs), capable of sensing
> their intended targets and making in-flight course corrections so as
> to insure direct hits; the "clustering" of many "bomblets" into dis-
> pensing systems that can explode them over a wide area; the use of
> new explosives and warhead technologies that can endow conven-
> tional arms with near-nuclear blast capabilities; and the introduction
> of new "target acquisition" systems that enable planes and helicop-

[62]*New York Times,* March 5, 1984; and Gordon Adams, Director, *The FY 1985
Defense Budget: The Buildup Continues* (Washington, D.C., 1984).
[63]These and the following data are from Christopher Paine, "Reaganomics, or How
to 'Prevail,'" *The Nation,* April 9, 1983, pp. 423–33, as well as other articles from
that Special Issue of *The Nation* on "the New Arms Technology and What it
Means," April 9, 1983.

ters to pinpoint enemy forces far behind the front lines for attack by PGMs and cluster munitions.[64]

As a new generation of high-powered conventional weapons are deployed, along with smaller, tactical nuclear weapons designed for battlefield use, the distinction between nuclear and conventional weapons becomes blurred. This makes it more likely that, in the event of a direct encounter between the United States and the Soviet Union, the conflict will escalate to the use of nuclear weapons.

(5) Chemical and germ weapons.

(6) An increase in the Navy from 400 to 700 ships.

(7) High-technology weapons. These include satellites capable of precise surveillance and reconnaissance from high altitudes, anti-satellite weapons (ASAT), robotic tanks, and other devices. This is capped by the militarization of space, advocated by President Reagan in 1983 as the Strategic Defense Initiative (SDI, popularly known as "star-wars"). The scheme is designed to destroy Soviet missiles on takeoff, in flight, or on reentry into the earth's atmosphere. The Star Wars R and D program was projected to cost over $24 billion between 1984 and 1989. Through surveillance equipment, earth- and space-based lasers, and hypervelocity spaced weapons, SDI aims to provide a shield around American cities or, more realistically, military installations.

Why do many military analysts consider that a "defensive" system increases the risk of war and serves offensive purposes? Critics charge that, by decreasing American vulnerability to the Soviet Union, at the same time that the Soviet Union remains highly vulnerable to American nuclear weapons, SDI creates a dangerous imbalance. If the United States were able to drastically reduce its military vulnerability, the Soviet Union might be driven to launch a preemptive strike in the long interim period while SDI technology is being developed and deployed. At the least, the Soviet Union will seek, as in past periods, to accelerate its arms buildup to nullify the American advantage.

(8) Increased spending for conventional weapons and forces. Nuclear weapons only account for about one tenth of American military spending. The rest goes for conventional weapons and

[64]Michael T. Klare, "The Conventional Arms Fallacy," *The Nation*, April 9, 1983, p. 438.

armed forces. One new development is the expansion of rapid deployment commando forces that can be airlifted, along with supplies and weapons, anywhere in the world within several days. These new forces are defended because of increasing instability in the Third World. The secretary of defense argued in the 1985 fiscal year budget report of the DOD, "Both an expansion of US interests in the Third World and an increase in Third World conflicts have forced us to focus more attention there." More generally, the secretary of defense argues, the United States needs "to reassume a leadership role recognized by our allies and friends, and our foes and potential enemies." This explains why the administration proposed a one-third increase for interventionary forces in 1985 alone.[65]

This brief review needs to be understood within the context of the new strategic doctrine elaborated to justify such an extraordinary military buildup. Among the innovations are:

(9) Using nuclear arms as tactical weapons. A shift from relying on nuclear weapons for *deterrence* to developing battlefield nuclear weapons that can be delivered from an artillery launcher.

(10) Limited nuclear war. Quite distinct from tactical nuclear weapons is preparation for limited nuclear war, which would involve more powerful nuclear weapons, such as the warheads on the Pershing II and cruise missiles stationed in Western Europe. These weapons are designed for destroying targets in the Soviet Union, although they are not part of the American strategic triad of ICBMs stationed in the United States, ALCMs on long-range bombers, and SLCMs on Trident submarines.

Preparing for limited nuclear war represents a basic shift in American military doctrine. Formerly, nuclear weapons were designed to be a deterrent—that is, not to be used. Since a nuclear attack by one country on the other would immediately be met by a devastating nuclear retaliation, it was in neither country's interest to unleash a nuclear attack. This was the doctrine of Mutual Assured Destruction—MAD.

However, United States nuclear planners decided that nuclear weapons were too valuable to be reserved for a deterrent. In order

---

[65]Michael T. Klare, "May the Force Project Us," *The Nation*, February 25, 1984, pp. 216–17. Also see Klare, "Building a Fortress America," *The Nation*, March 23, 1985, pp. 321, 337–39.

to devise nuclear weapons that could be *used*, they succeeded in designing smaller and more precise nuclear weapons that could be targeted not on Soviet cities (the previous counter-city stance) but on Soviet military targets (counter-force). The consequence is to make nuclear weapons appear to serve the traditional purpose of weakening the opponent's military forces rather than targeting them against cities as a means to deter nuclear attack.

American military planners began preparing for limited nuclear war in the last few years; they now speak of the ability to "prevail" in such an encounter. Other steps toward this end are reinforcing the American C^3I capacity, which might be endangered in a nuclear exchange, and improved civil defense facilities.

Paradoxically, by seeking to limit nuclear war, the new strategy makes it more likely. As nuclear war becomes more "thinkable," it becomes closer. Moreover, it is quite likely that a nuclear exchange that began as "limited" would quickly escalate to involve the use of strategic forces that cause widespread destruction. Contrary to some strategists, it is doubtful that a nuclear exchange could be made as precise as a ping-pong match on an intercontinental scale. This is because nuclear weapons inevitably cause widespread damage; it seems unlikely that limited nuclear war could remain confined to the precise limits imposed by military strategists.

(11) Preparation for a first strike. Until the late 1970s, American strategic efforts aimed at developing a second strike capability adequate to deter any possible Soviet attack. (A second strike is a strategic force sufficiently invulnerable and powerful that it could survive a nuclear attack and inflict crushing damage.) A second strike capability is designated for the defensive purpose of deterring a nuclear attack; since the attacker risks certain destruction, there is nothing to be gained from attacking first.

Until the late 1970s, the United States nuclear arsenal was designed as a second-strike force. It was highly destructive but not sufficiently precise to be used in a fine-tuned strike against Soviet military forces. The argument to move to a new generation of weapons, especially the MX mobile missile, was that a "window of vulnerability" was developing, in which Soviet missiles were becoming sufficiently accurate to destroy the American land-based missiles while they were in their silos—thus ending the deterrent value of this leg of the strategic triad. To close this purported window, the Air Force advocated developing a new missile that was less vulnerable, so that the Soviet Union could not be sure of destroying it in a first strike.

However, note that the USSR has always had such a window of vulnerability—and that it is larger on the Soviet side. The reason is that, whereas about two-thirds of the 7,500 Soviet strategic nuclear warheads are located on vulnerable land-based missiles, only one-fourth of the 9,200 United States strategic warheads are on land-based missiles. The remainder are ACLMs and SCLMs (sited in long-range bombers and submarines), which are far less vulnerable to Soviet attack.[66]

The traditional strategic doctrine of mutual deterrence was built on the fact that the destructive potential of nuclear retaliation deterred each nation from launching a nuclear attack on the other. "As long as each side knows that it can gain little or nothing from striking first and also knows that it can respond with a devastating blow [after a first strike by the other side], there is mutual deterrence."[67]

Major responsibility for destabilizing this mutual "balance of terror" lies within the United States through the development of new military technology and doctrine. The innovations in weaponry include antiballistic missile defenses, antisatellite weapons, warheads of pinpoint accuracy, and missiles that reach their targets swiftly and with little warning. Once deployed, these weapons make MAD obsolete. And the shift is packaged in new military doctrines of limited nuclear war, in which United States strategists argue that nuclear exchanges might occur without escalation to widespread destruction. Thus, rather than the American nuclear effort being directed exclusively to defensive and deterrent purposes, strategists now create scenarios for the use of nuclear weapons in a variety of situations.

Lurking behind the new developments is the strong possibility that the United States is seeking a *first-strike* capability: the ability to launch a preemptive strike against the USSR's second-strike force and thus eliminate the threat of a Soviet counterattack. A key development in these preparations is the deployment of the MX missile, a precise, long-range weapon able to destroy Soviet mili-

[66]Paine, p. 430.
[67]Leslie H. Gelb, "Is the Nuclear Threat Manageable?" *New York Times Magazine,* March 4, 1984, p. 34.

tary installations, including missile sites and command headquarters. Another element is the use of antisatellite weapons and other high-tech weapons to deprive Soviet leaders of their communications and command capability ("decapitation" of C^3I, in the current military jargon). Finally, a first-strike capability would be increased through the development of star-wars technology to detect and destroy any Soviet missiles that escaped initial destruction and were launched in response to an American attack.

The United States does not yet have such a first-strike capacity and it probably will never have a fully effective one. Even if 95 percent of all Soviet nuclear missiles could be destroyed (a far higher level than is conceivable short of fundamental new advances), the remaining 5 percent, consisting of several hundred missiles, could destroy the United States many times over.

What is significant about recent United States efforts is not that a first strike would actually be launched. Rather, developing the elements for a first strike is probably intended to provide American leaders with an additional means to intimidate the Soviet Union.

The consequence, as with past American attempts to develop and maintain nuclear superiority, has been precisely the opposite. In the past, American innovations did not compel the Soviet Union to accept its inferior position but rather spurred Soviet efforts to narrow the military gap. The same pattern is being repeated with the newest technological innovations in the 1980s.

At the extreme, if the United States were to move close to a first-strike capability, the Soviet Union might be tempted to launch a desperate attack to prevent the United States from gaining such a decisive advantage. Thus, the American attempt to achieve greater military security has in fact produced greater insecurity and instability. Moreover, the new generation of weapons increase the risk of nuclear disaster. For example, the time from the launching of nuclear missiles to their impact has been cut from over half an hour to about ten minutes. This means that leaders in each nation have but a few minutes to interpret radar and satellite information indicating a possible attack before deciding whether to launch a retaliatory response.

Although both the United States and the Soviet Union have elaborate safeguards to prevent accidental nuclear detonations, this horrifying possibility cannot be completely dismissed. Given the tens of thousands of nuclear warheads and missiles on each side, even a statistically miniscule risk poses a significant danger. Lest one be complacent about fail-safe procedures, one should recall civilian industrial catastrophes, including the near-meltdown of the Three Mile Island nuclear power plant, the Bhopal chemical disaster, and the meltdown of the Soviet nuclear plant at Cherno- byl. There have been numerous incidents through the years of mishaps involving nuclear weapons. In 1985 alone, a Soviet dummy missile flew out of control over Finland and Norway, and the engine of an American Pershing II missile burned while being unpacked in the Federal Republic of Germany. (In typical Pentagon double- talk, an Army major described the incident as "an unplanned rapid ignition of solid fuel.") An additional danger is that the blurring of the distinction between nuclear and non-nuclear weapons increases the chances of escalating past the nuclear threshold if a conflict were to break out between the two superpowers in Europe, the Middle East, or elsewhere.

The American expansion of the arms race beginning in the late 1970s provoked a sharp response. In addition to the dangers de- scribed previously, new scientific evidence accumulated that the damage of large-scale nuclear war would be far greater than the millions of people burned to death, maimed, and injured by the nuclear blast. Summing up these wider effects, astrophysicist Carl Sagan suggests that "the long-term consequence of a nuclear war could constitute a global climatic catastrophe."[68] About half the world's population would be immediately affected by a major nu- clear exchange—and the remaining half would be affected within a short time.

A major nuclear war would provoke massive fires that would have two devastating effects. First, they would cause immense clouds of radioactive dust, soot, and smoke that would block sun- light, causing a drop in temperature ("nuclear winter") that would destroy crops. Second, once these clouds settled, the sun's ultra violet rays could penetrate the earth's surface because the fire- storms would reduce the earth's protective ozone shield in the strat- osphere. The result would soon be to endanger nucleic acids and proteins, the "fundamental molecules for life on Earth."[69]

[68]Carl Sagan, "Nuclear War and Climatic Catastrophe," *Foreign Affairs,* vol. 62, no. 2 (Winter 1983/84), p. 259. Also see *New York Times,* September 22, 1985.
[69]Sagan, p. 263.

The biological effects of these developments would include widespread famine and malnutrition from inadequate food and water, genetic damage, and radiation sickness. According to a panel of eminent biologists convened to study the effects of nuclear war, the result could be the extinction of human life.

As a response to the dangers of nuclear war, as well as other aspects of American foreign policy, including intervention in Third World nations like Nicaragua, a broad range of forces organized within the United States and abroad. In Western Europe, the peace movement mobilized millions of citizens to protest American actions, probably the largest grass-roots movement in history. In 1985, the government of New Zealand banned the visit of American nuclear-armed warships, and Australia refused to make tracking facilities available for testing the MX missile.

Within the United States, groups have worked for a nuclear "freeze," which would stabilize spending for nuclear arms. (Three-quarters of the electorate support such a freeze, according to a public opinion poll, and referenda advocating a freeze were approved in nine states, many cities, and the House of Representatives.)[70] Given the enormous increases in military spending in recent years, to freeze spending at existing levels would still represent an extraordinary expenditure. However, it is significant that widespread support exists for a measure so contrary to President Reagan's policies.

Groups have also opposed CIA-sponsored subversion of the Sandinista regime in Nicaragua as well as shipments of arms to other nations in Central America. (United States aid to El Salvador increased from $6 million in 1980 to $200 million in 1984.)

Congress responded to popular pressure. On many issues, large minorities or majorities in Congress opposed the administration's military proposals. Congress narrowly approved military aid to the "Contras" in Nicaragua, ordered a reduction in the pace of R and D and deployment of new weapons like the MX and star-wars technology, and voted smaller increases in military spending.

In response to political pressure, the Reagan administration entered into arms limitations negotiations with the Soviet Union and President Reagan met with Soviet leader Mikhail S. Gor-

[70]Gordon Adams, "Restructuring National Defense Policy," in Alan Gartner, Colin Greer, and Frank Riessmann, eds., *Beyond Reagan: Alternatives for the '80s* (New York, 1984), pp. 167–92.

bachev in 1985 and 1986 to seek an agreement reducing nuclear weapons. In the 1960s and 1970s, treaties banned above-ground nuclear tests, limited the number of offensive strategic warheads, and limited antiballistic missile systems. The process of arms limitations was halted in the late 1970s with the resumption of cold war tensions and resumed only in 1985. Further, the Reagan administration used the desire for arms limitations talks to extract further funds for military purposes. President Reagan warned Congress, "Rejecting the peacekeeper [the president's curious designation for the MX missile] will knock the legs from under the negotiating table."[71] In close congressional votes, the president obtained authorization for most new weapons systems, although the pace of development and deployment is slowed.

CONCLUSION

As in domestic policy, the Reagan administration sought to sponsor a substantial reorientation of American foreign policy. The two areas are somewhat related: reductions in welfare spending and the assault on the working class, described in other chapters, sought to increase American productivity and help the United States regain economic dominance over Western Europe and Japan. However, given the administration's conservative economic policies (for example, high interest rates, which made the dollar overvalued), American industry has not reaped the fruits of increased productivity. The overvalued dollar means that the prices of American exports remain higher than comparable goods produced by other industrialized capitalist nations. Thus, the very means used to restore American capitalism have prevented the United States from regaining international economic dominance.

In the military realm, the Reagan administration also succeeded in sponsoring a substantial shift, yet this did not enable it to achieve the goal of ending challenges to American military supremacy. Although the immense arms buildup widened the American military edge over the Soviet Union, this was not equivalent to

[71]*Newsweek,* March 8, 1985, p. 9.

increased security. In fact, the new weaponry and doctrines have produced greater instability and insecurity. Likewise, the expansion of American rapid deployment forces for intervention in the Third World did not ensure compliant procapitalist regimes. As the Vietnam tragedy demonstrated, American intervention on a vast scale can fail to achieve its military goal while convulsing American society.

conclusion

11

the reagan revolution and the future of american politics

The second edition of this book was published in 1979, soon before incumbent President Jimmy Carter was defeated for reelection by Ronald Reagan. We are struck by the fact that the issues and trends just emerging in the late 1970s—economic instability, cutbacks in federal spending for domestic programs, deregulation, hikes in military spending, and heightened political activity by business—have dominated the political agenda in the 1980s. Further, the new trends of that period have become embedded in political institutions and practice. As the 1980s draw to a close, the political structure of the United States (used in a broad sense to encompass political institutions, the economy, the party system, and social structure) is dramatically different than it was at the beginning of the decade.

Or is it? Some have asserted that the much-discussed right turn in American politics is illusory—that neither policies nor opinions have changed much in the present decade. Although we have presented abundant material in preceding chapters that documents important shifts, it is worth presenting the case for stability. Our aim in this concluding chapter is to analyze the extent of change within American political patterns and the probability that recent changes will persist into the future. One can discern two quite different scholarly perspectives on the issue of how deep and durable has been the transformation of American politics in the recent past. In order to illustrate the different positions, we summarize influential examples of each. David Stockman's *The Triumph of Politics,* written by President Reagan's first director of the Office of Budget and Management, seeks to prove that the "Reagan Revolution" to dismantle the welfare state failed because of bedrock realities and continuities within American politics; Thomas Byrne Edsall's *The New Politics of Inequality* argues, on the contrary, that Reagan administration policies and other changes within the past decade have produced a substantial redistribution of income and power away from workers, the poor, and the middle class to the affluent minority.[1] The future of American politics depends in good measure on which interpretation of the Reagan era proves correct.

THE TRIUMPH OF (TRADITIONAL) POLITICS

For David Stockman, the Reagan Revolution promised a fundamental realignment of the American political economy, involving the implementation of supply-side economics. Stockman calls the supply-side doctrine a "sweeping austere ideological blueprint," whose essence was "capitalist prosperity and shrinking government." The two were linked, for, according to supply-side theory, government intervention cannot help but distort market forces, thereby reducing potential economic output. Ever since the New Deal, the development of the welfare state has imposed massive burdens on market forces.

The Reagan Revolution promised a break with this tradition;

---

[1]David A. Stockman, *The Triumph of Politics: Why the Reagan Revolution Failed* (New York, 1986); Thomas Byrne Edsall, *The New Politics of Inequality* (New York, 1984).

it advocated "minimalist government—a spare and stingy creature, which offered even-handed public justice, but no more. Its vision of the good society rested on the strength and productive potential of free men in free markets. . . . It envisioned a land the opposite of the coast-to-coast patchwork of dependencies, shelters, protections, and redistributions that the nation's politicians had brokered over the decades." In the supply-side approach, all groups—even those at the lower end of the income pyramid—would benefit from tax incentives to the wealthy and from reducing government assistance. In an often-used image, the economy could be represented by a sea; once government no longer hindered its movement, the rising tide of economic growth would uplift all groups, even the poor.[2]

Reagan's supply-side revolution rested on three bold initiatives: a sweeping across-the-board cut in personal income taxes, in order to free income and savings for productive investment; a substantial cut in welfare-state programs and expenditures, in order to eliminate the myriad government subsidies that impeded market forces, as well as compensate for the tax cut; and a policy that restrained monetary growth in order to reduce inflation. (Monetary policy was under the control of the independent Federal Reserve Board, but President Reagan enthusiastically endorsed its commitment to tight money.)

The Reagan Revolution initially appeared to be a brilliant success for, in his first year in office, President Reagan achieved his principal goals. However, from the very beginning, Stockman laments, the revolution lacked rigor and it soon foundered on the shoals of American politics. "What had started out as an idea-based Reagan Revolution," Stockman ruefully observes, "ended up as an unintended exercise in free lunch economics." Political and socioeconomic forces, skillfully exploiting the decentralized and complex political system (especially Congress) quickly blocked extensive domestic spending cutbacks and devised myriad new loopholes that, added to the supply-side income-tax reduction, severely eroded the government's revenue base. The inevitable result was soaring federal deficits (exceeding $100 billion annually), which Stockman believes constitute a grave peril facing the American nation. Thus, although the new initiatives were inadequate to reverse the trend toward a welfare state built on a patchwork of

[2]Stockman, pp. 43, 47, 9.

government programs and tax concessions, they produced unprecedentedly high deficits that have undermined economic stability.[3]

According to Stockman, "The Reagan Revolution . . . required a frontal assault on the American welfare state. That was the only way to pay for the massive [personal income] tax cut. Accordingly, forty years' worth of promises, subventions, entitlements, and safety nets issued by the federal government to every component and stratum of American society would have to be scrapped. . . ." Instead, only modest cuts were made. The revolution foundered on the conservative institutional forces of American politics: the system of divided powers, checks and balances, Congressional power, and the like. However, more fundamentally, Stockman notes, the revolution failed not for institutional reasons but because of the democratic character of American politics. Not only elected politicians but, more importantly, the American people opposed the basic goal of the Reagan Revolution: to dismantle the welfare state and return to a situation of unfettered capitalism. Differently put, it was so difficult to dislodge the welfare state not because of the undemocratic (unrepresentative) character of American political institutions but precisely because the welfare state enjoyed widespread support among the American people.[4]

Stockman's book is a fascinating, self-serving, and depressing account of how Reagan's ideologically committed and politically blind advisers produced the skyrocketing federal deficits that resulted from the Reagan administration's policies. According to Stockman, the deficits derived from three factors. First, the Reagan administration sponsored a series of tax cuts that reduced the federal government's revenue base. These included a 23 percent permanent personal income-tax cut, a reduction in business taxes through accelerated business depreciation allowance, and the creation of numerous tax loopholes. Second, congressional opposition prevented the administration from achieving the enormous cuts in federal domestic spending needed to avoid the deficits that loomed because of the tax cuts. An even more important reason for the burgeoning deficit was that the administration sponsored the largest peacetime increase in military spending in history. Third, deficits were so high because the administration projected an

[3] *Ibid.*, p. 8.
[4] *Ibid.*

unrealistically large increase in economic growth. (Rapid growth would mean greater tax revenues.) In fact, given the tight money policies of the Federal Reserve Board, a severe recession developed in the early 1980s, which eroded tax revenues and increased the costs of welfare programs (for example, unemployment insurance), thereby further increasing the deficit. The result of these factors was that, whereas the highest deficit before President Reagan was the $68 billion run up by Jimmy Carter in 1980, President Reagan has run up annual deficits of over $200 billion.

Stockman describes how the administration slowly and painfully grasped the magnitude of the problem. Although it succeeded in legislating an across-the-board income-tax cut, it was also forced to offer additional tax cuts to particular groups that distorted the coherence of the initial plan. And, following the administration's initial success in sponsoring $47 billion in spending cuts, it ran up against a stone wall of opposition to new cuts. Whereas the Reagan Revolution envisioned wholesale abolition of the welfare state, constituency after constituency (or interest group after interest group) mobilized congressional protection for its favored program. Although several of Reagan's advisers believed that great savings could be achieved merely by eliminating "fraud, waste, and abuse" in federal programs, Stockman recognized the necessity for "drastic reductions in dozens of programs. It amounted to a substantial retraction of welfare state benefits. . . ."[5]

The Reagan administration's basic problem, according to Stockman, was that it sought simultaneously to cut taxes, raise defense spending, and balance the budget. As one opponent remarked, this could only be done with smoke and mirrors—that is, through subterfuge. Stockman notes that, since the administration was raising defense spending and cutting taxes by a total of 6 percent of gross national product, nearly half the federal government's domestic spending (which consumed about 15 percent of GNP) would have to be cut to avoid budget deficits. Not surprisingly, the attempt to do so was a dismal failure.

At first, the administration obscured the implications of its reform program by projecting unrealistically high rates of economic growth and inflation, which in turn inflated estimates of future tax revenues. By this sleight-of-hand, "nearly 200 billion of

[5] *Ibid.*, p. 90.

phantom [tax] revenues tumbled into our budget computer in one fell swoop. The massive deficit inherent in the true supply-side fiscal equation was substantially covered up." But the rude awakening was not long in coming: instead of the rosily optimistic growth rate of over 5 percent that the administration forecast for 1982, the economy *contracted* by 1.5 percent. At the same time, many of the proposed spending cuts were abandoned in face of opposition from the bureaucracy, Congress, and interest groups. Thus, the administration "succeeded only on paper, not in the real world of politics." Stockman describes his dread when he grasped that a $130 billion budget deficit lay in store for 1982. Rather than divulging the bad news, however, "I soon became a veritable incubator of shortcuts, schemes, and devices to overcome the truth. . . ."[6]

He eventually came to realize that failure was inevitable. His basic dilemma: "There was no economic magic. The success of the Reagan Revolution depended upon the willingness of the politicians to turn against their own handiwork—the bloated budget of the American welfare state." Thus, "politics as usual" quickly followed the administration's stunning success in gaining congressional approval for the first round of cuts. As a result, the politics of compromise and pro-welfare–state policies triumphed to defeat the Reagan Revolution. "The borders of the American welfare state had been redefined, but they had been only slightly and symbolically shrunken from where they had stood before."[7]

The basic cleavage was that "supply-siders were dedicated to capitalist wealth creation whereas the politicians were dedicated to socialist wealth redistribution. That was the fundamental axis of the struggle for the Reagan Revolution." Since most members of Congress were opposed to the supply-side vision of a dynamic capitalist economy unrestrained by government, legislative support had to be "purchased," notably through tax loopholes and government subsidies for well situated interests. However, "the payments inherently shattered the fiscal equation. They caused the budget reduction package to shrink and the tax cut package to expand. Winning any battle, perforce, meant losing the war."[8]

[6]*Ibid.*, pp. 97, 113, 123.
[7]*Ibid.*, pp. 135, 228.
[8]*Ibid.*, pp. 236, 251.

Stockman argues that the fundamental goal of the supply-side vision and the Reagan Revolution was to change expectations, so that people would rely on market forces rather than government. "The supply-side revolution was in the final analysis a political revolution." Conversely, the failure of the Reagan Revolution— notably, its inability to eliminate the patchwork of government subsidies and tax loopholes that constitute the welfare state—was due to the triumph of the democratic process. For, following the initial round of budget cuts, "The American welfare state had found its permanent boundaries and the politicians had drawn their defensive perimeters." Not that nothing had changed: ". . . The revolution had not been a total failure. We had tightened the money supply, sharply reduced inflation, and were making some progress on deregulation. For the first time in modern American politics, we had actually put the spending constituencies on the defensive. That was no mean feat." However, these changes, that Stockman considers positive, were purchased at a heavy price: "a fiscal and political disorder that was probably beyond correction" and "a lapse into fiscal indiscipline on a scale never before experienced in peacetime."[9]

The Reagan administration learned too late the depth of the American people's attachment to the welfare state. This commitment collided with the supply-side vision of free-market forces unrestrained by government. "The abortive Reagan Revolution proved that the American electorate wants a moderate social democracy to shield it from capitalism's rougher edges." The administration was blind to political realities: "The Reagan Revolution was radical, imprudent, and arrogant. . . . It mistakenly presumed that a handful of ideologues were right and all the politicians were wrong about what the American people wanted from government." In brief, the welfare state is deeply embedded in American political economy and culture. It reflects a quite conscious choice fundamentally at odds with the supply-side vision of unrestrained capitalism.

As Stockman describes it, "The triumphant welfare state principle means that economic governance must consist of a fundamental trade-off between capitalist prosperity and social security. As a nation we have chosen to have less of the former in order to have

---

[9]*Ibid.*, pp. 304, 341–42, 348, 376, 378.

more of the latter." He confesses that he belatedly appreciated the value of the welfare state: "Although it is riddled with inefficiency and injustice, the American welfare state does fulfill at least some of its promises." The triumph of politics also involved the education of David Stockman.[10]

Assessing Stockman

Two questions can be raised regarding Stockman's approach. First, how valid is his analysis of economic theory and American politics? Second, has he correctly identified the significance and impact of the Reagan Revolution? Regarding economic theory, Stockman suggests that, although supply-side economic theory provides the best guide to maximizing economic growth, the American people prefer a trade-off between economic efficiency and social equity. Thus, they reject the harsh demands of supply-side economics in favor of a policy orientation that, although less able to maximize output, provides protection from market forces. However, this argument fails on two counts.

First, the core claim of supply-side theory—that an unregulated capitalism is best able to maximize wealth—ignores the contribution that government makes to assisting capitalist efficiency. (Consider where many business firms would be without government programs of employment training, physical infrastructure, research and development, and so on.) Welfare-state programs also indirectly contribute to capitalist efficiency by strengthening social stability. Stockman ignores the fact that the development of the welfare state following the Second World War accompanied an unprecedented rise in economic productivity and output. Granted that, since the 1970s, a further expansion of the welfare state has been associated with a decline in productivity, the relation between social welfare and economic efficiency is far more complex than Stockman suggests. Moreover, he barely mentions that the United States has among the smallest welfare state sectors of any capitalist democracy, and he mistakenly classifies all domestic spending as part of the welfare state. Federal spending for the FBI, farm-price support programs, interest payments on the federal debt,

[10]*Ibid.,* pp. 394, 395, 391.

and congressional staff salaries hardly qualify as welfare-state expenditures.

Stockman's portrayal of American politics, centering on an endless array of political forces, all of which are equally able to pursue their interests, is also questionable. For this approach obscures biases in government activity, which reflects the fact that the capacity of groups differs enormously according to their structural situation and resources. In particular, business interests can extract disproportionate benefits from government, while workers, racial minorities, and women are politically underrepresented. This oversight is surprising in view of Stockman's own failure when budget director to achieve government spending cuts that would treat groups even-handedly.

In the first months of the Reagan administration, Stockman met frequently with *Washington Post* reporter William Grieder to share his confidential observations of the process of preparing tax and budget reforms. When Grieder published a report of these talks in the December 1981 issue of the *Atlantic Monthly,* they created a political bombshell. One reason was Stockman's bitter remarks about the greed of business interests and their power to block tax increases or government spending cuts of programs that were in their interest. When the tax cut bill passed, "Stockman participated in the trading—special tax concessions for oil-lease holders and real-estate tax shelters, and generous loopholes that virtually eliminated the corporate income tax. Stockman sat in the room and saw it happen. 'Do you realize the greed that came to the forefront?' Stockman asked with wonder. 'The hogs were really feeding. The greed level, the level of opportunism, just got out of control," '[11] Yet in *The Triumph of Politics*, Stockman describes government programs as providing something (and about as much) for everyone. In fact, a title that would better reflect Stockman's earlier insight than *The Triumph Politics* would be *The Triumph of Business*.

What about the impact of the Reagan Revolution? Stockman implies that relatively little changed within American politics during the 1980s and whatever changes did occur affected all groups

---

[11]William Greider, "The Education of David Stockman," *The Atlantic Monthly,* December 1981, p. 51.

about equally. From his account, the major consequence of Reagan's fiscal (tax and spending) reforms was soaring federal deficits. Stockman fails to examine other, at least equally significant, results of fiscal changes in the 1980s. Moreover, according to Stockman, the Reagan administration's attempt to dismantle the welfare state failed; thus, the collision between the Reagan Revolution and the American political system left the latter quite untouched.

THOMAS EDSALL AND THE NEW POLITICS OF INEQUALITY

Washington Post reporter Thomas Byrne Edsall squarely challenges this view in *The New Politics of Inequality.* Edsall's argument is concisely summarized on the book's cover: "A quiet transfer of power has taken place in the nation's capital." The opening words of the introduction are even more emphatic: "This book attempts to describe a major shift in the balance of power in the United States over the past decade. . . . There has been a significant erosion of the power of those on the bottom half of the economic spectrum, an erosion of the power not only of the poor but of those in the working and middle classes. At the same time, there has been a sharp increase in the power of economic elites, of those who fall in the top 15 percent of the income distribution."[12]

In an approach parallel to that we have adopted in this text, Edsall explores the changed balance of power within the United States by describing such shifts as the transformation of the party system in a way that increases the conservative thrust and capacity of the Republican party, the increased power and political activism of business, the decline of organized labor, increased class disparities in voting turnout patterns, and the turn to the right in government policies. The consequence of these shifts has been an increase in economic and political inequalities within the United States. Although Edsall argues that Reagan's electoral victory and his conservative policies were a product of prior socioeconomic changes

[12]Edsall, p. 13.

in the 1970s, he emphasizes the Reagan administration's contribution to intensifying inequalities within the United States.

In sharp contrast to Stockman, Edsall argues that a basic shift occurred in the character of American politics within the past decade. "For nearly fifty years, since the formation of the New Deal coalition in the 1930s, there had been a sustained base of support for both social spending programs and a tax system that modestly redistributed income and restricted the concentration of wealth in the hands of the few. These deeply rooted liberal traditions were abandoned during the late 1970s in favor of policies calling for a major reduction of the tax burden on income derived from capital, and for reductions in domestic spending programs directed toward the poor and the working poor."

Edsall sees a basic shift to the right occurring in American politics that originated prior to the 1980s, but accelerated in the Reagan era. In the 1980s, Congress passed "legislation that would have been politically inconceivable at any time during the previous fifty years." As a result of the new policy mix, conservative forces have gained "what amounts to veto power both over the scope of issues admitted to national political discourse and over congressional legislation likely to achieve victory."[13]

Edsall accords close attention to the tax cuts described in *The Triumph of Politics.* Yet whereas Stockman considers their major significance to lie in the creation of budget deficits, Edsall emphasizes their substantial impact on the distribution of power and income. Parallel to our discussion in Chapter 3, Edsall documents the uneven impact of tax cuts on different income groups. Rather than all groups benefiting (or losing) about equally from the tax changes, Edsall demonstrates the handsome benefits that they provided to the small minority (about 15 percent of the population) within high income brackets, and the even larger benefits reaped by the tiny percent of the population at the top of the income pyramid. In reviewing the net effect of tax reform, Edsall analyzes the importance of a reduction of the top income tax bracket and a rise in Social Security taxes (neither of which is mentioned by Stockman). These changes added up to an additional bonus for the

[13] *Ibid.,* p. 15.

very wealthy and a penalty for the working and middle classes, thus further intensifying income inequalities in the United States.

A similar difference between Stockman and Edsall concerns their analysis of budget cuts. Whereas Stockman minimizes their impact, Edsall emphasizes the magnitude of the cuts, which "eliminated the entire public service jobs program, eliminated the Social Security minimum benefit, and reduced or eliminated welfare and Medicaid benefits for the working poor. . . . The cuts, in effect, chipped away at the margin of the most marginal incomes." In brief, Edsall strongly disagrees with Stockman that the forces supporting Reagan failed to achieve their fiscal goal: "From the vantage point of those seeking a reversal of past progressive redistributional policies in both tax and spending programs, this drive was an extraordinary success."[14]

Edsall points to other changes wrought by the Reagan Revolution that do not figure in Stockman's account. For example, Edsall (and we) consider "one of the major policy initiatives of the Reagan administration [to be] . . . the across-the-board drive to reduce the scope and content of the federal regulation of industry, the environment, the workplace, health care, and the relationship between buyer and seller." It is curious that Stockman does not analyze deregulation for, from the viewpoint of the pro-business Reagan constituency, it was a stunning success. This omission is especially curious since the Office of Management and Budget that Stockman directed played a key role in dismantling federal regulation.[15]

Edsall's basic approach differs from Stockman's in that he interprets the Reagan Revolution in class terms. For example, Edsall identifies an overall goal of the Reagan Revolution—one not even mentioned by Stockman—as follows: "More than any other president since Franklin Delano Roosevent [but in an opposite manner], Ronald Reagan has consciously set out to use the federal government to alter the balance of power between labor and management. . . ." Edsall sees a class bias underlying Reagan's policy orientation. For example, "The cuts in food stamps and welfare were just a part of a much larger pattern of spending reductions, reductions that functioned more to alter the political balance of power

---

[14]*Ibid.*, pp. 17, 204.
[15]*Ibid.*, p. 66. We analyze deregulation in Chapter 3.

than to reduce the size of the deficit." In brief, rather than a revolution, the Reagan program might better be interpreted as an attempted *counter*-revolution, aiming to replace the postwar alliance of organized labor and large-scale capital by a governing coalition more openly skewed toward capital. A key element of the new approach was an assault on organized labor and lower income groups.[16]

How influential was the policy shift? What has been its impact on American politics? Edsall considers the Reagan Revolution largely to have accomplished both its immediate and long-term goals. He points out that the spending cuts "represent an ideological victory that runs even deeper than the numbers themselves. Perhaps one of the most substantial achievements of the policy changes in the Reagan administration has been to consistently weaken the governmental base of support provided organized labor in its dealings with management. . . ." Edsall believes that the policy reorientation of the 1980s will endure far into the future. "The Reagan administration achieved a number of key, long-range victories, changes that will survive to influence policy significantly no matter what the elective future of the GOP. . . . The most important of these victories was . . . what amounts to continued conservative domination of the federal agenda . . . Even if the Democratic party were to regain power, the centrality of the deficit will obstruct all efforts to seek to provide benefits to such key Democratic voting blocks as blacks, women, and workers in distressed industries."[17]

We believe that Edsall places the emphasis where it belongs: on how the Reagan administration's policies have redistributed power within the United States. "The shifts in power that have taken place over the last decade suggest that the changes in tax and spending policies . . . benefiting the affluent will remain in place regardless of which party takes control of the White House. . . ." Edsall concludes with an even more disturbing suggestion, one that is consistent with our own analysis: "The power shift that produced the fundamental policy realignment of the past decade did not result from a conservative or Republican realignment of the voters; nor did it produce such a realignment after the tax and spending

[16]*Ibid.*, pp. 28, 228.
[17]*Ibid.*, pp. 232, 33.

legislation of 1981 was enacted. Rather, these policy changes have grown out of pervasive distortions in this country's democratic political process." And we join Edsall in the sentence that closes the book: "As long as the balance of political power remains so heavily weighed toward those with economic power, national economic policy will remain distorted, regardless of which party is in control of the federal government."[18]

WHOSE FUTURE?

In one important respect, our analysis is closer to that of Stockman than that of Edsall: whereas Stockman believes that the welfare state continues to enjoy strong support, Edsall appears to believe that the drive to reshape the socioeconomic and political structure represented a definitive defeat for workers, the poor, and the middle class. However, despite the sharp changes in the content and distributional impact of government policies in the 1980s, which Edsall highlights, a near-consensus continues to exist within the United States on maintaining and even expanding the welfare state. Public opinion polls regularly produce large majorities in support of programs that were favorite targets of the Reagan administration's assault. This not only helps to explain why the Reagan administration failed to achieve cutbacks in the welfare state on the scale that it envisaged but contains important implications for future possibilities in American politics.

In a detailed examination of public opinion in the Reagan years, political scientists Thomas Ferguson and Joel Rogers reach quite unexpected conclusions.[19] Take federal regulation of the environment and workplace, which the Reagan administration charged represented a menace to freedom and productivity. A 1982 poll found that the proportion of respondents who favored "keeping" rather than "easing" federal regulation of the environment

[18]*Ibid.*, pp. 241, 242.
[19]All poll data reported here are taken from Thomas Ferguson and Joel Rogers, "The Myth of America's Turn to the Right," *The Atlantic Monthly*, May 1986, pp. 43–53. Also see, Ferguson and Rogers, *Right Turn: The Decline of the Democrats and the Future of American Politics* (New York, 1986).

was 49 to 28 percent, industrial safety (66 to 18), automobile emission and safety standards (59 to 29), and offshore oil drilling (46 to 29). Moreover, support for environmental regulation *increased* during the early 1980s, at a time when the Reagan administration was claiming a mandate to deregulate.

Similarly for social spending. Between 1981 and 1983, the proportion of respondents who agreed that Reagan "was going too far in attempting to cut back or eliminate government social programs" increased from 37 to 52 percent. In 1983, an overwhelming majority (74 percent) supported a government employment program even if it increased the federal deficit. A CBS/*New York Times* poll conducted after the 1984 presidential election observed, "There is no suggestion in this poll that the American public has grown more conservative during the [first] four years of the Reagan administration. If anything, there is more willingness now to spend money on domestic programs. . . ." Significantly, even programs targeted for the poor—the object of Reagan's greatest wrath— were supported by two-thirds of the respondents.

What about social issues? Is there evidence of a conservative turn to "traditional" values on questions like religion, abortion, and women's rights? Here again, polls show virtually no evidence of greater conservatism; quite the contrary. For example, large majorities support women's right to elect abortion; indeed, fewer than one-third of those voting for Reagan in 1984 approved of his antiabortion position. Majorities of Americans oppose mandatory school prayer, and support both the Equal Rights Amendment and a federal law requiring affirmative action programs for women and minorities in employment and education.

Ferguson and Rogers note several trends that point in the opposite direction, for example, increased support for harsh criminal punishment and, during a brief period (between 1976 and 1981), support for increased military spending. (By 1983, however, only 13 percent of the respondents favored further military spending.) Yet these are quite isolated exceptions to the prevalent—and increasingly—liberal mood.

As Ferguson and Rogers observe, "On virtually all the important issues identified with the 'Reagan revolution' in public policy, public opinion ran against the president." Further, the "great communicator" was singularly unsuccessful at persuading Americans to accept his conservative ideas: "If American public opinion drifted anywhere over Reagan's first term [and probably over his second term], it was toward the left."[20] Ferguson and Rogers argue that Reagan's popularity was due mainly to his personality and the evolution of the economy rather than to his policies. Reagan's standing in public opinion polls was extremely low until the recovery from the severe recession of the early 1980s. Moreover, widespread esteem for Reagan's personal qualities should not be confused with support for his conservative approach.

The fact that, after two terms of a conservative president, the American people are more attached than ever to the welfare state has important consequences for analyzing future trends in American politics. In brief, the substantial redistribution of economic resources and political power to the most affluent Americans in the past decade has intensified rather than diminished the strain between capitalism and democracy. However, in the absence of an effective organizational vehicle and plausible policy proposals, there is little prospect of electing a government responsive to a progressive majority.

A critically important ingredient in the conservative renaissance beginning in the late 1970s was a wave of scholarship challenging established policies and ideas associated with the welfare state and proposing alternative policy directions. Similarly, a progressive revival will require fresh ideas and proposals. The broad direction is clear: just as the new right proposed to resolve the strain between capitalism and democracy by restricting the public, democratic sphere, so a progressive approach requires deepening the democratic elements within the American political economy.

[20]Ferguson and Rogers, "Myth," pp. 49, 51.

selected
bibliography

*The following bibliography indicates some of the most important work in the field. Additional works are cited in footnotes throughout the text. Books indicated by * are available in paperback.*

CHAPTER 1

Barber, Benjamin. *Strong Democracy: Participatory Politics for a New Age.* Berkeley: University of California Press, 1984.
Barber presents a vigorous case on behalf of a conception of democracy that moves beyond representation to the active participation of citizens in self-government.

*Dahl, Robert A. *Dilemmas of Pluralist Democracy.* New Haven: Yale University Press, 1982.
In this exploration of the role of large-scale organizations and interest groups, Dahl asks how much autonomy they should have in a democracy, and he advocates a decentralized socialist economy as a way of securing democracy and its values.

*Mansbridge, Jane J. *Beyond Adversary Democracy.* Chicago: University of Chicago Press, 1984.
The book shows that there are two different basic kinds of democracy: face-to-face situations in which individuals seek to arrive at a consensus after discussion, and representative democracy in which institutions are designed as forums for the resolution of conflicting interests.

*Pateman, Carole. *Participation and Democratic Theory.* Cambridge: Cambridge University Press, 1970.
In this analysis of the role of participation in democratic theory, the author emphasizes the work of political theorist Jean Jacques Rousseau.

*Pitkin, Hanna. *The Concept of Representation.* Berkeley: University of California Press, 1967.
An important statement by a political theorist on the central role played by the concept of representation in constructing a critical approach to democracy.

399

CHAPTER 2

*Bluestone, Barry and Bennett Harrison. *The Deindustrialization of America: Plant Closings, Community Abandonment, and the Dismantling of Basic Industry.* New York: Basic Books, 1982.
The social and economic costs of regional shifts by industry. The authors document how jobs created through the location of new industries in the Northeast have led to a decline in skill levels and wages.

*Bowles, Samuel, David M. Gordon, and Thomas E. Weisskopf. *Beyond the Wasteland: A Democratic Alternative to Economic Decline.* New York: Doubleday Anchor, 1983.
A detailed analysis of the enormous waste (about one-half of Gross National Product) associated with American capitalist production and proposals to reverse economic decline through democratizing production.

*Melman, Seymour. *Profits Without Production.* New York: Knopf, 1983.
Melman asserts that financial manipulation to maximize profits takes precedence over developing a useful, efficient productive system.

Mintz, Beth, and Michael Schwartz. *The Power Structure of American Business.* Chicago: University of Chicago Press, 1985.
Case studies of several large industrial corporations, which suggest the leading role played by financial firms.

Useem, Michael. *The Inner Circle: Large Corporations and the Rise of Business Political Activity in the U.S. and U.K.* New York: Oxford University Press, 1983.
Useem asserts that large corporations have recently developed a coordinated and aggressive approach to defending their political interests.

CHAPTER 3

*Carnoy, Martin, Derek Shearer, and Russell Rumberger. *A New Social Contract: The Economy and Government After Reagan.* New York: Harper & Row, 1983.
A critical analysis of economic decline in the Reagan era and proposals for revival.

*Edsall, Thomas Byrne. *The New Politics of Inequality.* New York: W. W. Norton, 1984.
Edsall analyzes the ways that government policies have increased inequalities in the 1980s.

*O'Connor, James. *The Fiscal Crisis of the State.* New York: St. Martin's Press, 1973.
O'Connor analyzes various sectors of the economy, discusses the role of government in maintaining capitalism, and describes contradictions in American economic and political development.

*_____. *Accumulation Crisis.* London: Basil Blackwell, 1984.
For O'Connor, individualist values have led to economic crisis.

Page, Benjamin I. *Who Gets What from Government?* Berkeley: University of California Press, 1983.
Page analyzes the ways that government policies reinforce existing income and class inequalities.

Wolfe, Alan. *America's Impasse: The Rise and Fall of the Politics of Growth.* New York: Pantheon Books, 1981.
Wolfe argues that American political development has been blocked by the refusal to choose between democratic and capitalist priorities.

CHAPTER 4

*Barber, James David, ed. *Choosing the President.* Englewood Cliffs, N.J.: Prentice-Hall, 1974.
Essays on various aspects of presidential selection, including procedures, strategy, symbolic aspects, and recent trends.

Lowi, Theodore. *The Personal President: Power Invested, Promise Unfulfilled.* Ithaca: Cornell University Press, 1985.
Presidents raise expectations as intermediary institutions wither; the inevitable result is deceit and failure.

Pious, Richard M. *The American Presidency.* New York: Basic Books, 1979.
A thorough account of the attempts by presidents to stretch the constitutional limits of their power.

Stockman, David. *The Triumph of Politics: Why the Reagan Revolution Failed.* New York: Harper & Row, 1986.
An insider's account of how President Reagan's anti-welfare state priorities collided with dominant American political forces.

*Tugwell, Rexford G., and Thomas E. Cronin, eds. *The Presidency Reappraised.* New York: Praeger, 1974.
These essays challenge the earlier scholarly consensus on the value of a strong president.

CHAPTER 5

*Brenner, Philip. *The Limits and Possibilities of Congress.* New York: St. Martin's Press, 1983.
Utilizing case studies of American relations with Cuba and the restructuring of higher education, Brenner shows that Congress occupies the contradictory position of strengthening the existing society, and its inequalities, and opening the way for substantive change.

*Fenno, Richard, Jr. *Home Style: House Members in Their Districts.* Boston: Little, Brown, 1978.
An analytical and ethnographic work that details the ways in which representatives relate to the districts from which they are elected.

Fiorina, Morris P. *Congress: Keystone of the Washington Establishment*. New Haven: Yale University Press, 1977.

The book treats the interrelated questions of the decline of marginal congressional seats, the changing responsibilities of members of Congress, and the consequences for democratic practices and the making of public policy.

Ferejohn, John. *Pork Barrel Politics: Rivers and Harbors Legislation*. Stanford: Stanford University Press, 1974.

In his treatment of the role of Congress in managing federal programs to specific constituencies such as dam and post office construction, the author examines the relationships between Congress and the relevant bureaucracies in the executive branch.

*Orfield, Gary. *Congressional Power: Congress and Social Change*. New York: Harcourt Brace Jovanovich, 1975.

Though the book acknowledges that Congress rarely leads on controversial social issues, it argues that the role of Congress has been underplayed by much recent scholarship.

CHAPTER 6

*Emerson, Thomas I. *The System of Freedom of Expression*. New York: Vintage Books, 1970.

A comprehensive analysis of civil liberties and the First Amendment, the book covers such subjects as libel, freedom of speech, academic freedom, and laws to protect national security.

*Friedman, Lawrence. *A History of American Law*. New York: Simon and Schuster, 1985.

Now updated, this volume remains the best one-volume legal history of the United States covering the eighteenth and nineteenth centuries.

*Goldman, Sheldon. *Constitutional Law and Supreme Court Decision-Making*. New York: Harper & Row, 1982.

This overview shows how the Supreme Court establishes the limits within which other branches of government work by defining the meaning and content of the Constitution.

*Horwitz, Morton. *The Transformation of American Law, 1780–1860*. Cambridge: Harvard University Press, 1977.

Horwitz, who works in the critical legal studies tradition, argues that American law changed in the early years of the Republic to an instrument facilitating capitalist economic development.

Hurst, James Willard. *Law and Social Order in the United States*. Ithaca, New York: Cornell University Press, 1977.

A sensitive and literate treatment of the relationship between the law, the economy, and social change in nineteenth- and twentieth-century America. The discussion of science and technology is especially original.

CHAPTER 7

Aronowitz, Stanley. *Working Class Hero: A New Strategy for Labor.* New York: The Pilgrim Press, 1983.
American labor is in trouble. Aronowitz explains what he thinks to be the origins of the crisis and suggests ways of reinvigorating the labor movement.

*Degler, Carl. *At Odds: Women and the Family in America from the Revolution to the Present.* New York: Oxford University Press, 1980.
A major, general history of American women, focusing on the tensions and possibilities inherent in family relations and the quest for equality.

*Lieberson, Stanley. *A Piece of the Pie: Blacks and White Immigrants Since 1880.* Berkeley: University of California Press, 1980.
This is the most detailed and thoughtful analytical comparison we have on the subject of why white immigrants to the United States have done better economically than American blacks.

*Lipset, Seymour Martin. *Unions in Transition: Entering the Second Century.* San Francisco: Institute for Contemporary Studies, 1986.
This collection of essays asks why the labor movement has been in a period of decline and what role labor unions might assume in the future.

*Wilson, William Julius. *The Declining Significance of Race: Blacks and Changing American Institutions.* Chicago: University of Chicago Press, 1978.
This controversial book argues that the major impediments to black economic progress after the civil rights revolution are rooted more in the class structure of the United States than in race relations as such.

CHAPTER 8

Chubb, John E., and Paul E. Peterson, eds. *The New Direction in American Politics.* Washington, D.C.: Brookings, 1985.
Describes changes in political parties, institutions, and policies.

Eldersveld, Samuel J. *Political Parties in American Society.* New York: Basic Books, 1982.
Detailed analysis of American party history, structure, and functioning.

Ferguson, Thomas, and Joel Rogers. *Right Turn: The Decline of the Democrats and the Future of American Politics.* New York: Hill & Wang, 1986.
The decline of the Democratic party is due to the fact that party leaders have adopted the conservative policy orientations of the Republican party on the mistaken assumption that American public opinion has shifted drastically to the Right.

Kayden, Xandra, and Eddie Mahe, Jr. *The Party Goes On: The Persistence of the Two-Party System in the United States.* New York: Basic Books, 1985.
Discusses the persistence and rebirth of political parties in the 1980s.

Mayhew, David R. *Placing Parties in American Politics: Organization, Electoral Settings, and Government Activity in the Twentieth Century.* Princeton: Princeton University Press, 1986.
Study of American party organization.

Sorauf, Frank J. *Party Politics in America,* Fifth ed. Boston: Little, Brown, 1984.
Comprehensive description of American political parties.

Wattenberg, Martin P. *The Decline of American Political Parties, 1952–1980.* Cambridge: Harvard University Press, 1984.
Wattenberg surveys American political parties' declining capacity to organize, mobilize, and represent.

CHAPTER 9

*Gronbjerg, Kirsten, David Street and Gerald D. Suttles. *Poverty and Social Change.* Chicago: University of Chicago Press, 1978.
The authors provide a history of the development of the American welfare state and argue that the United States lacks a comprehensive theory of welfare and of the role of government in dealing with inequalities in the society.

Levitan, Sar A., and Robert Taggart. *The Promise of Greatness: The Social Programs of the Past Decade and Their Major Achievements.* Cambridge: Harvard University Press, 1976.
The book argues that the programs initiated in the Great Society of the 1960s have had major successes and that their shortcomings are the result of underfunding.

*Murray, Charles. *Losing Ground: American Social Policy, 1950–1980.* New York: Basic Books, 1984.
By contrast, Murray argues that the social policies of the Great Society have failed and, moreover, are major causes of current social problems.

*Piven, Frances Fox, and Richard Cloward. *The New Class War: Reagan's Attack on the Welfare State and its Consequences.* New York: Pantheon Books, 1982.
These two scholars and activists interpret the Reagan administration's assault on the welfare state and map out a strategy, hinging on a relationship between welfare state bureaucrats and clients, to build a more humane politics.

CHAPTER 10

Klare, Michael T. *American Arms Supermarket.* Austin: University of Texas Press, 1984.
How the United States is the world's leading arms merchant.

*Halliday, Fred. *The Making of the Second Cold War.* London: Verso, 1983.
Halliday argues that the revival of cold war tensions since the late 1970s was a product of American policymakers' attempt to reestablish United States international dominance.

*Melman, Seymour. *Our Depleted Society.* New York: Holt, Rinehart & Winston, 1965.

*_____. *Pentagon Capitalism: The Political Economy of War.* New York: McGraw Hill, 1970.

*_____. *The Permanent War Economy.* Boston: Simon and Schuster, 1974.
In these books Melman argues that the Department of Defense controls a private constituency (whose most notable members are giant military producers) favorable to military production. He traces the damaging effects on the rest of the economy.

CHAPTER 11

*Benjamin, Roger, and Stephen L. Elkin, eds. *The Democratic State.* Lawrence: University Press of Kansas, 1985.
This unusually provocative volume of essays examines the tensions inherent in the relationship of political democracy, liberalism, and advanced capitalism.

*Edsall, Thomas Byrne. *The New Politics of Inequality.* New York: W. W. Norton, 1984.
Edsall shows how changes in the two major parties, labor unions, and the business community have promoted a shift to the Right in American politics.

Kloppenberg, James T. *Uncertain Victory: Social Democracy and Progressivism in European and American Thought, 1870–1920.* New York: Oxford University Press, 1986.
This history of social thought underpinning the development of the modern welfare state casts much light on the terms of current debates about the role of the state.

*Stockman, David J. *The Triumph of Politics: Why the Reagan Revolution Failed.* New York: Harper & Row, 1986.
President Reagan's first budget director argues that the administration's failures to confront interest group liberalism created massive budget deficits and left big government intact.

index

Note: Page numbers in italics refer to tables or figures.

406

A 7
B 8
C 9
D 0
E 1
F 2
G 3
H 4
I 5
J 6

EP 62